D0368121

AiON

Volume 1
Created by
Yuna Kagesaki

HAMBURG // LONDON // LOS ANGELES // TOKYO

AiON Volume 1
Created by Yuna Kagesaki

Translation - Katherine Schilling
English Adaptation - J. Doe
Retouch and Lettering - Star Print Brokers
Production Artist - Rui Kyo
Graphic Designer - Al-Insan Lashley

Editor - Asako Suzuki
Print Production Manager - Lucas Rivera
Managing Editor - Vy Nguyen
Senior Designer - Louis Csontos
Art Director - Al-Insan Lashley
Director of Sales and Manufacturing - Allyson De Simone
Associate Publisher - Marco F. Pavia
President and C.O.O. - John Parker
C.E.O. and Chief Creative Officer - Stu Levy

A TOKYOPOP Manga

TOKYOPOP and are trademarks or registered trademarks of TOKYOPOP Inc.

TOKYOPOP Inc.
5900 Wilshire Blvd. Suite 2000
Los Angeles, CA 90036

E-mail: info@TOKYOPOP.com
Come visit us online at www.TOKYOPOP.com

HEKIKAI NO AION Volume 1 © 2009 YUNA KAGESAKI
First published in Japan in 2009
by FUJIMISHOBO CO., LTD., Tokyo.
English translation rights arranged
with KADOKAWA SHOTEN Publishing Co., Ltd., Tokyo
through TUTTLE-MORI AGENCY, INC., Tokyo.
English text copyright © 2011 TOKYOPOP Inc.

ISBN: 978-1-4278-3187-3

First TOKYOPOP printing: January 2011
10 9 8 7 6 5 4 3 2 1
Printed in the USA

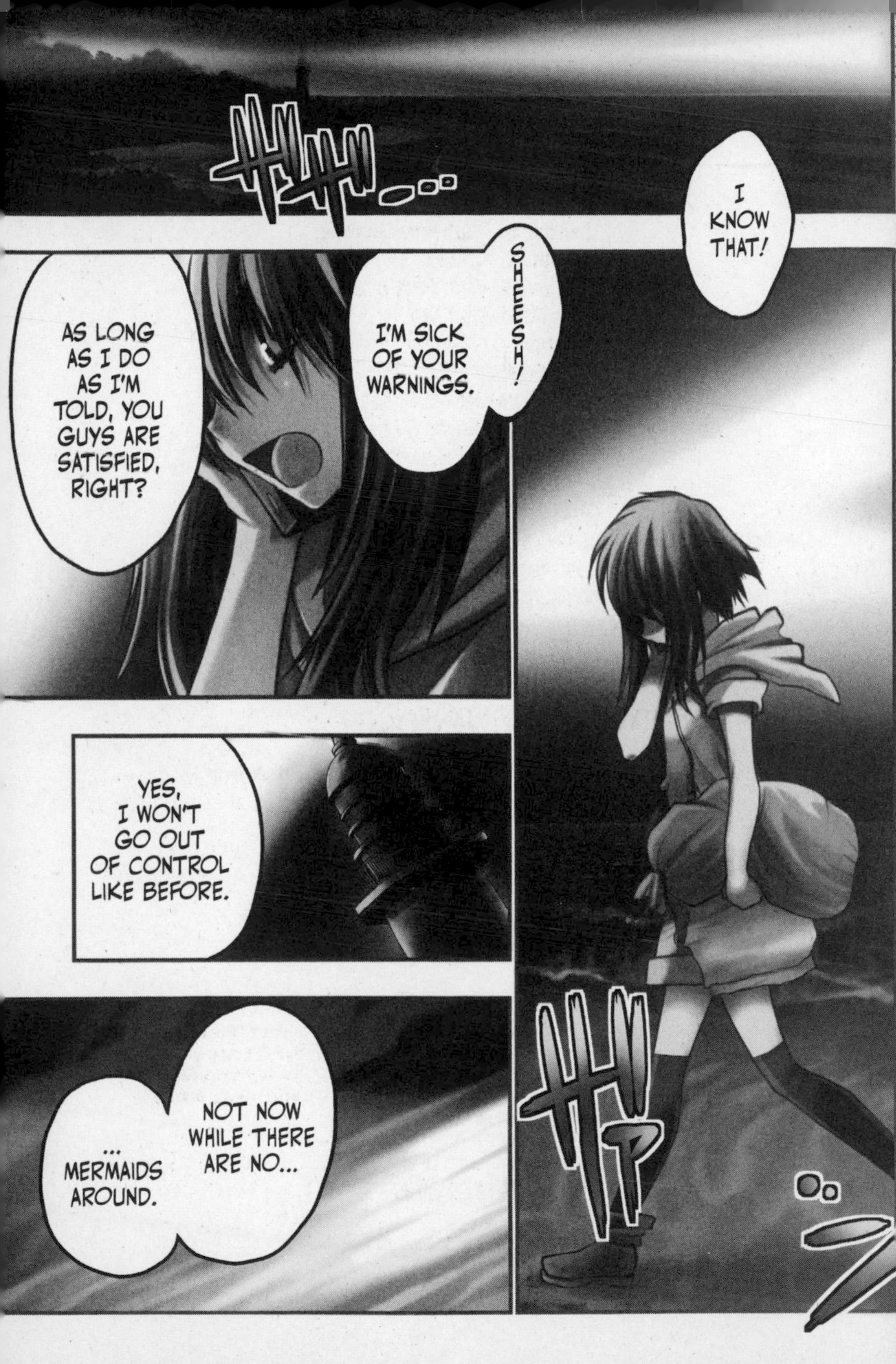
I KNOW THAT!
SHEESH!
I'M SICK OF YOUR WARNINGS.
AS LONG AS I DO AS I'M TOLD, YOU GUYS ARE SATISFIED, RIGHT?
YES, I WON'T GO OUT OF CONTROL LIKE BEFORE.
NOT NOW WHILE THERE ARE NO...
...MERMAIDS AROUND.

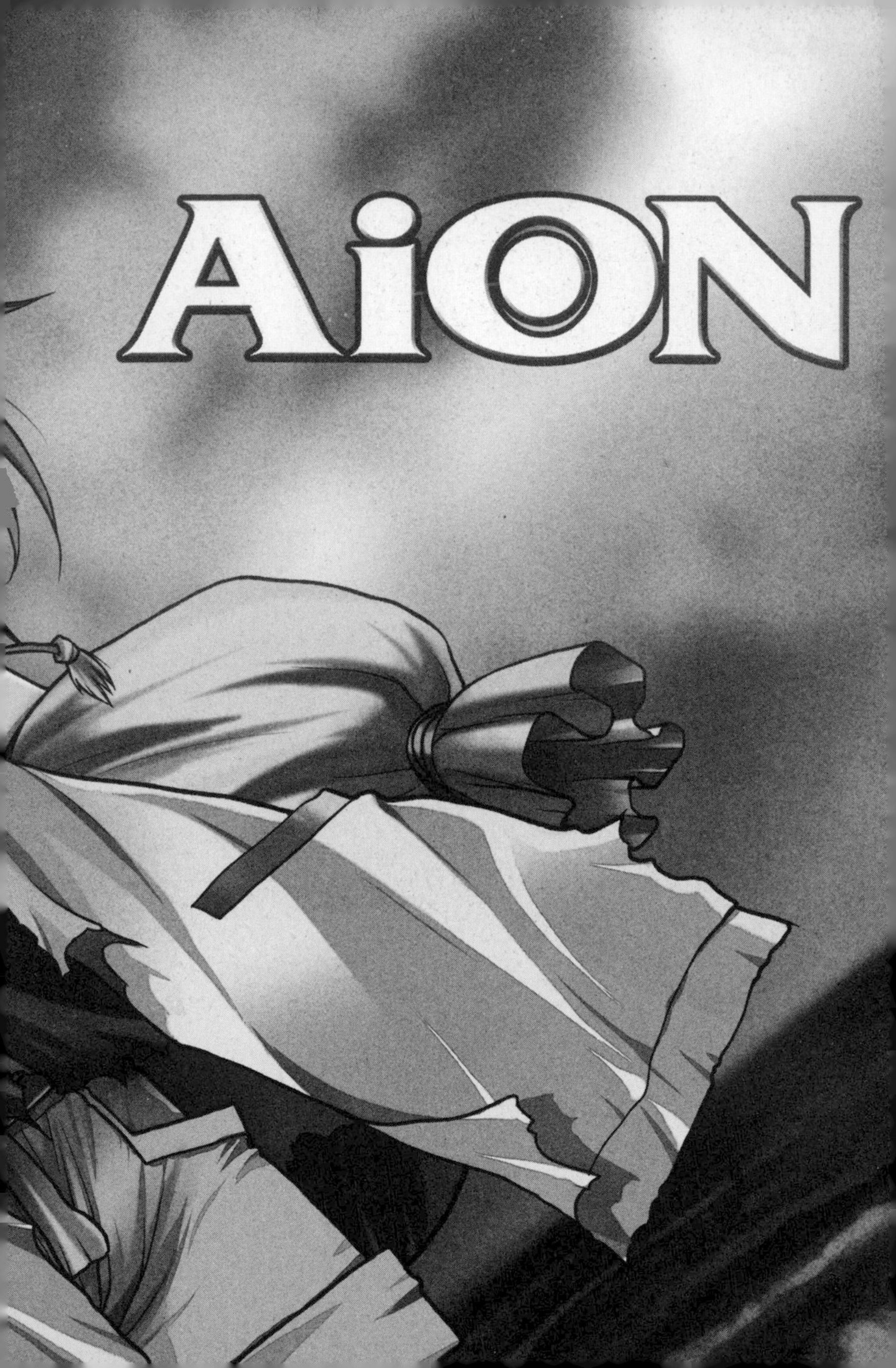
AiON

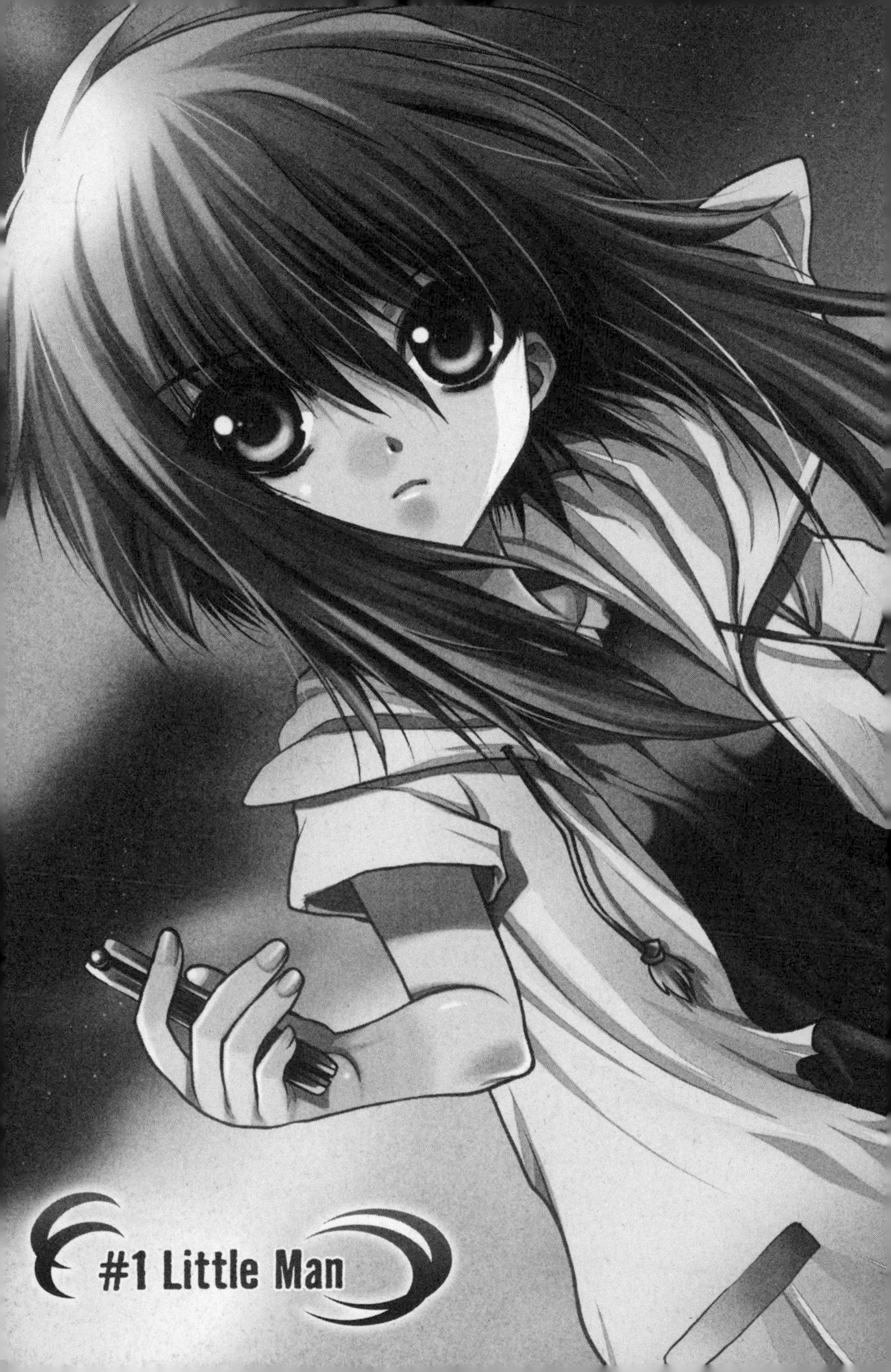

#1 Little Man

CONTENTS

AiON

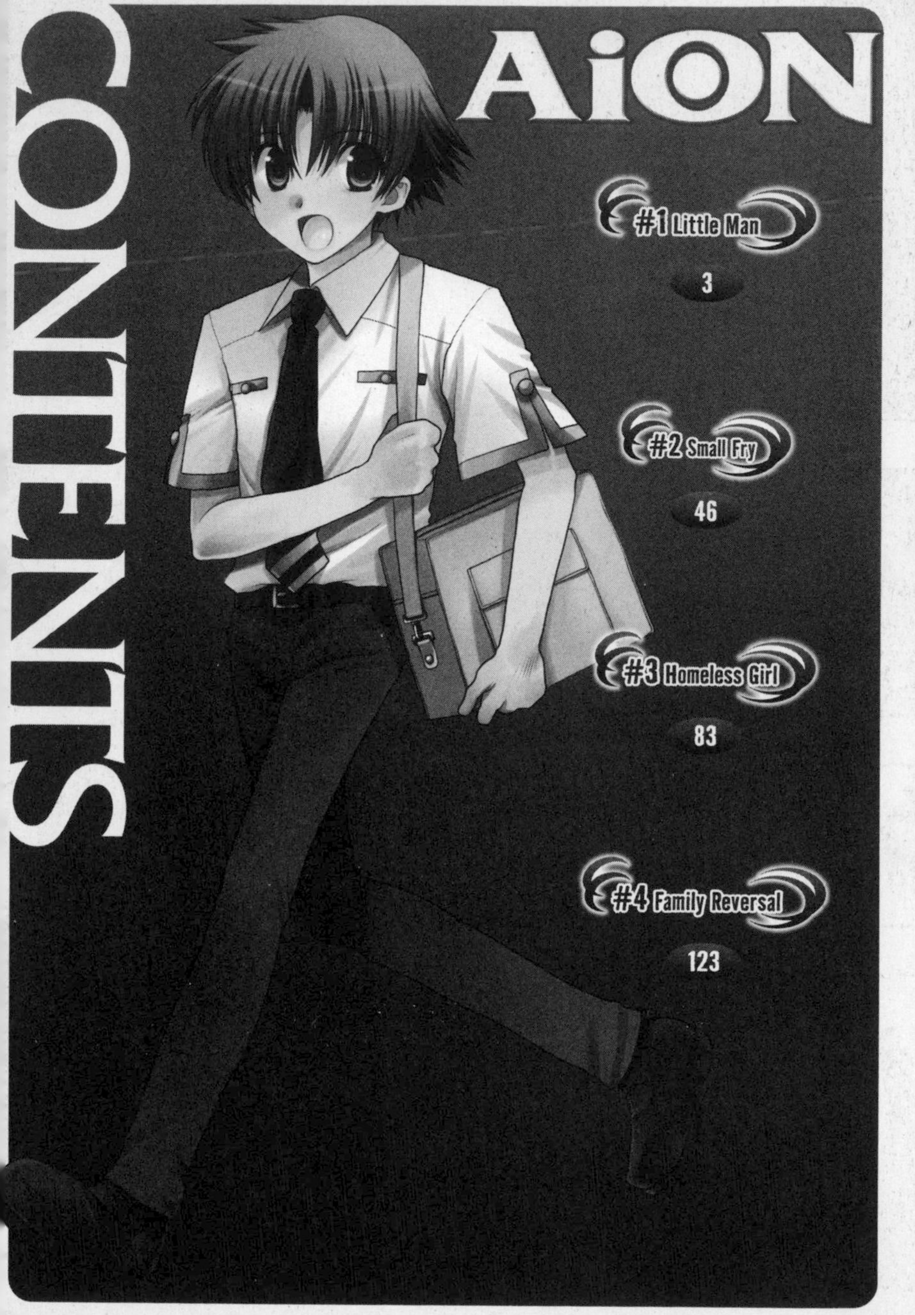

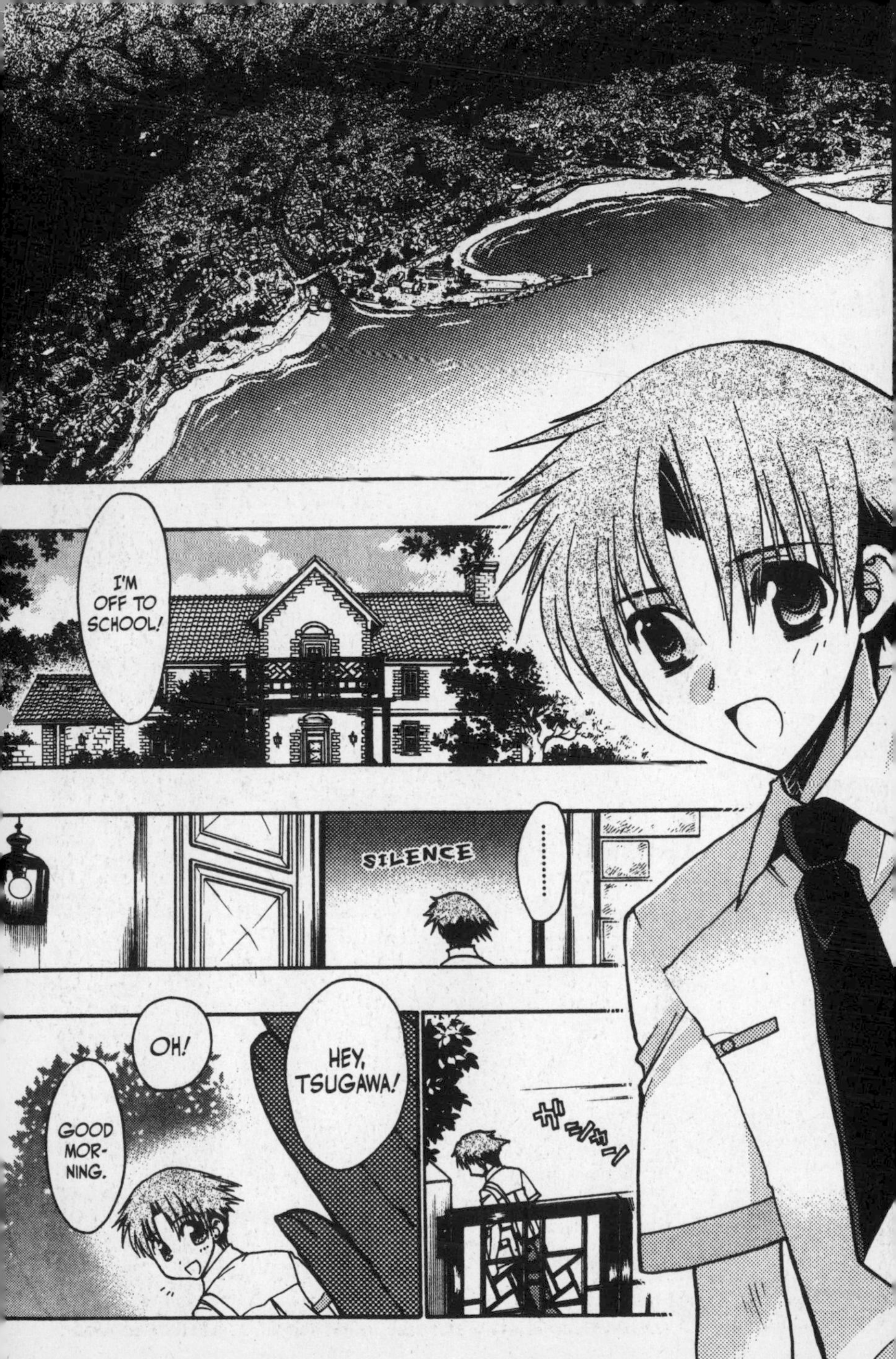
I'M OFF TO SCHOOL!
SILENCE
......
HEY, TSUGAWA!
OH!
GOOD MOR-NING.

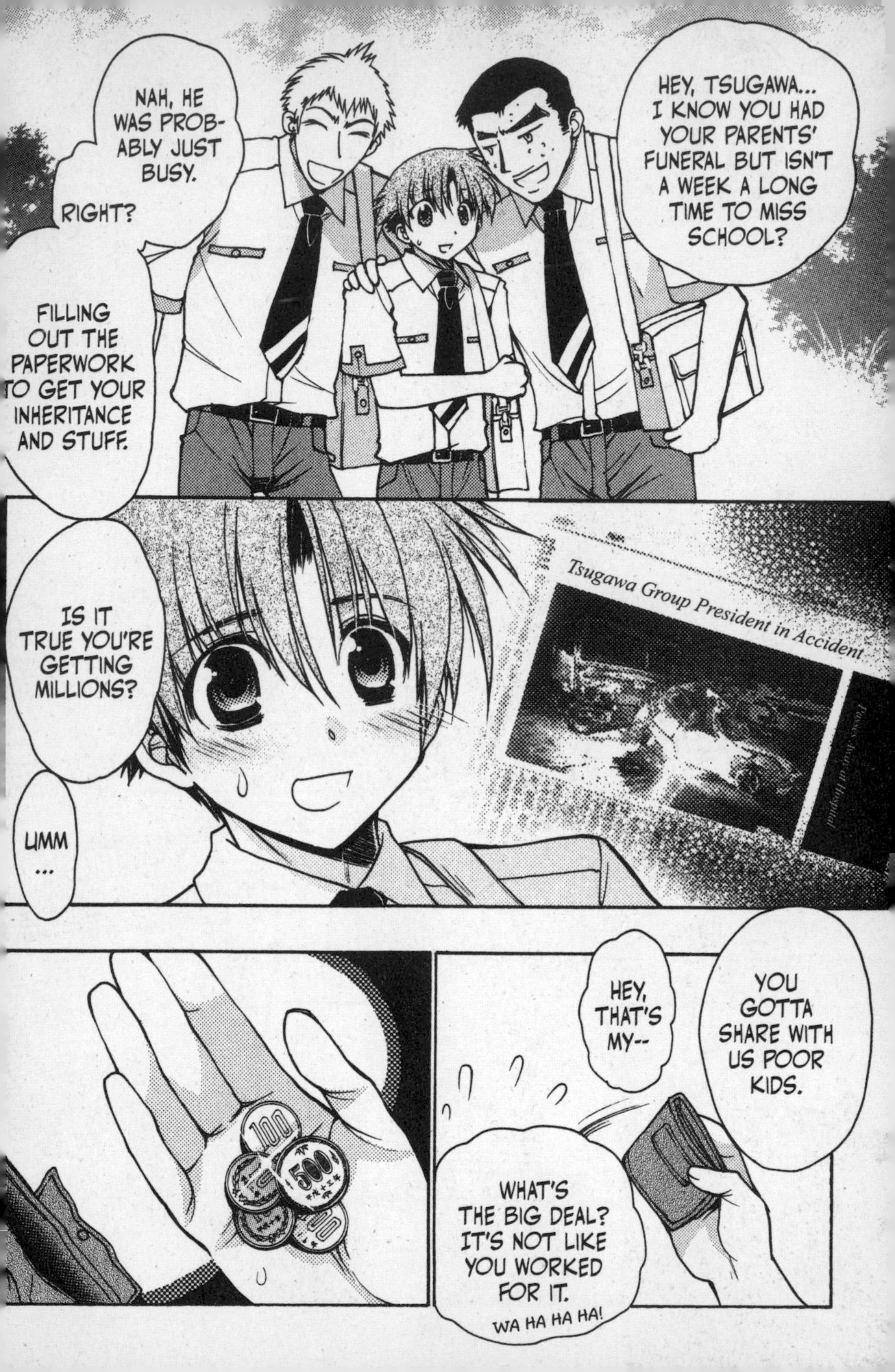
HEY, TSUGAWA... I KNOW YOU HAD YOUR PARENTS' FUNERAL BUT ISN'T A WEEK A LONG TIME TO MISS SCHOOL?
NAH, HE WAS PROB-ABLY JUST BUSY.
RIGHT?
FILLING OUT THE PAPERWORK TO GET YOUR INHERITANCE AND STUFF.
Tsugawa Group President in Accident
IS IT TRUE YOU'RE GETTING MILLIONS?
UMM ...
YOU GOTTA SHARE WITH US POOR KIDS.
HEY, THAT'S MY--
WHAT'S THE BIG DEAL? IT'S NOT LIKE YOU WORKED FOR IT.
WA HA HA HA!

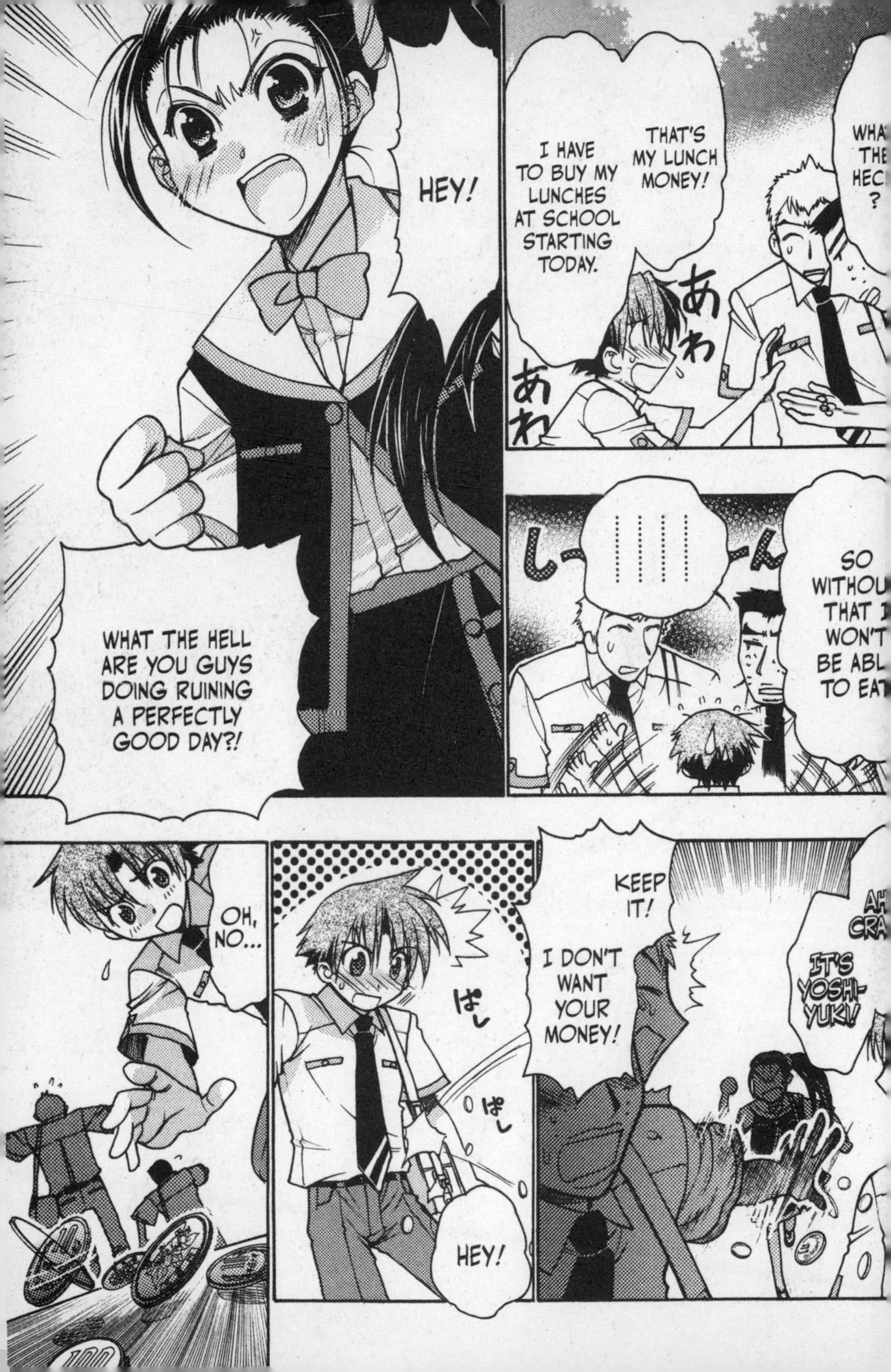
WHA THE HEC ?
THAT'S MY LUNCH MONEY!
I HAVE TO BUY MY LUNCHES AT SCHOOL STARTING TODAY.
あわ
あわ
SO WITHOU THAT I WON'T BE ABL TO EAT
......
しーーん
HEY!
WHAT THE HELL ARE YOU GUYS DOING RUINING A PERFECTLY GOOD DAY?!
AH CRA
IT'S YOSHI-YUKI!
KEEP IT!
I DON'T WANT YOUR MONEY!
ぱし
ぱし
HEY!
OH, NO...

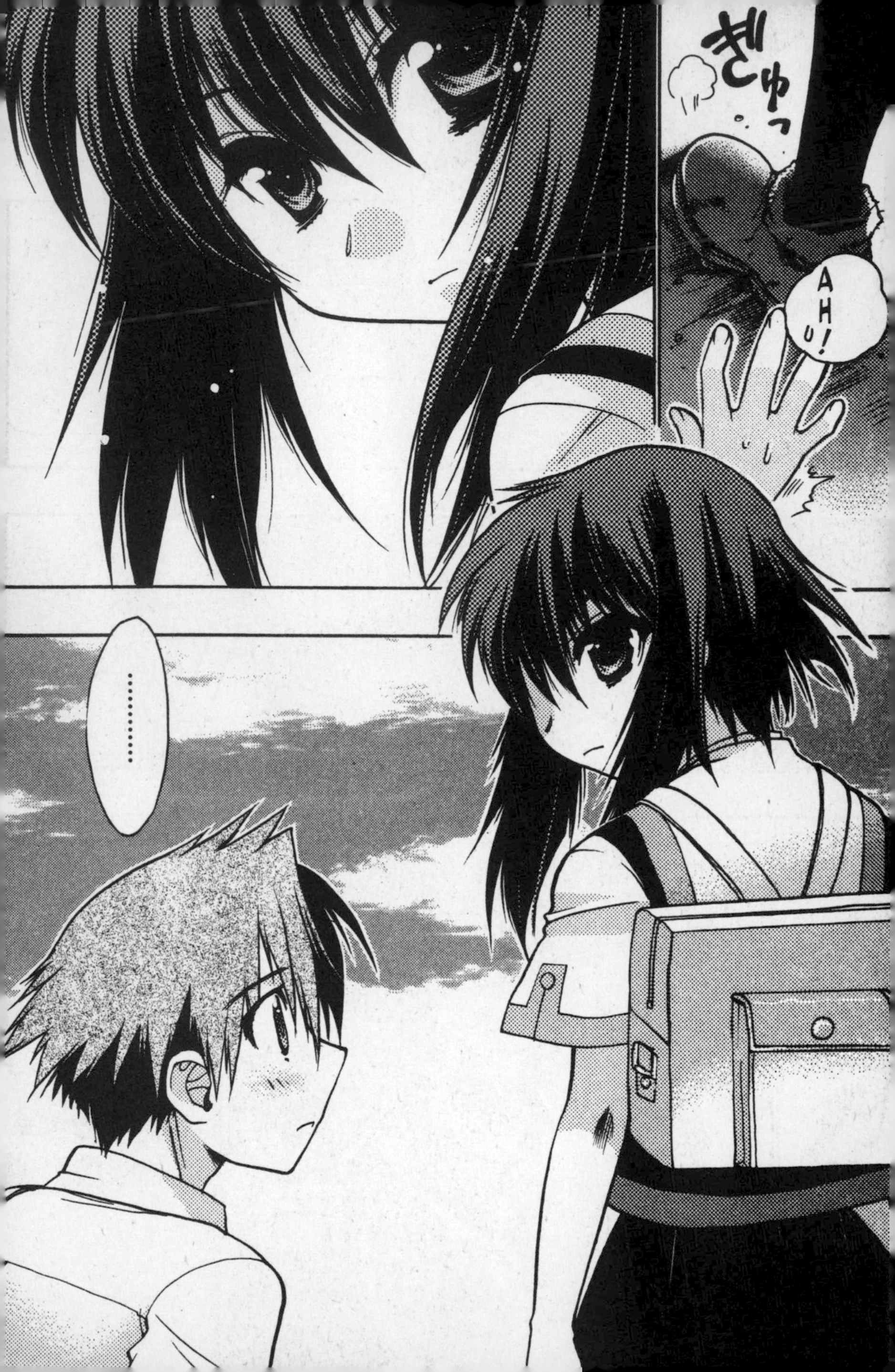
ぎゅっ
AHU!
....

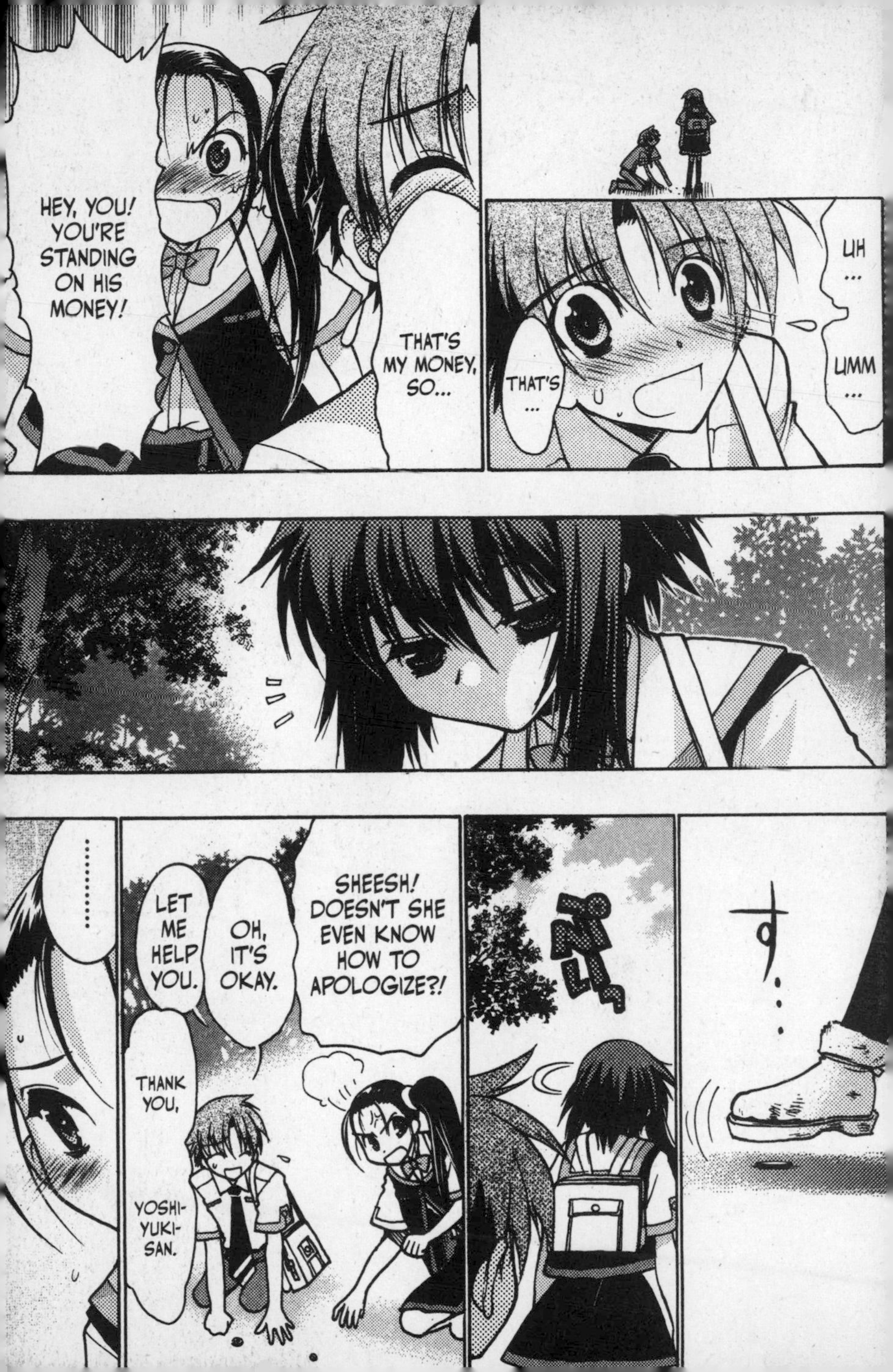
UH ... UMM ...
THAT'S ...
THAT'S MY MONEY, SO...
HEY, YOU! YOU'RE STANDING ON HIS MONEY!
す...
SHEESH! DOESN'T SHE EVEN KNOW HOW TO APOLOGIZE?!
OH, IT'S OKAY.
LET ME HELP YOU.
THANK YOU, YOSHI-YUKI-SAN.
......

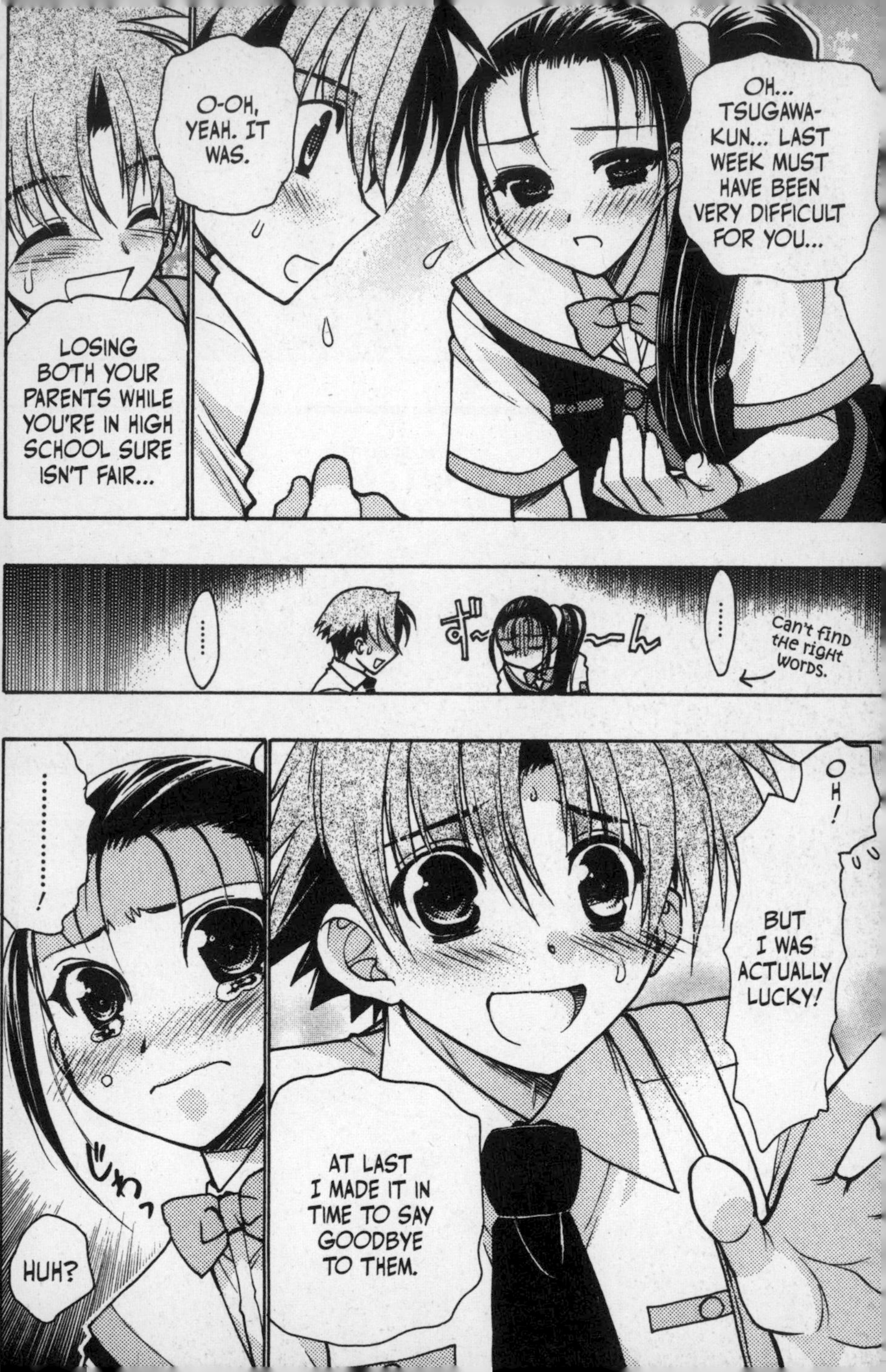
OH... TSUGAWA-KUN... LAST WEEK MUST HAVE BEEN VERY DIFFICULT FOR YOU...
O-OH, YEAH. IT WAS.
LOSING BOTH YOUR PARENTS WHILE YOU'RE IN HIGH SCHOOL SURE ISN'T FAIR...
......
Can't find the right words.
ず~~ん
......
OH!
BUT I WAS ACTUALLY LUCKY!
AT LAST I MADE IT IN TIME TO SAY GOODBYE TO THEM.
..........!
じわっ
HUH?

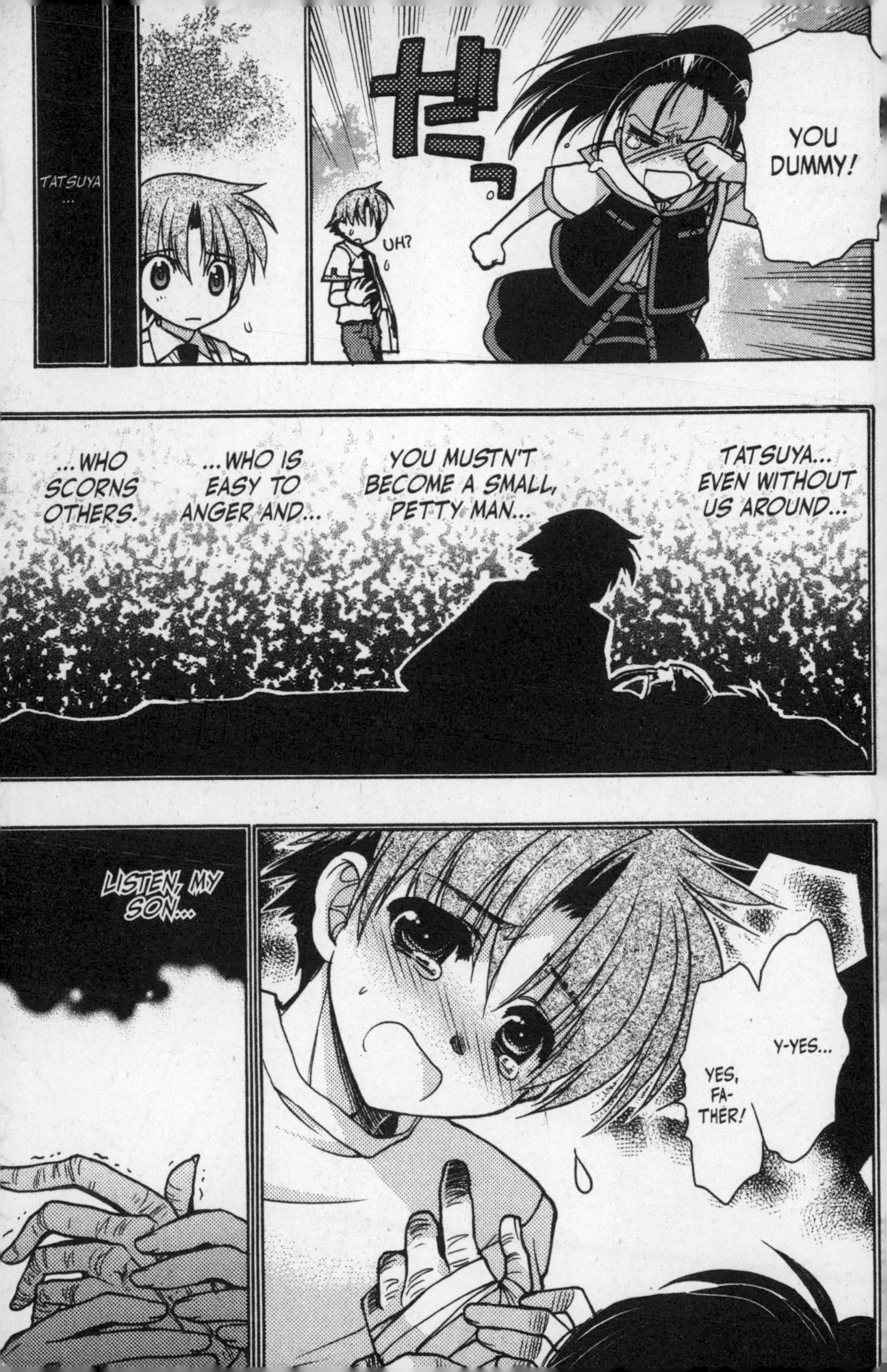
YOU DUMMY!
だっ
UH?
TATSUYA ...
TATSUYA... EVEN WITHOUT US AROUND...
YOU MUSTN'T BECOME A SMALL, PETTY MAN...
...WHO IS EASY TO ANGER AND...
...WHO SCORNS OTHERS.
Y-YES...
YES, FA-THER!
LISTEN, MY SON...

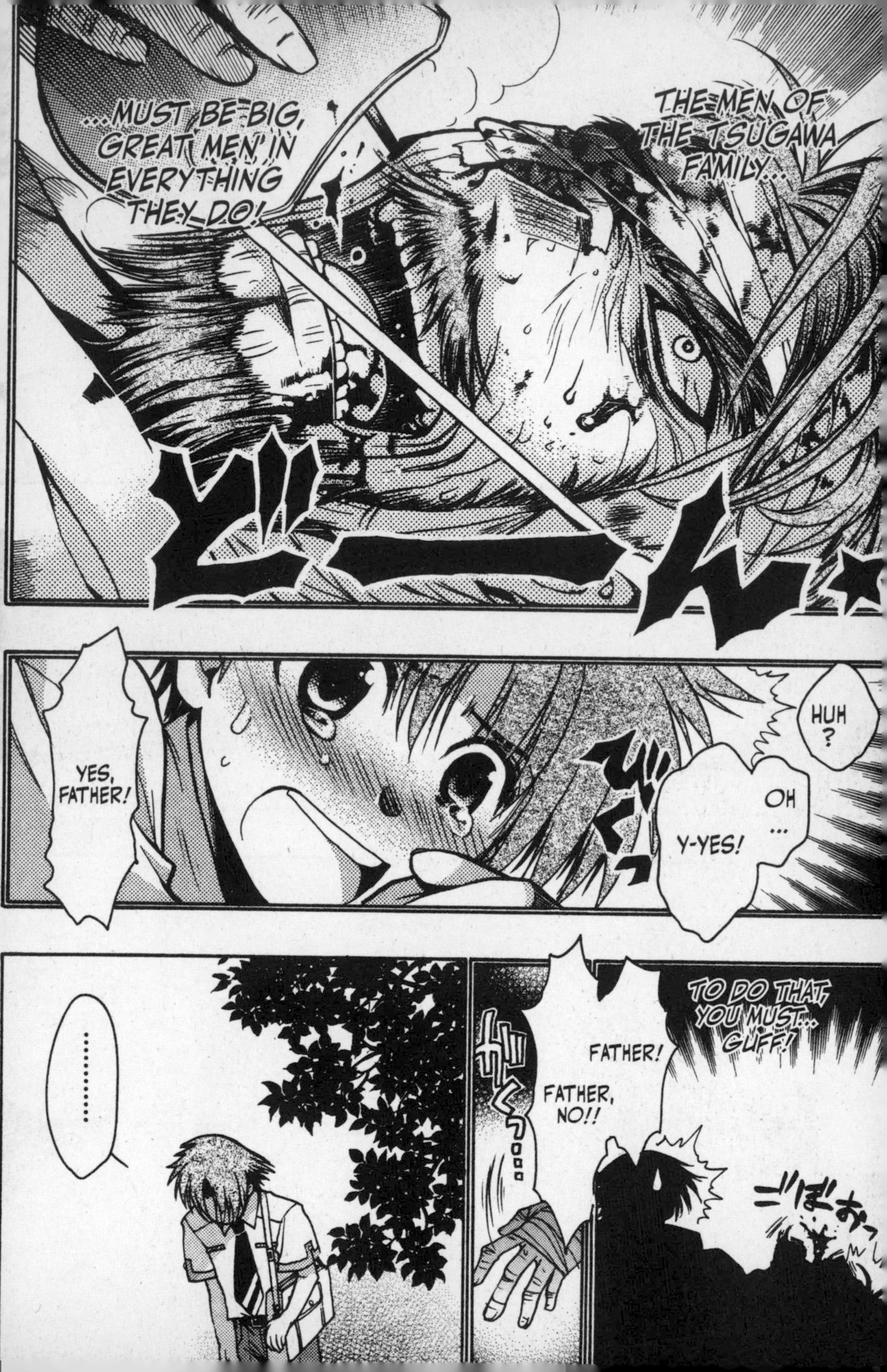
THE MEN OF THE TSUGAWA FAMILY...
...MUST BE BIG, GREAT MEN IN EVERYTHING THEY DO!
HUH?
OH... Y-YES!
YES, FATHER!
TO DO THAT, YOU MUST... GUFF!
FATHER!
FATHER, NO!!
......

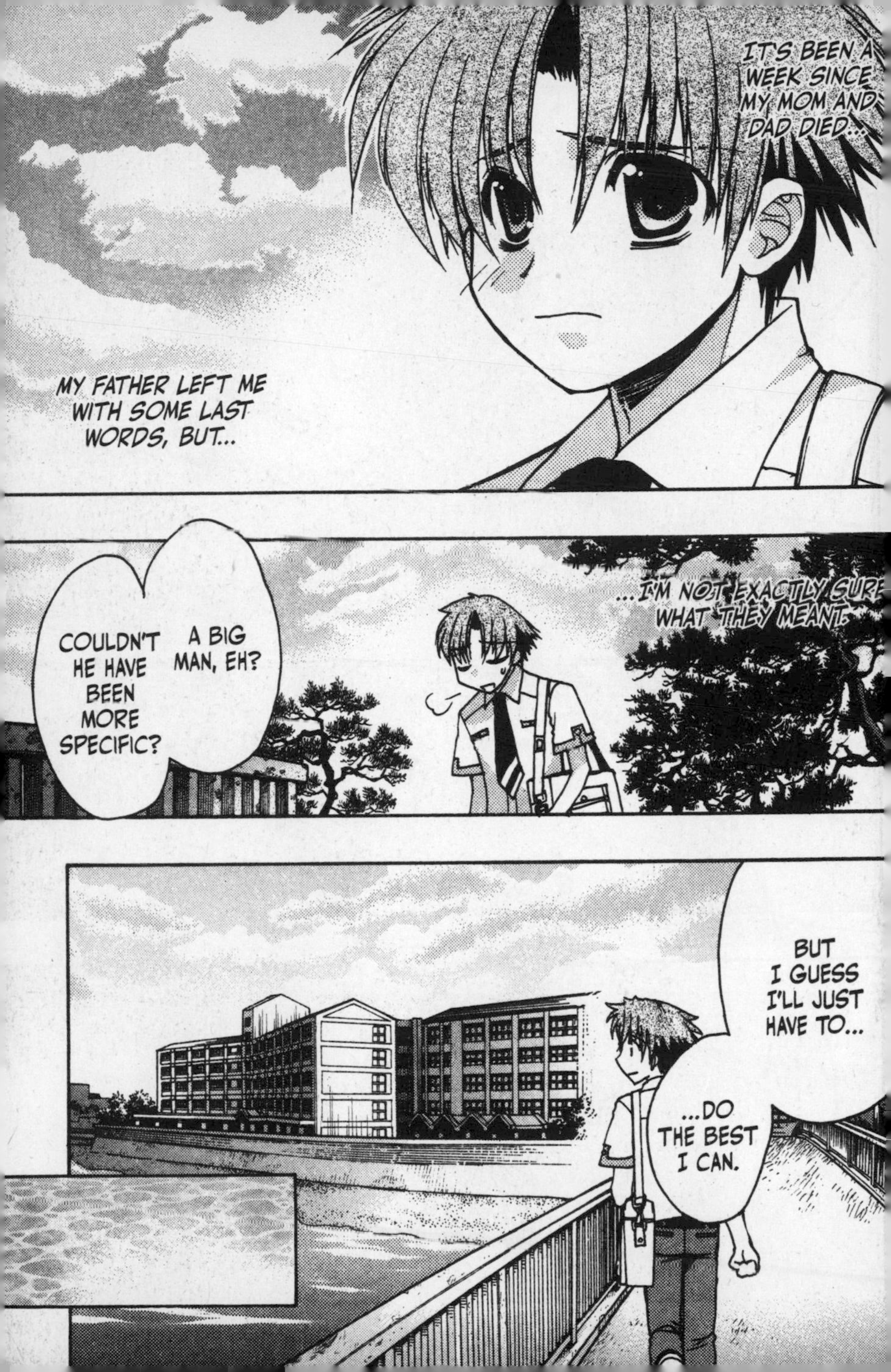
IT'S BEEN A WEEK SINCE MY MOM AND DAD DIED...
MY FATHER LEFT ME WITH SOME LAST WORDS, BUT...
...I'M NOT EXACTLY SURE WHAT THEY MEANT.
A BIG MAN, EH?
COULDN'T HE HAVE BEEN MORE SPECIFIC?
BUT I GUESS I'LL JUST HAVE TO...
...DO THE BEST I CAN.

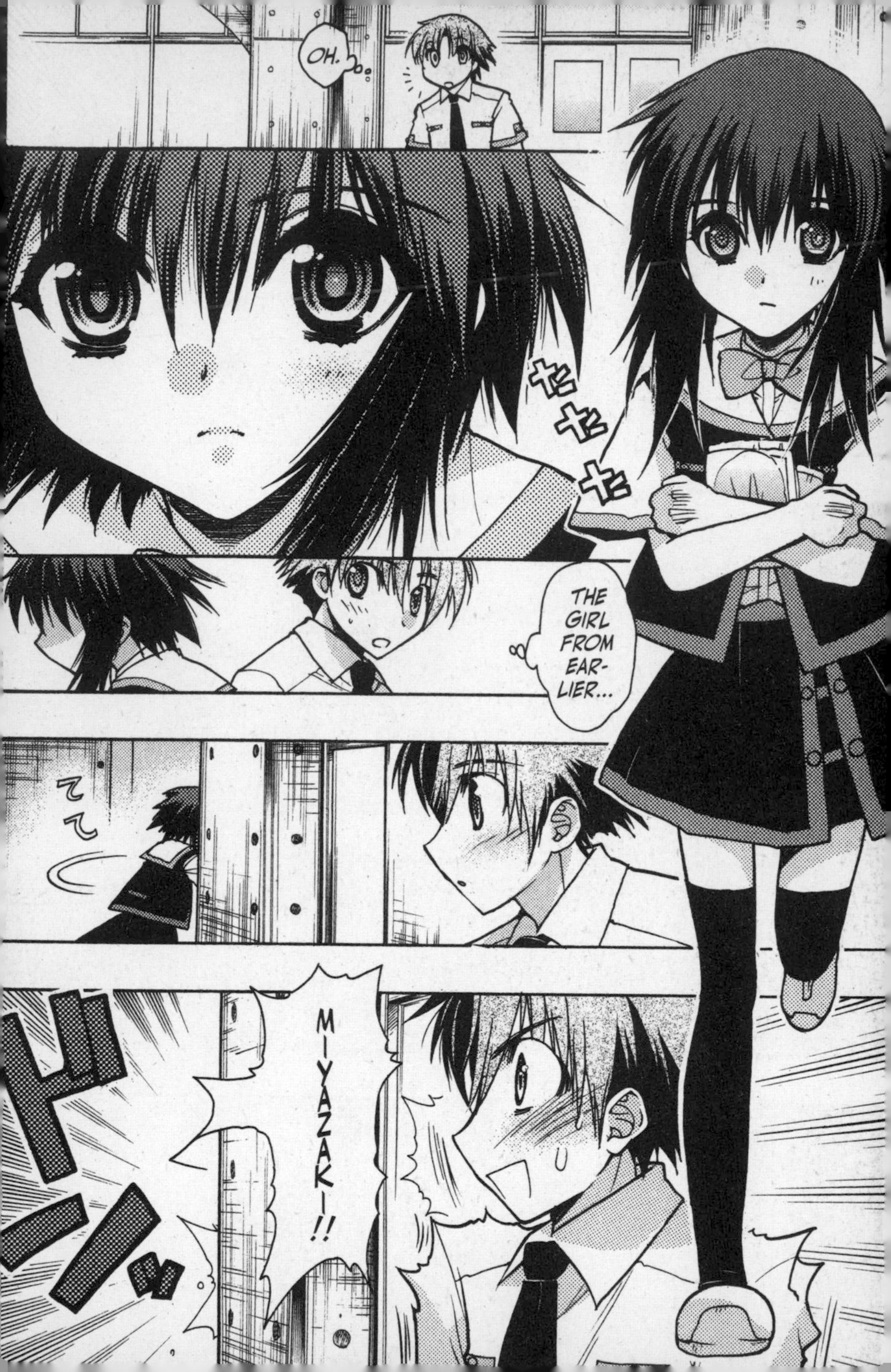
OH.
THE GIRL FROM EAR-LIER...
MIYAZAKI!!

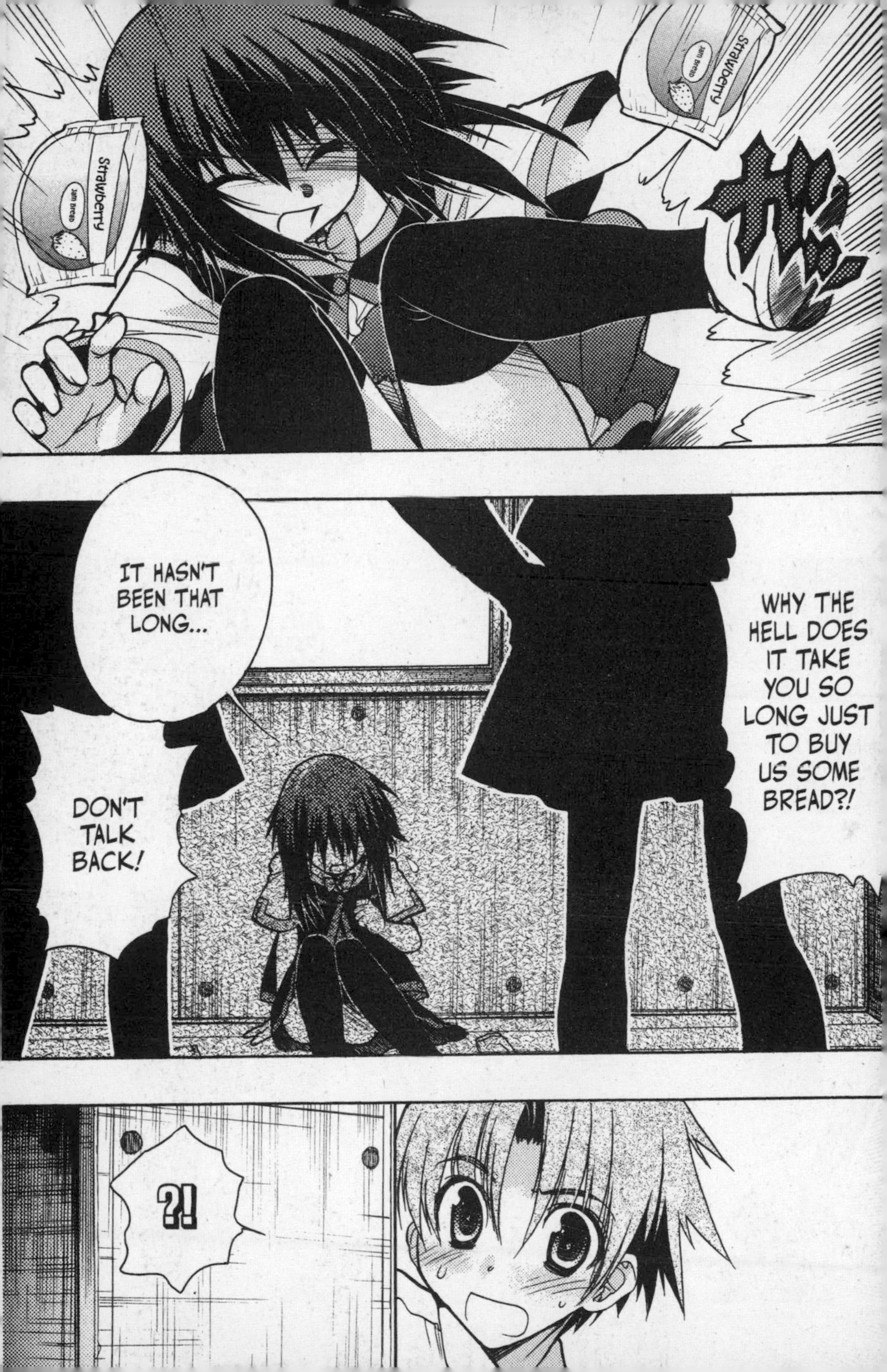
Strawberry
Jam Bread
Strawberry
Jam Bread
WHY THE HELL DOES IT TAKE YOU SO LONG JUST TO BUY US SOME BREAD?!
IT HASN'T BEEN THAT LONG...
DON'T TALK BACK!
?!

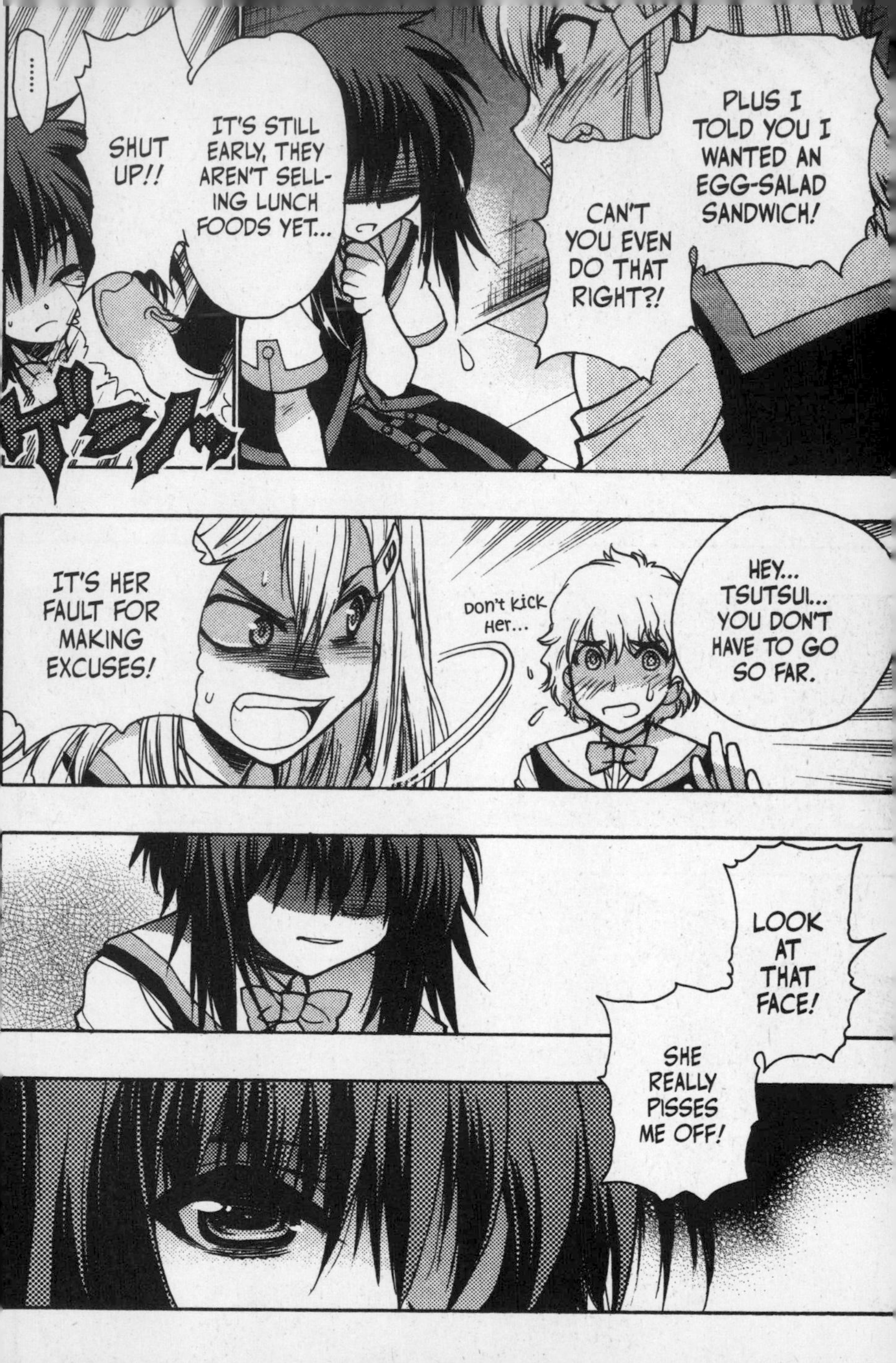
PLUS I TOLD YOU I WANTED AN EGG-SALAD SANDWICH!
CAN'T YOU EVEN DO THAT RIGHT?!
IT'S STILL EARLY, THEY AREN'T SELL-ING LUNCH FOODS YET...
SHUT UP!!
......
HEY... TSUTSUI... YOU DON'T HAVE TO GO SO FAR.
Don't kick her...
IT'S HER FAULT FOR MAKING EXCUSES!
LOOK AT THAT FACE!
SHE REALLY PISSES ME OFF!

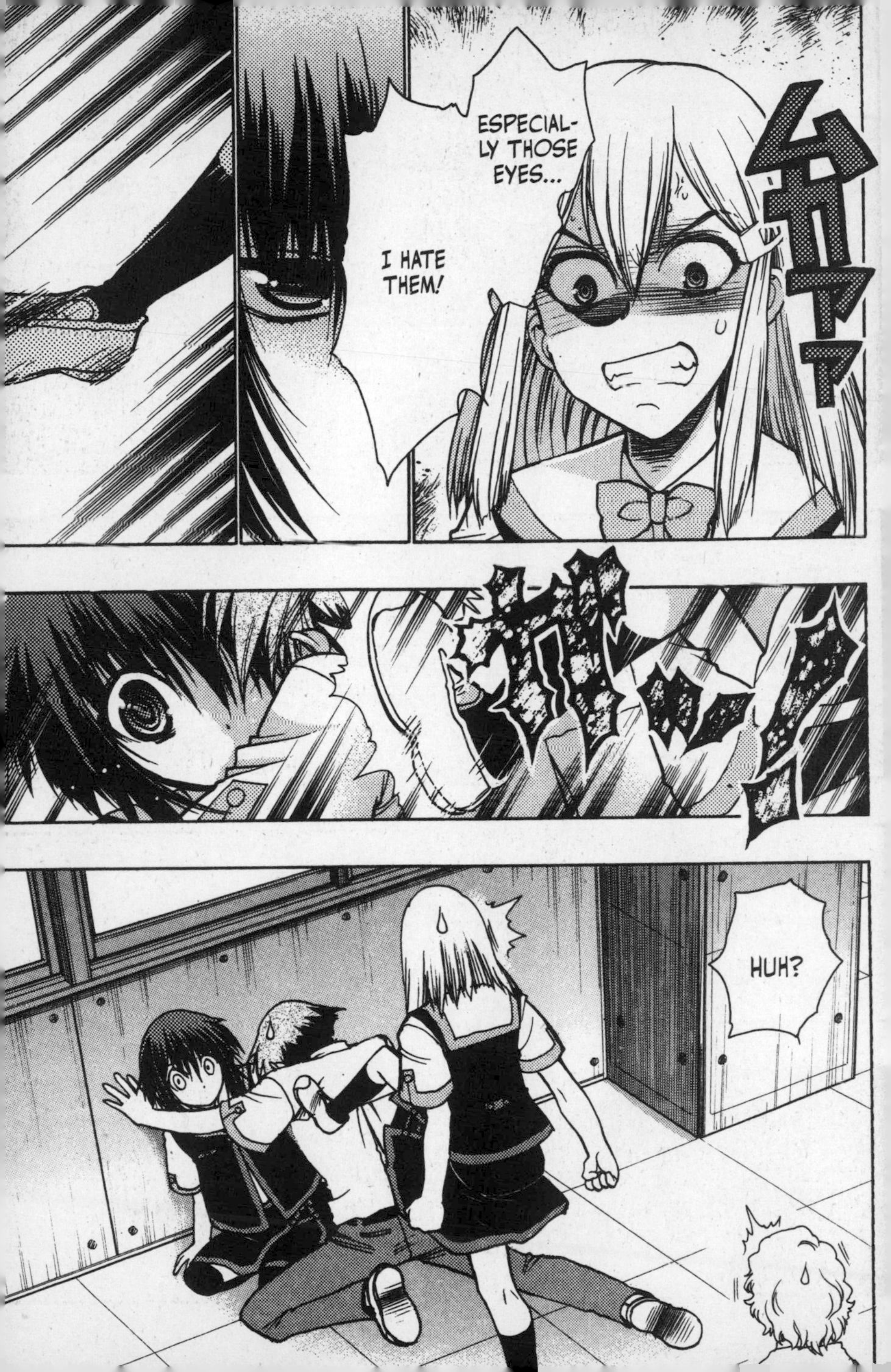
ESPECIAL-
LY THOSE
EYES...
I HATE
THEM!
HUH?

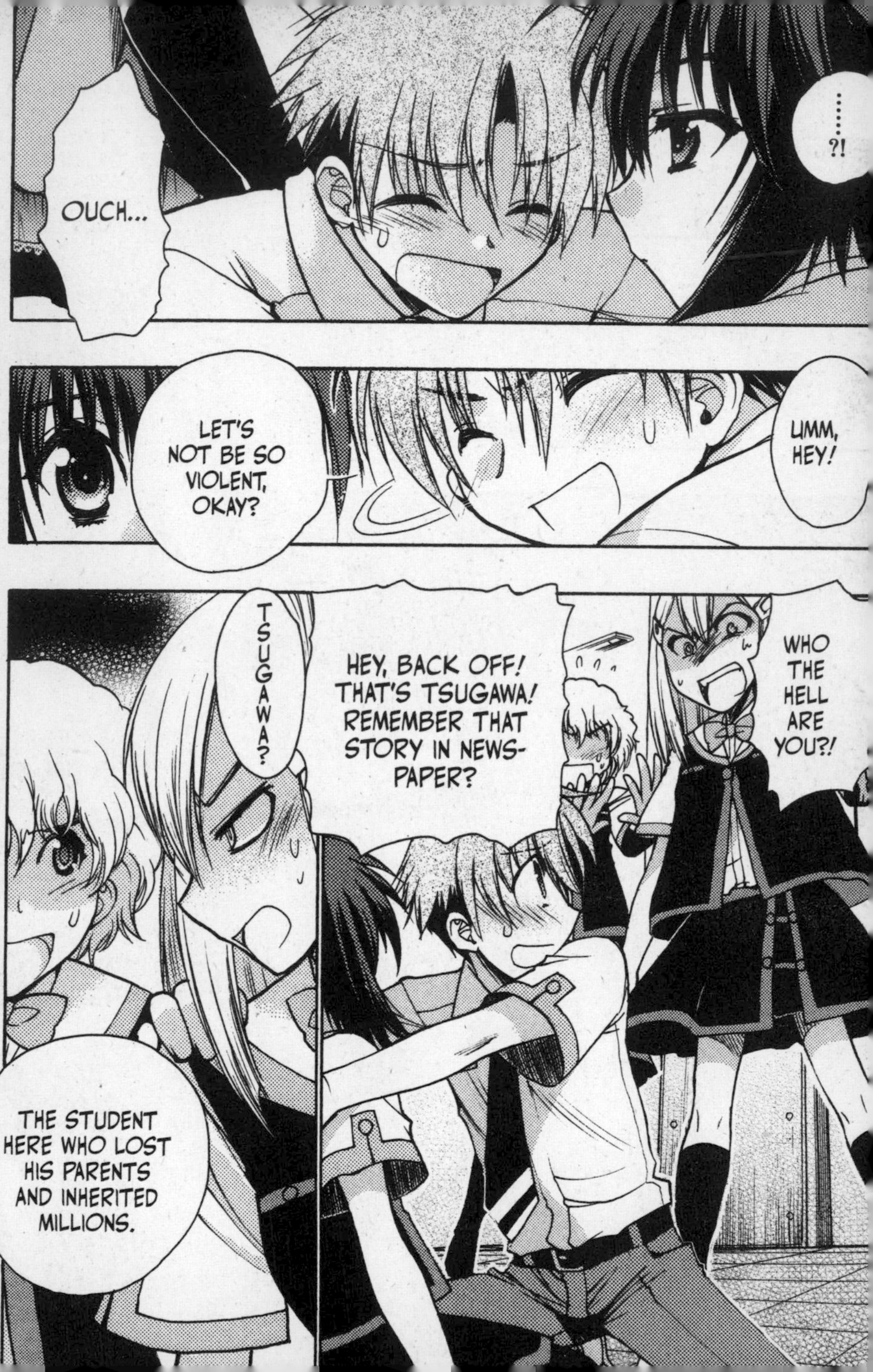
......?!
OUCH...
UMM, HEY!
LET'S NOT BE SO VIOLENT, OKAY?
WHO THE HELL ARE YOU?!
HEY, BACK OFF! THAT'S TSUGAWA! REMEMBER THAT STORY IN NEWS-PAPER?
TSUGAWA?
THE STUDENT HERE WHO LOST HIS PARENTS AND INHERITED MILLIONS.

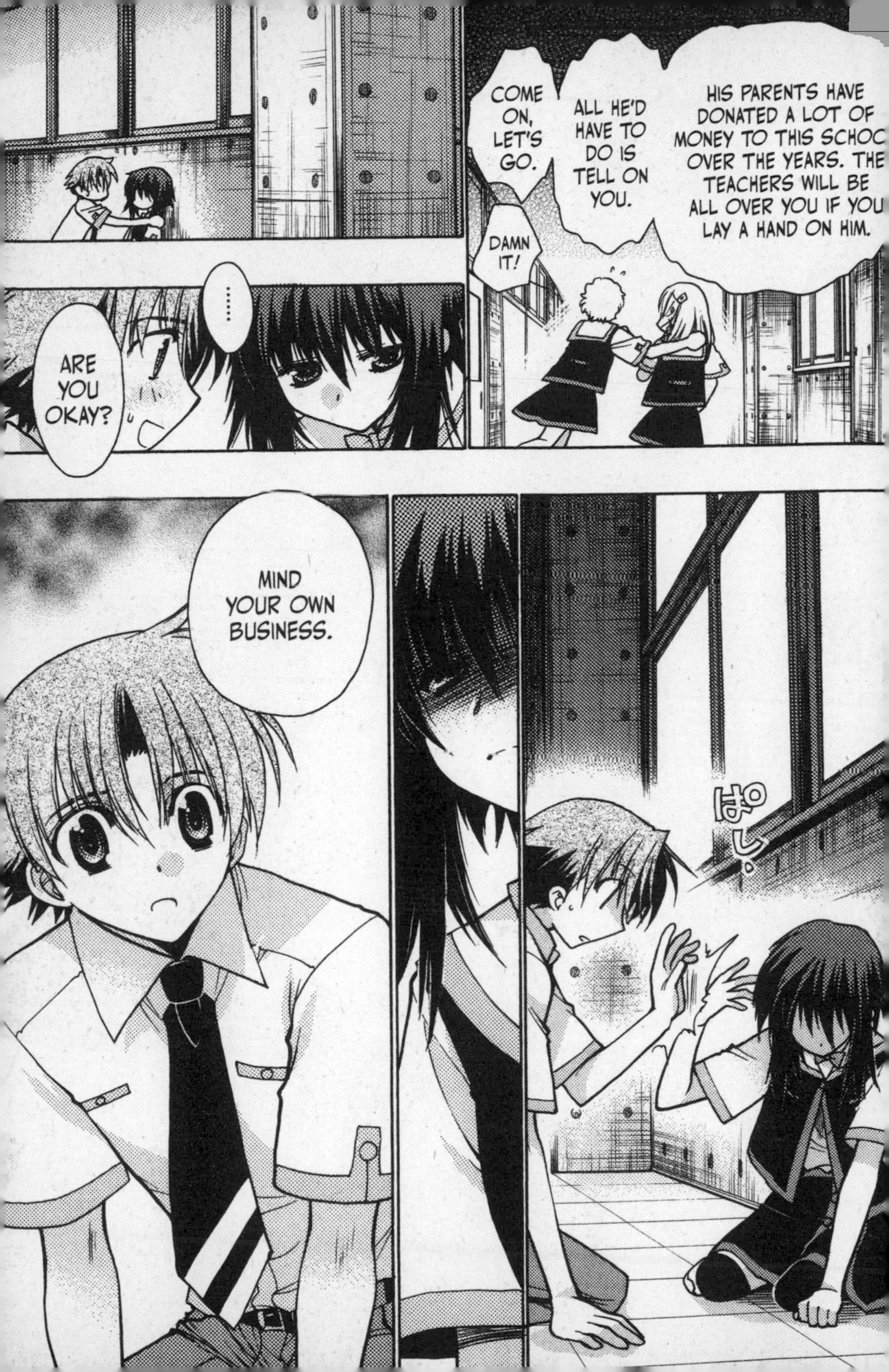
HIS PARENTS HAVE DONATED A LOT OF MONEY TO THIS SCHOO OVER THE YEARS. THE TEACHERS WILL BE ALL OVER YOU IF YOU LAY A HAND ON HIM.
ALL HE'D HAVE TO DO IS TELL ON YOU.
COME ON, LET'S GO.
DAMN IT!
......
ARE YOU OKAY?
ぱし
MIND YOUR OWN BUSINESS.

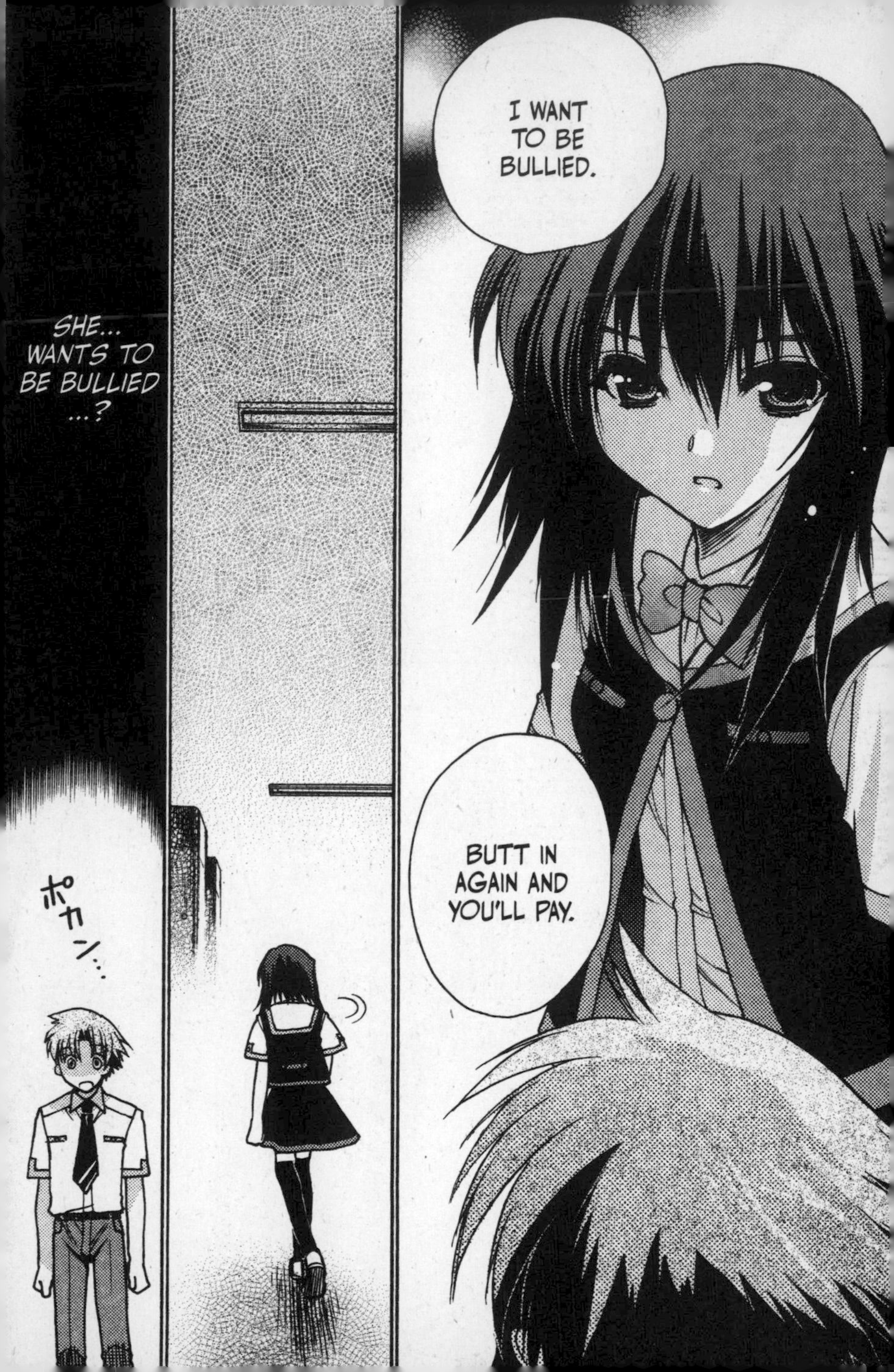
I WANT TO BE BULLIED.
BUTT IN AGAIN AND YOU'LL PAY.
SHE... WANTS TO BE BULLIED ...?
ポカン...

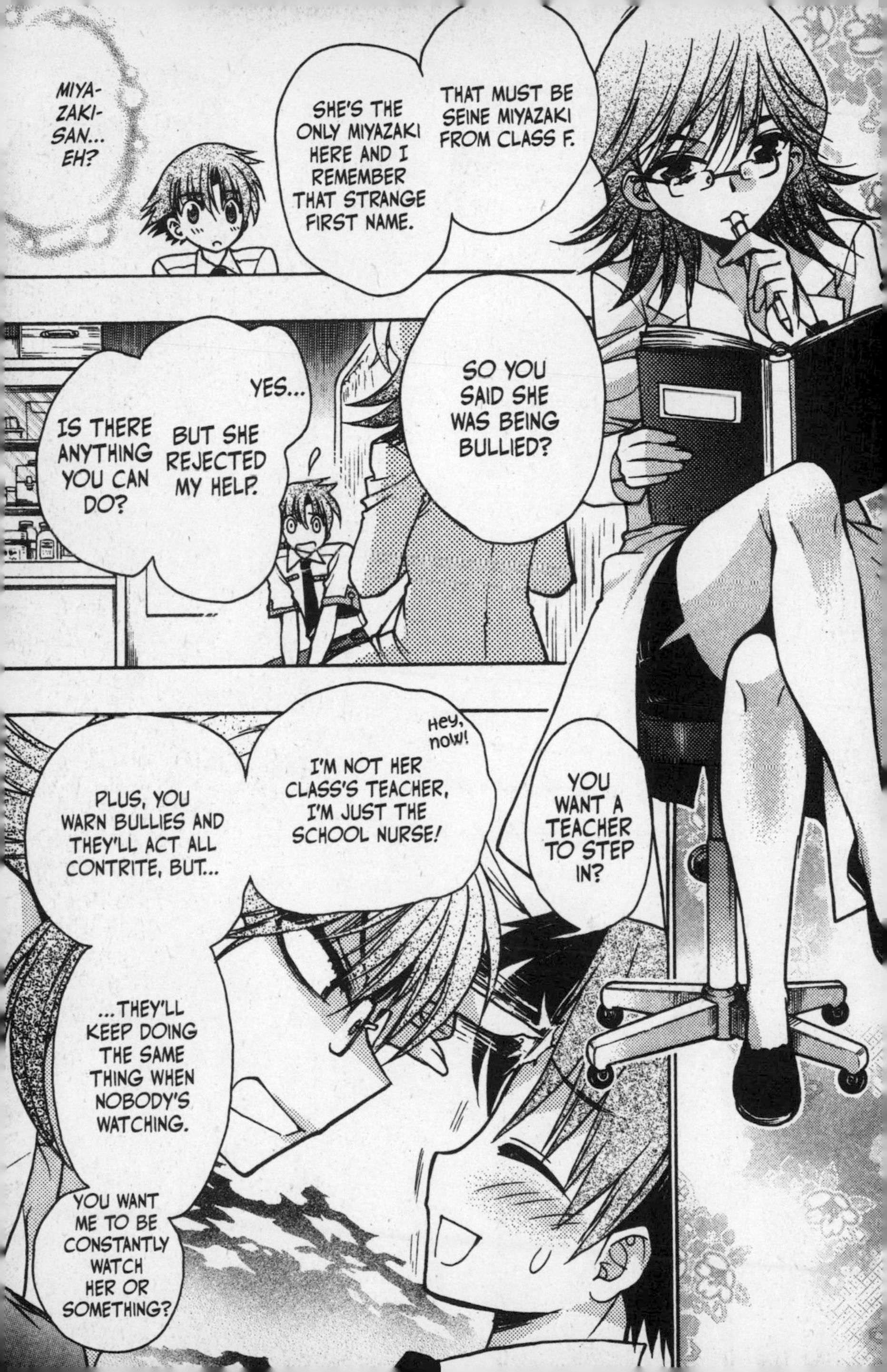
THAT MUST BE SEINE MIYAZAKI FROM CLASS F.
SHE'S THE ONLY MIYAZAKI HERE AND I REMEMBER THAT STRANGE FIRST NAME.
MIYA-ZAKI-SAN... EH?
SO YOU SAID SHE WAS BEING BULLIED?
YES...
BUT SHE REJECTED MY HELP.
IS THERE ANYTHING YOU CAN DO?
YOU WANT A TEACHER TO STEP IN?
Hey, now!
I'M NOT HER CLASS'S TEACHER, I'M JUST THE SCHOOL NURSE!
PLUS, YOU WARN BULLIES AND THEY'LL ACT ALL CONTRITE, BUT...
...THEY'LL KEEP DOING THE SAME THING WHEN NOBODY'S WATCHING.
YOU WANT ME TO BE CONSTANTLY WATCH HER OR SOMETHING?

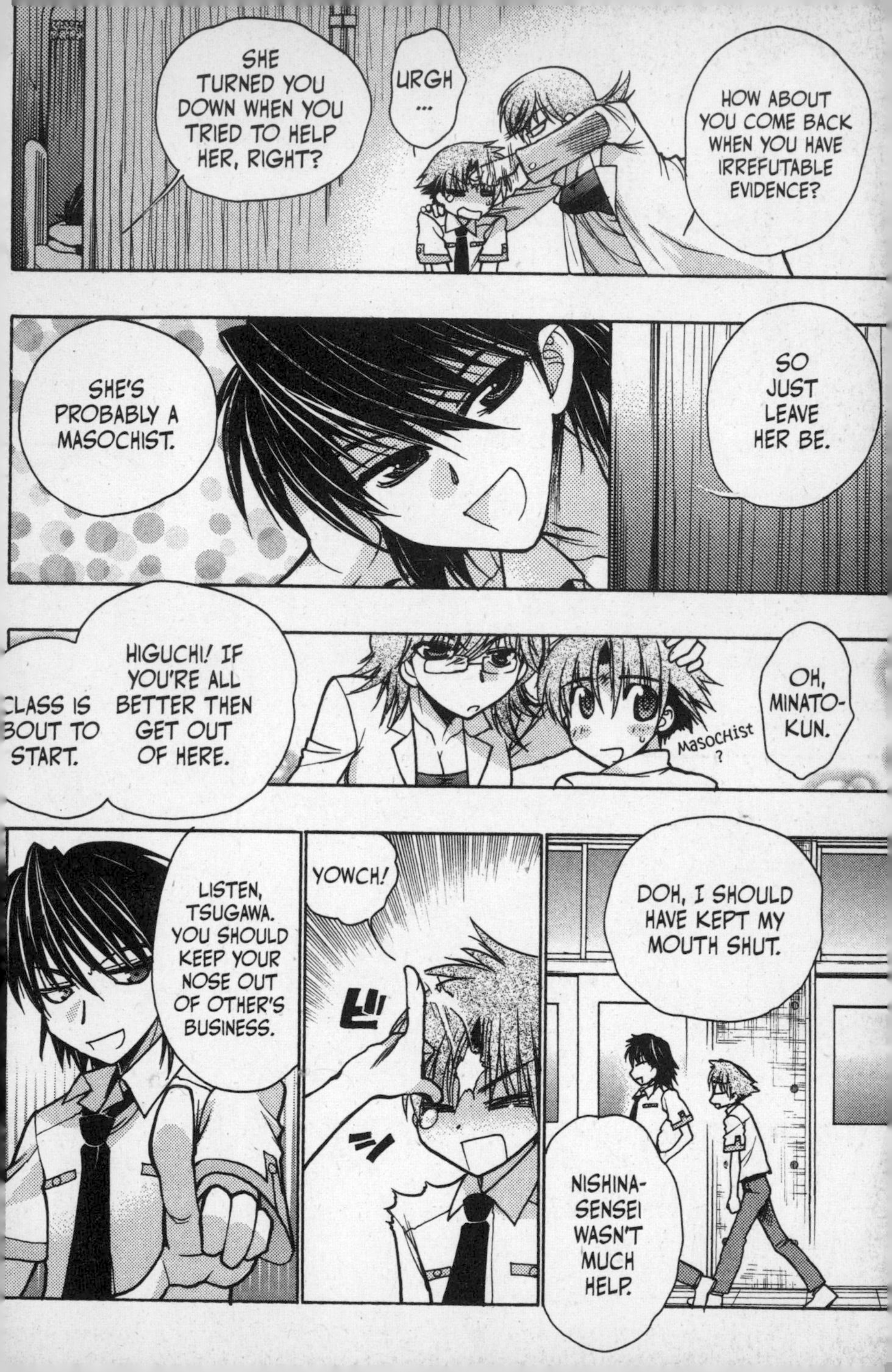
HOW ABOUT YOU COME BACK WHEN YOU HAVE IRREFUTABLE EVIDENCE?
URGH ...
SHE TURNED YOU DOWN WHEN YOU TRIED TO HELP HER, RIGHT?
SO JUST LEAVE HER BE.
SHE'S PROBABLY A MASOCHIST.
OH, MINATO-KUN.
Masochist ?
HIGUCHI! IF YOU'RE ALL BETTER THEN GET OUT OF HERE.
CLASS IS BOUT TO START.
DOH, I SHOULD HAVE KEPT MY MOUTH SHUT.
NISHINA-SENSEI WASN'T MUCH HELP.
YOWCH!
LISTEN, TSUGAWA. YOU SHOULD KEEP YOUR NOSE OUT OF OTHER'S BUSINESS.

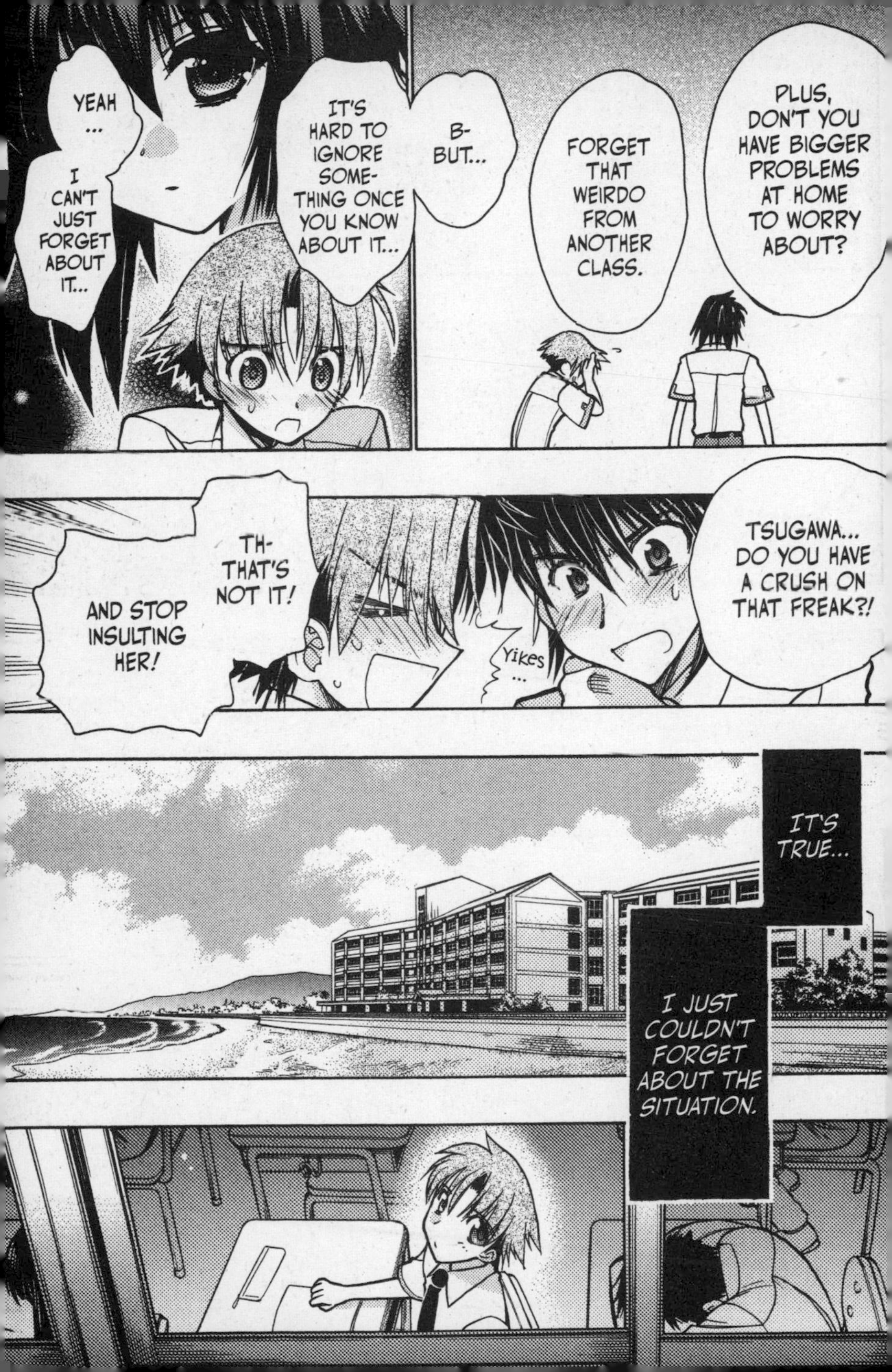
PLUS, DON'T YOU HAVE BIGGER PROBLEMS AT HOME TO WORRY ABOUT?
FORGET THAT WEIRDO FROM ANOTHER CLASS.
B-BUT...
IT'S HARD TO IGNORE SOME-THING ONCE YOU KNOW ABOUT IT...
YEAH ...
I CAN'T JUST FORGET ABOUT IT...
TSUGAWA... DO YOU HAVE A CRUSH ON THAT FREAK?!
Yikes ...
TH-THAT'S NOT IT!
AND STOP INSULTING HER!
IT'S TRUE...
I JUST COULDN'T FORGET ABOUT THE SITUATION.

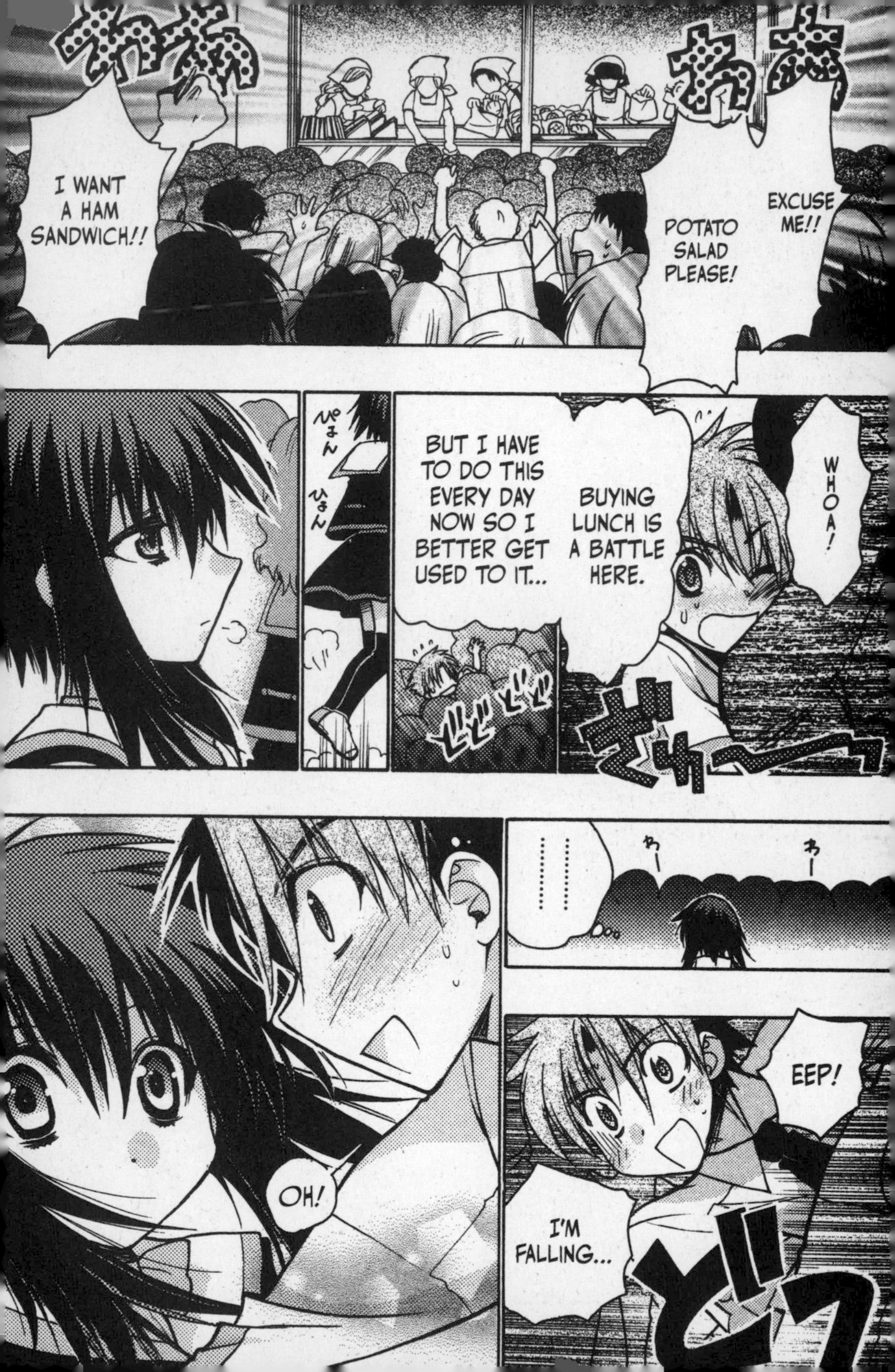
EXCUSE ME!!
POTATO SALAD PLEASE!
I WANT A HAM SANDWICH!!
WHOA!
BUYING LUNCH IS A BATTLE HERE.
BUT I HAVE TO DO THIS EVERY DAY NOW SO I BETTER GET USED TO IT...
ぴょん ぴょん
......
EEP!
I'M FALLING...
OH!

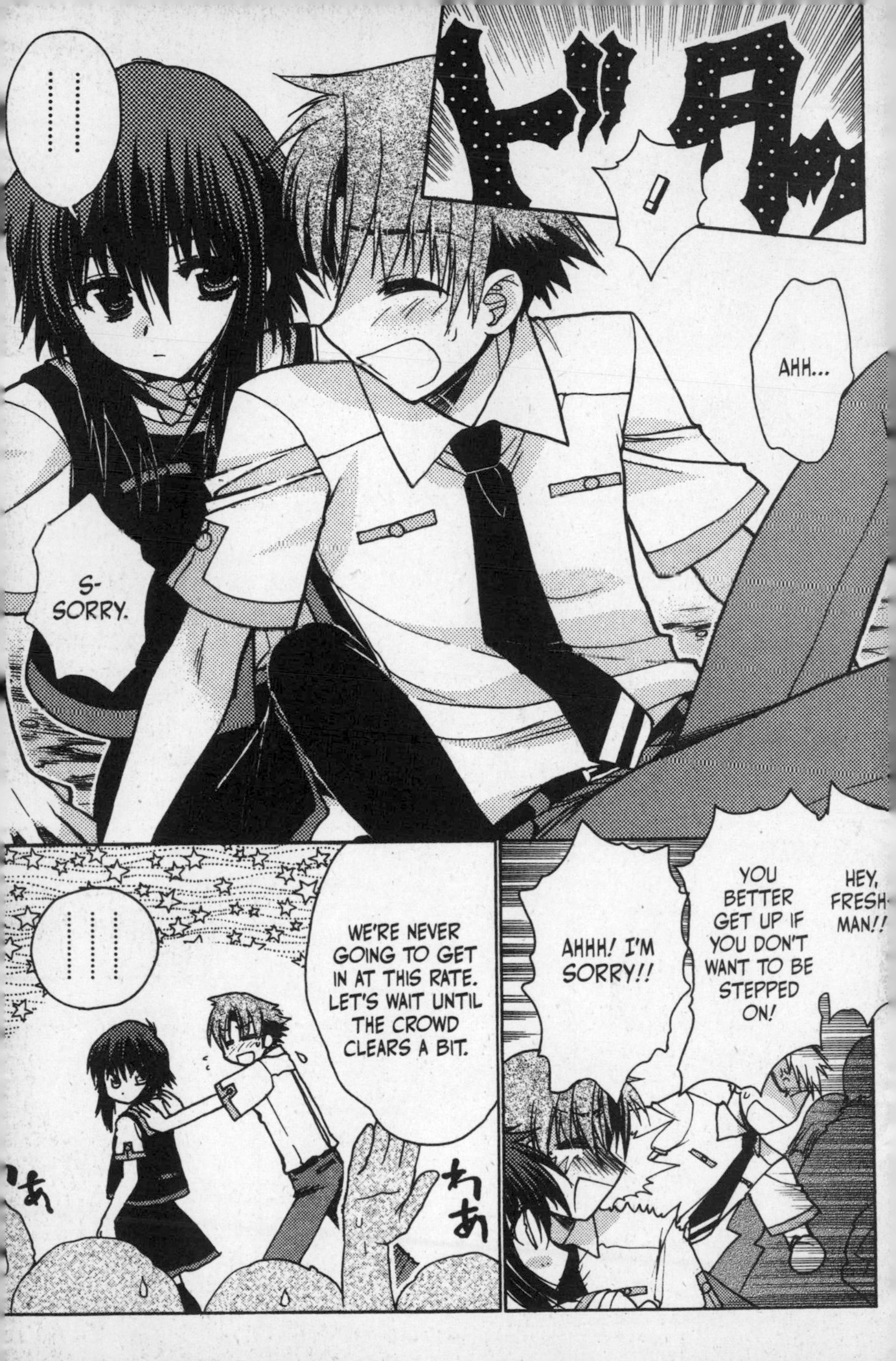

!
......
AHH...
S-SORRY.
HEY, FRESHMAN!!
YOU BETTER GET UP IF YOU DON'T WANT TO BE STEPPED ON!
AHHH! I'M SORRY!!
WE'RE NEVER GOING TO GET IN AT THIS RATE. LET'S WAIT UNTIL THE CROWD CLEARS A BIT.
......
わあ

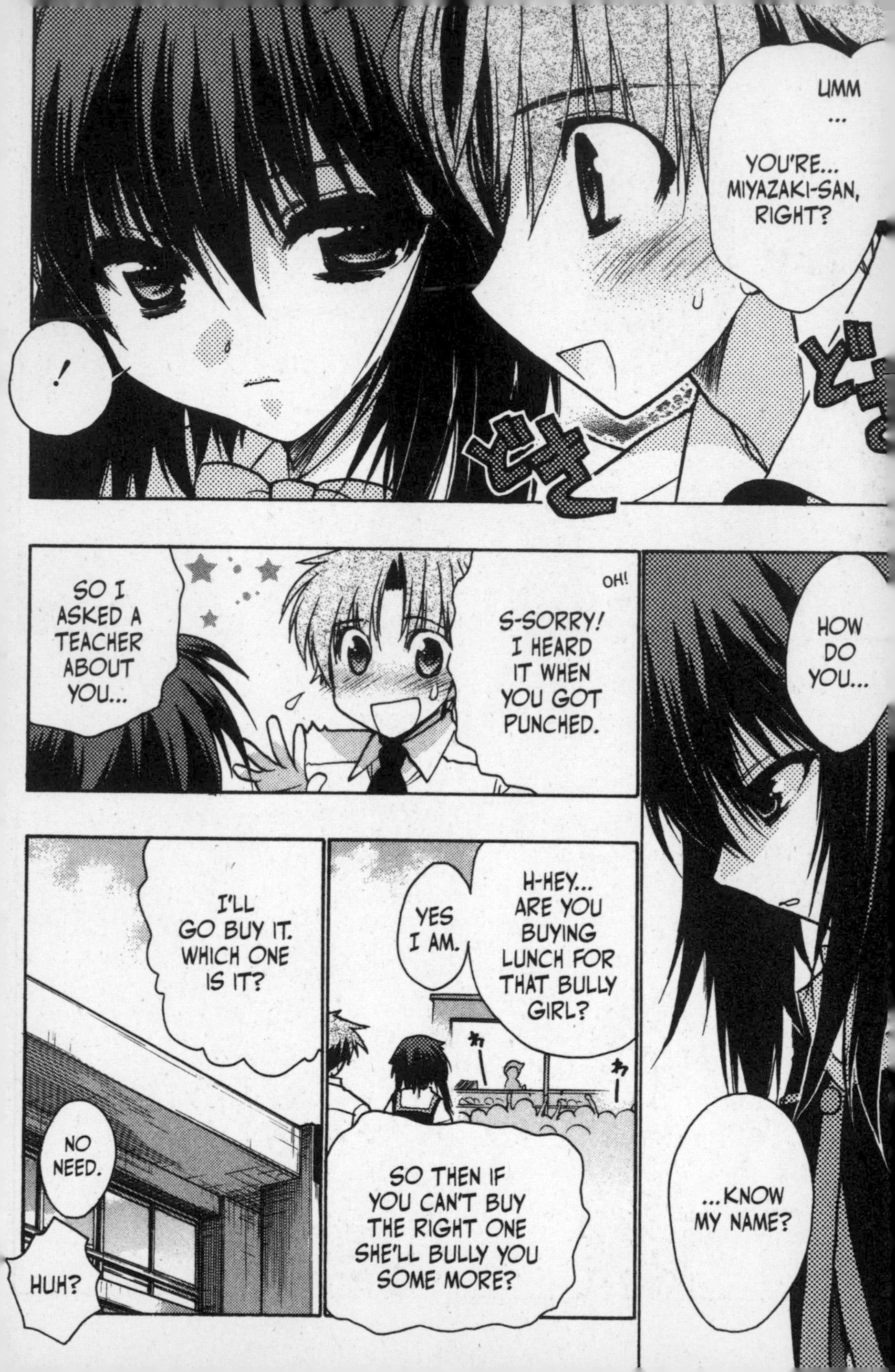
UMM ... YOU'RE... MIYAZAKI-SAN, RIGHT?
!
HOW DO YOU...
...KNOW MY NAME?
OH!
S-SORRY! I HEARD IT WHEN YOU GOT PUNCHED.
SO I ASKED A TEACHER ABOUT YOU...
H-HEY... ARE YOU BUYING LUNCH FOR THAT BULLY GIRL?
YES I AM.
SO THEN IF YOU CAN'T BUY THE RIGHT ONE SHE'LL BULLY YOU SOME MORE?
I'LL GO BUY IT. WHICH ONE IS IT?
NO NEED.
HUH?

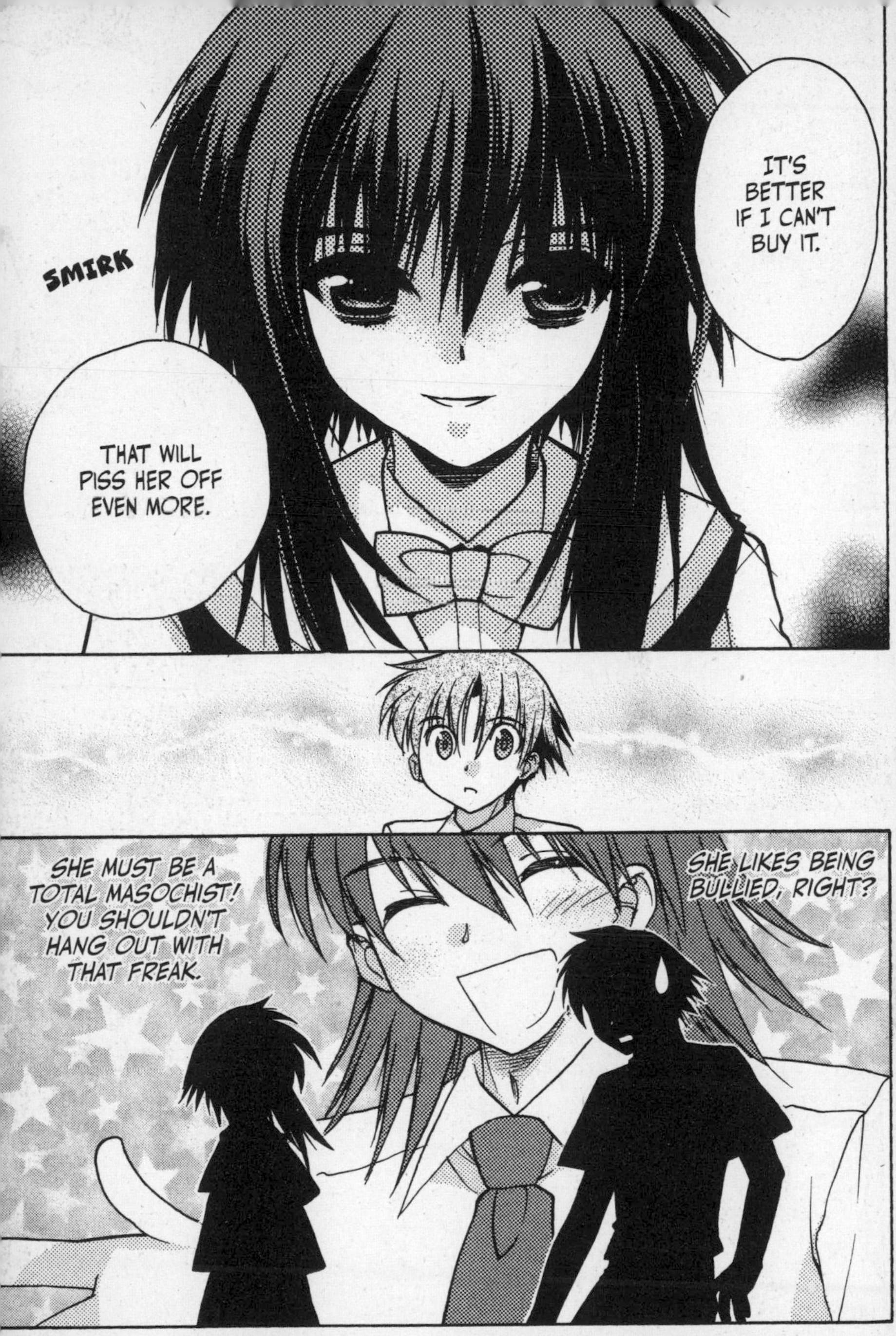
IT'S BETTER IF I CAN'T BUY IT.
SMIRK
THAT WILL PISS HER OFF EVEN MORE.
SHE LIKES BEING BULLIED, RIGHT?
SHE MUST BE A TOTAL MASOCHIST! YOU SHOULDN'T HANG OUT WITH THAT FREAK.

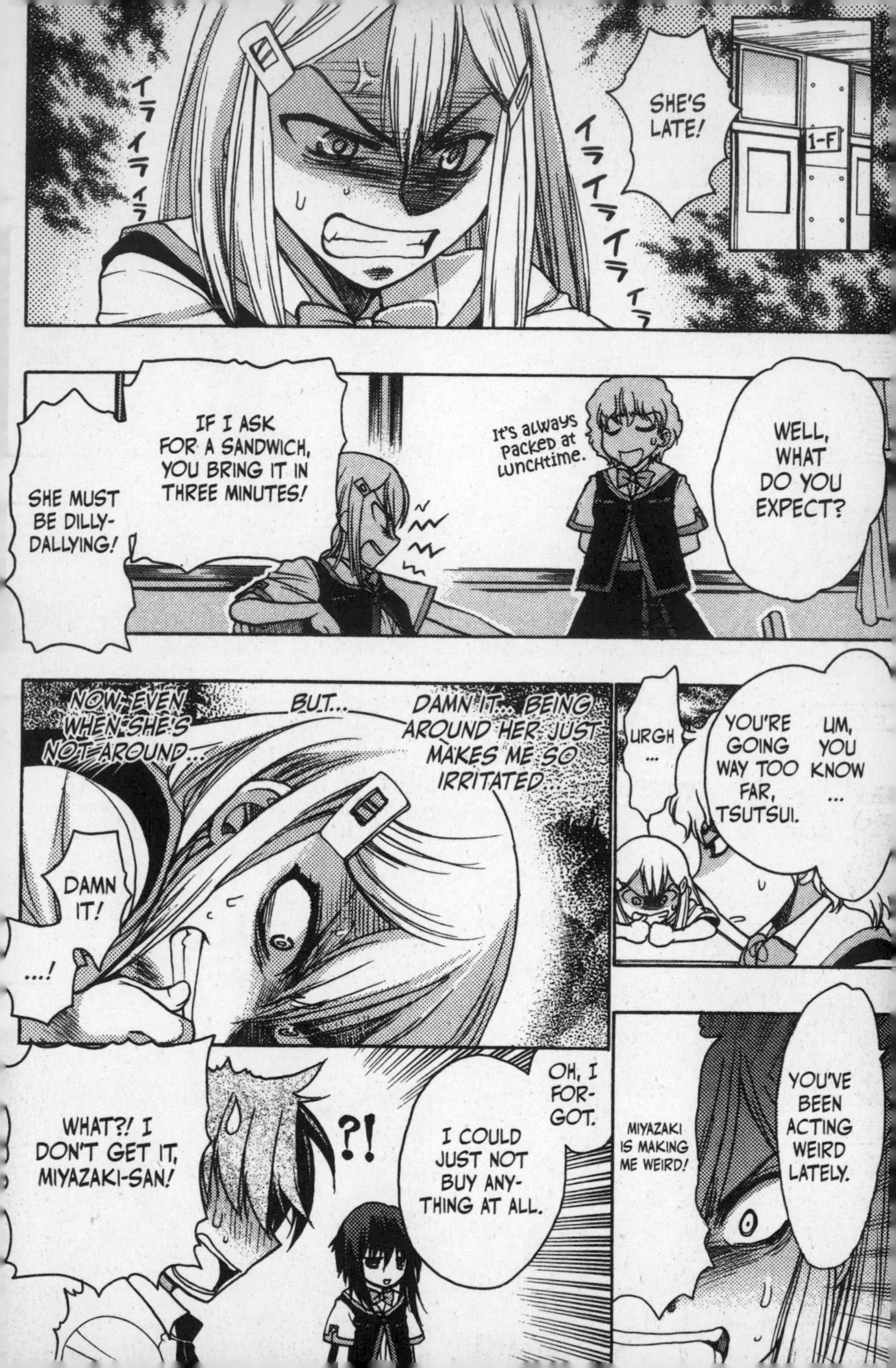
SHE'S LATE!
イライライライラ
イライライラ
WELL, WHAT DO YOU EXPECT?
It's always packed at lunchtime.
IF I ASK FOR A SANDWICH, YOU BRING IT IN THREE MINUTES!
SHE MUST BE DILLY-DALLYING!
UM, YOU KNOW ...
YOU'RE GOING WAY TOO FAR, TSUTSUI.
URGH ...
DAMN IT... BEING AROUND HER JUST MAKES ME SO IRRITATED...
BUT...
NOW EVEN WHEN SHE'S NOT AROUND...
DAMN IT!
...!
YOU'VE BEEN ACTING WEIRD LATELY.
MIYAZAKI IS MAKING ME WEIRD!
OH, I FOR-GOT.
I COULD JUST NOT BUY ANY-THING AT ALL.
?!
WHAT?! I DON'T GET IT, MIYAZAKI-SAN!

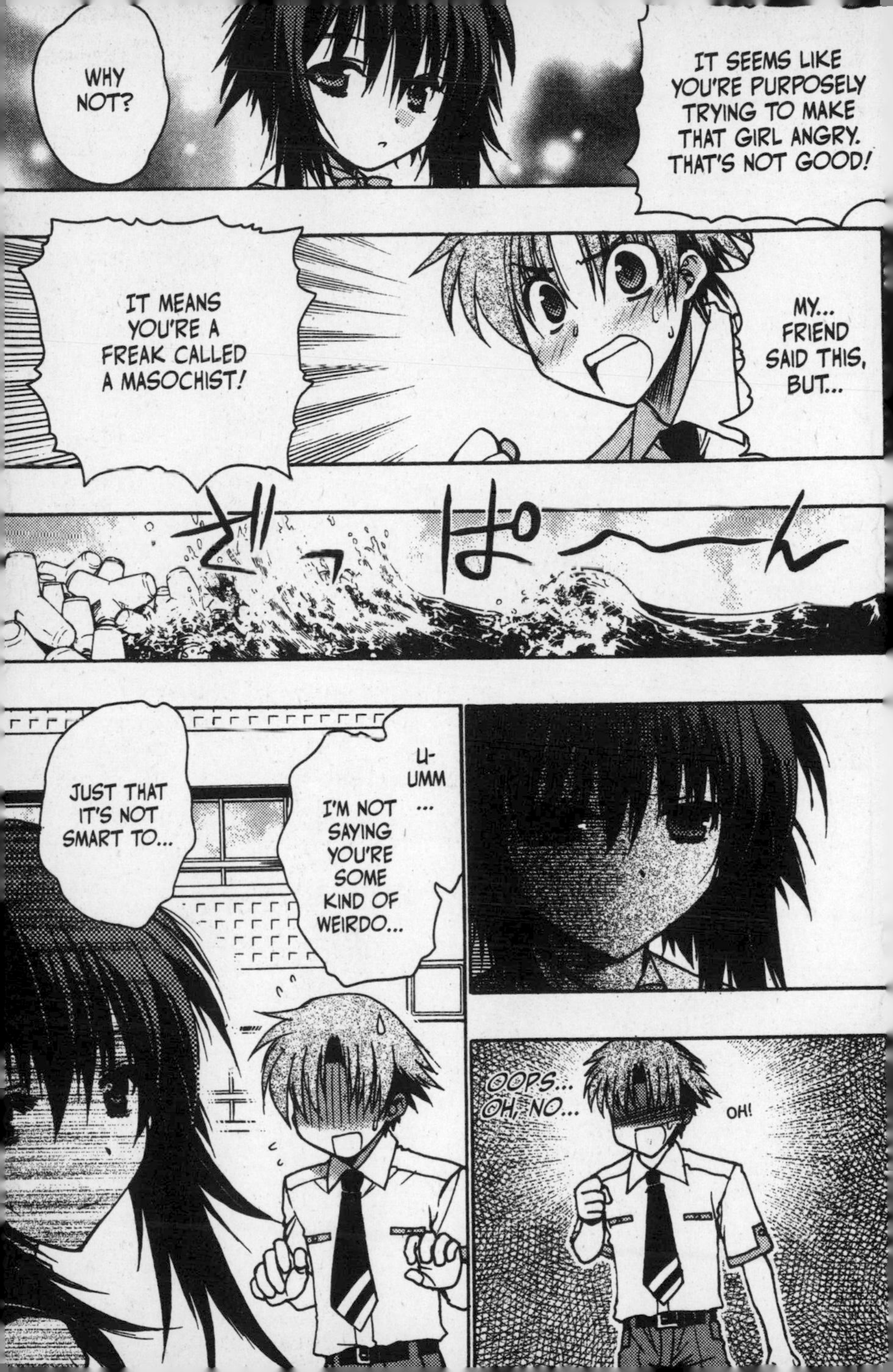
IT SEEMS LIKE YOU'RE PURPOSELY TRYING TO MAKE THAT GIRL ANGRY. THAT'S NOT GOOD!
WHY NOT?
MY... FRIEND SAID THIS, BUT...
IT MEANS YOU'RE A FREAK CALLED A MASOCHIST!
ざっぱ～ん
OH!
OOPS... OH, NO...
U-UMM...
I'M NOT SAYING YOU'RE SOME KIND OF WEIRDO...
JUST THAT IT'S NOT SMART TO...

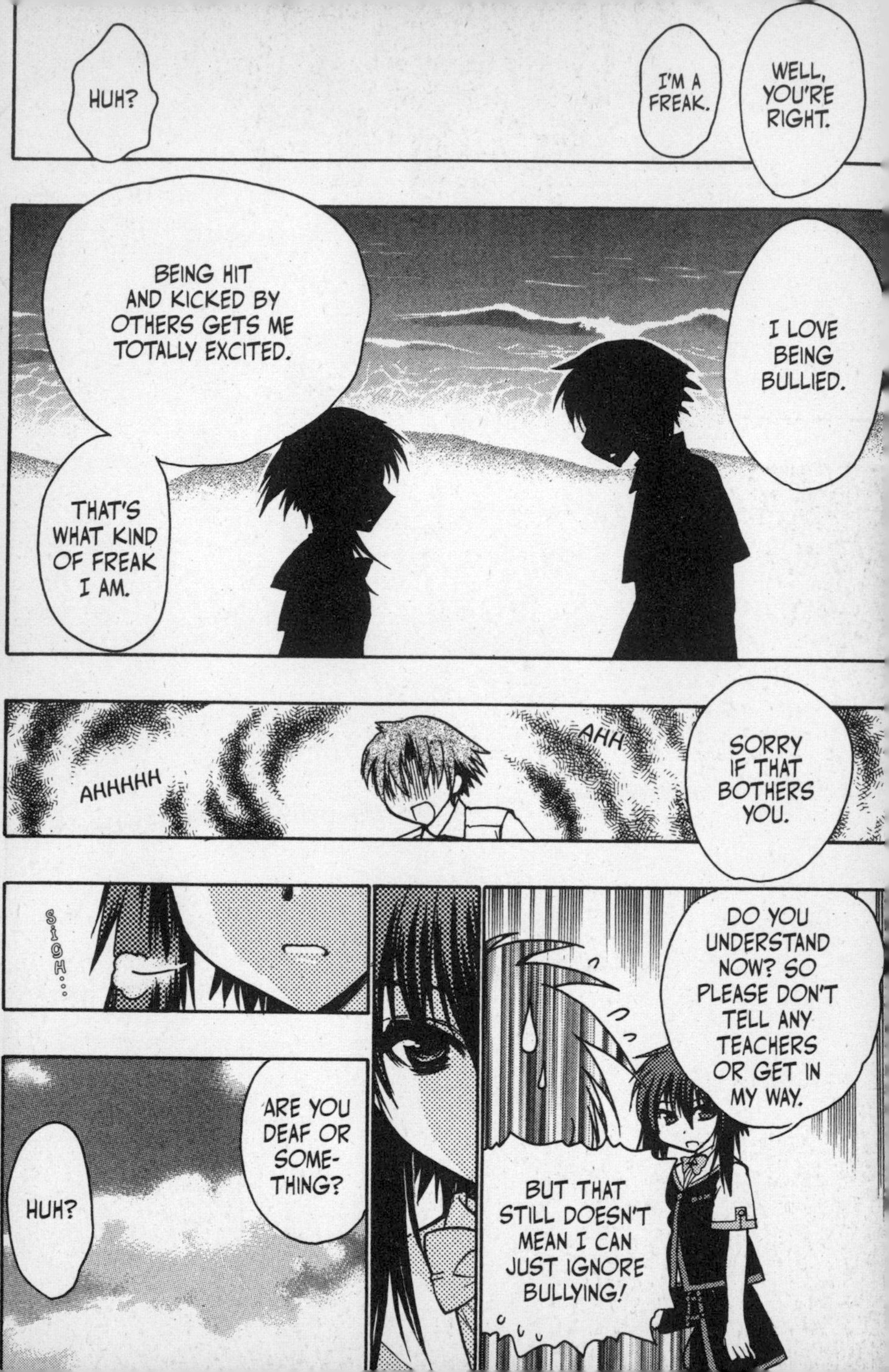
WELL, YOU'RE RIGHT.
I'M A FREAK.
HUH?
I LOVE BEING BULLIED.
BEING HIT AND KICKED BY OTHERS GETS ME TOTALLY EXCITED.
THAT'S WHAT KIND OF FREAK I AM.
SORRY IF THAT BOTHERS YOU.
AHH
AHHHHH
DO YOU UNDERSTAND NOW? SO PLEASE DON'T TELL ANY TEACHERS OR GET IN MY WAY.
BUT THAT STILL DOESN'T MEAN I CAN JUST IGNORE BULLYING!
SIGH...
ARE YOU DEAF OR SOME-THING?
HUH?

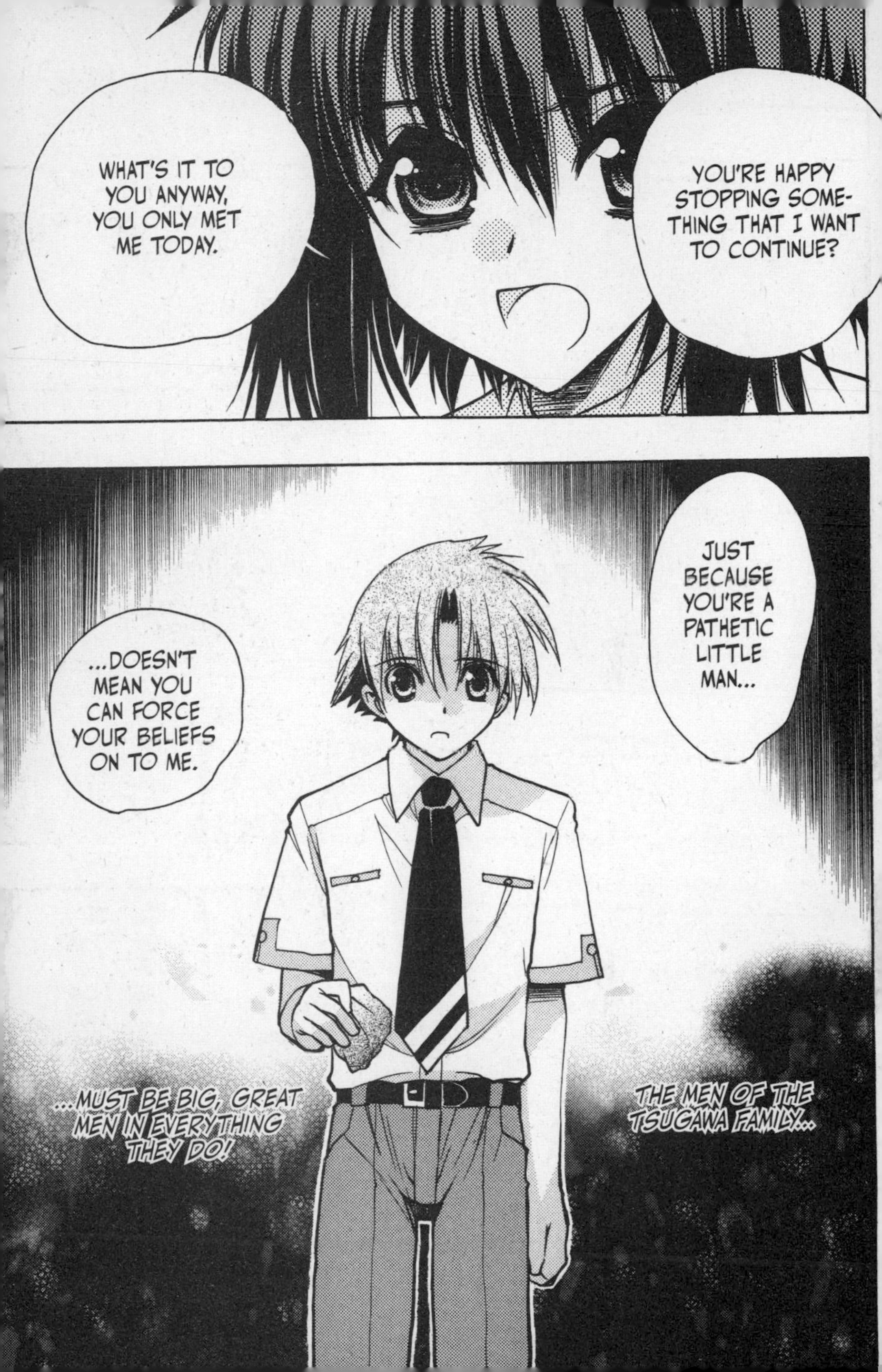
YOU'RE HAPPY STOPPING SOME-THING THAT I WANT TO CONTINUE?
WHAT'S IT TO YOU ANYWAY, YOU ONLY MET ME TODAY.
JUST BECAUSE YOU'RE A PATHETIC LITTLE MAN...
...DOESN'T MEAN YOU CAN FORCE YOUR BELIEFS ON TO ME.
THE MEN OF THE TSUGAWA FAMILY...
...MUST BE BIG, GREAT MEN IN EVERYTHING THEY DO!

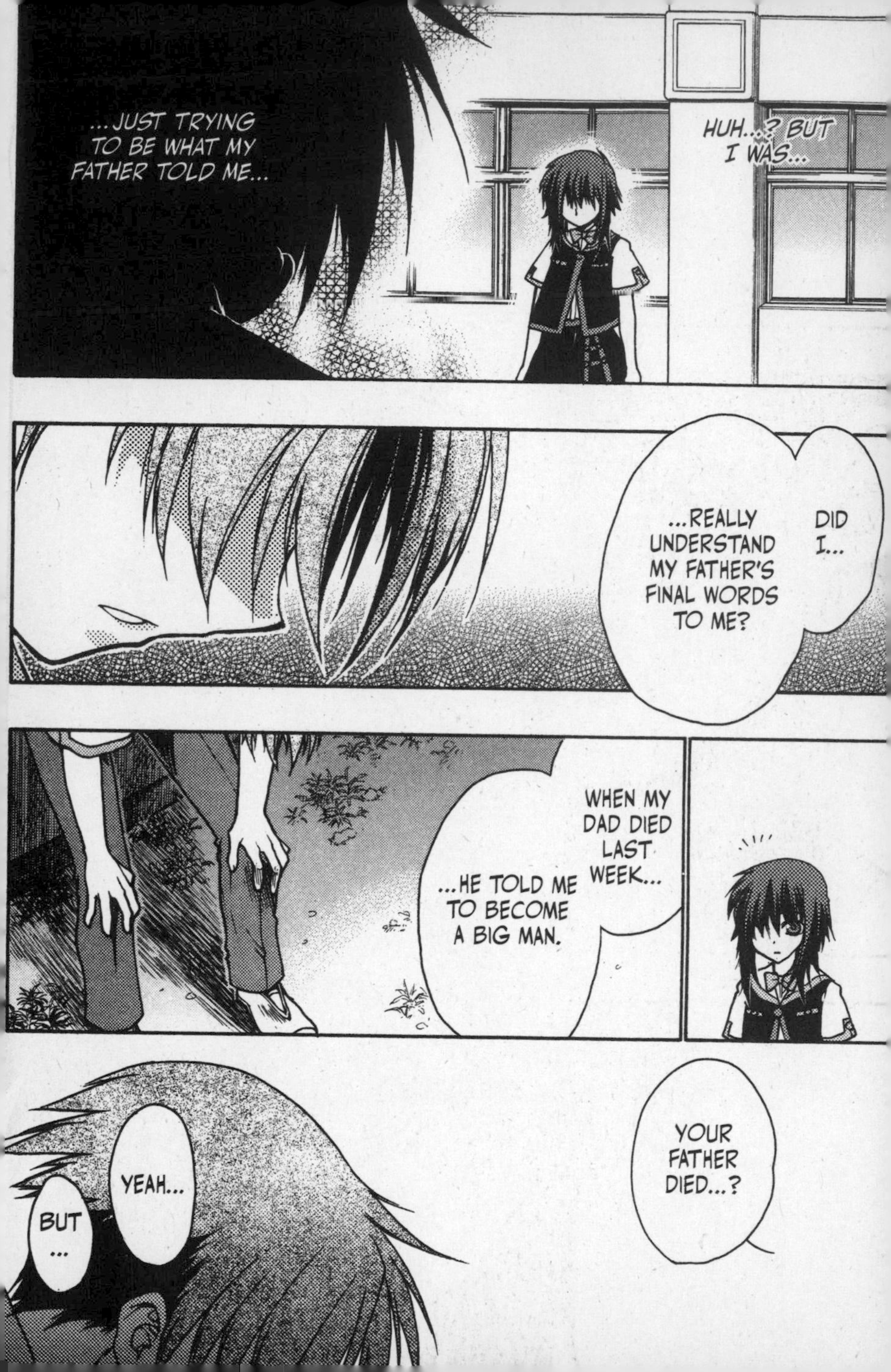
HUH...? BUT I WAS...
...JUST TRYING TO BE WHAT MY FATHER TOLD ME...
DID I...
...REALLY UNDERSTAND MY FATHER'S FINAL WORDS TO ME?
WHEN MY DAD DIED LAST WEEK...
...HE TOLD ME TO BECOME A BIG MAN.
YOUR FATHER DIED...?
YEAH...
BUT ...

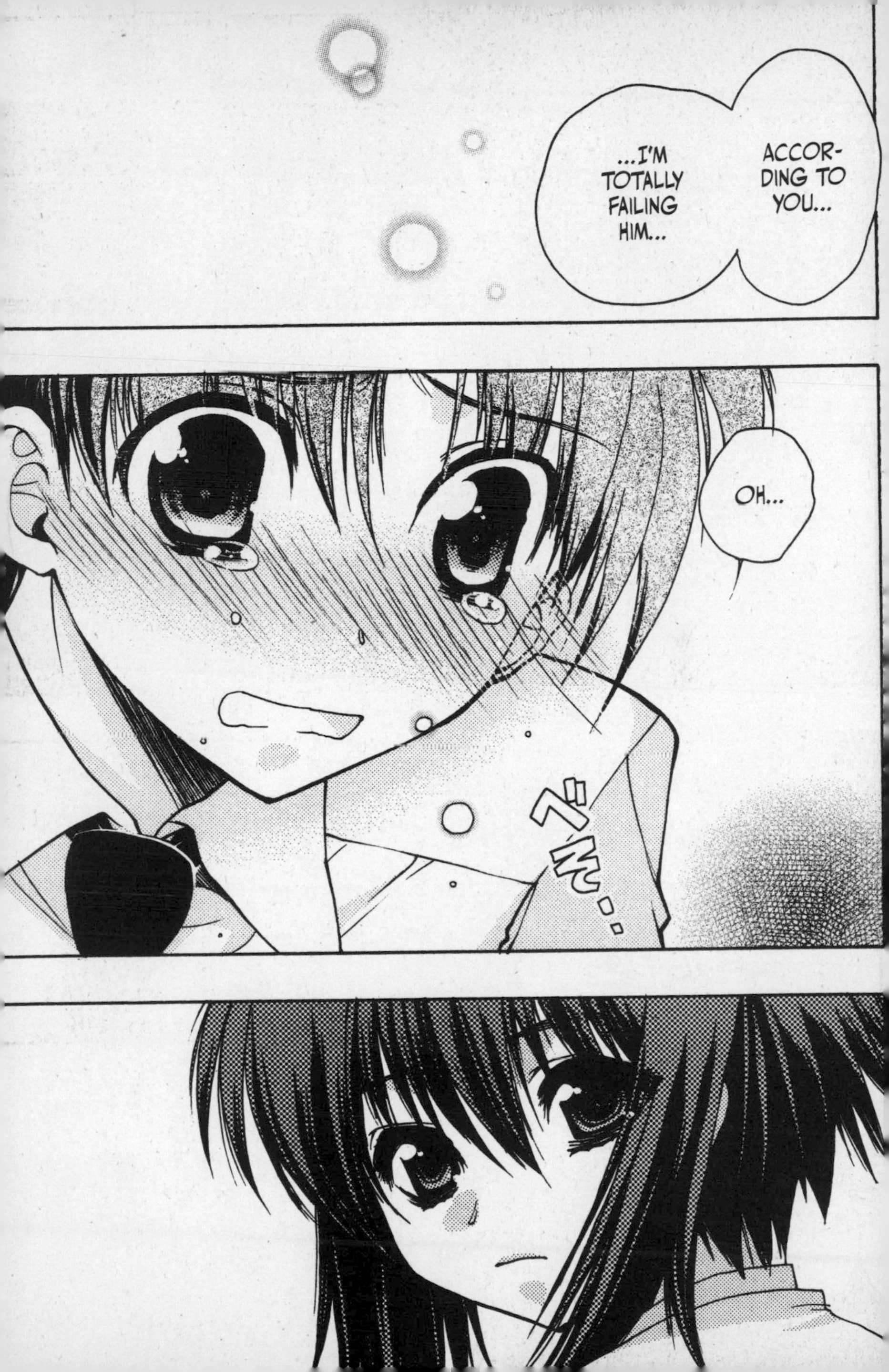
ACCORDING TO YOU...
...I'M TOTALLY FAILING HIM...
OH...

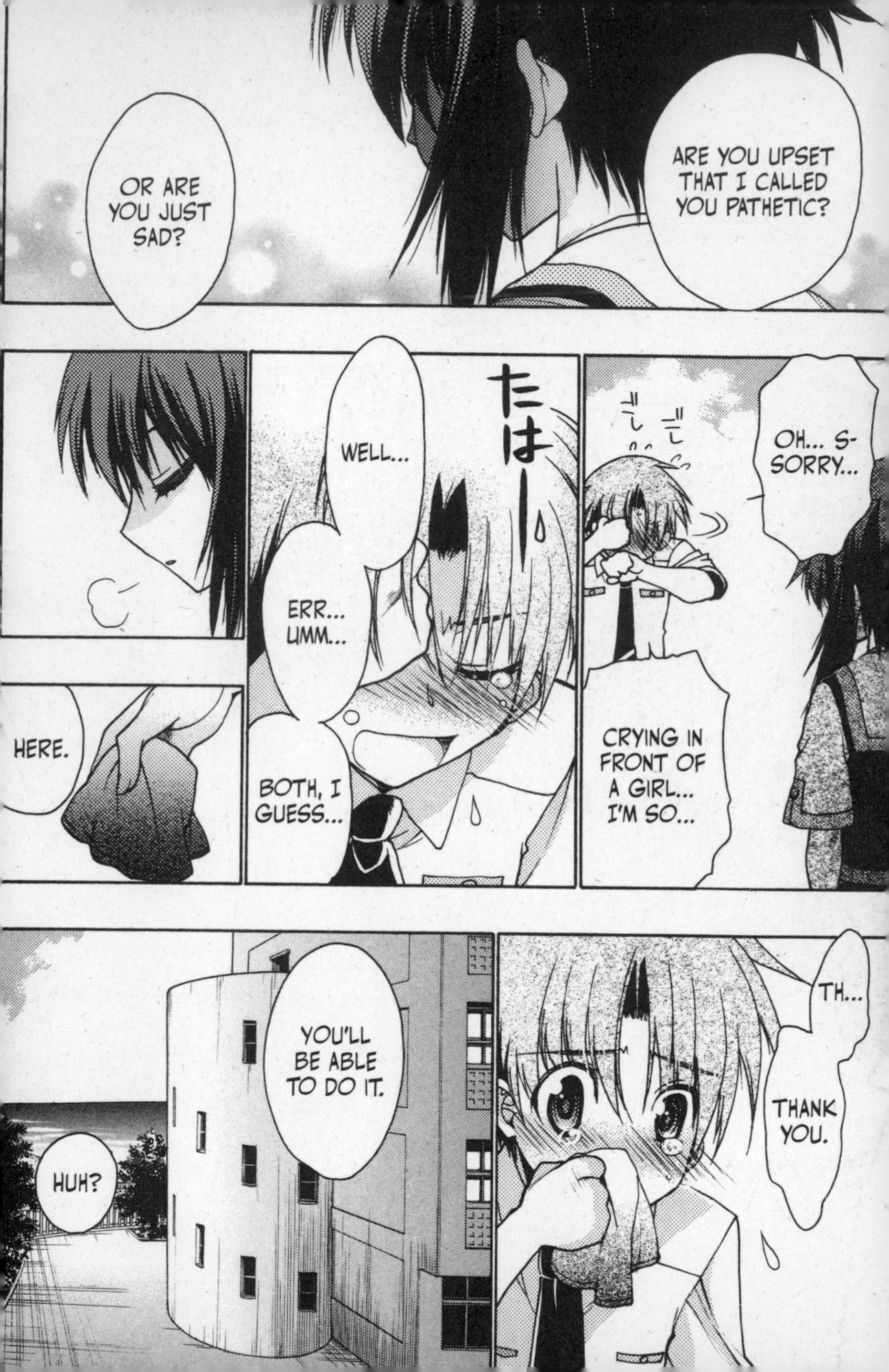

ARE YOU UPSET THAT I CALLED YOU PATHETIC?
OR ARE YOU JUST SAD?
ごし ごし
OH... S-SORRY...
CRYING IN FRONT OF A GIRL... I'M SO...
たはー
WELL...
ERR... UMM...
BOTH, I GUESS...
HERE.
TH...
THANK YOU.
YOU'LL BE ABLE TO DO IT.
HUH?

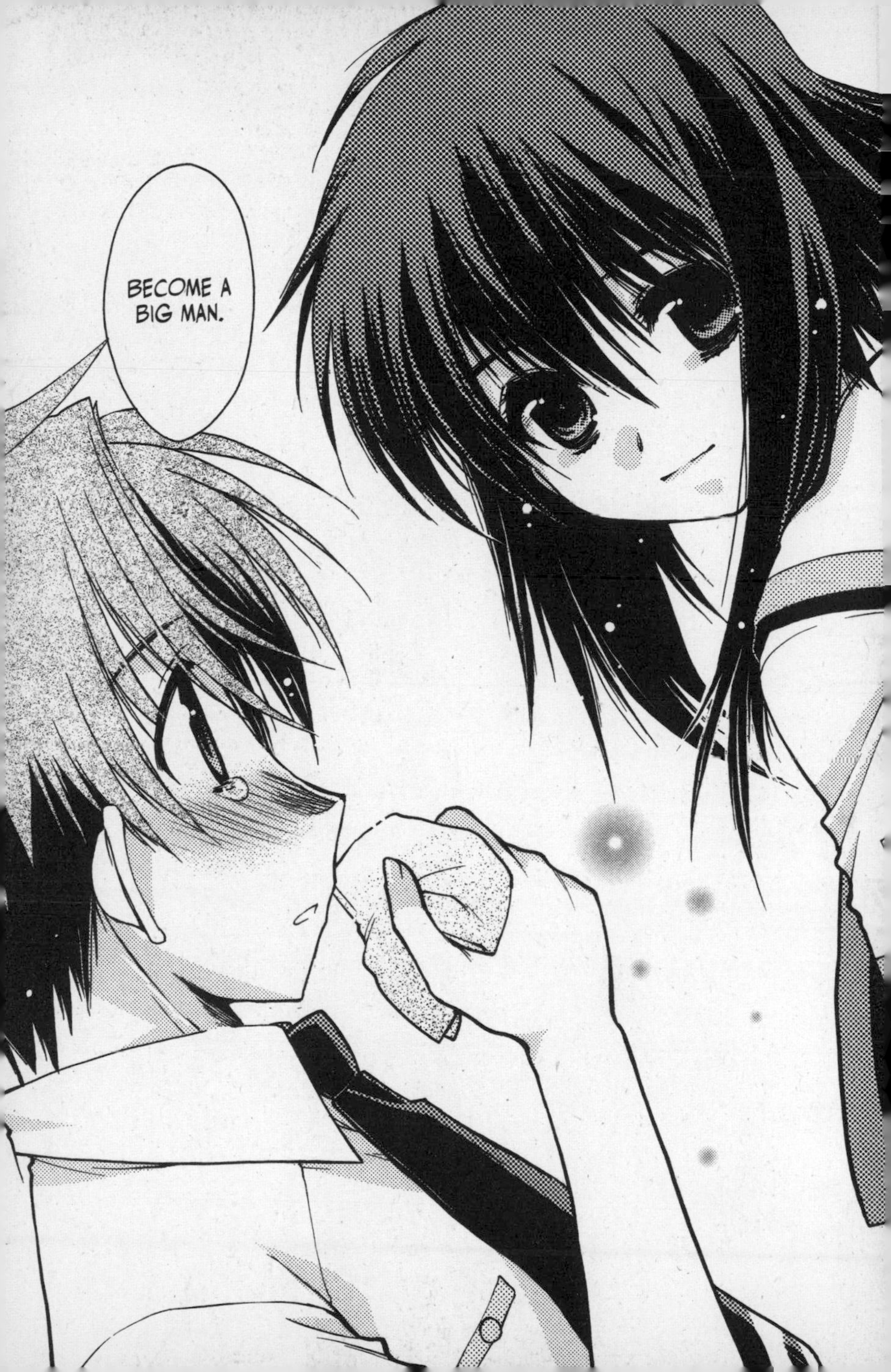
BECOME A BIG MAN.

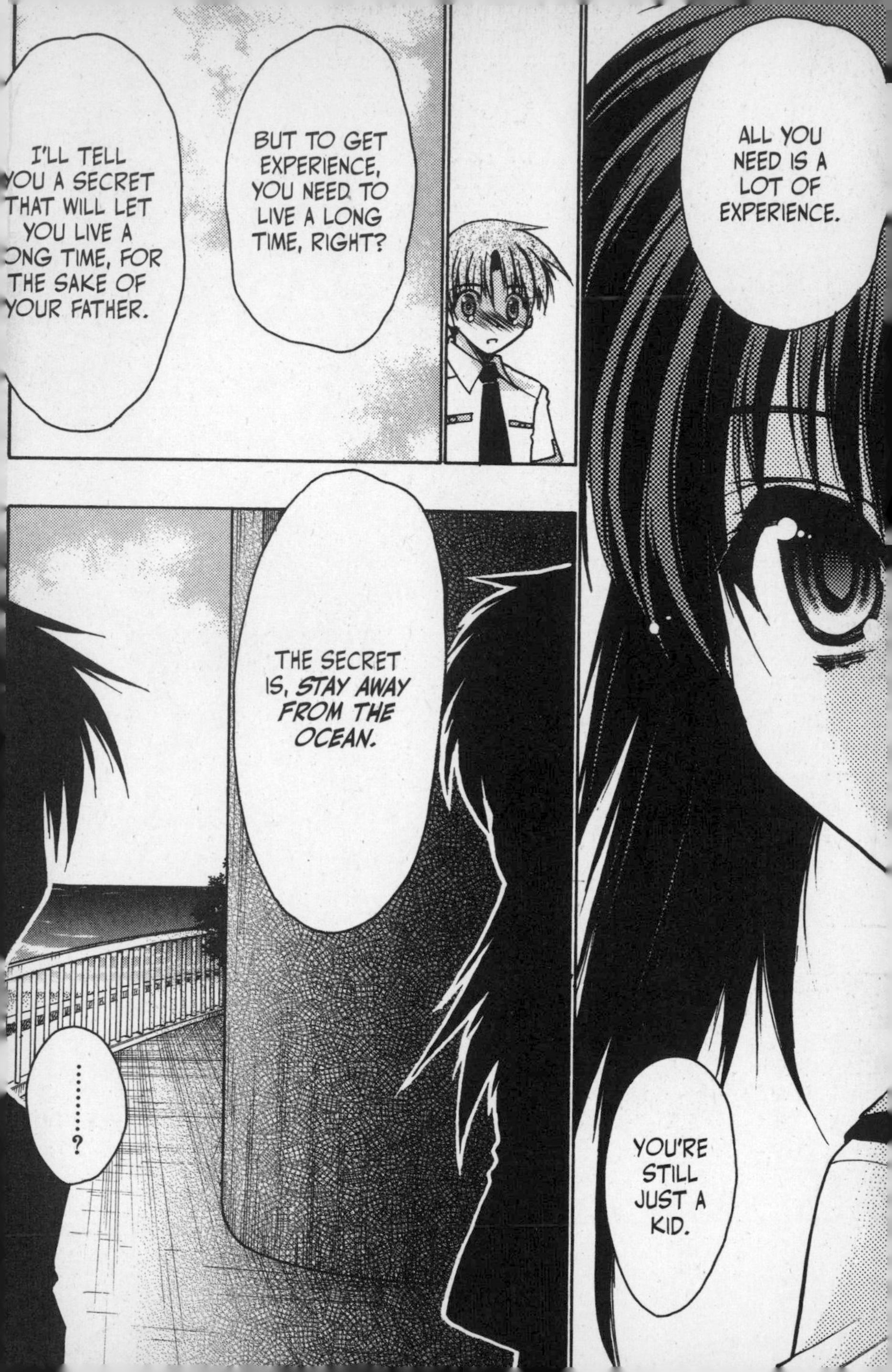
ALL YOU NEED IS A LOT OF EXPERIENCE.
YOU'RE STILL JUST A KID.
BUT TO GET EXPERIENCE, YOU NEED TO LIVE A LONG TIME, RIGHT?
I'LL TELL YOU A SECRET THAT WILL LET YOU LIVE A ONG TIME, FOR THE SAKE OF YOUR FATHER.
THE SECRET IS, *STAY AWAY FROM THE OCEAN.*
......?

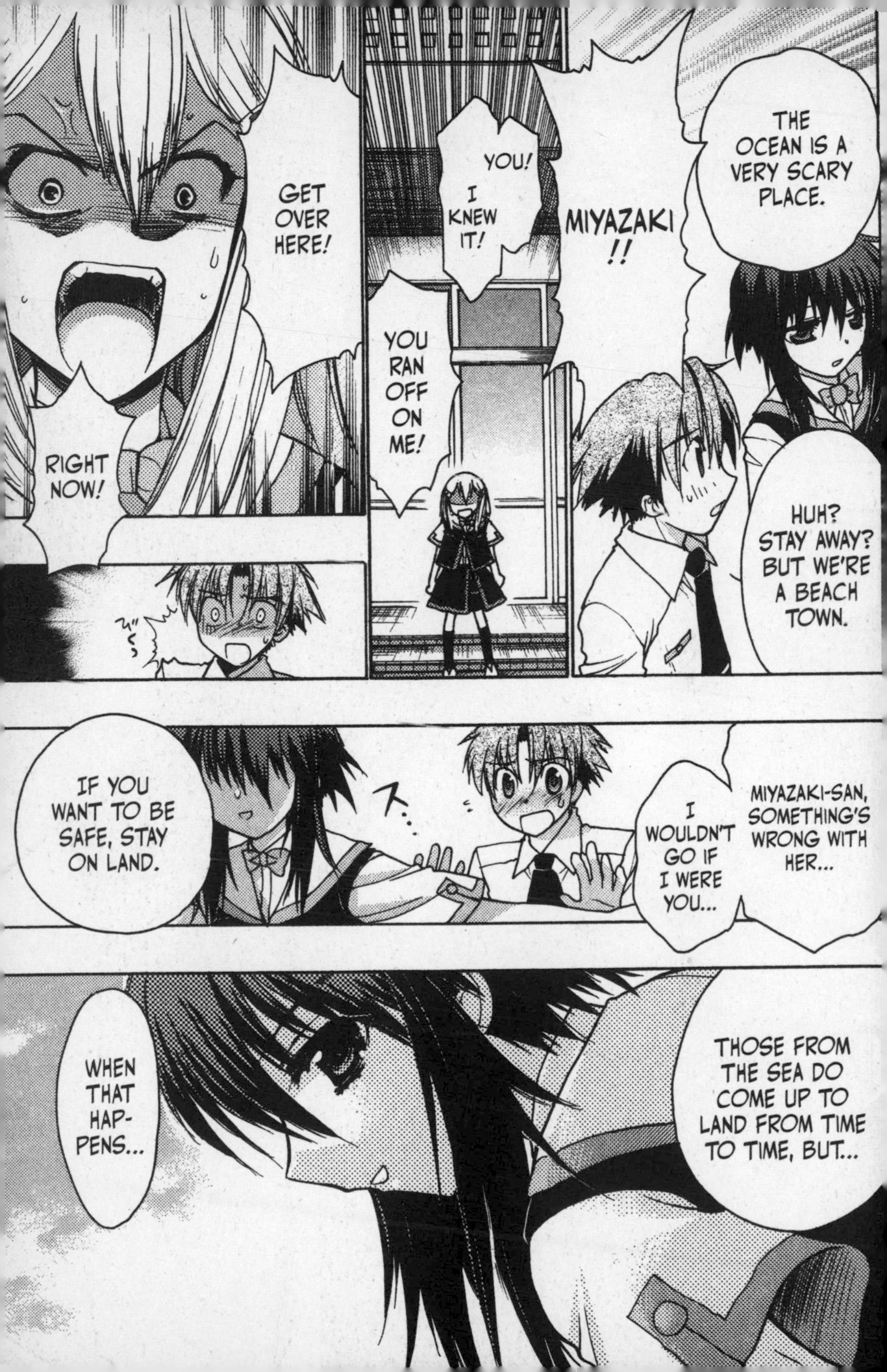
THE OCEAN IS A VERY SCARY PLACE.
HUH? STAY AWAY? BUT WE'RE A BEACH TOWN.
MIYAZAKI!!
YOU! I KNEW IT!
YOU RAN OFF ON ME!
GET OVER HERE!
RIGHT NOW!
MIYAZAKI-SAN, SOMETHING'S WRONG WITH HER...
I WOULDN'T GO IF I WERE YOU...
IF YOU WANT TO BE SAFE, STAY ON LAND.
THOSE FROM THE SEA DO COME UP TO LAND FROM TIME TO TIME, BUT...
WHEN THAT HAP- PENS...

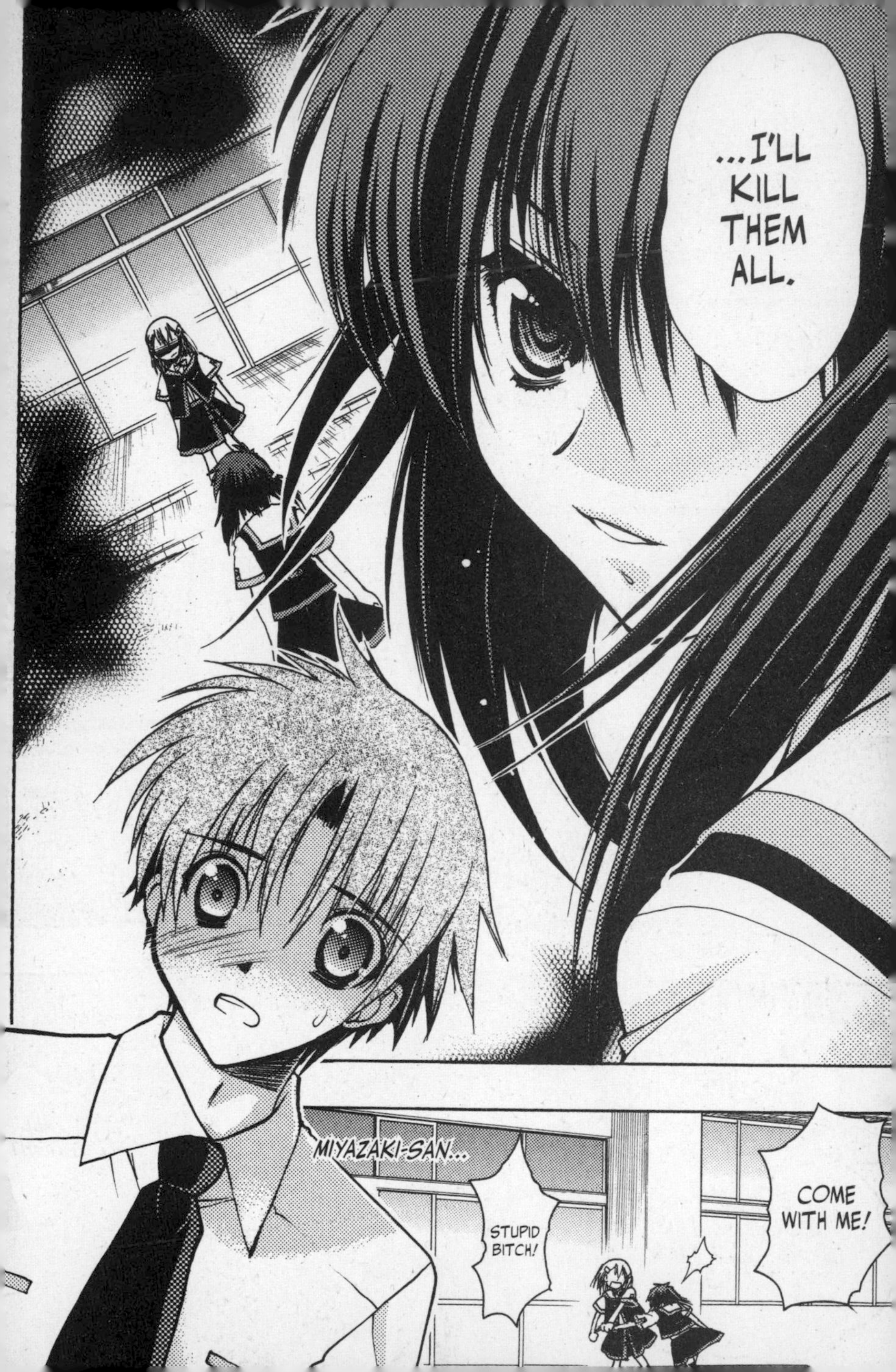
...I'LL KILL THEM ALL.
COME WITH ME!
STUPID BITCH!
MIYAZAKI-SAN...

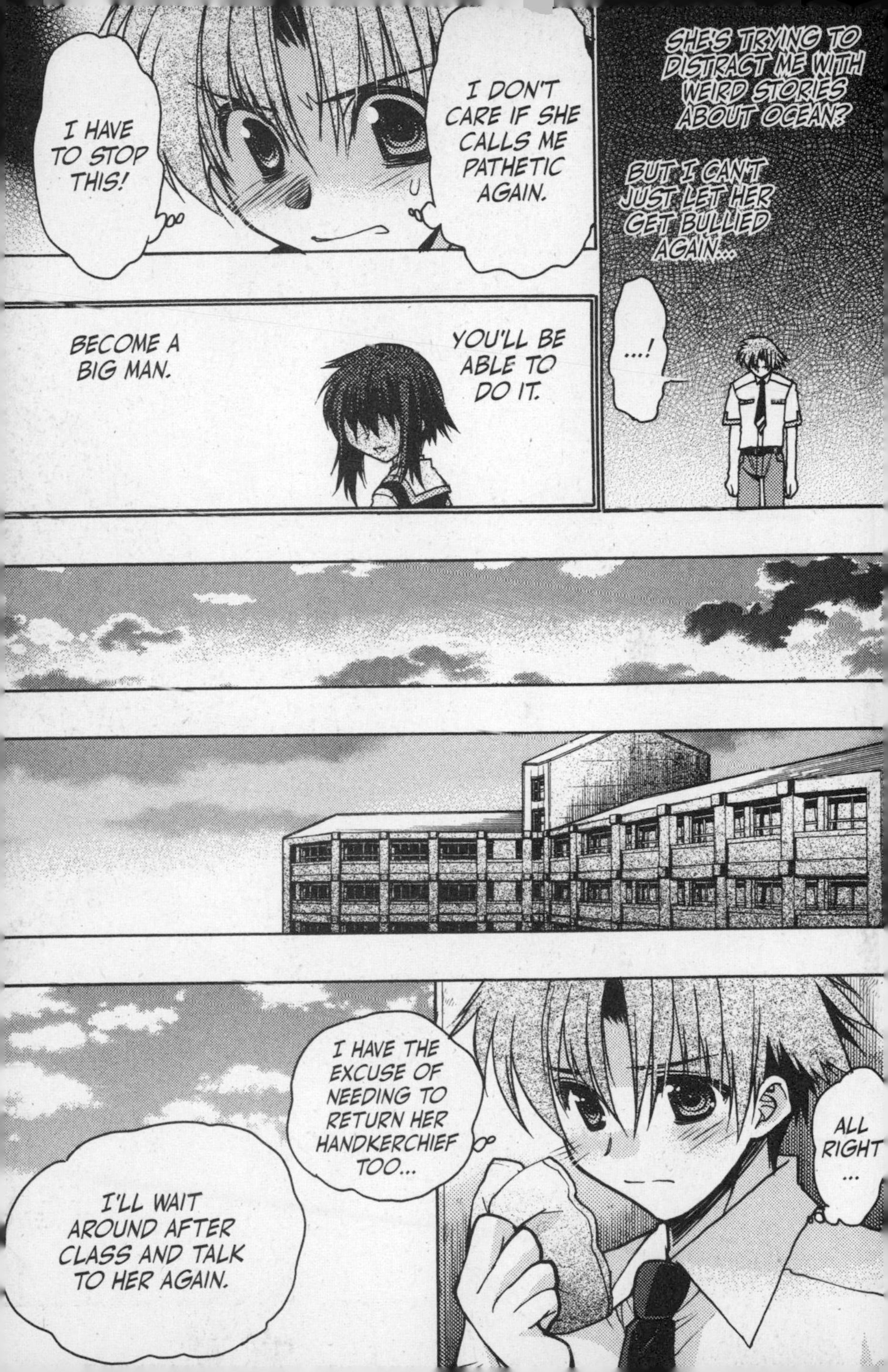
SHE'S TRYING TO DISTRACT ME WITH WEIRD STORIES ABOUT OCEAN?
BUT I CAN'T JUST LET HER GET BULLIED AGAIN...
...!
I DON'T CARE IF SHE CALLS ME PATHETIC AGAIN.
I HAVE TO STOP THIS!
YOU'LL BE ABLE TO DO IT.
BECOME A BIG MAN.
ALL RIGHT...
I HAVE THE EXCUSE OF NEEDING TO RETURN HER HANDKERCHIEF TOO...
I'LL WAIT AROUND AFTER CLASS AND TALK TO HER AGAIN.

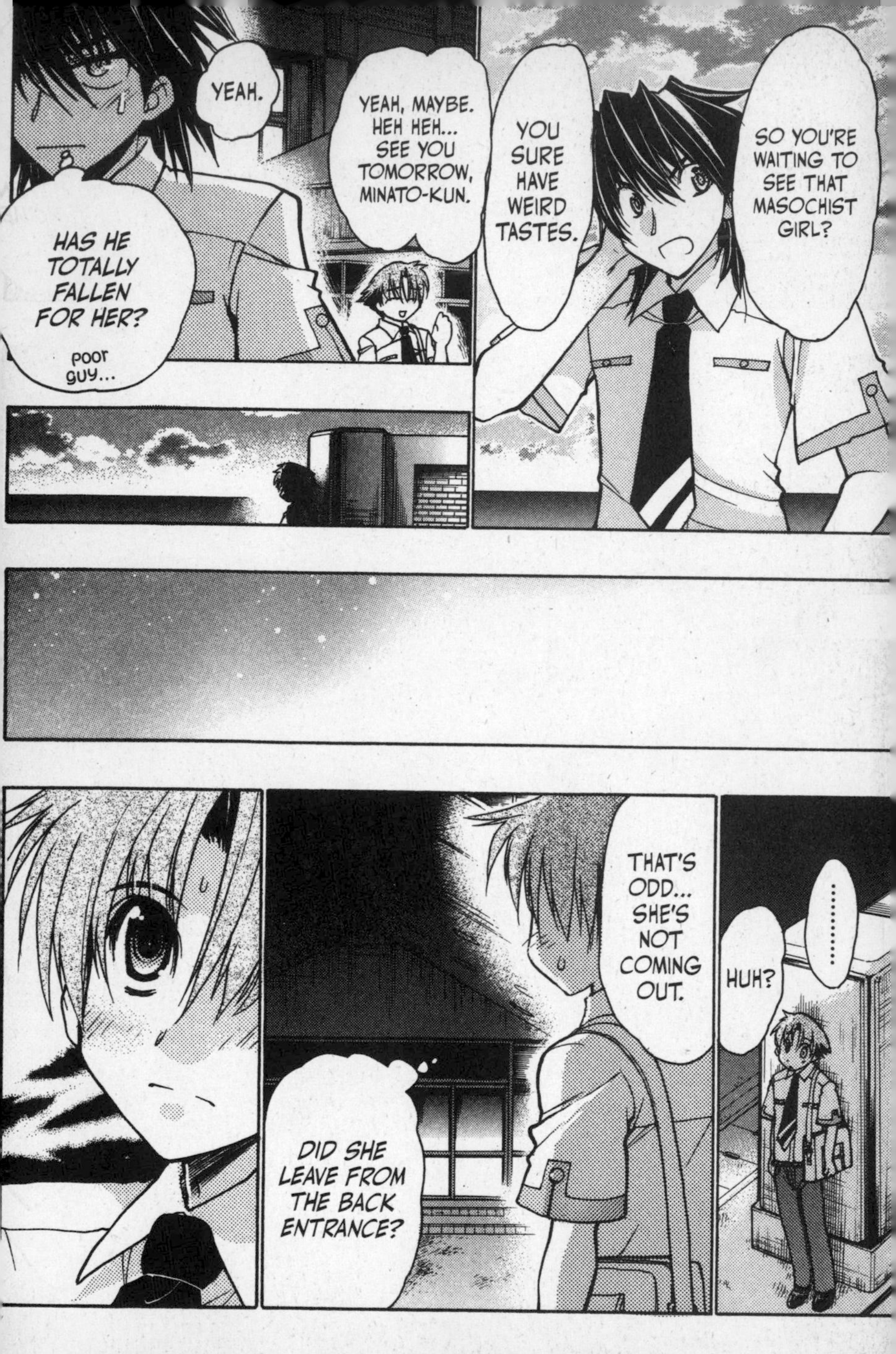
SO YOU'RE WAITING TO SEE THAT MASOCHIST GIRL?
YOU SURE HAVE WEIRD TASTES.
YEAH, MAYBE. HEH HEH... SEE YOU TOMORROW, MINATO-KUN.
YEAH.
HAS HE TOTALLY FALLEN FOR HER?
poor guy...
......
HUH?
THAT'S ODD... SHE'S NOT COMING OUT.
DID SHE LEAVE FROM THE BACK ENTRANCE?

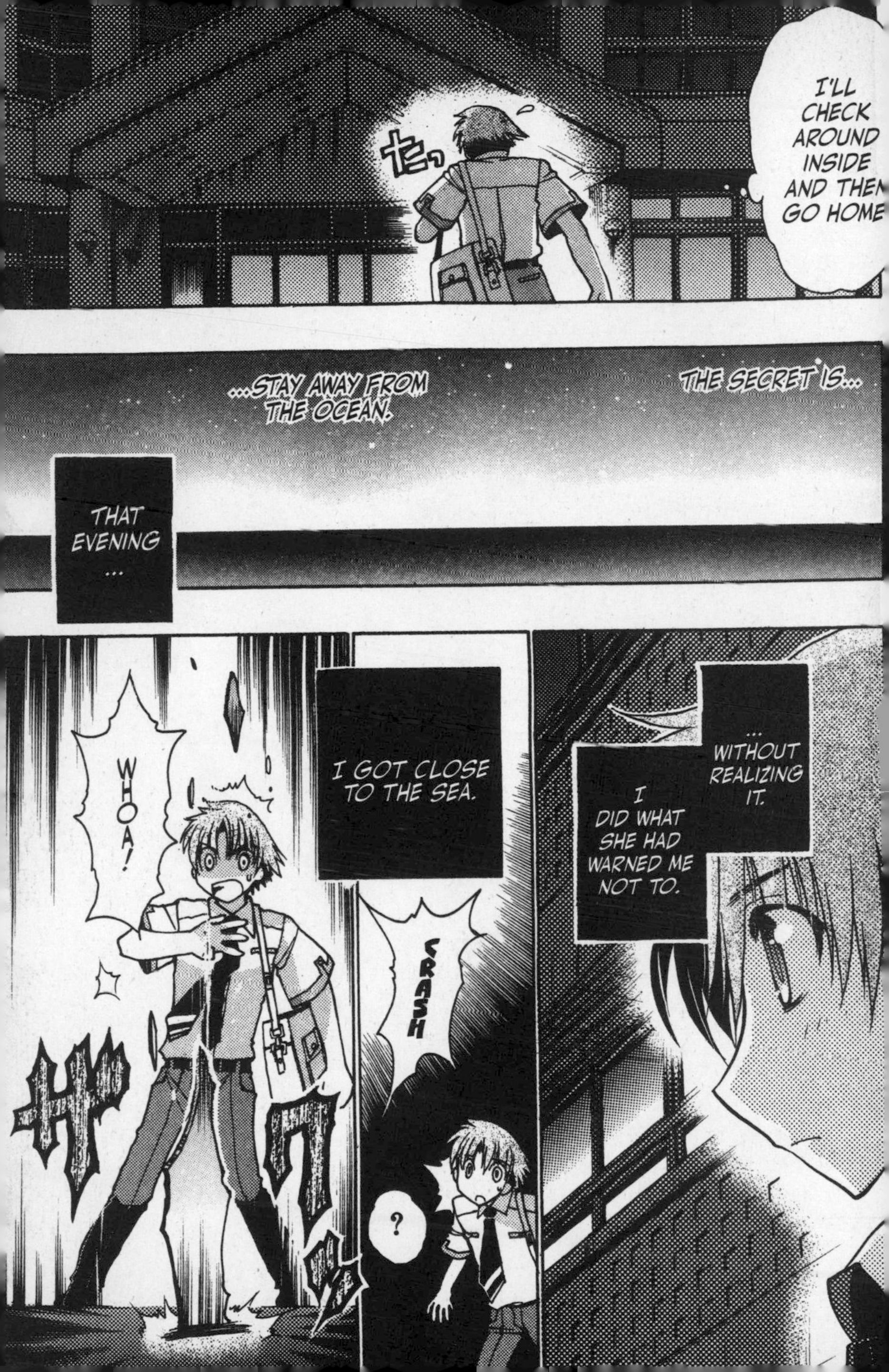

I'LL CHECK AROUND INSIDE AND THEN GO HOME
たっ
THE SECRET IS...
...STAY AWAY FROM THE OCEAN.
THAT EVENING...
...WITHOUT REALIZING IT.
I DID WHAT SHE HAD WARNED ME NOT TO.
I GOT CLOSE TO THE SEA.
CRASH
?
WHOA!

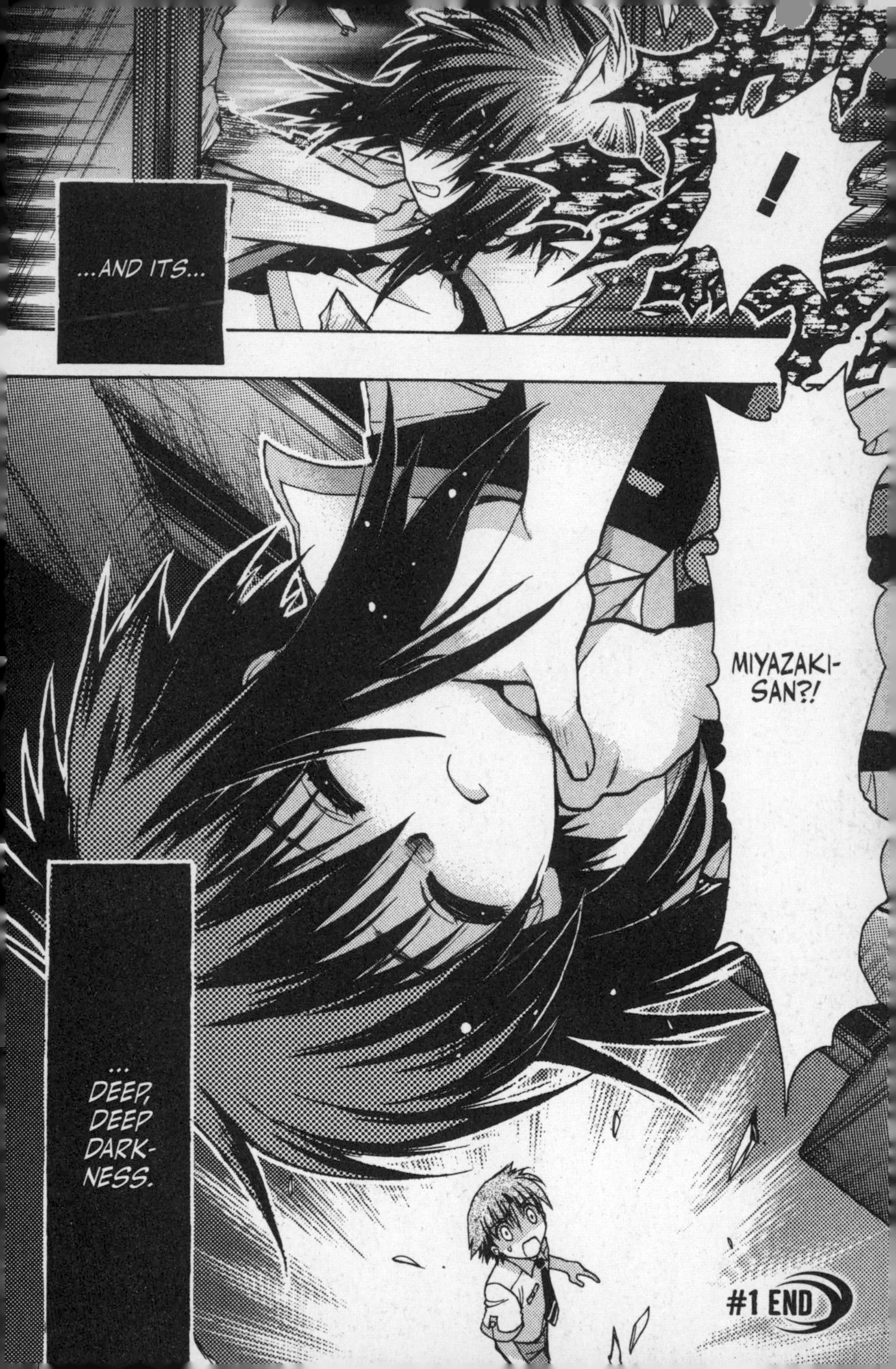
!
...AND ITS...
MIYAZAKI-SAN?!
... DEEP, DEEP DARKNESS.
#1 END

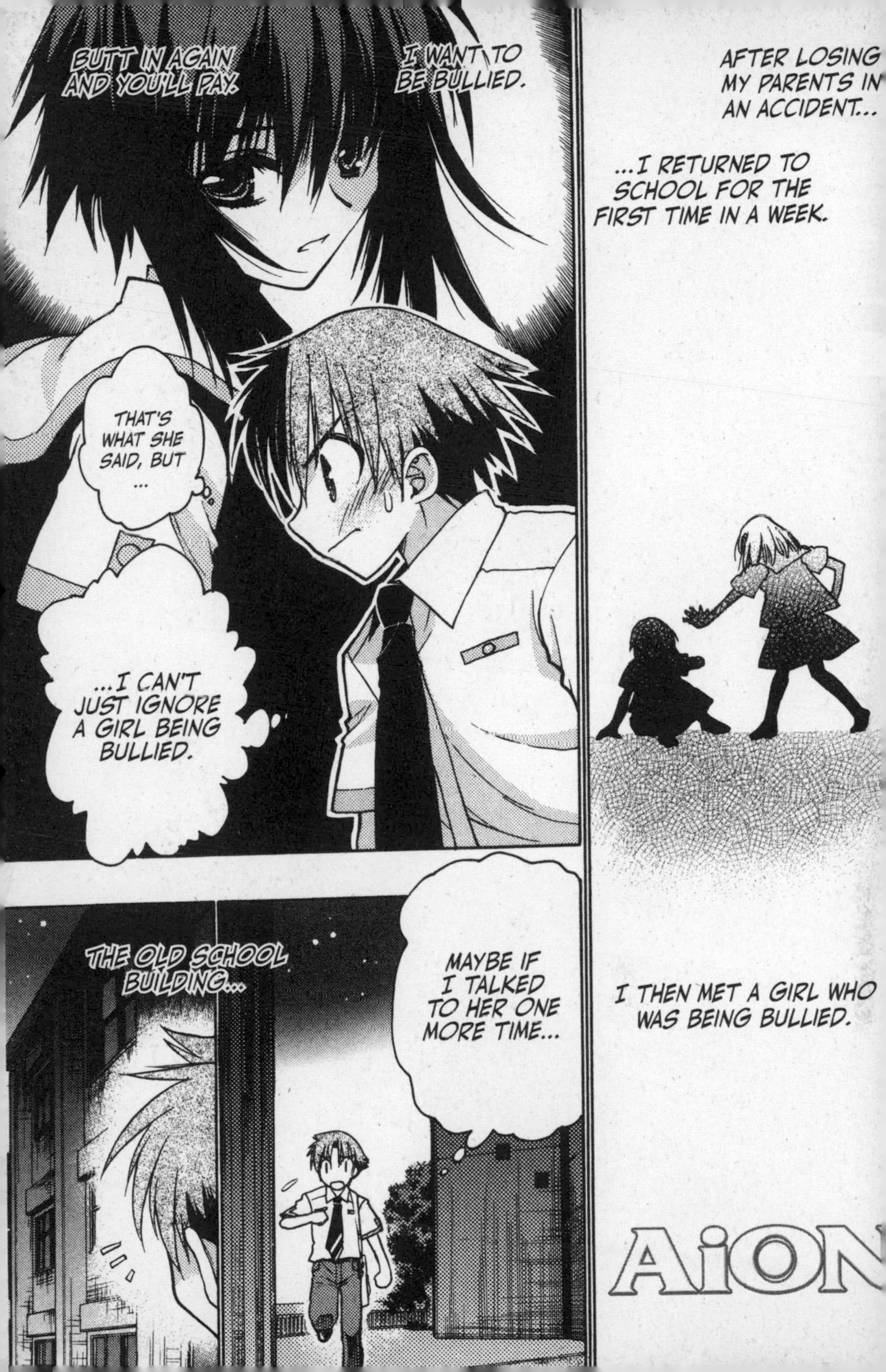
AFTER LOSING MY PARENTS IN AN ACCIDENT...
...I RETURNED TO SCHOOL FOR THE FIRST TIME IN A WEEK.
I THEN MET A GIRL WHO WAS BEING BULLIED.
AiON
I WANT TO BE BULLIED.
BUTT IN AGAIN AND YOU'LL PAY.
THAT'S WHAT SHE SAID, BUT ...
...I CAN'T JUST IGNORE A GIRL BEING BULLIED.
MAYBE IF I TALKED TO HER ONE MORE TIME...
THE OLD SCHOOL BUILDING...

#2 Small Fry

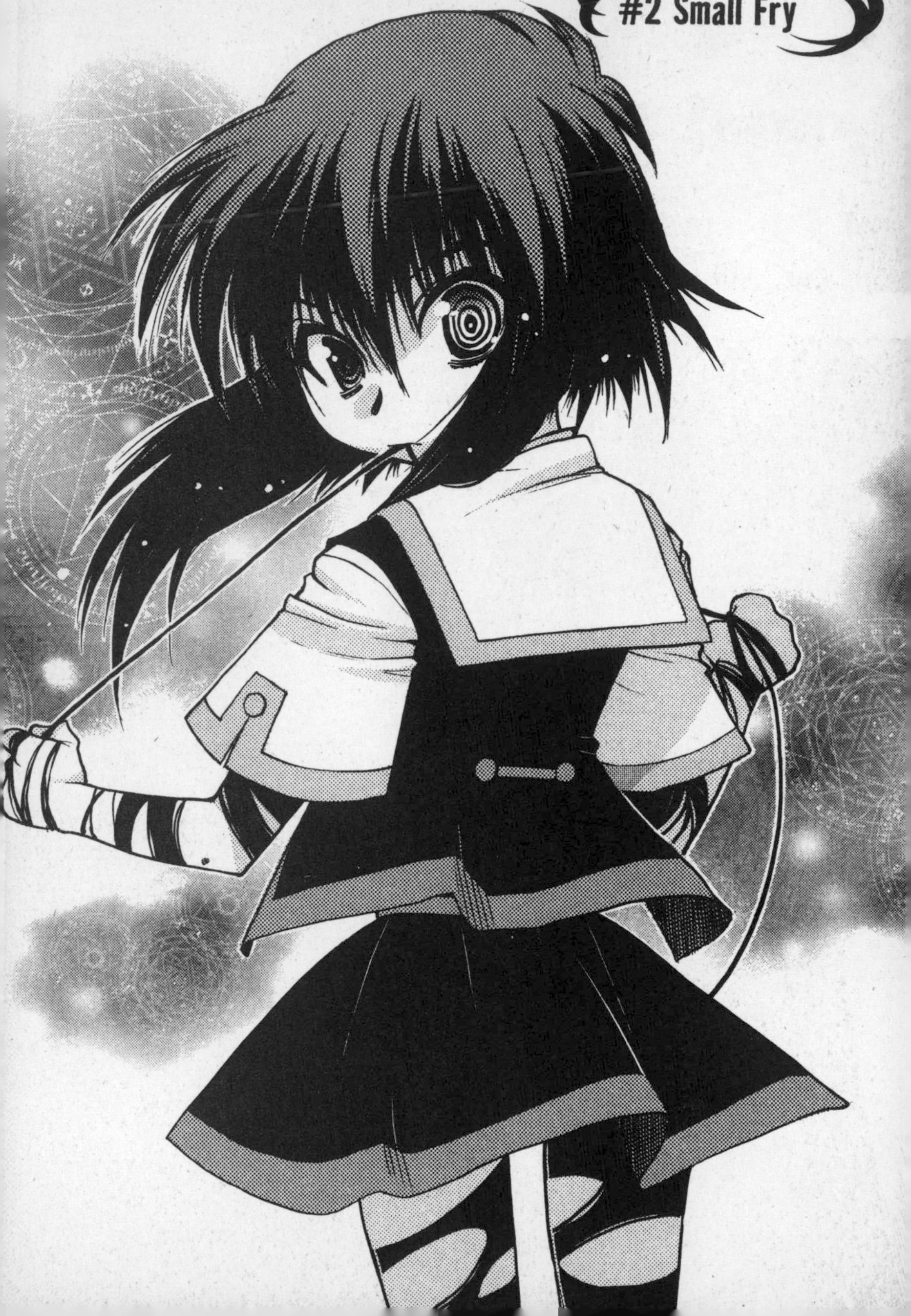

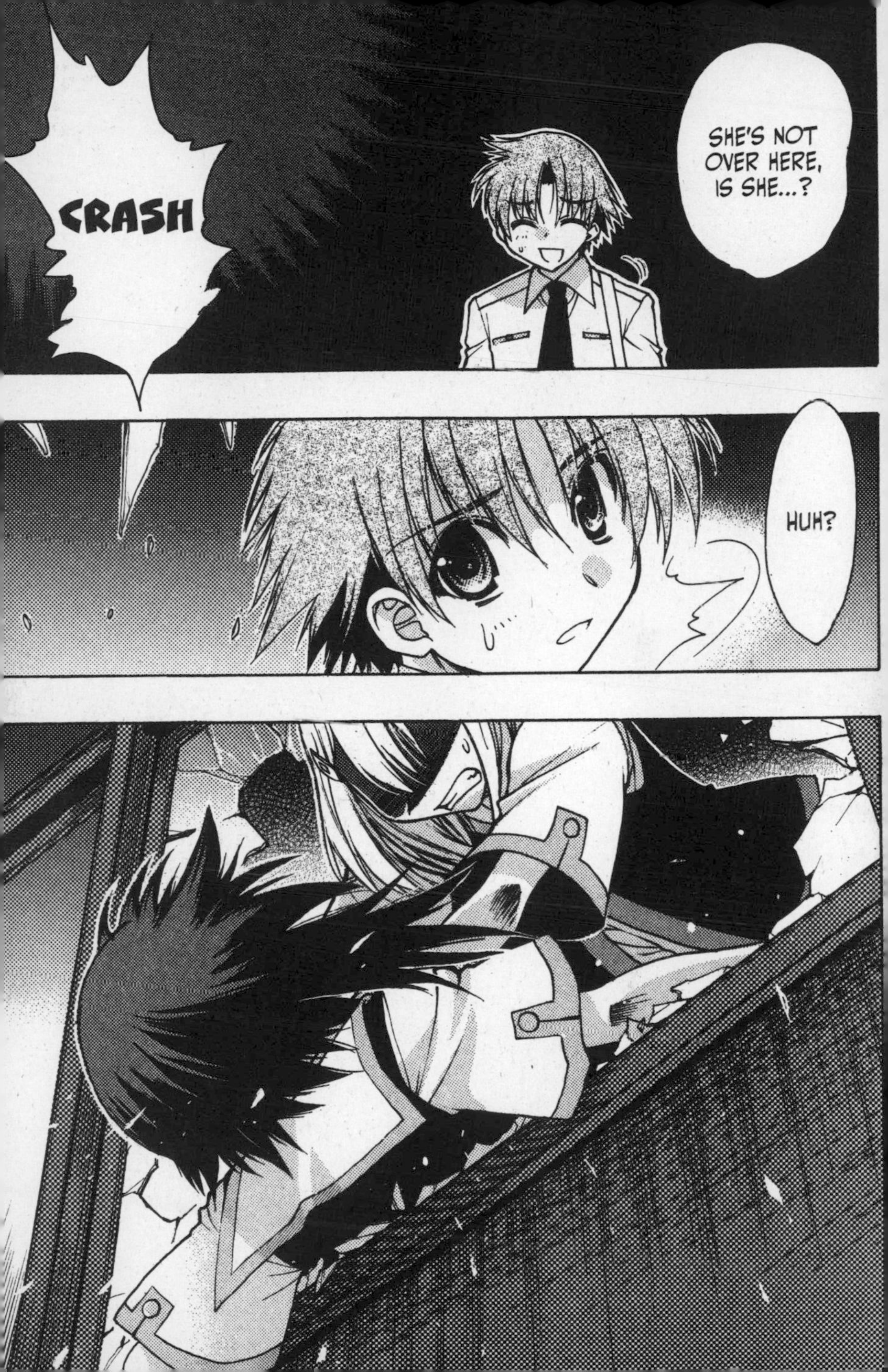
SHE'S NOT OVER HERE, IS SHE...?
CRASH
HUH?

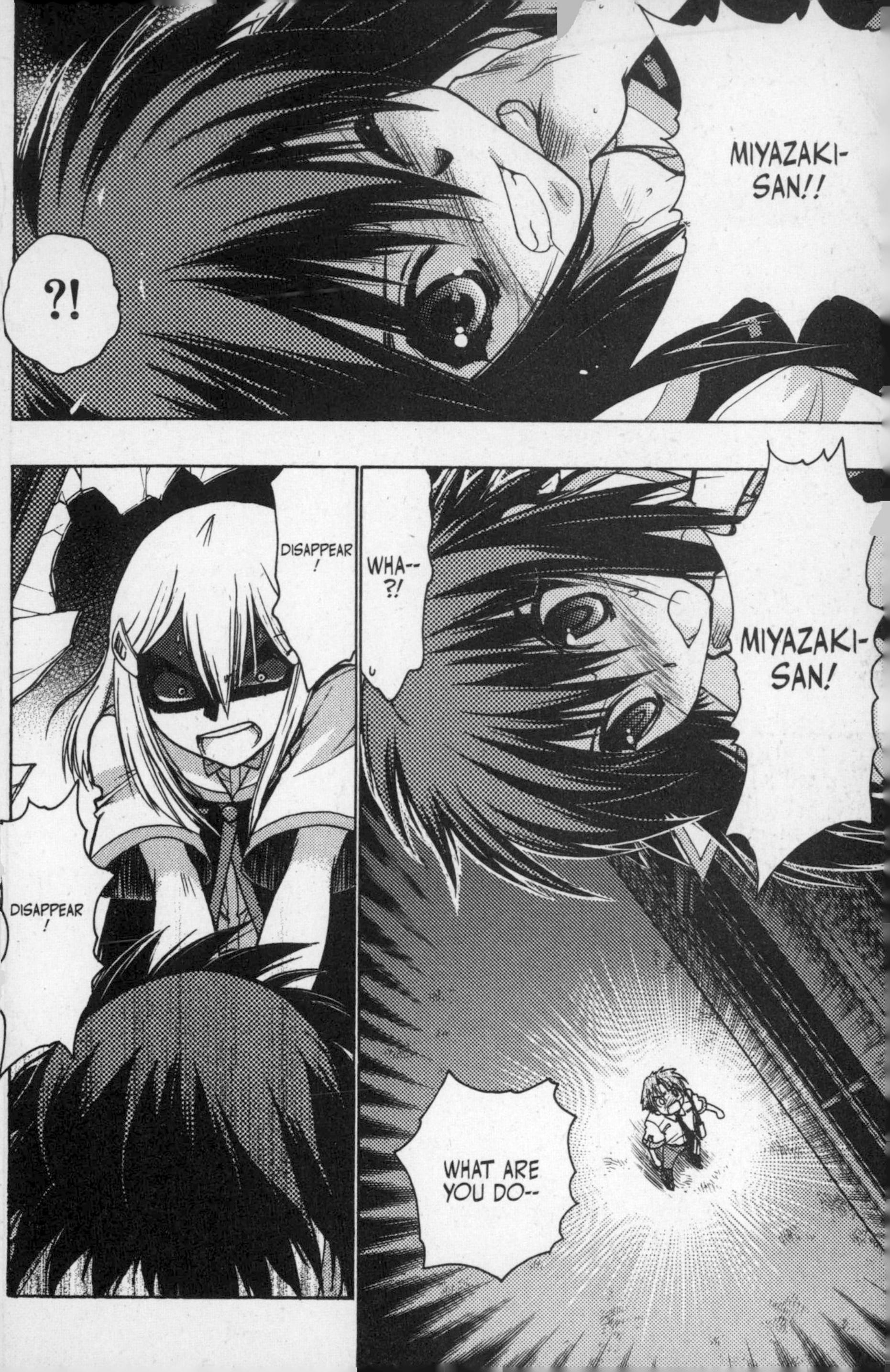
MIYAZAKI-SAN!!
?!
MIYAZAKI-SAN!
WHA-- ?!
WHAT ARE YOU DO--
DISAPPEAR!
DISAPPEAR!

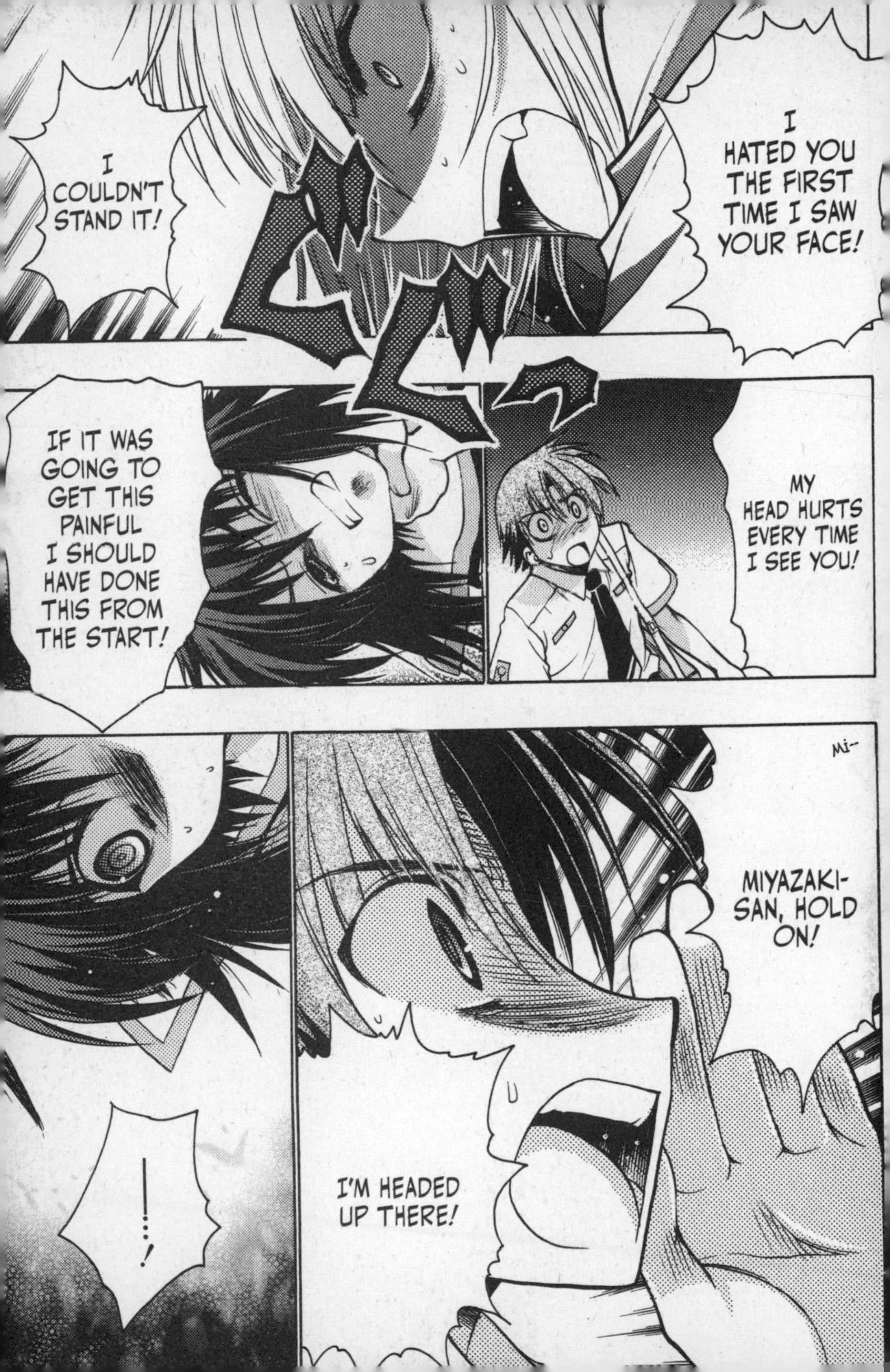
I HATED YOU THE FIRST TIME I SAW YOUR FACE!
I COULDN'T STAND IT!
MY HEAD HURTS EVERY TIME I SEE YOU!
IF IT WAS GOING TO GET THIS PAINFUL I SHOULD HAVE DONE THIS FROM THE START!
Mi--
MIYAZAKI-SAN, HOLD ON!
I'M HEADED UP THERE!
...!

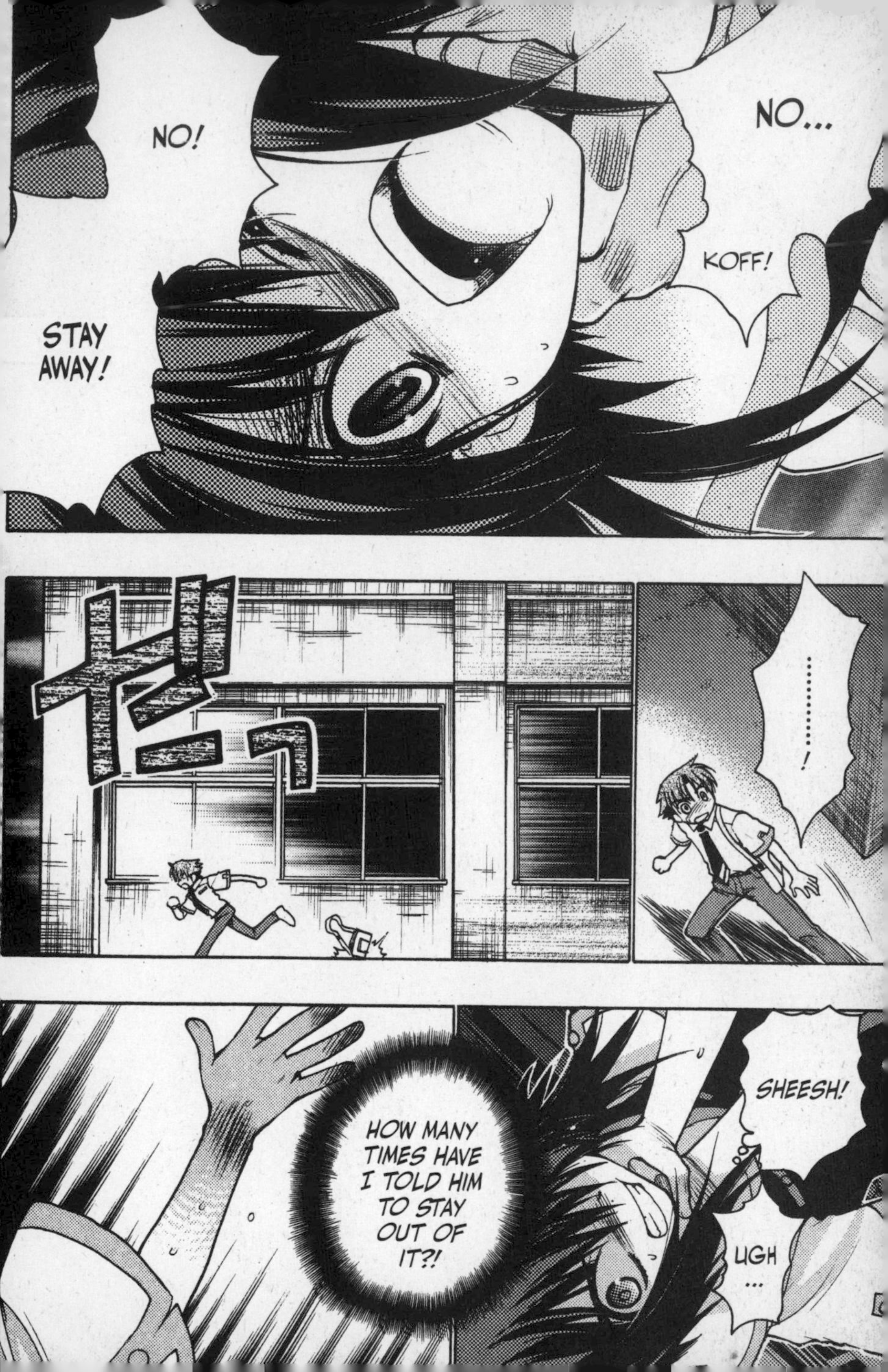
NO...
KOFF!
NO!
STAY AWAY!
......!
ダーッ
SHEESH!
UGH ...
HOW MANY TIMES HAVE I TOLD HIM TO STAY OUT OF IT?!

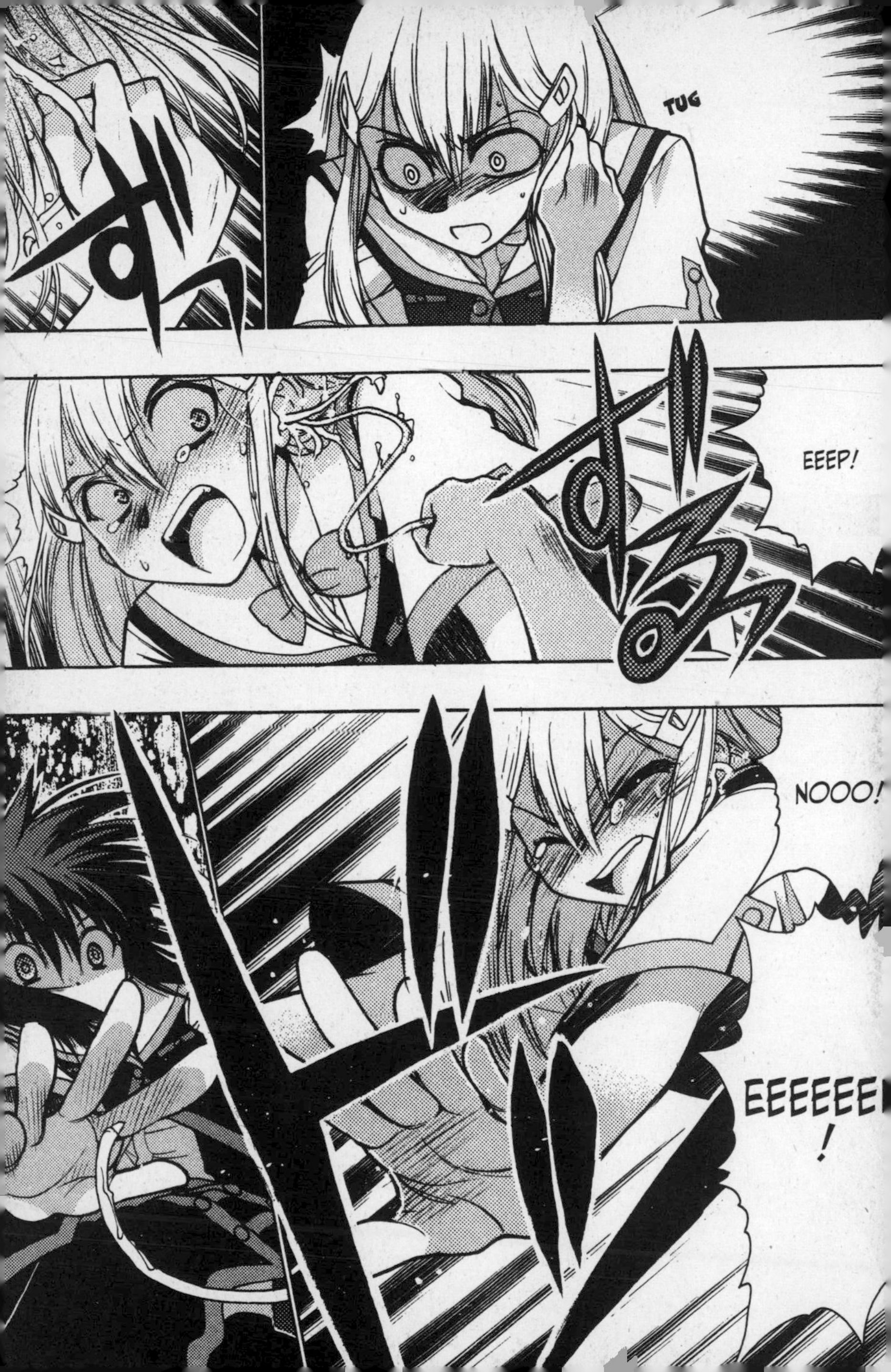
TUG
EEEP!
NOOO!
EEEEEE!

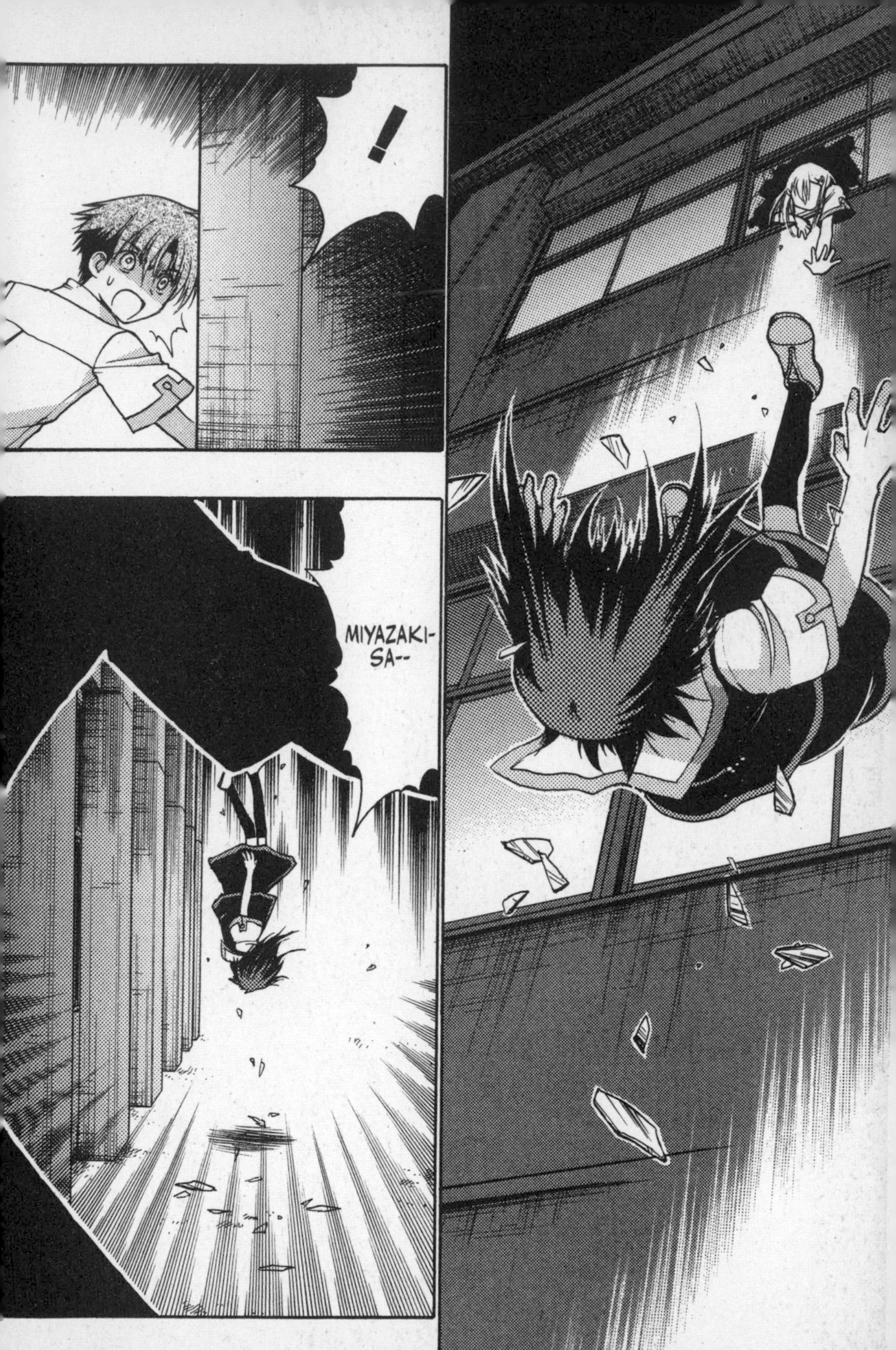
!
MIYAZAKI-SA--

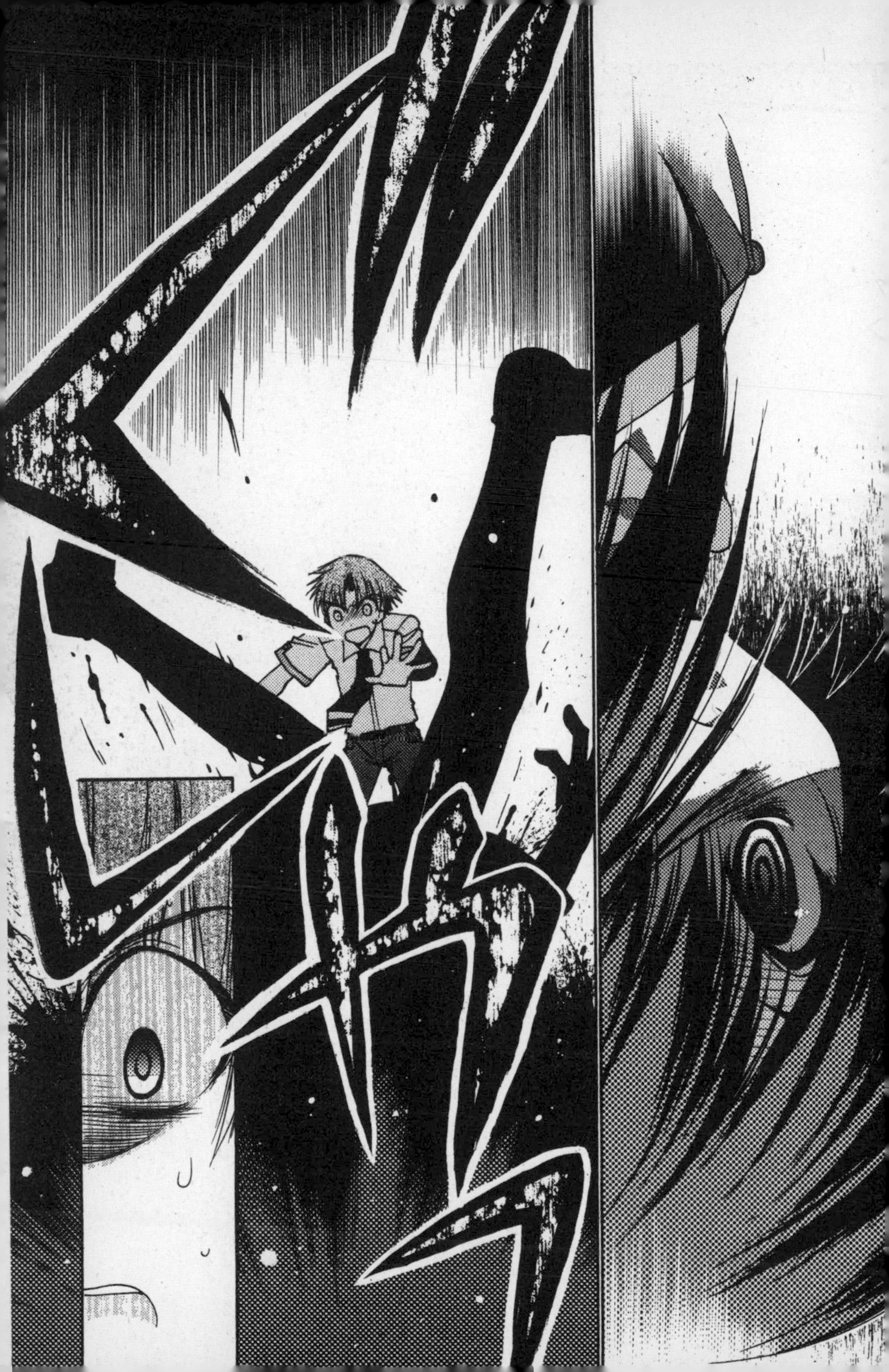

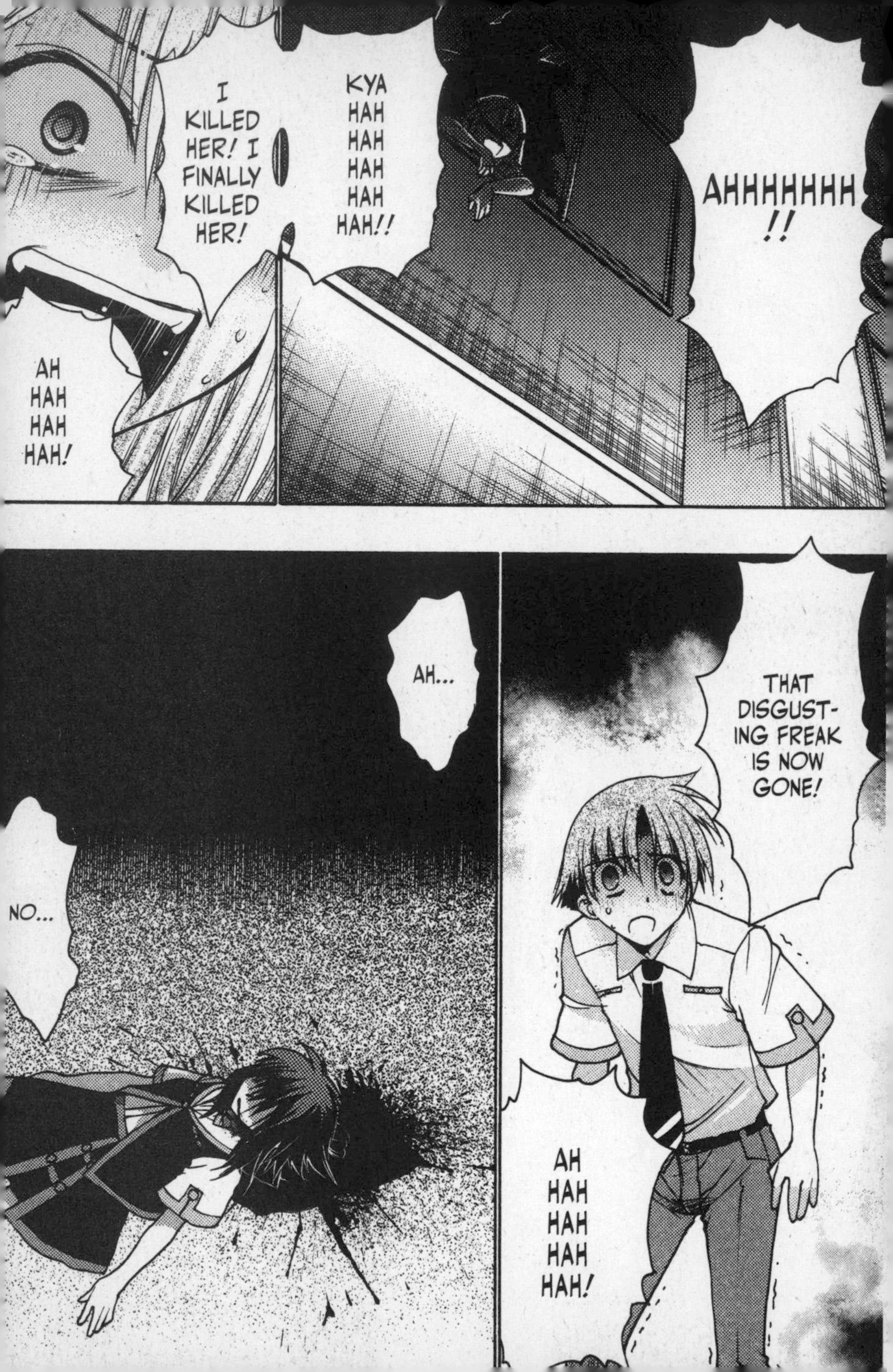

AHHHHHHH!!
KYA HAH HAH HAH HAH HAH!!
I KILLED HER! I FINALLY KILLED HER!
AH HAH HAH HAH!
THAT DISGUST-ING FREAK IS NOW GONE!
AH HAH HAH HAH HAH!
AH...
NO...

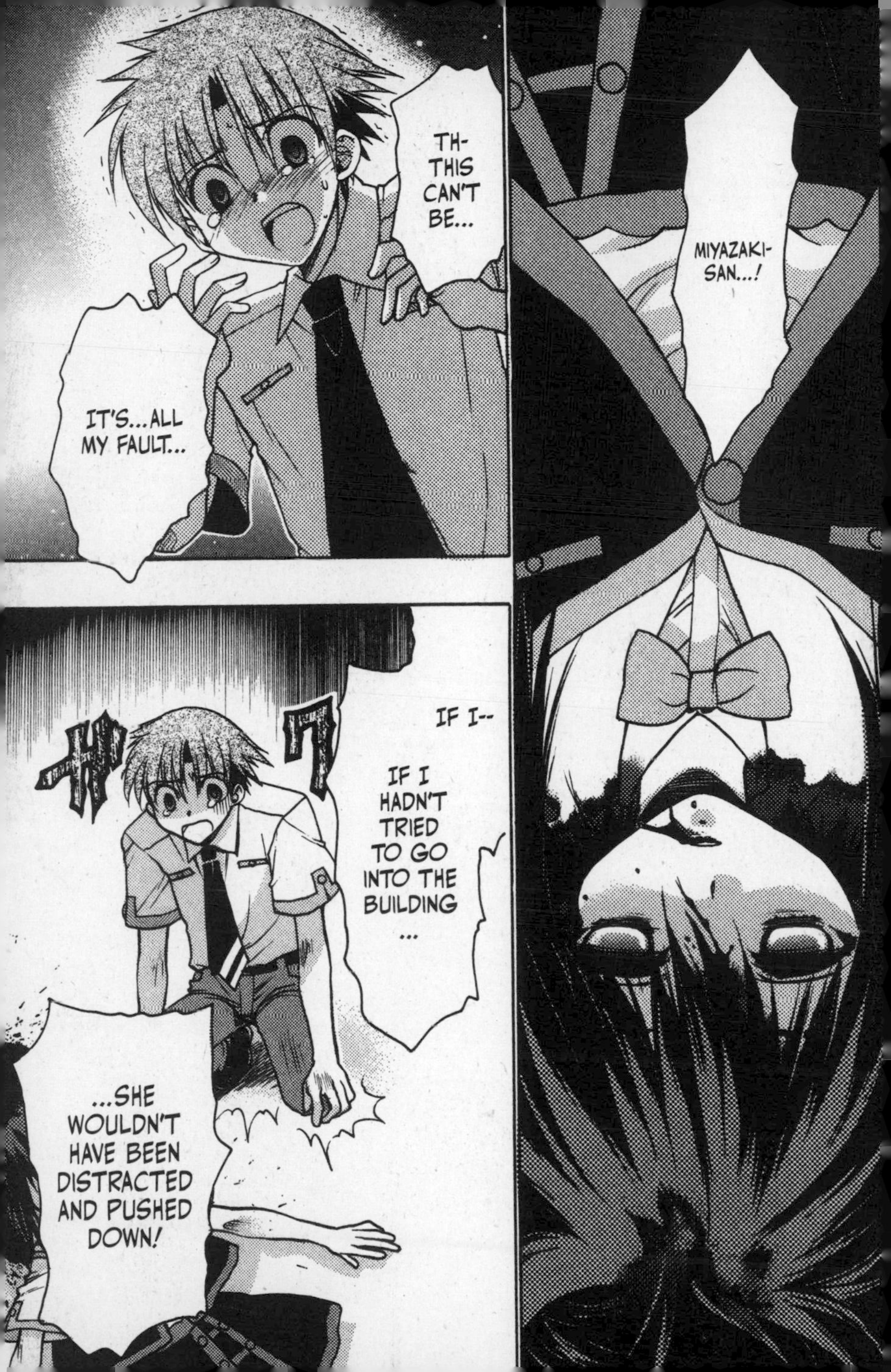
MIYAZAKI-SAN...!
TH- THIS CAN'T BE...
IT'S...ALL MY FAULT...
IF I--
IF I HADN'T TRIED TO GO INTO THE BUILDING ...
...SHE WOULDN'T HAVE BEEN DISTRACTED AND PUSHED DOWN!

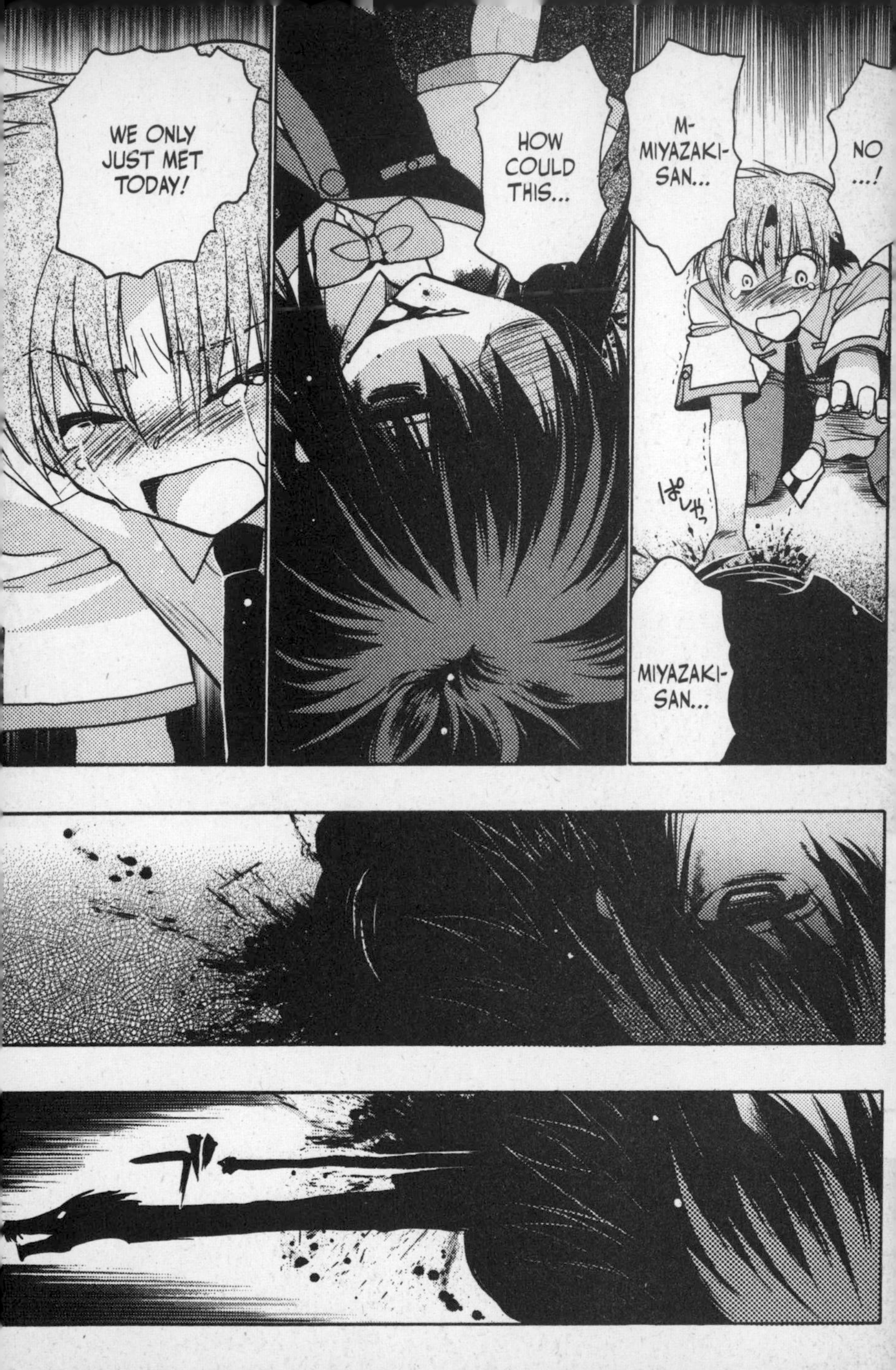
NO ...!
M-MIYAZAKI-SAN...
ぱしゃ
MIYAZAKI-SAN...
HOW COULD THIS...
WE ONLY JUST MET TODAY!

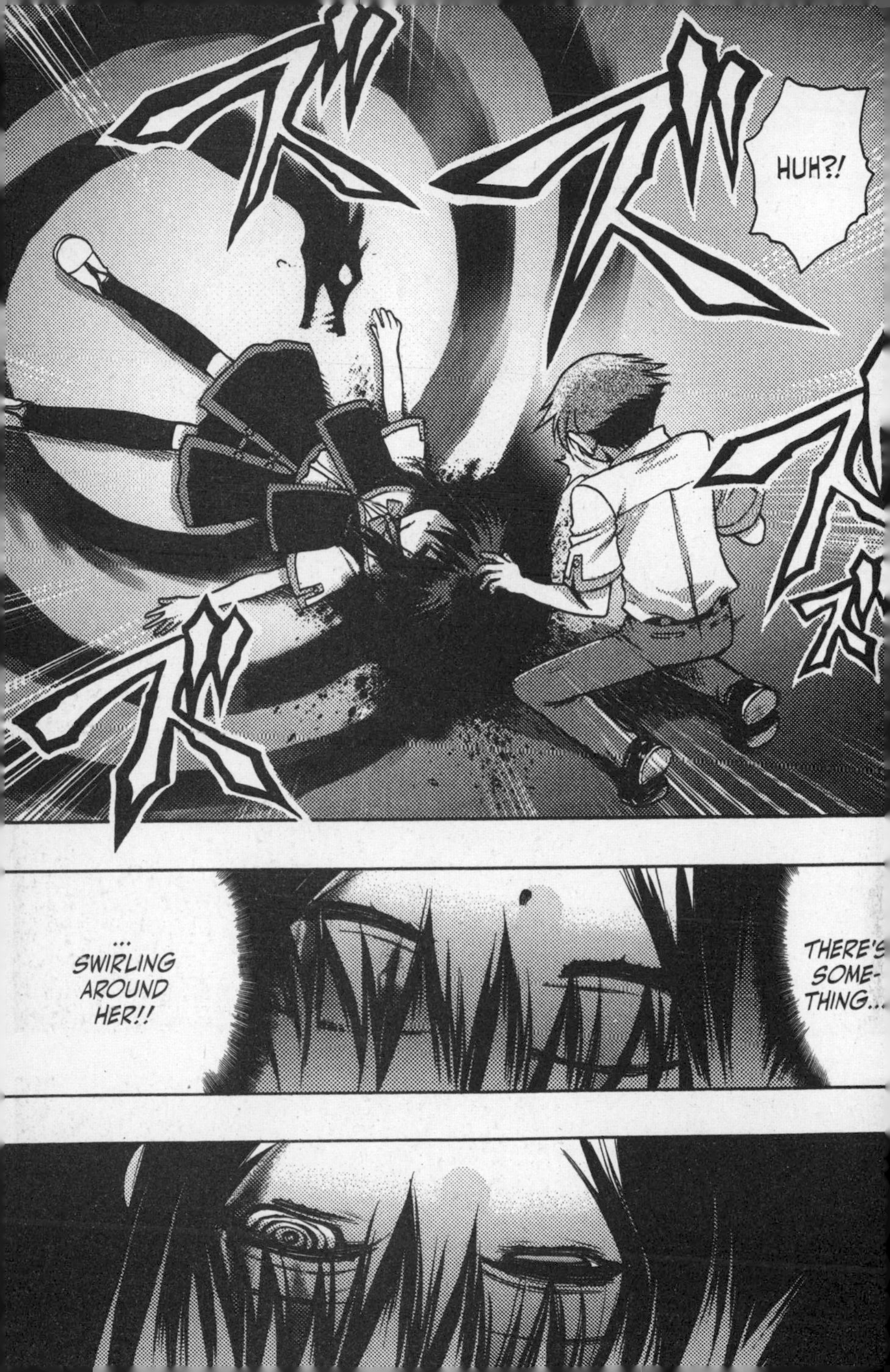
HUH?!
THERE'S SOME-THING...
... SWIRLING AROUND HER!!

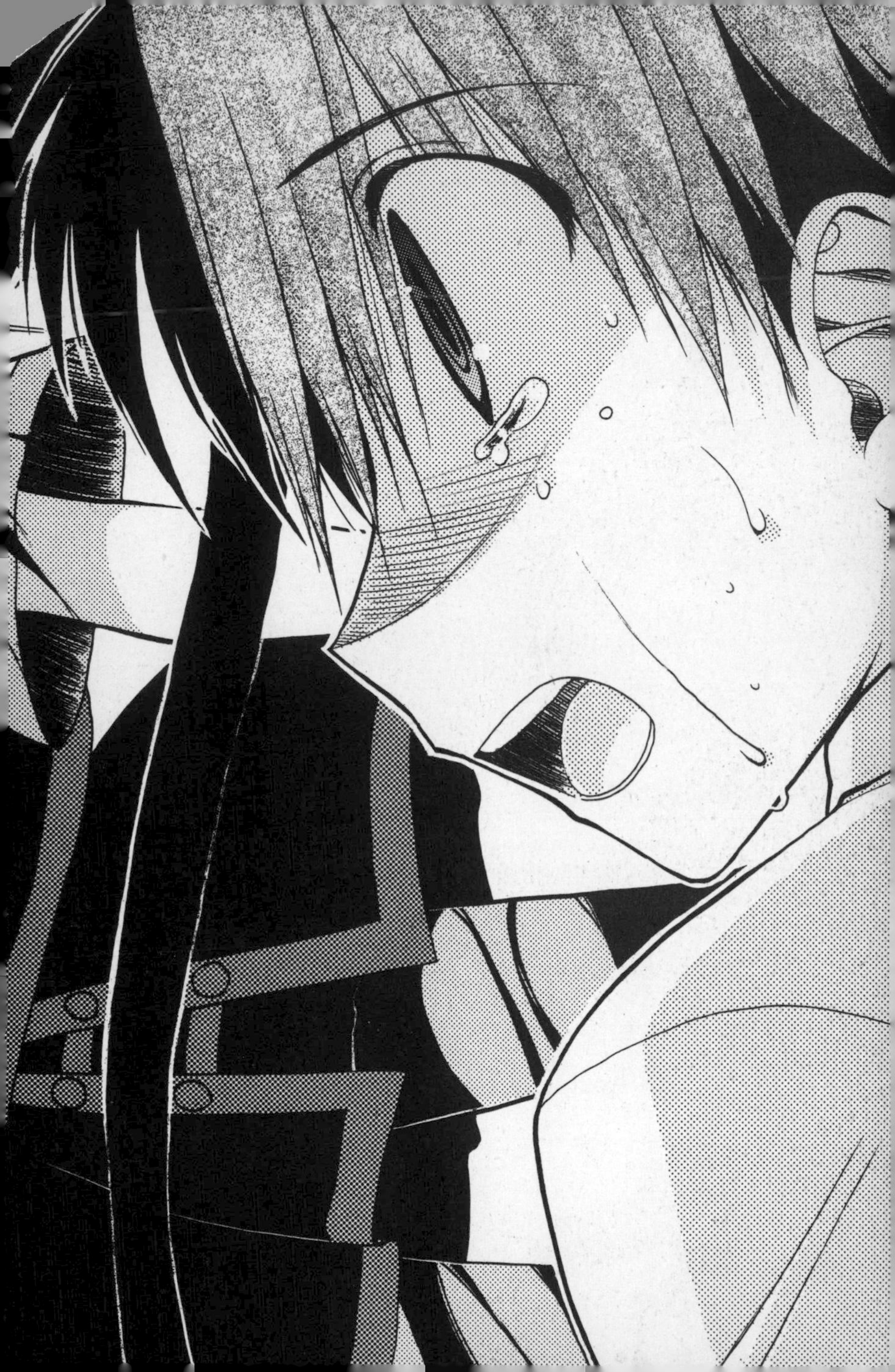

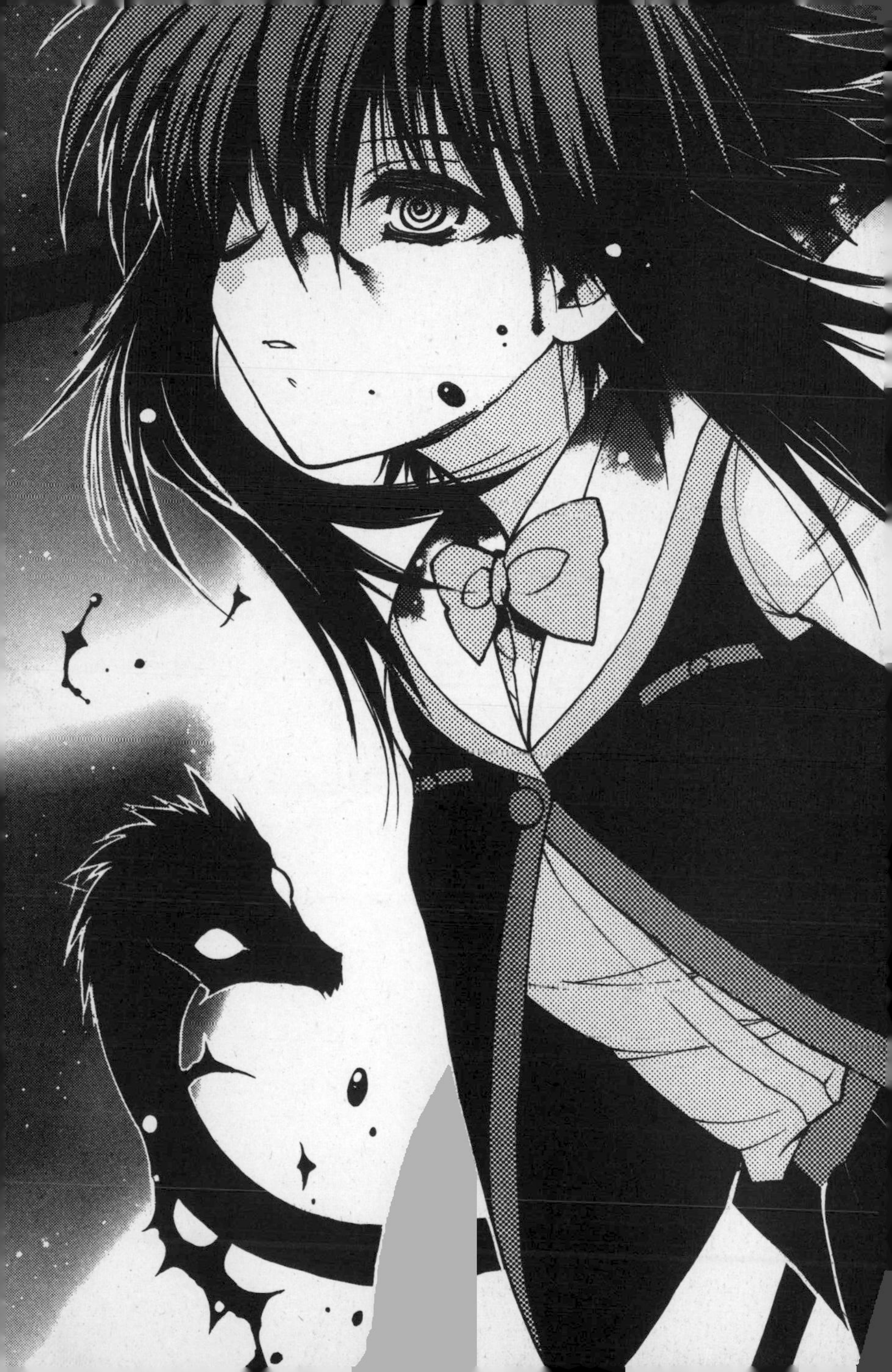

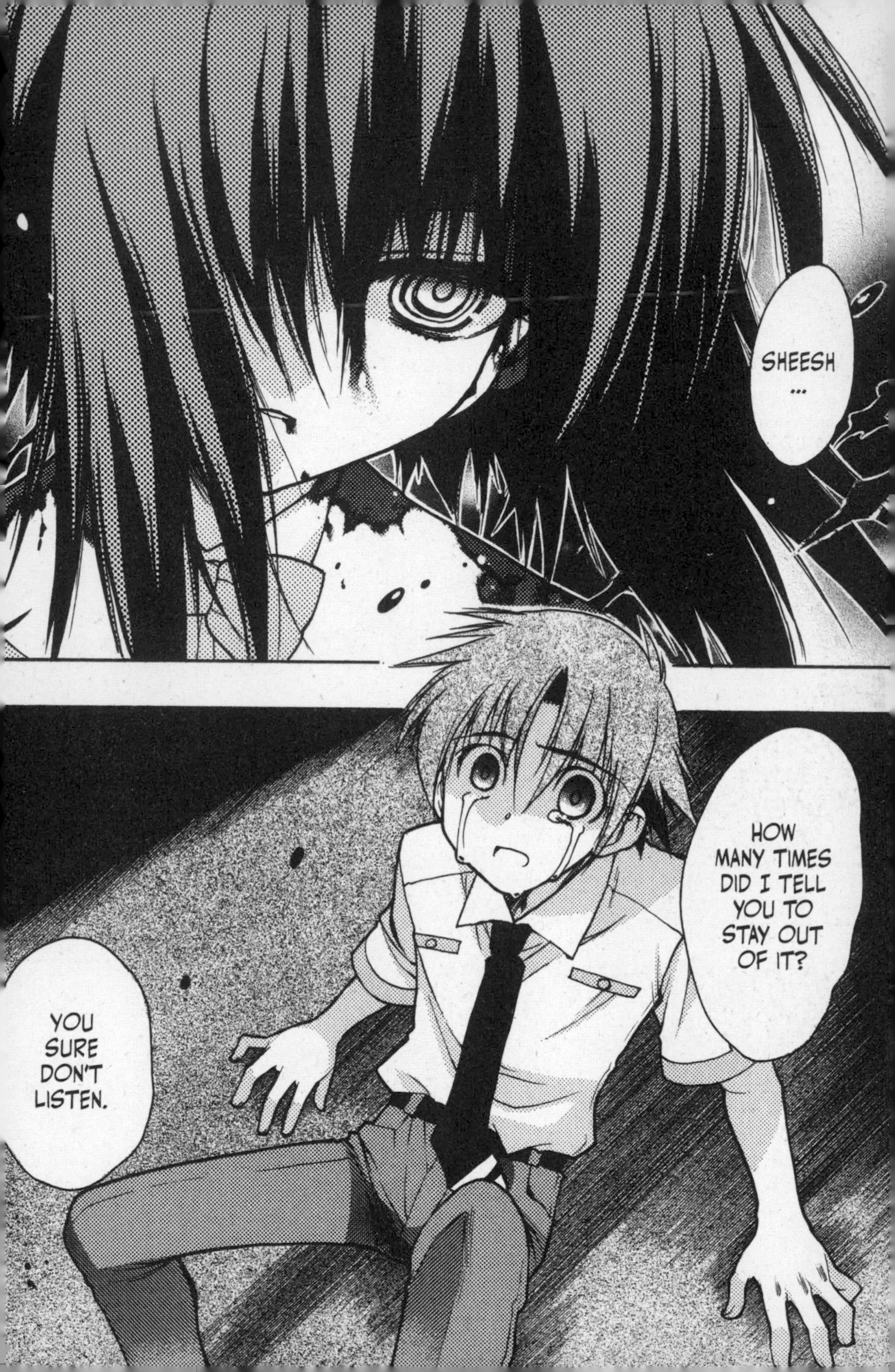
SHEESH ...
HOW MANY TIMES DID I TELL YOU TO STAY OUT OF IT?
YOU SURE DON'T LISTEN.

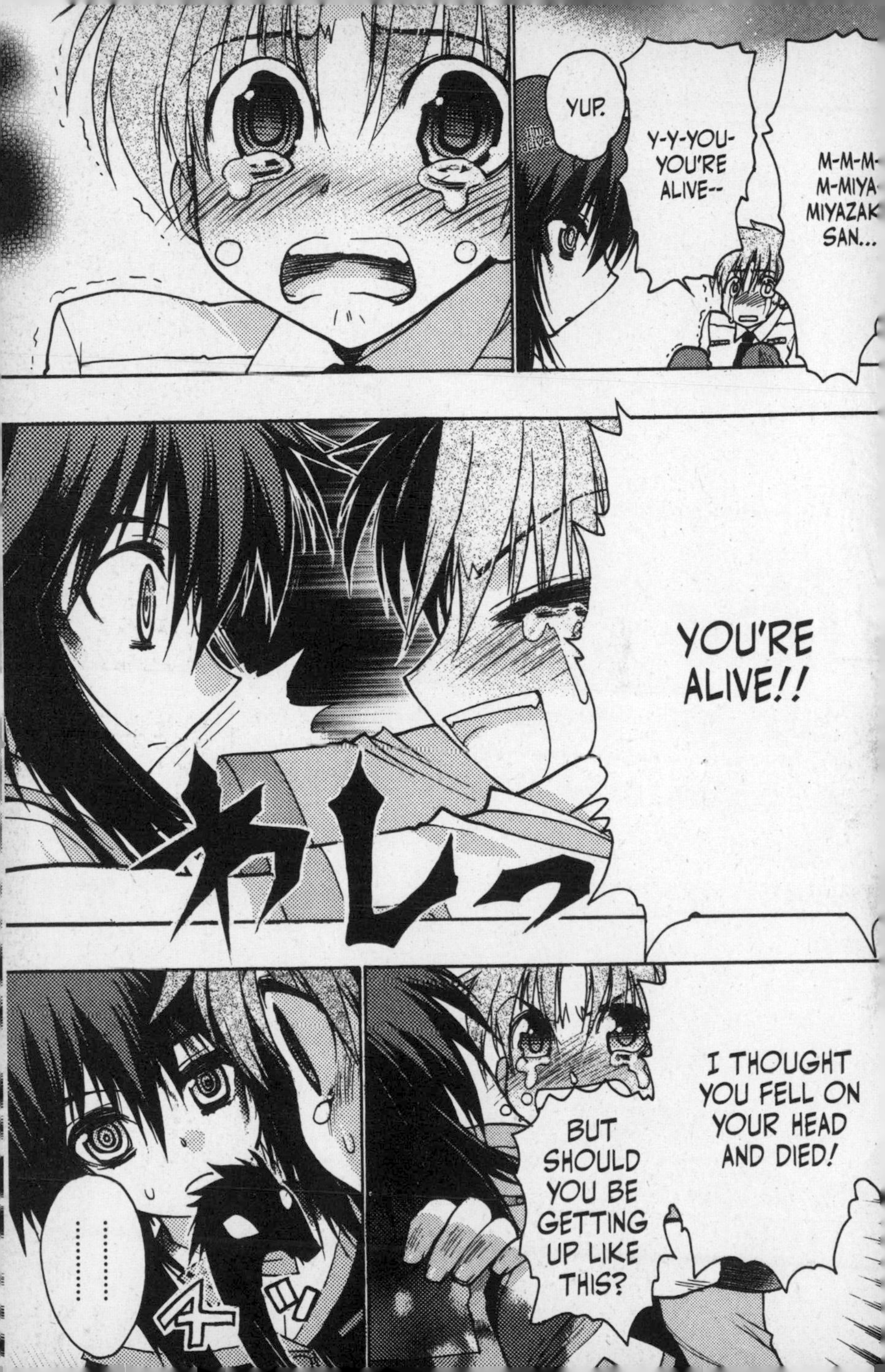
M-M-M-M-MIYA-MIYAZAK-SAN...
Y-Y-YOU-YOU'RE ALIVE--
YUP.
I'm alive
YOU'RE ALIVE!!
I THOUGHT YOU FELL ON YOUR HEAD AND DIED!
BUT SHOULD YOU BE GETTING UP LIKE THIS?
......

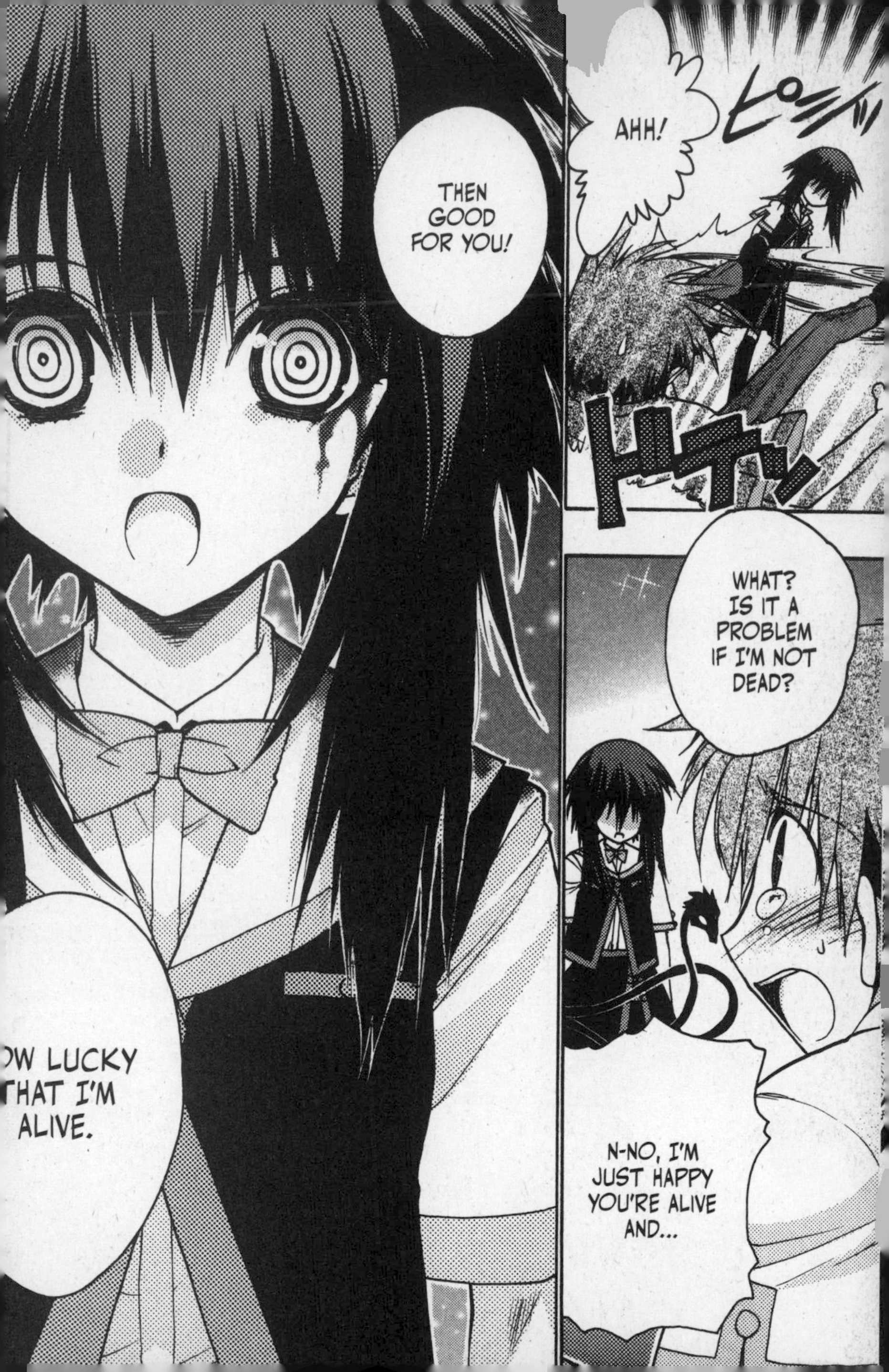
AHH!
WHAT? IS IT A PROBLEM IF I'M NOT DEAD?
N-NO, I'M JUST HAPPY YOU'RE ALIVE AND...
THEN GOOD FOR YOU!
OW LUCKY THAT I'M ALIVE.

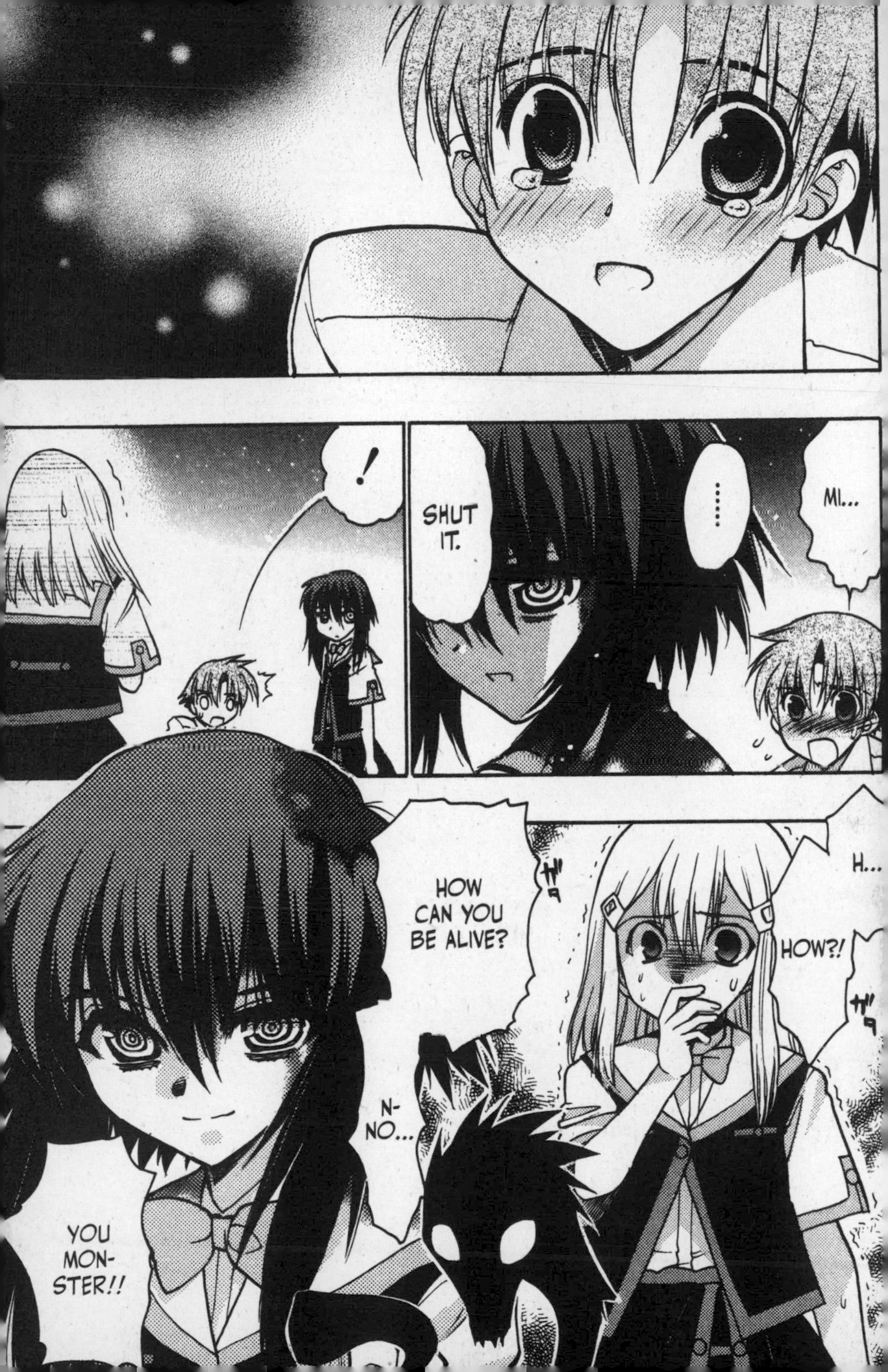
MI...
......
SHUT IT.
!
H...
HOW?!
HOW CAN YOU BE ALIVE?
N-NO...
YOU MONSTER!!

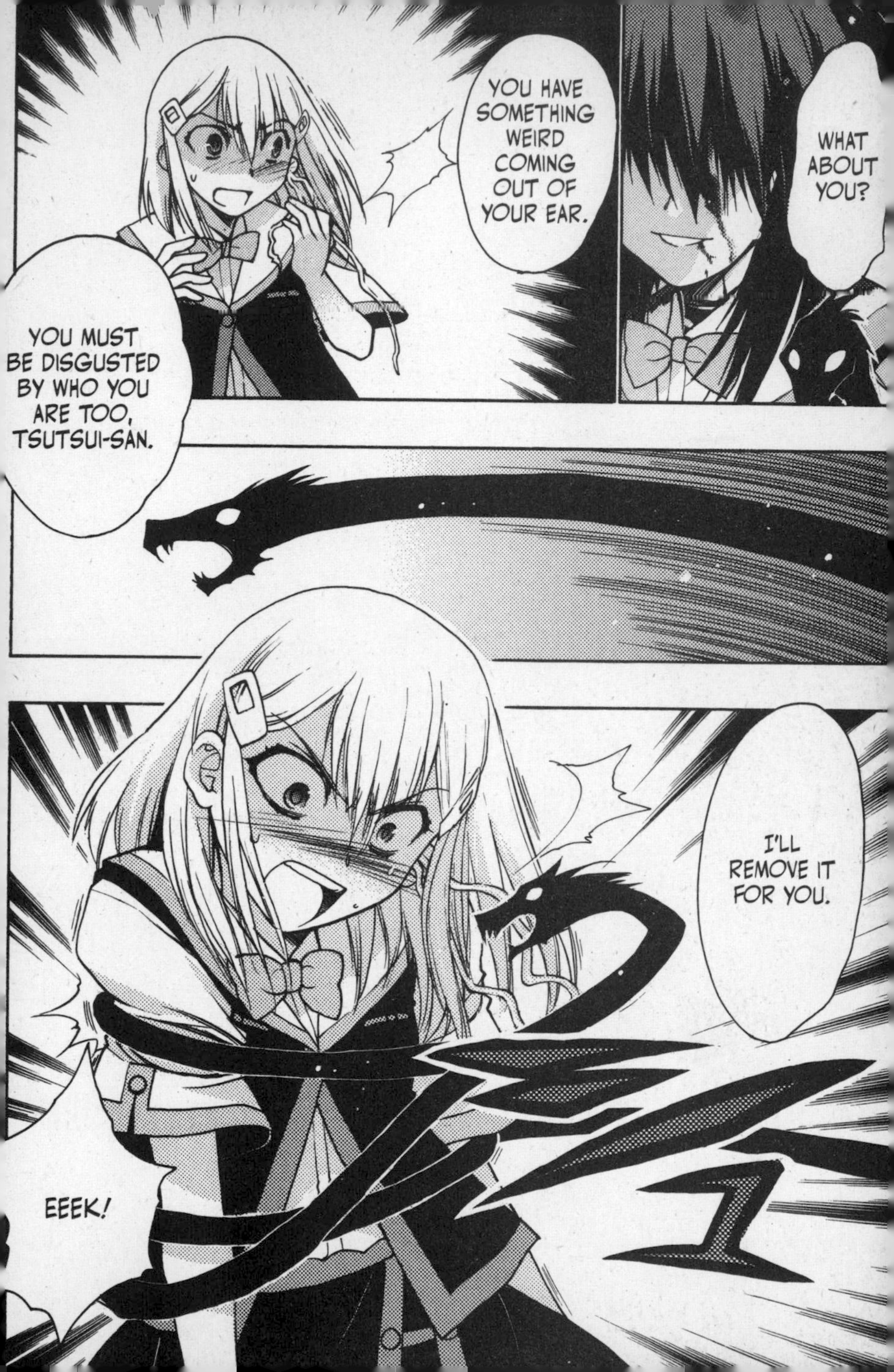
WHAT ABOUT YOU?
YOU HAVE SOMETHING WEIRD COMING OUT OF YOUR EAR.
YOU MUST BE DISGUSTED BY WHO YOU ARE TOO, TSUTSUI-SAN.
I'LL REMOVE IT FOR YOU.
EEEK!

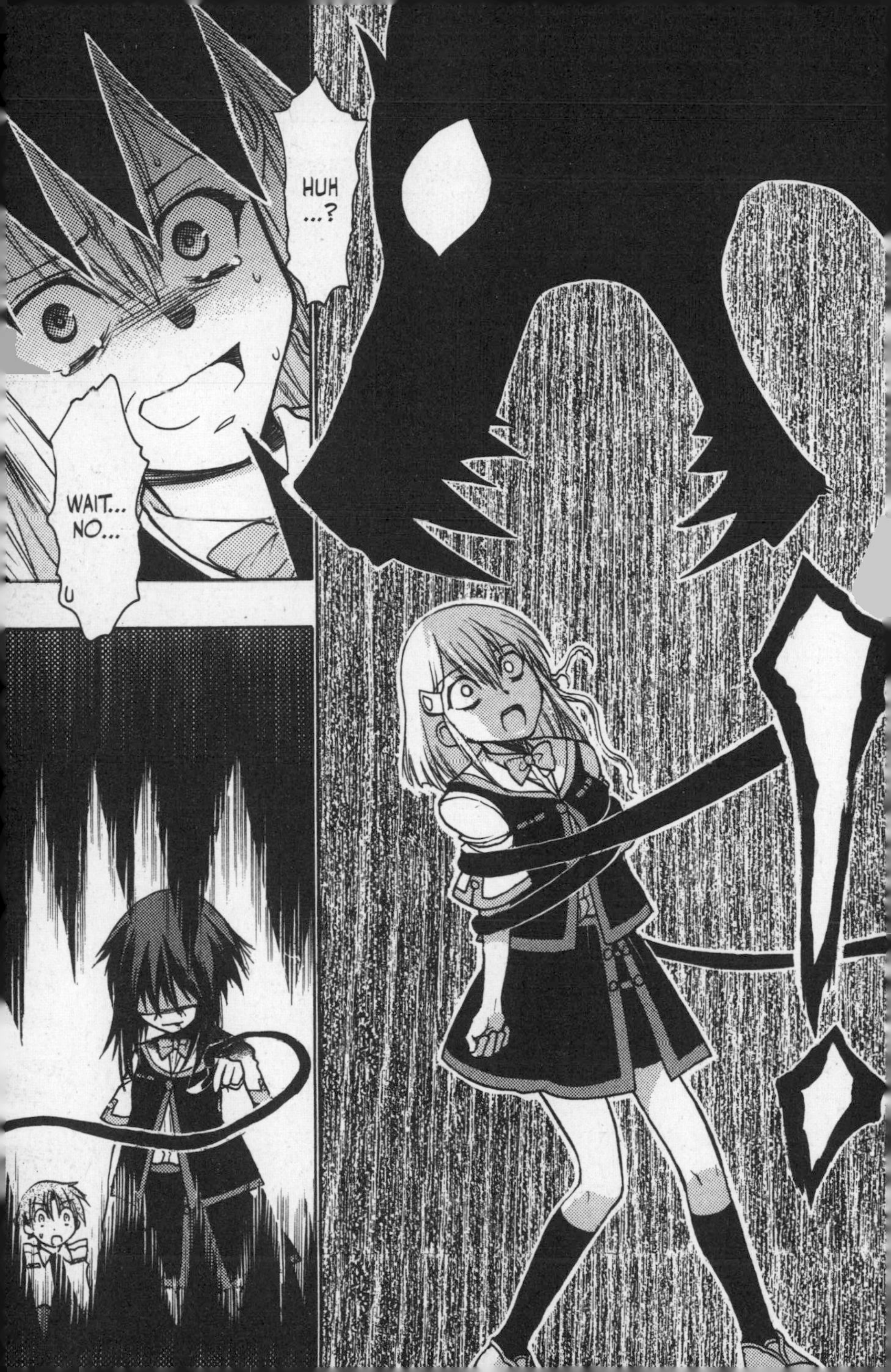
HUH ...?
WAIT... NO...

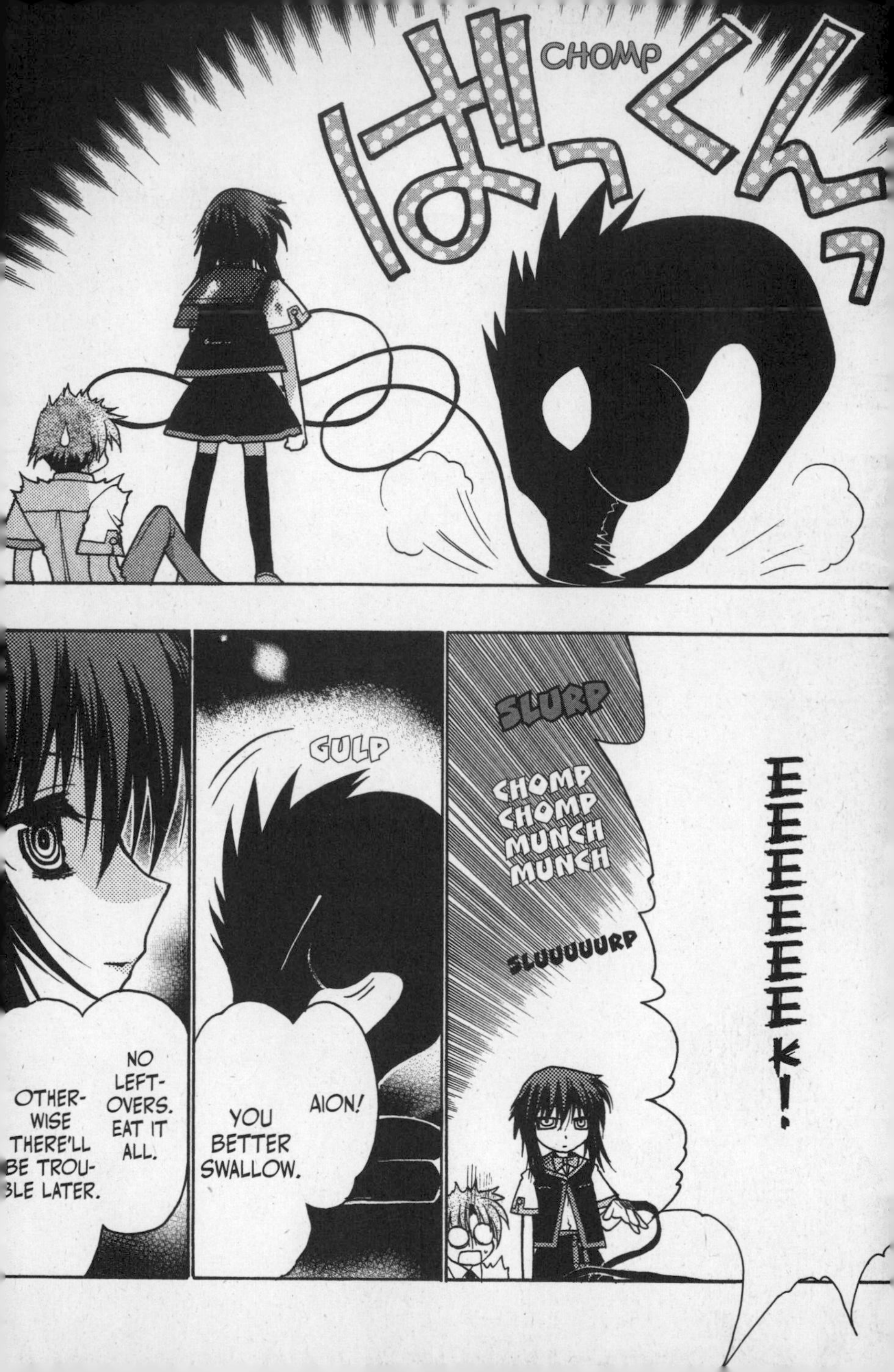
ぱっくん～
CHOMP
EEEEEEK!
SLURP
CHOMP CHOMP MUNCH MUNCH
SLUUUUURP
AION!
YOU BETTER SWALLOW.
GULP
NO LEFT-OVERS. EAT IT ALL.
OTHER-WISE THERE'LL BE TROU-BLE LATER.

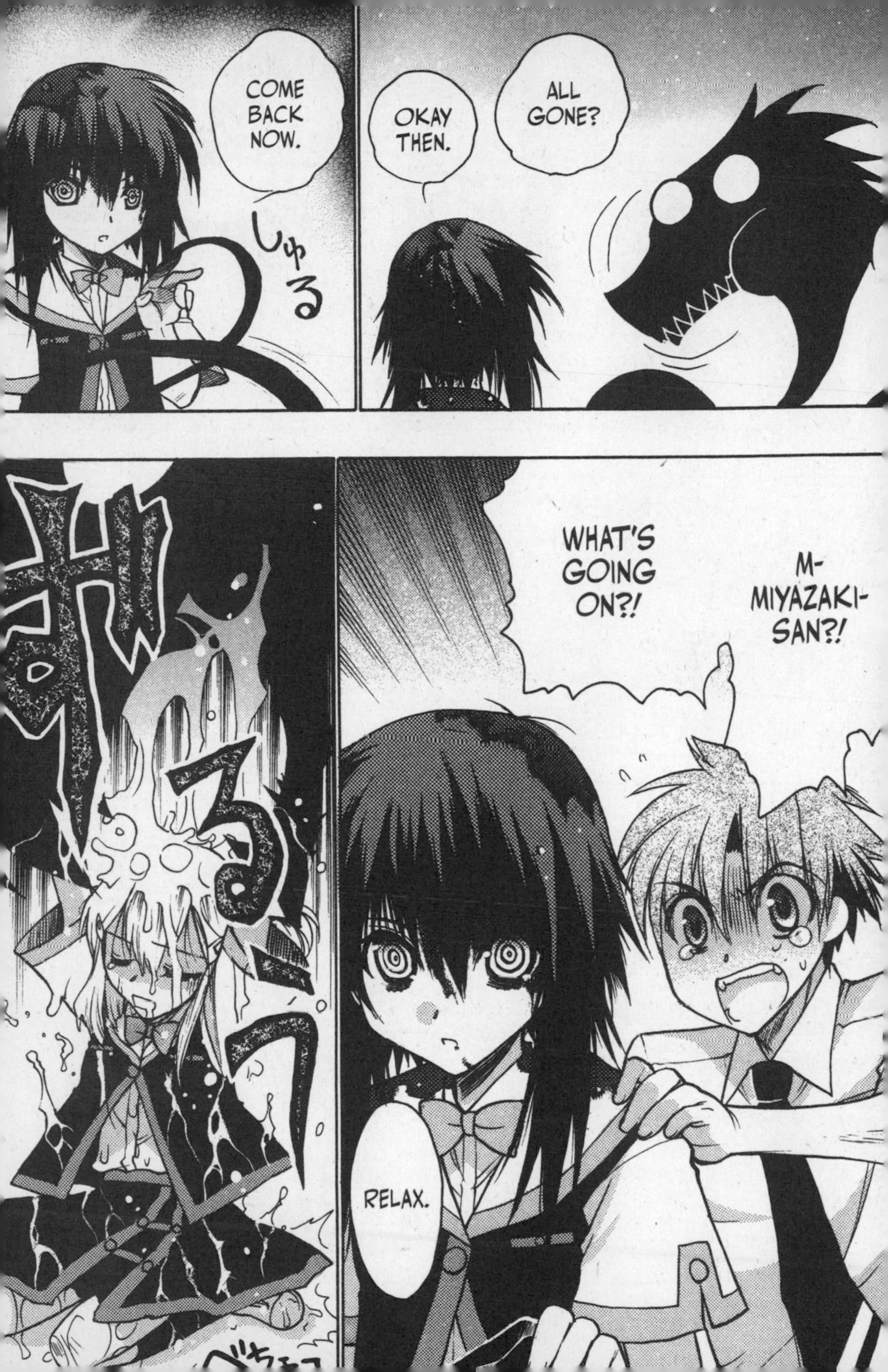
ALL GONE?
OKAY THEN.
COME BACK NOW.
しゅる
M-MIYAZAKI-SAN?!
WHAT'S GOING ON?!
RELAX.

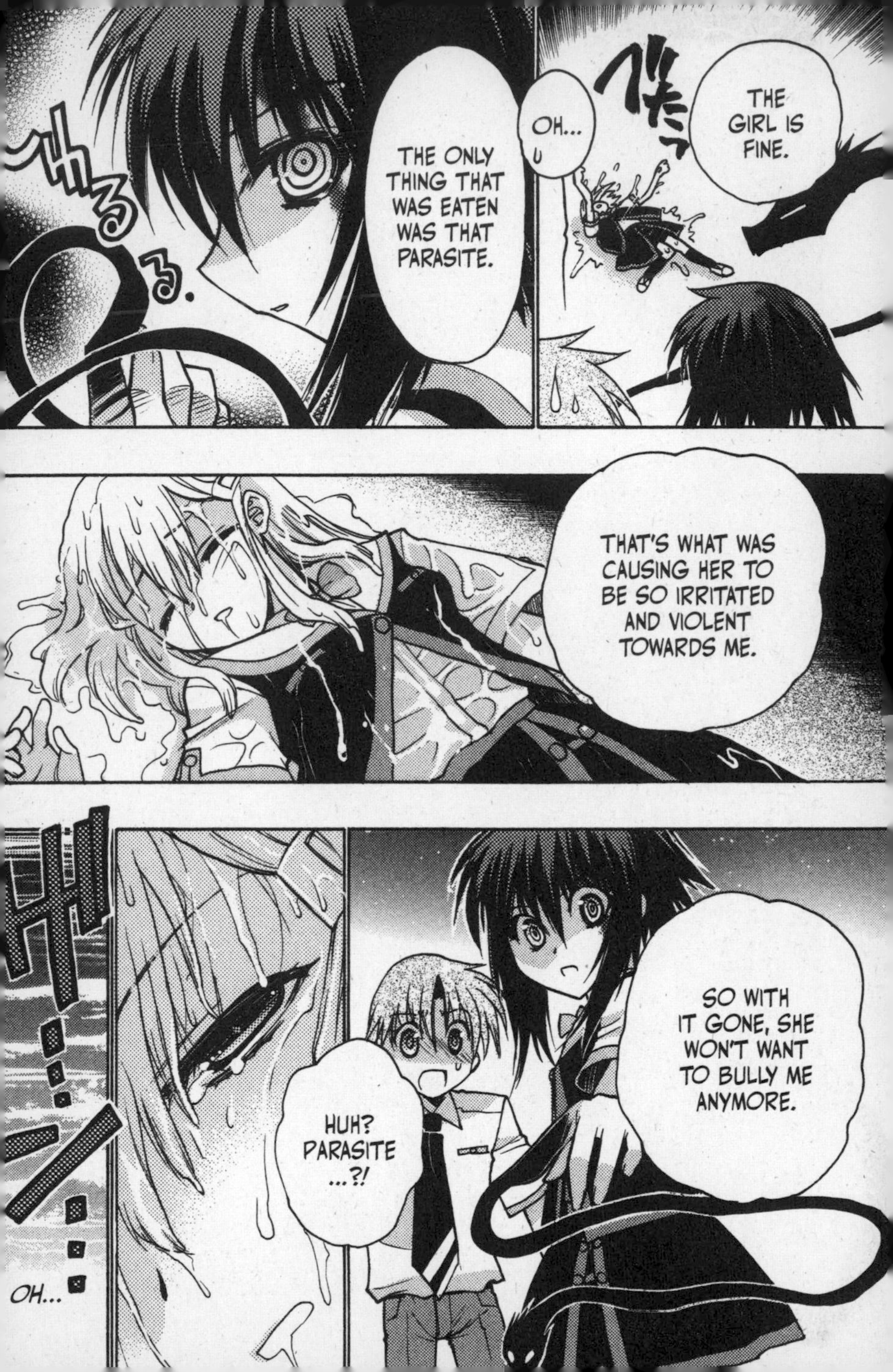
THE GIRL IS FINE.
OH...
THE ONLY THING THAT WAS EATEN WAS THAT PARASITE.
THAT'S WHAT WAS CAUSING HER TO BE SO IRRITATED AND VIOLENT TOWARDS ME.
SO WITH IT GONE, SHE WON'T WANT TO BULLY ME ANYMORE.
HUH? PARASITE ...?!
OH...

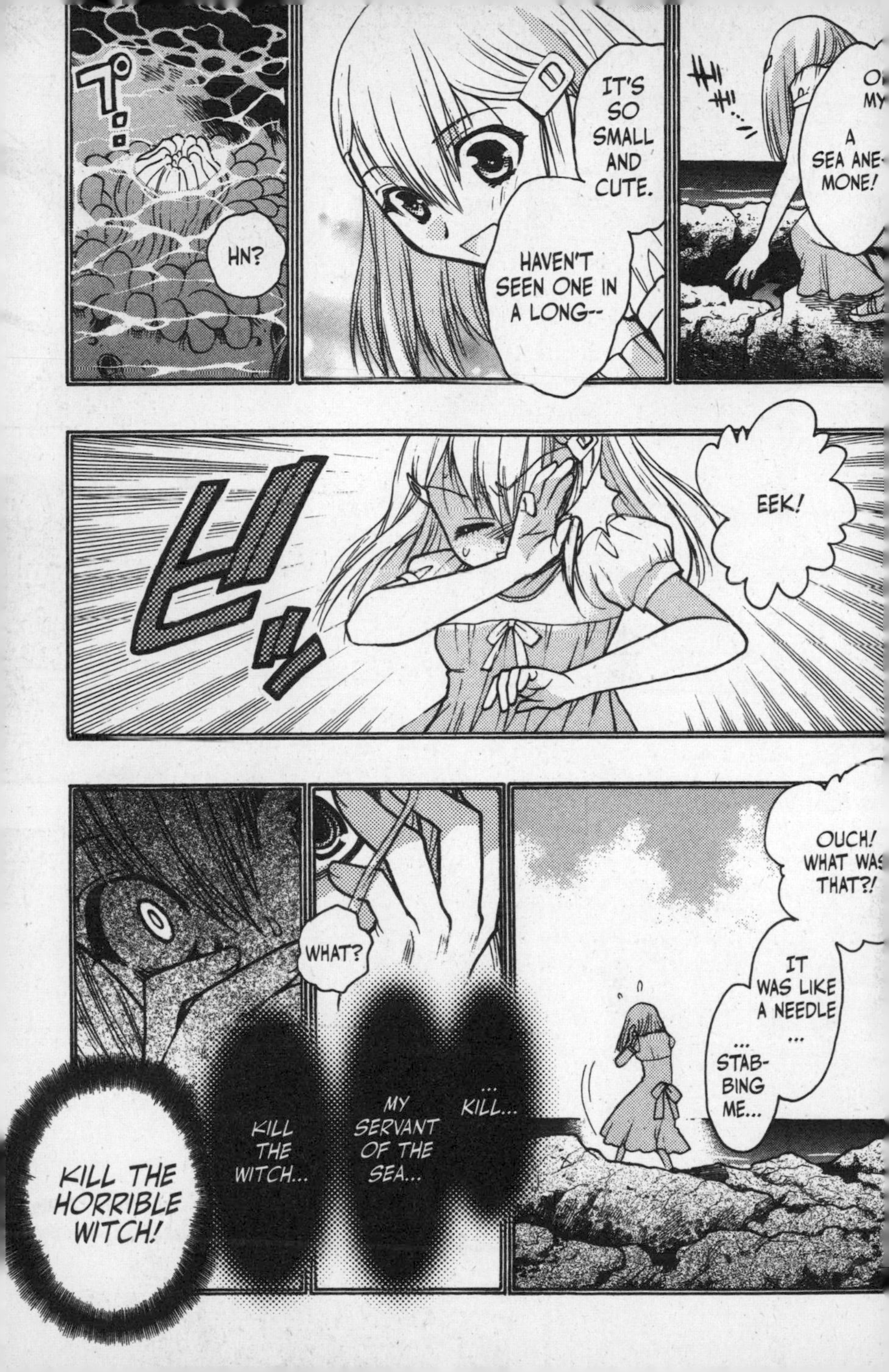

O MY
A SEA ANE-MONE!
IT'S SO SMALL AND CUTE.
HAVEN'T SEEN ONE IN A LONG--
HN?
EEK!
OUCH! WHAT WAS THAT?!
IT WAS LIKE A NEEDLE...
... STAB-BING ME...
WHAT?
... KILL...
MY SERVANT OF THE SEA...
KILL THE WITCH...
KILL THE HORRIBLE WITCH!

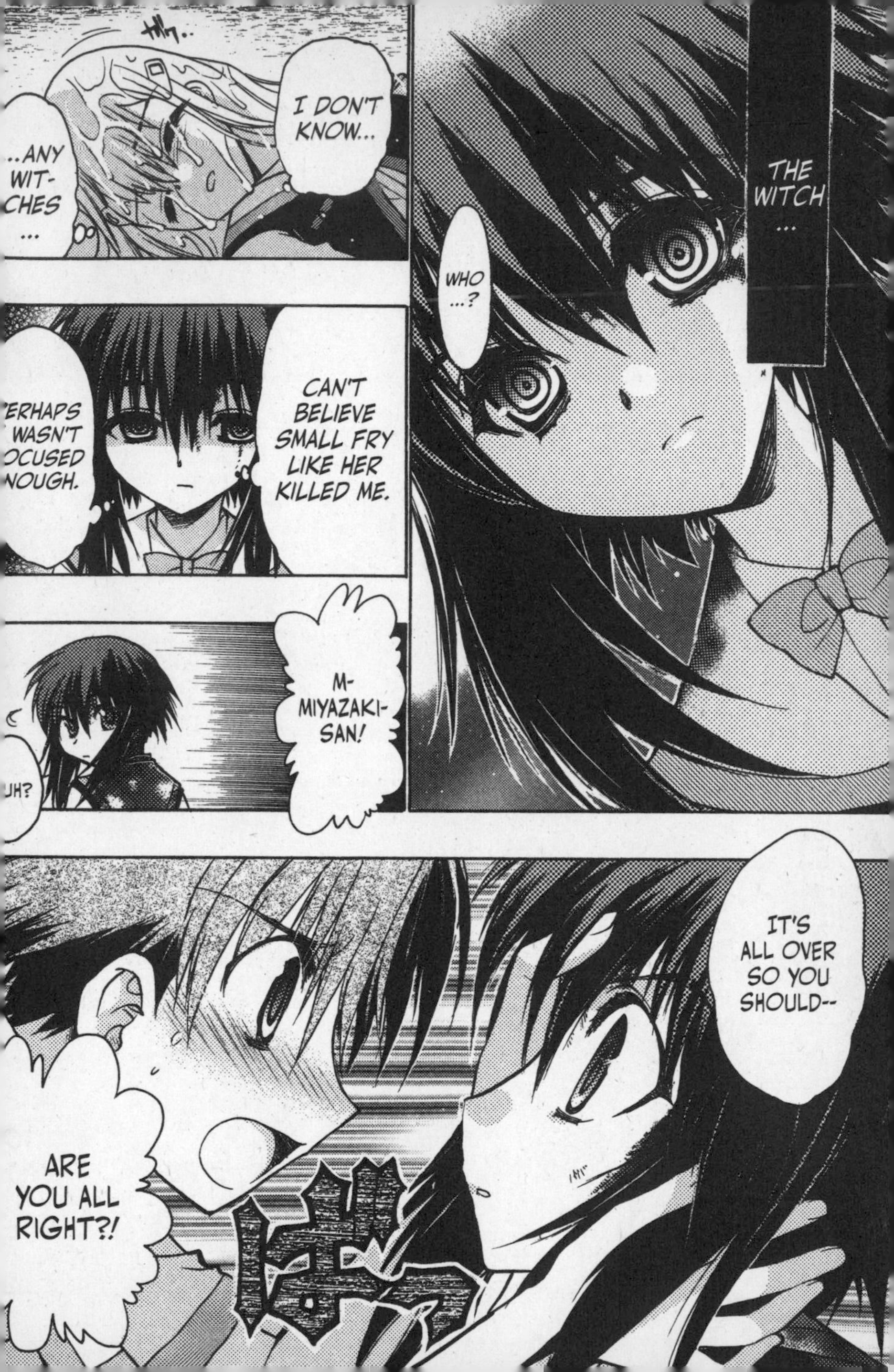
THE WITCH ...
WHO ...?
I DON'T KNOW...
...ANY WIT-CHES ...
CAN'T BELIEVE SMALL FRY LIKE HER KILLED ME.
ERHAPS WASN'T OCUSED NOUGH.
M-MIYAZAKI-SAN!
JH?
IT'S ALL OVER SO YOU SHOULD--
ARE YOU ALL RIGHT?!

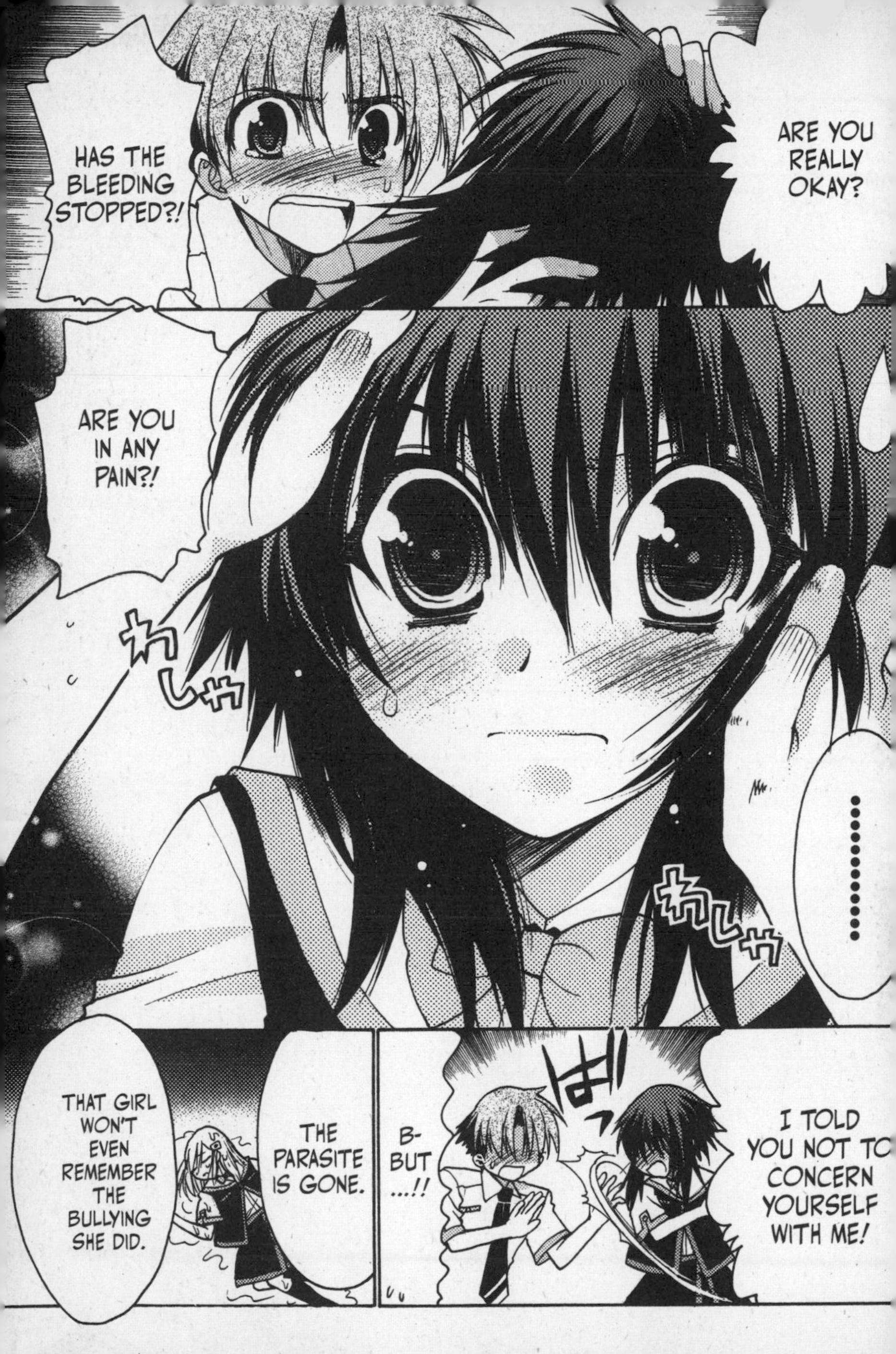
ARE YOU REALLY OKAY?
HAS THE BLEEDING STOPPED?!
ARE YOU IN ANY PAIN?!
わしゃ
わしゃ
....
I TOLD YOU NOT TO CONCERN YOURSELF WITH ME!
はっ
B-BUT ...!!
THE PARASITE IS GONE.
THAT GIRL WON'T EVEN REMEMBER THE BULLYING SHE DID.

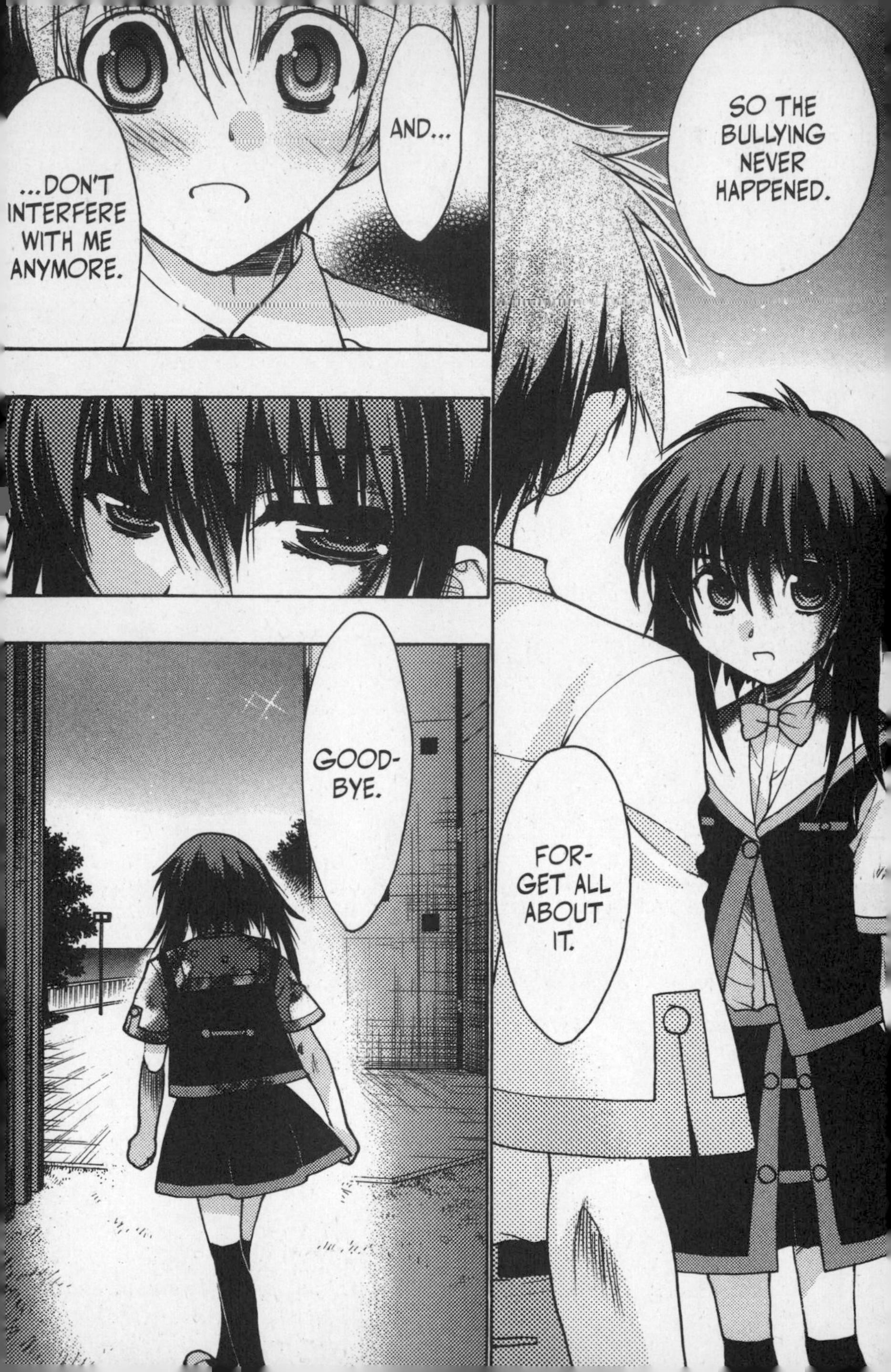
SO THE BULLYING NEVER HAPPENED.
FOR-GET ALL ABOUT IT.
AND...
...DON'T INTERFERE WITH ME ANYMORE.
GOOD-BYE.

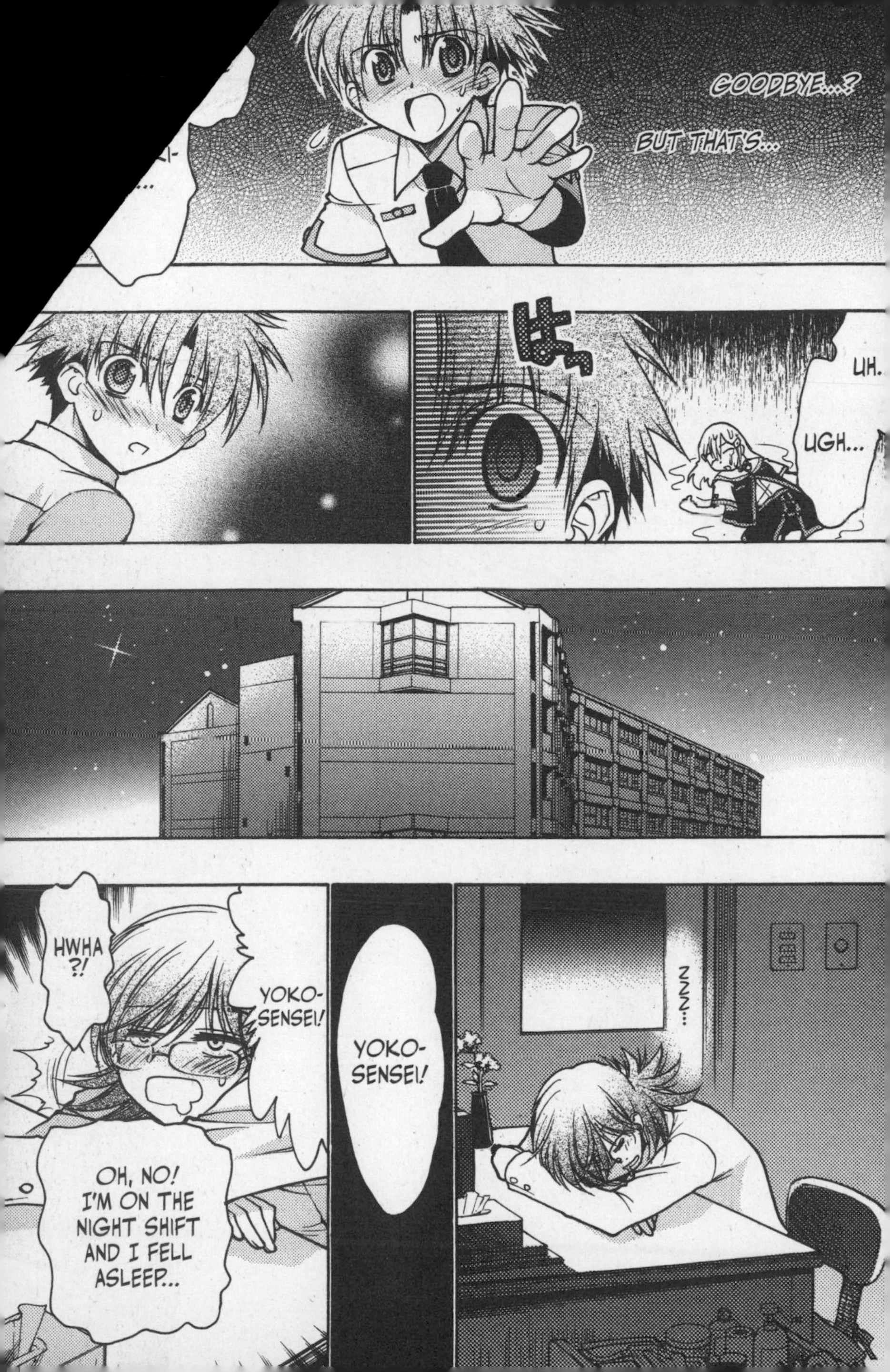
GOODBYE...?
BUT THAT'S...
UH.
UGH...
はっ
ZZZ...
YOKO-SENSEI!
YOKO-SENSEI!
HWHA?!
OH, NO! I'M ON THE NIGHT SHIFT AND I FELL ASLEEP...

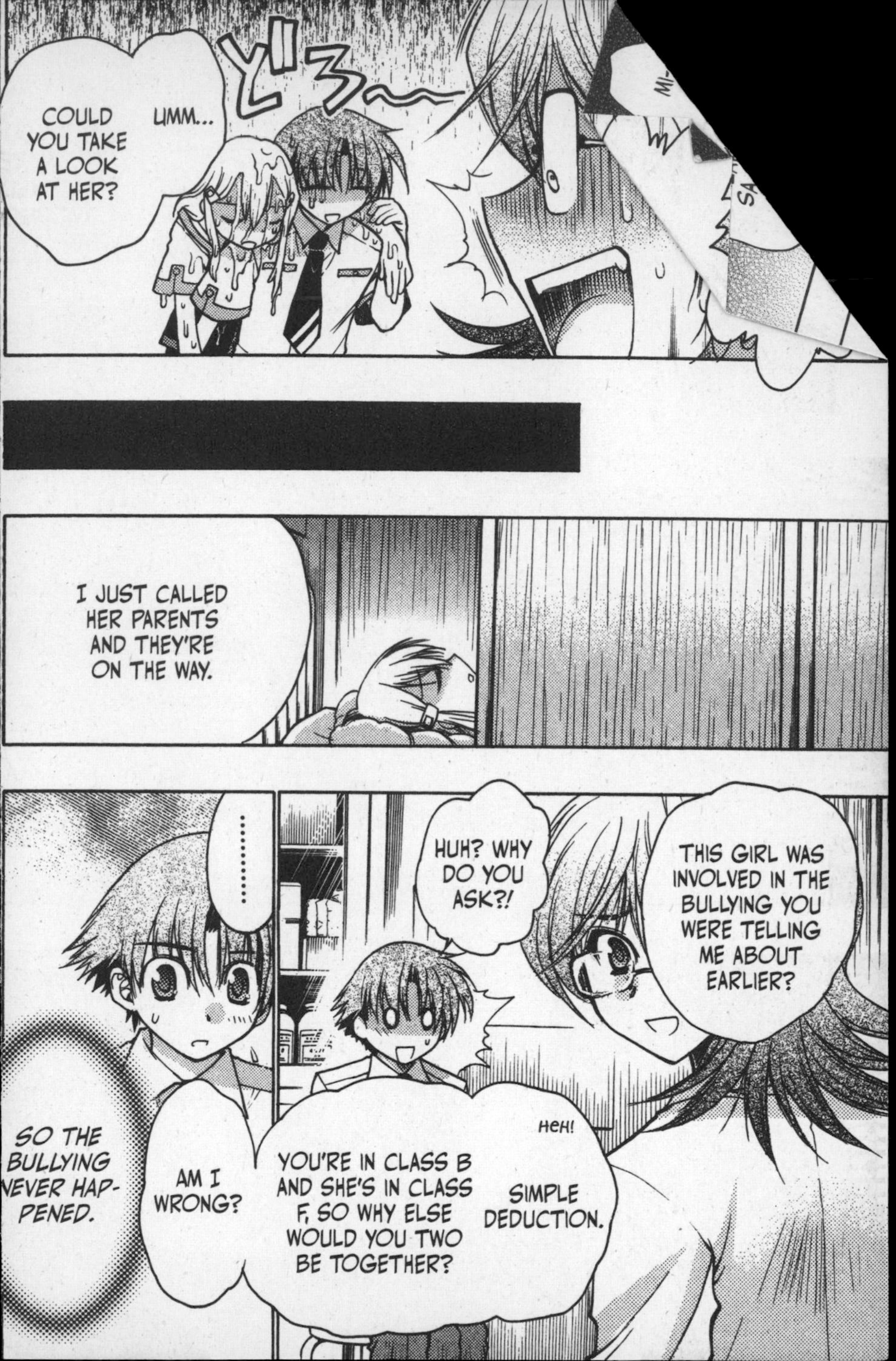
どろ〜〜
UMM...
COULD YOU TAKE A LOOK AT HER?
I JUST CALLED HER PARENTS AND THEY'RE ON THE WAY.
THIS GIRL WAS INVOLVED IN THE BULLYING YOU WERE TELLING ME ABOUT EARLIER?
HUH? WHY DO YOU ASK?!
......
HEH!
SIMPLE DEDUCTION.
YOU'RE IN CLASS B AND SHE'S IN CLASS F, SO WHY ELSE WOULD YOU TWO BE TOGETHER?
AM I WRONG?
SO THE BULLYING NEVER HAPPENED.

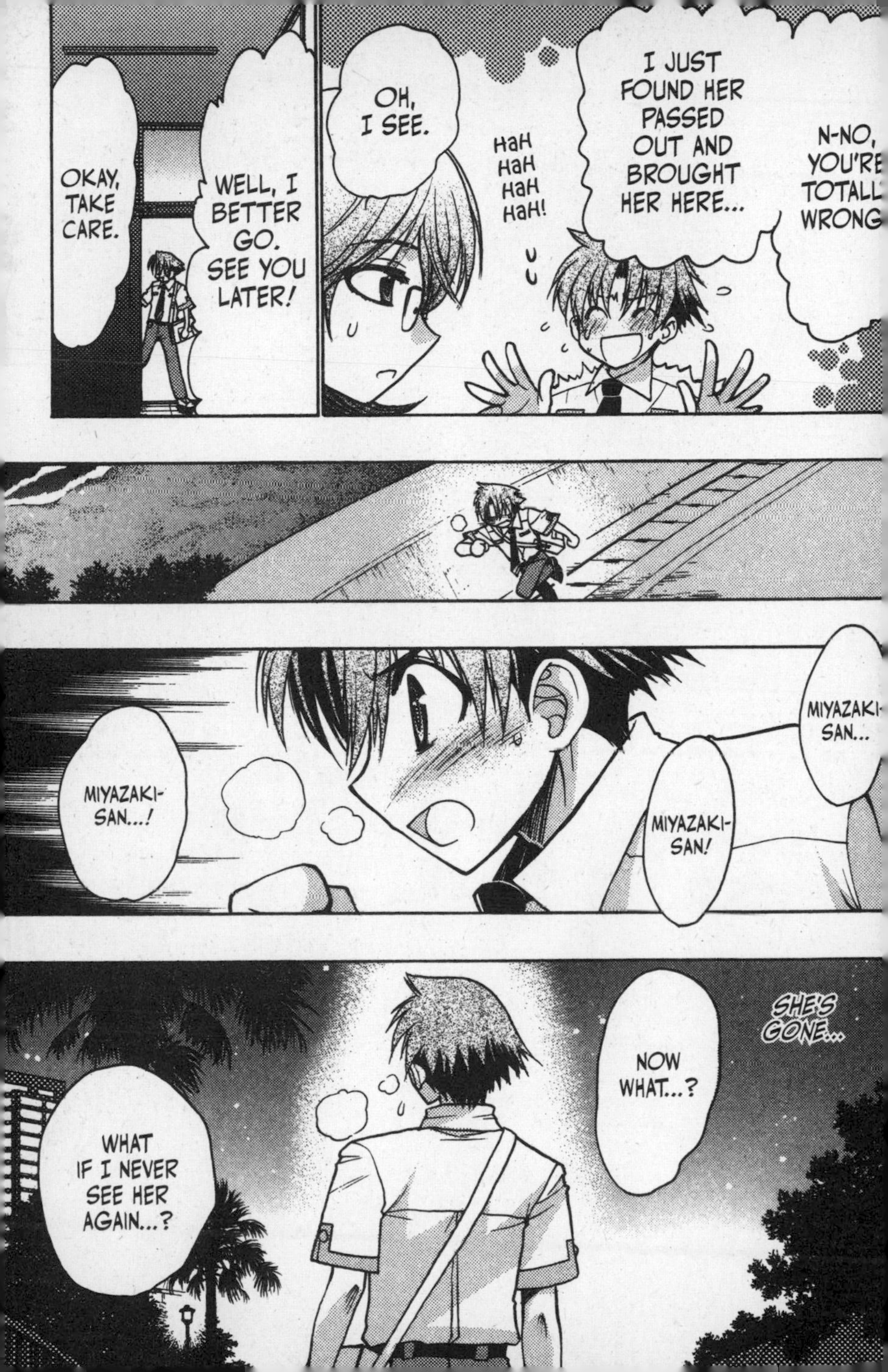
N-NO, YOU'RE TOTALL WRONG
I JUST FOUND HER PASSED OUT AND BROUGHT HER HERE...
HaH HaH HaH HaH!
OH, I SEE.
WELL, I BETTER GO. SEE YOU LATER!
OKAY, TAKE CARE.
MIYAZAKI-SAN...
MIYAZAKI-SAN!
MIYAZAKI-SAN...!
SHE'S GONE...
NOW WHAT...?
WHAT IF I NEVER SEE HER AGAIN...?

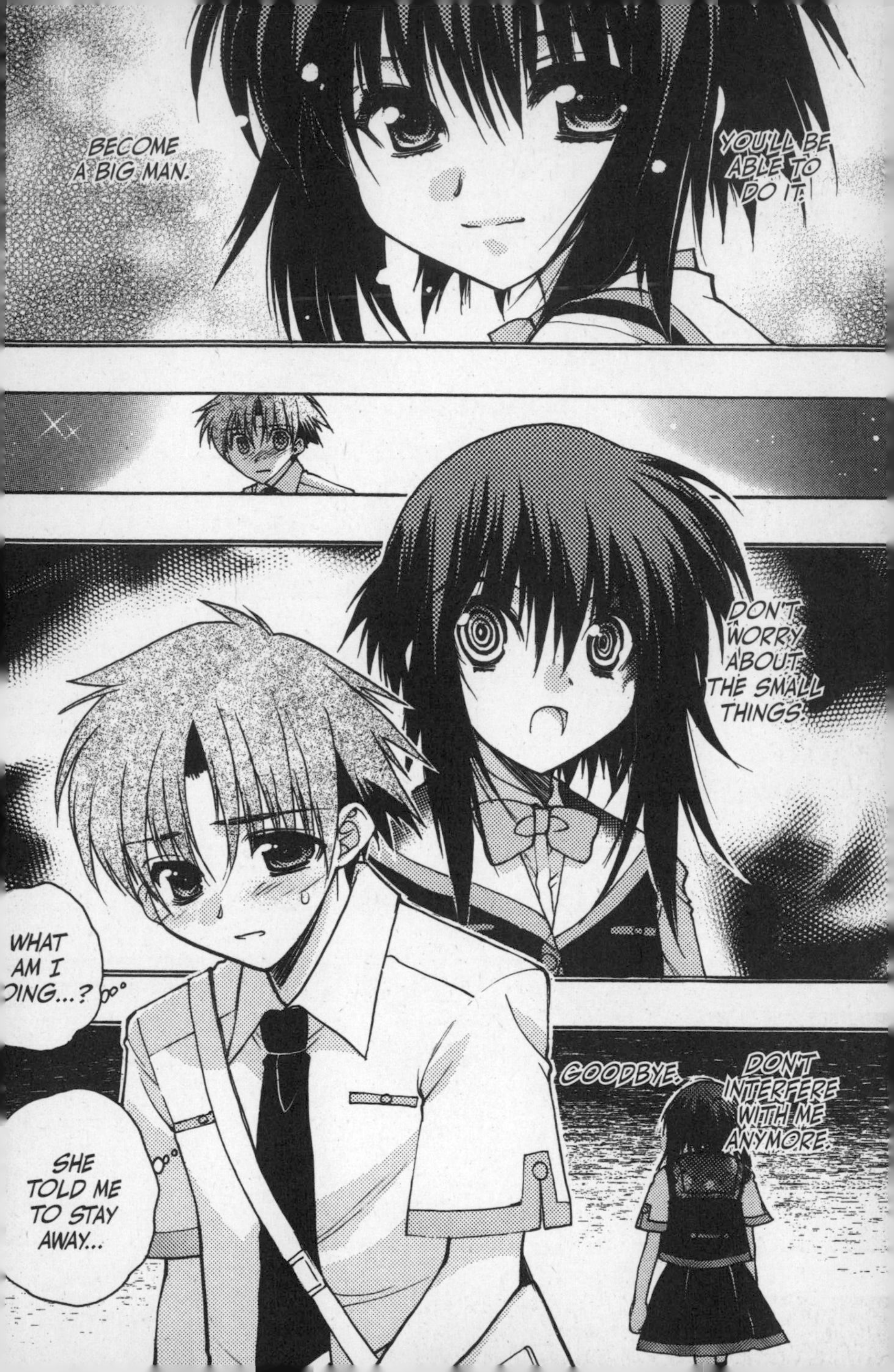
YOU'LL BE ABLE TO DO IT.
BECOME A BIG MAN.
DON'T WORRY ABOUT THE SMALL THINGS.
DON'T INTERFERE WITH ME ANYMORE.
GOODBYE.
WHAT AM I OING...?
SHE TOLD ME TO STAY AWAY...

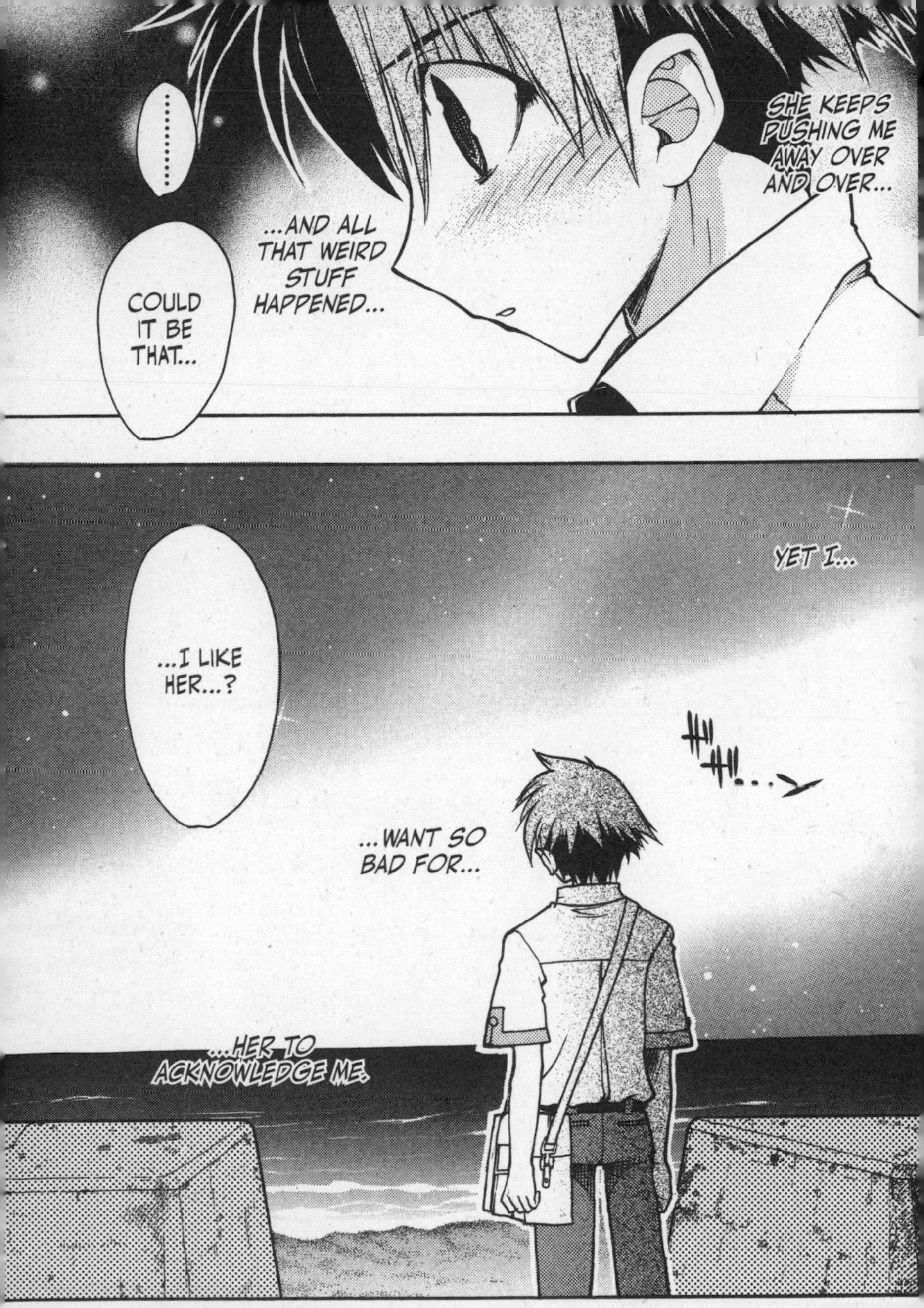
SHE KEEPS PUSHING ME AWAY OVER AND OVER...
...AND ALL THAT WEIRD STUFF HAPPENED...
......
COULD IT BE THAT...
YET I...
...I LIKE HER...?
...WANT SO BAD FOR...
...HER TO ACKNOWLEDGE ME.

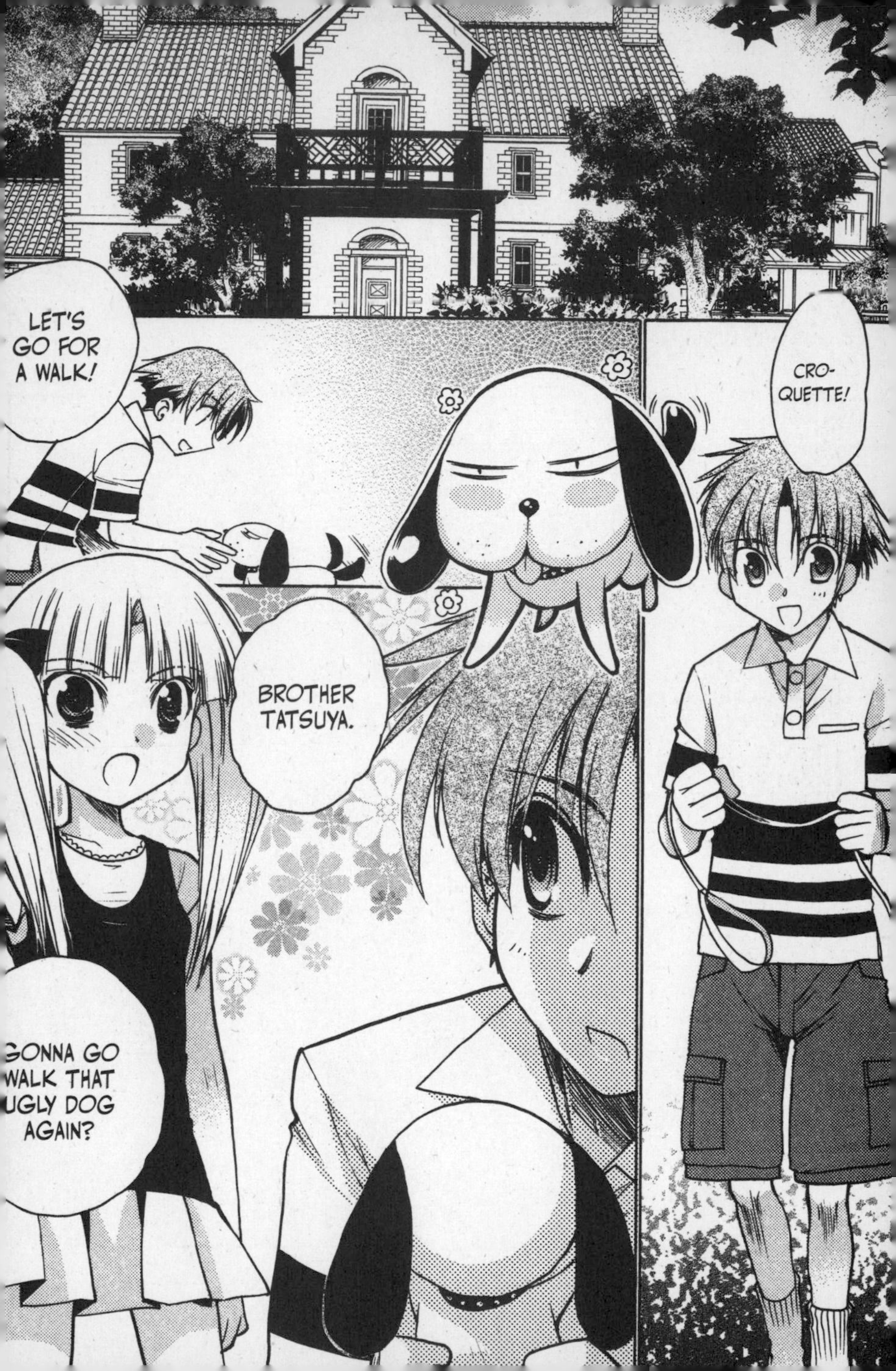
CRO-QUETTE!
LET'S GO FOR A WALK!
BROTHER TATSUYA.
GONNA GO WALK THAT UGLY DOG AGAIN?

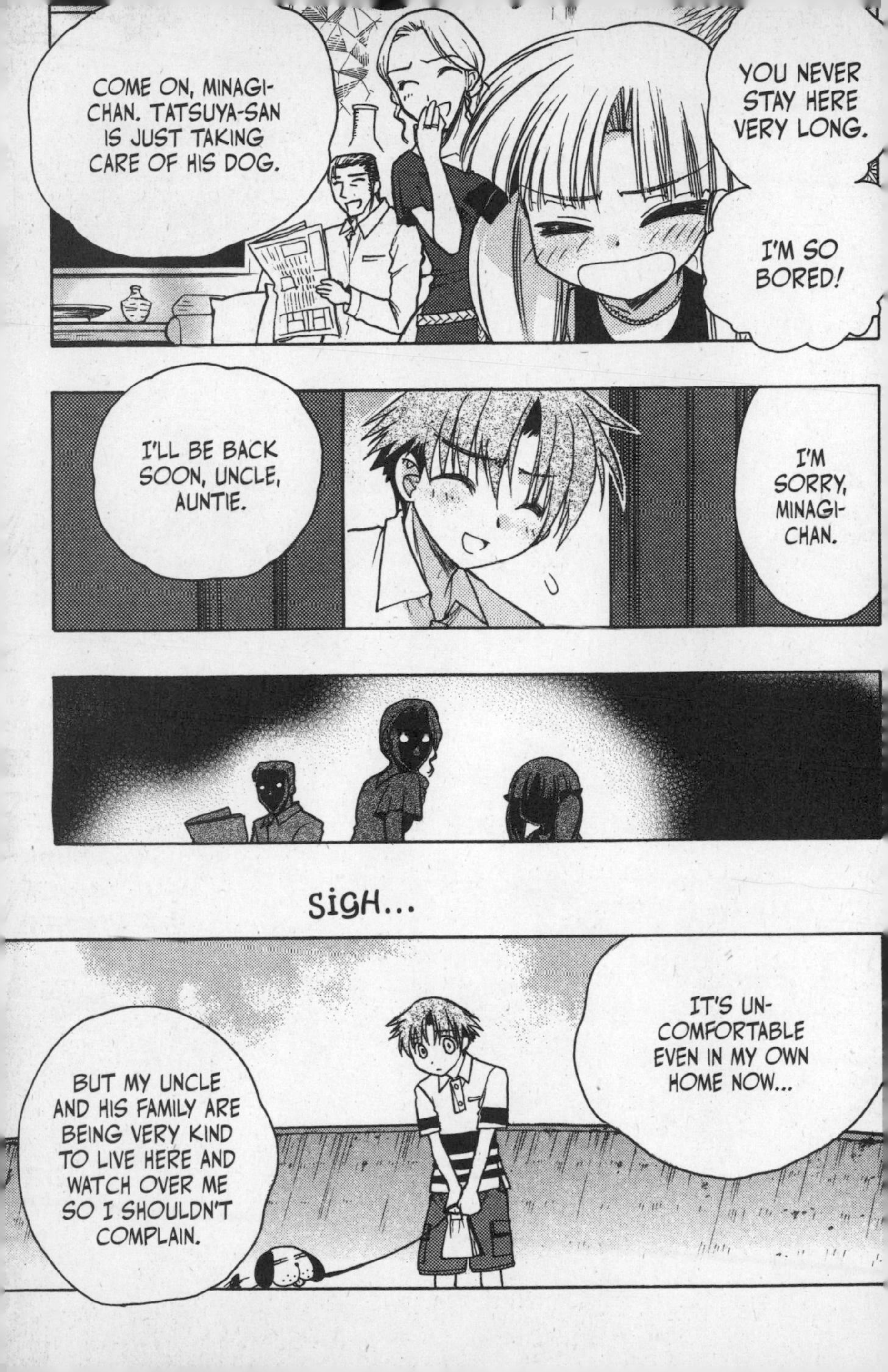
YOU NEVER STAY HERE VERY LONG.
I'M SO BORED!
COME ON, MINAGI-CHAN. TATSUYA-SAN IS JUST TAKING CARE OF HIS DOG.
I'M SORRY, MINAGI-CHAN.
I'LL BE BACK SOON, UNCLE, AUNTIE.
SIGH...
IT'S UN-COMFORTABLE EVEN IN MY OWN HOME NOW...
BUT MY UNCLE AND HIS FAMILY ARE BEING VERY KIND TO LIVE HERE AND WATCH OVER ME SO I SHOULDN'T COMPLAIN.

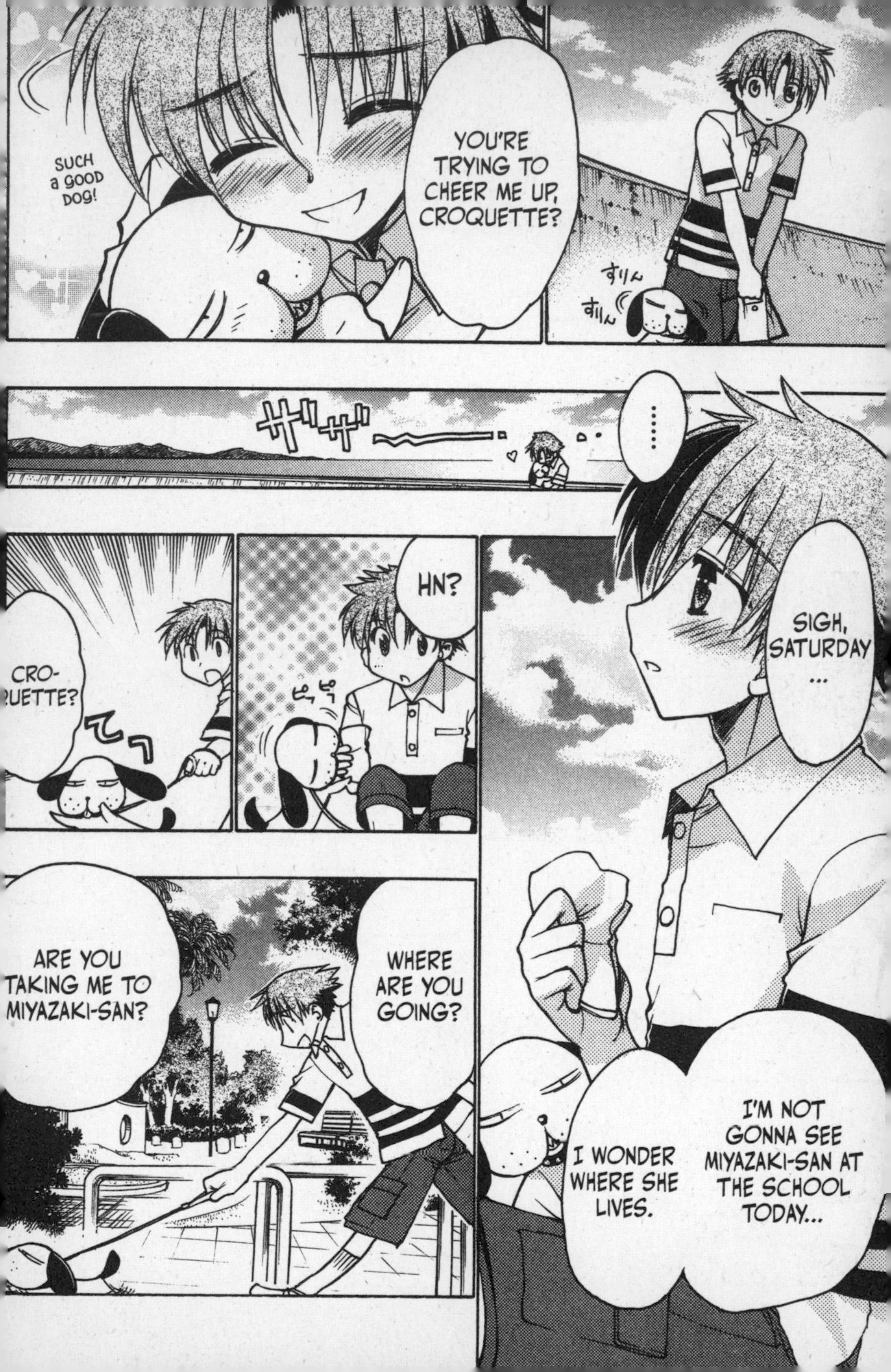
すりん
すりん
YOU'RE TRYING TO CHEER ME UP, CROQUETTE?
SUCH a GOOD DOG!
......
SIGH, SATURDAY ...
I'M NOT GONNA SEE MIYAZAKI-SAN AT THE SCHOOL TODAY...
I WONDER WHERE SHE LIVES.
HN?
CRO- UETTE?
WHERE ARE YOU GOING?
ARE YOU TAKING ME TO MIYAZAKI-SAN?

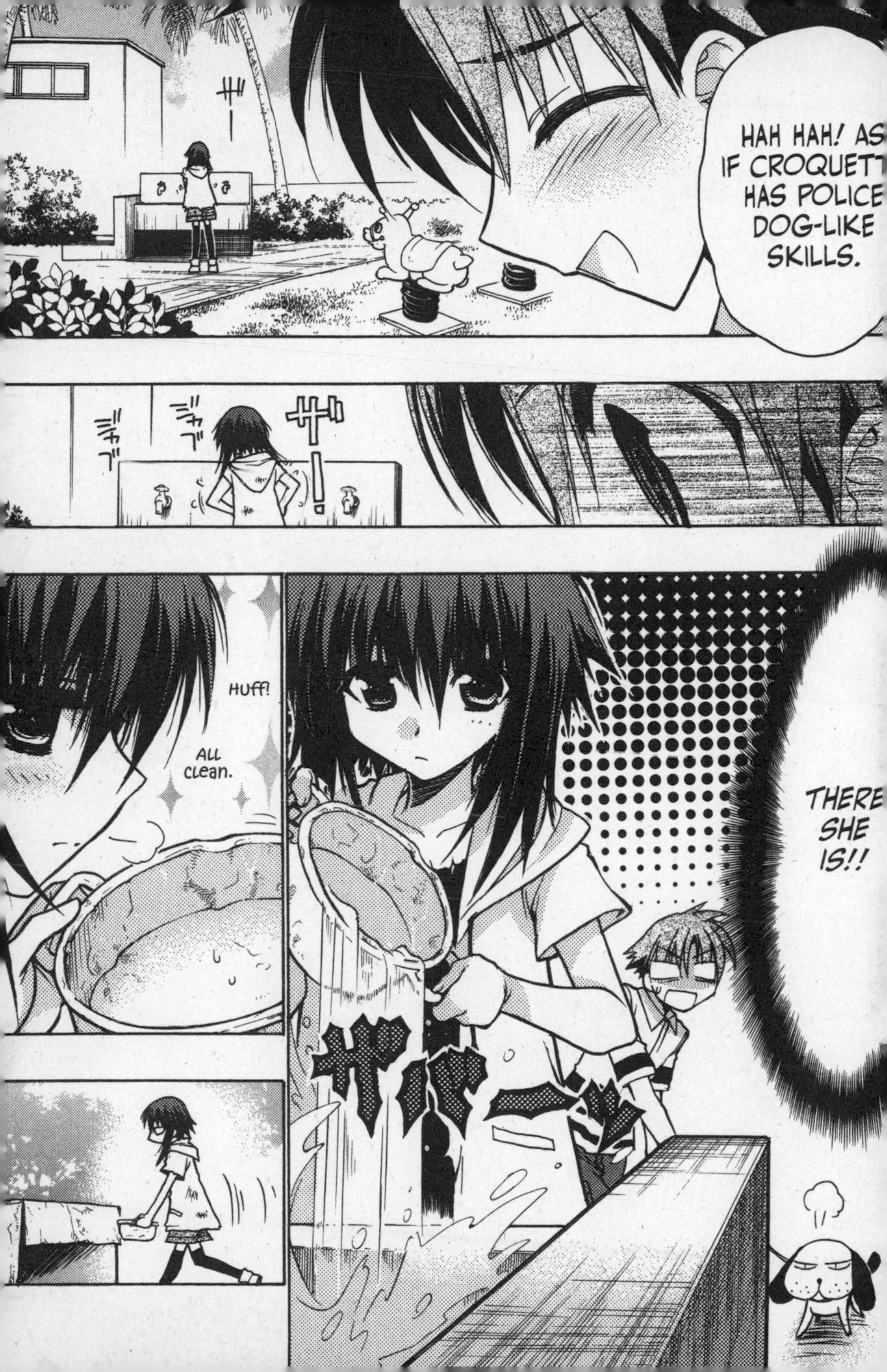
HAH HAH! AS IF CROQUETT HAS POLICE DOG-LIKE SKILLS.
THERE SHE IS!!
HUFF!
ALL clean.

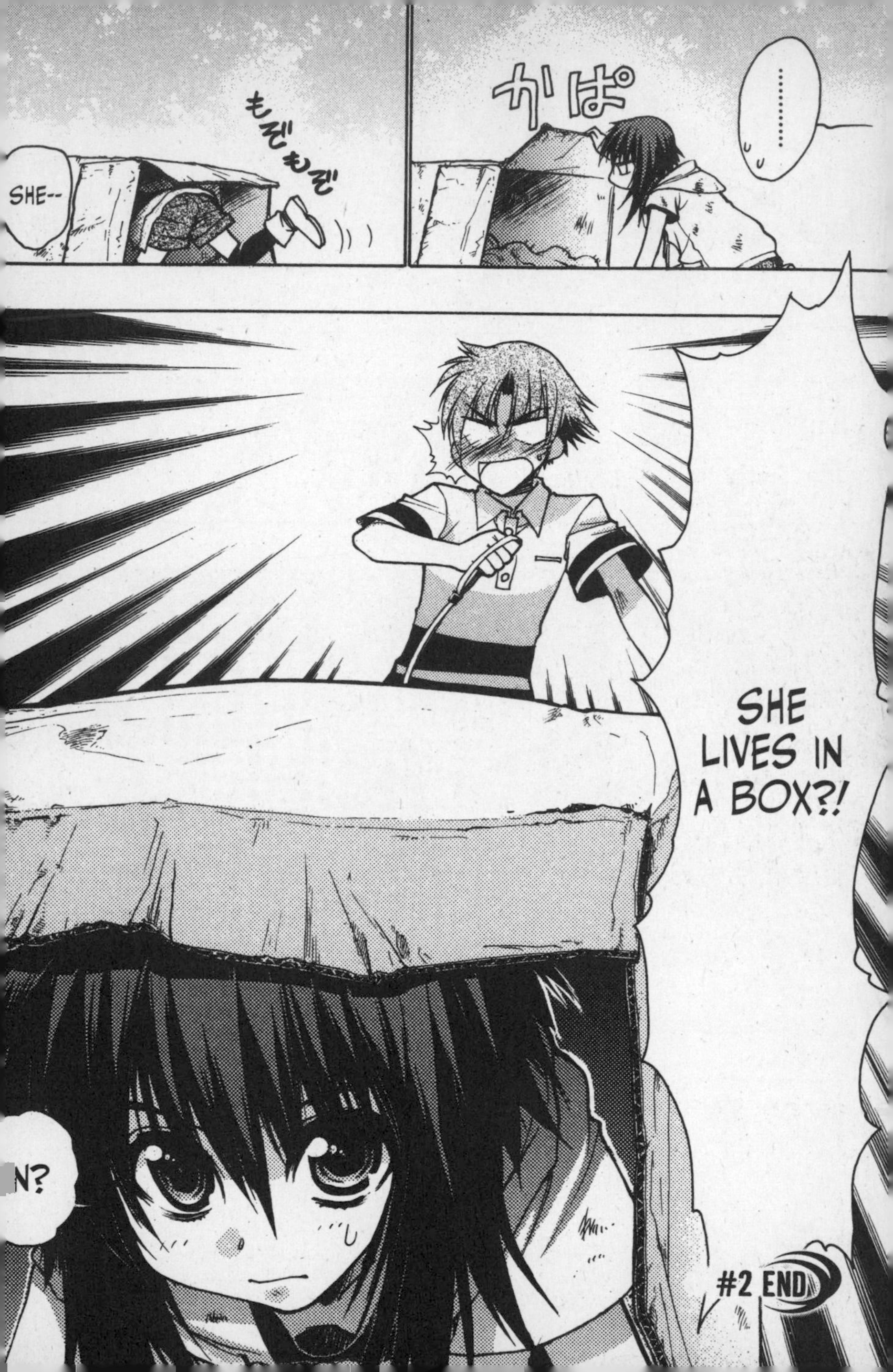
かぱ
......
もぞもぞ
SHE--
SHE LIVES IN A BOX?!
N?
#2 END

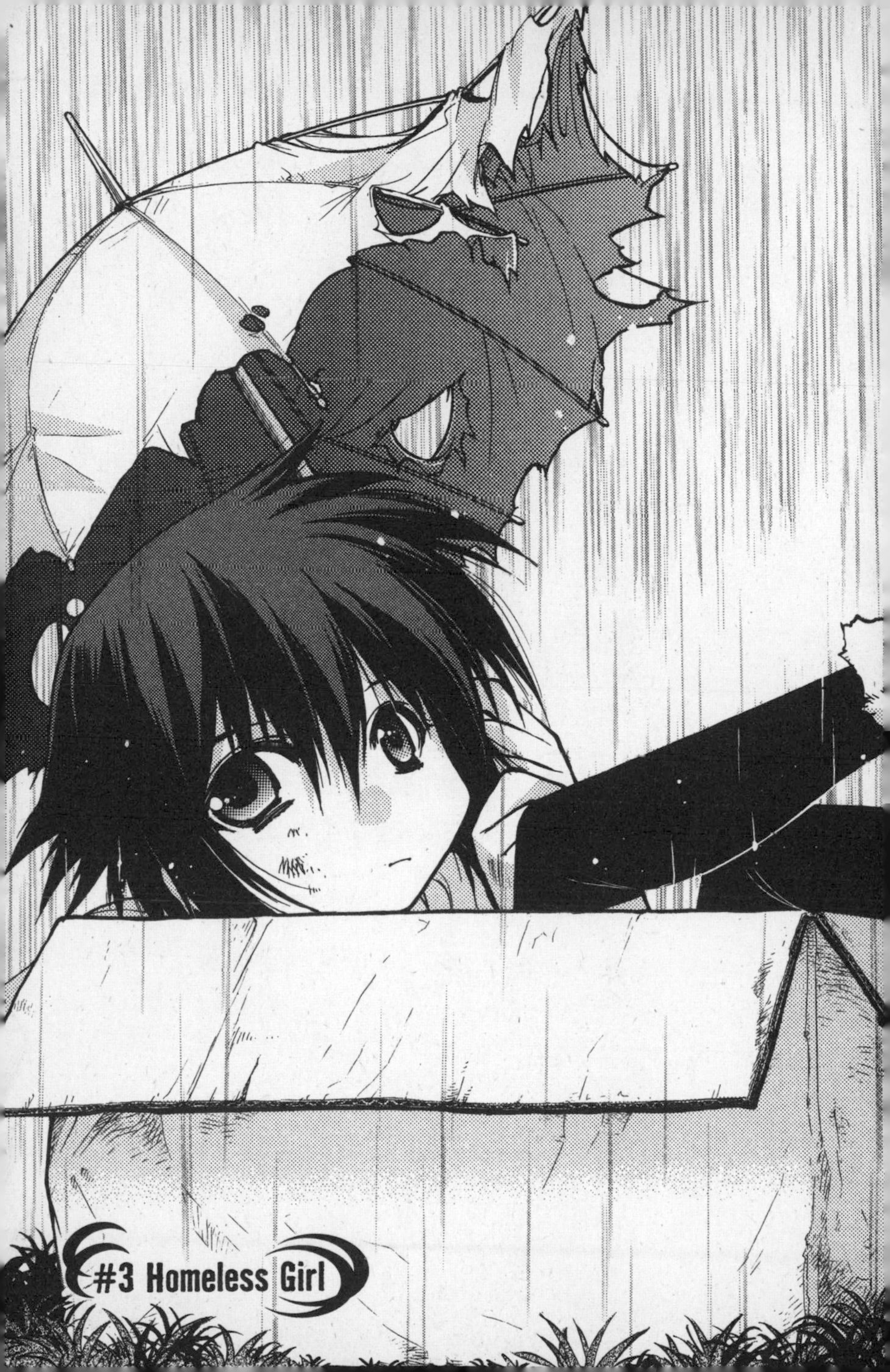
#3 Homeless Girl

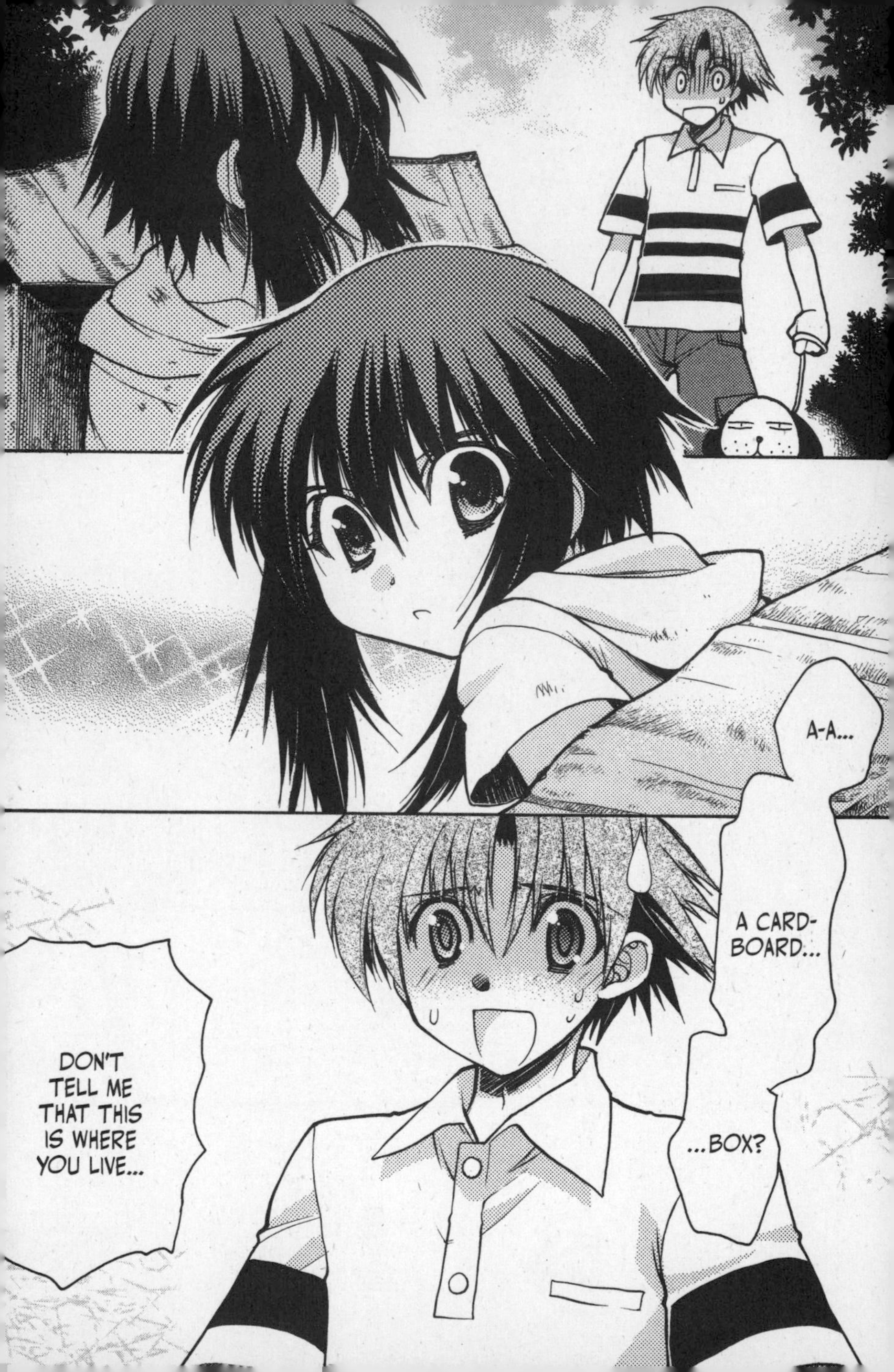
A-A...
A CARD-BOARD...
...BOX?
DON'T TELL ME THAT THIS IS WHERE YOU LIVE...

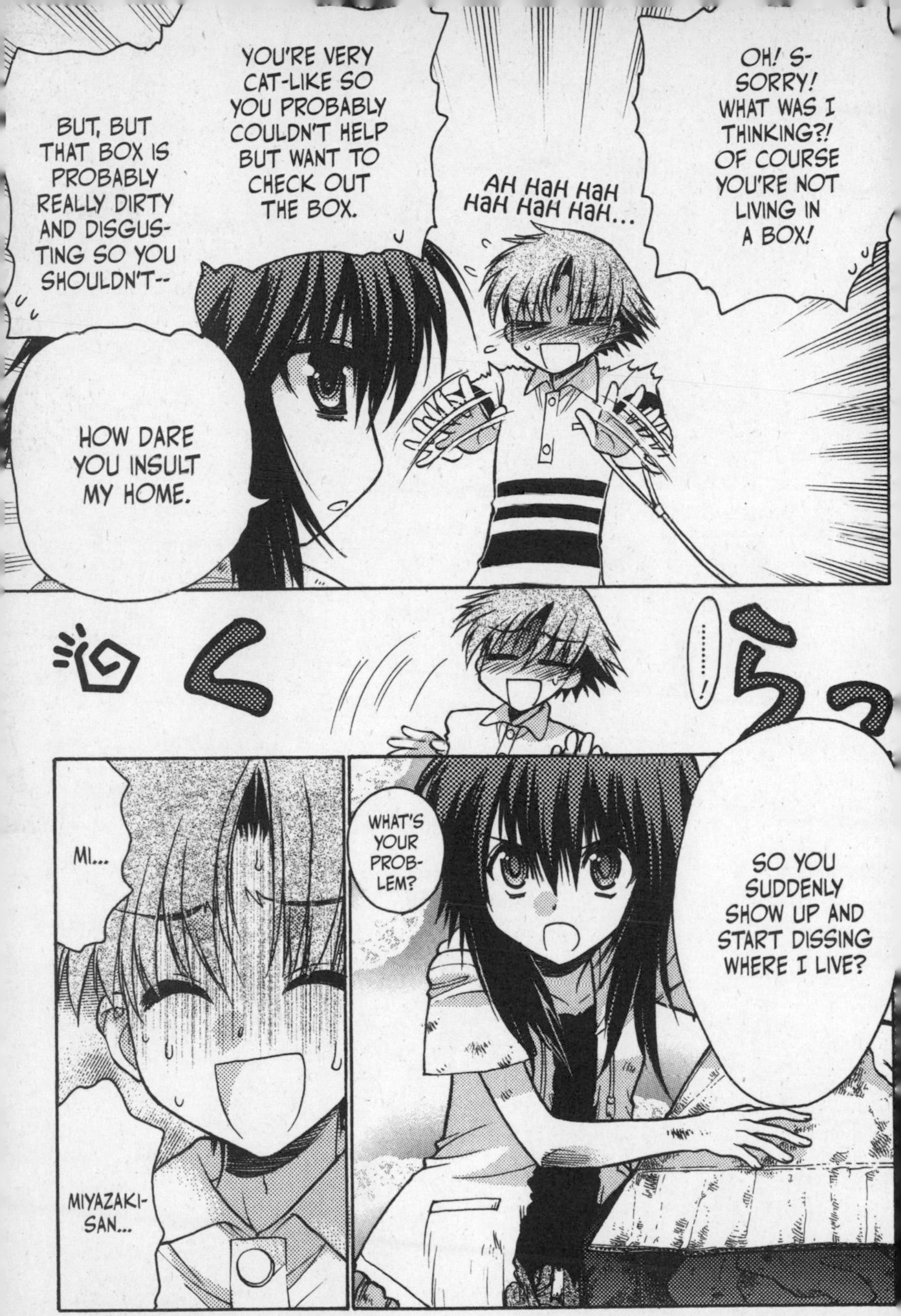
OH! S-SORRY! WHAT WAS I THINKING?! OF COURSE YOU'RE NOT LIVING IN A BOX!
AH HAH HAH HAH HAH HAH...
YOU'RE VERY CAT-LIKE SO YOU PROBABLY COULDN'T HELP BUT WANT TO CHECK OUT THE BOX.
BUT, BUT THAT BOX IS PROBABLY REALLY DIRTY AND DISGUS-TING SO YOU SHOULDN'T--
HOW DARE YOU INSULT MY HOME.
くらっ
......!
SO YOU SUDDENLY SHOW UP AND START DISSING WHERE I LIVE?
WHAT'S YOUR PROB-LEM?
MI...
MIYAZAKI-SAN...

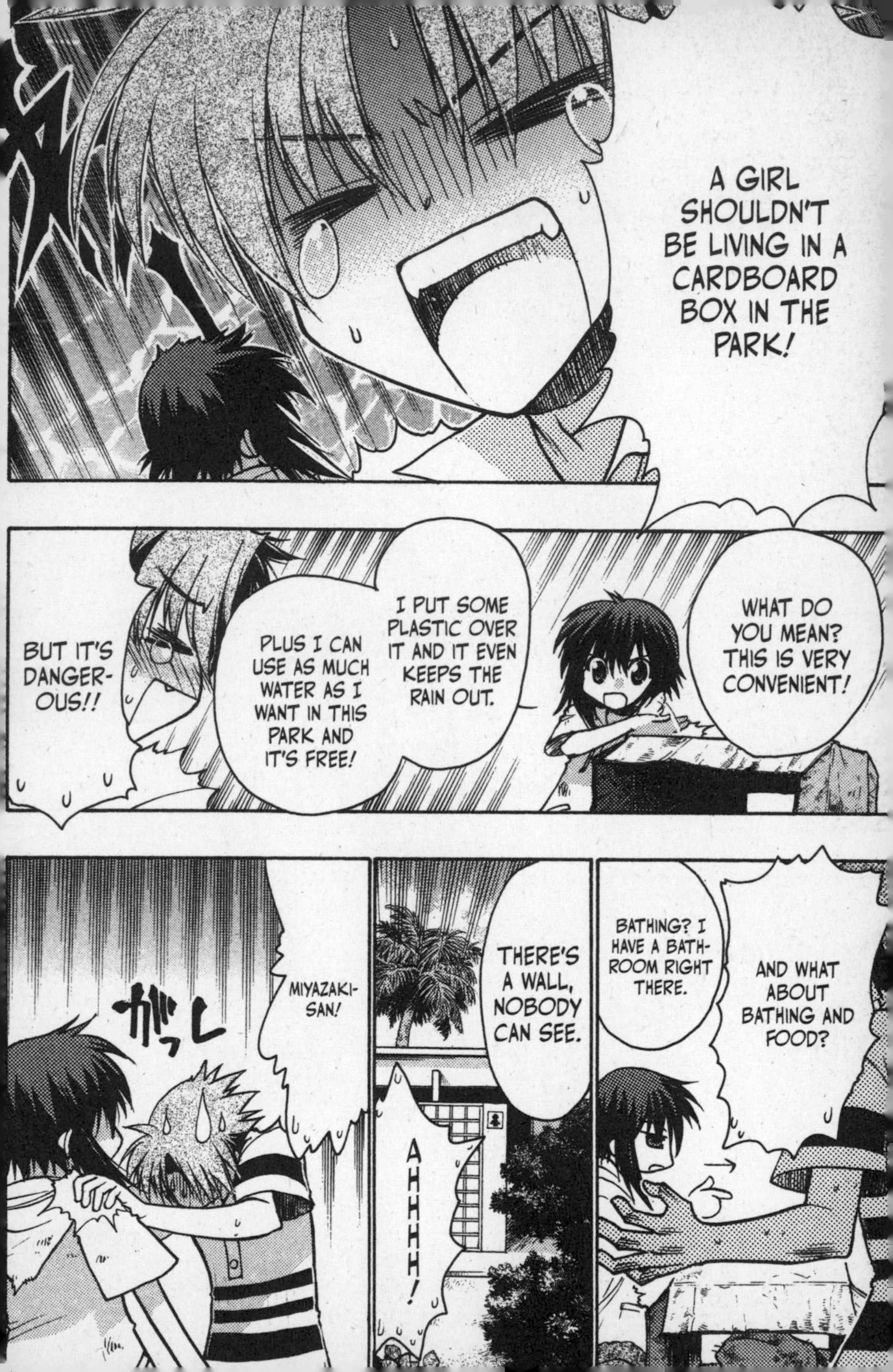
A GIRL SHOULDN'T BE LIVING IN A CARDBOARD BOX IN THE PARK!
WHAT DO YOU MEAN? THIS IS VERY CONVENIENT!
I PUT SOME PLASTIC OVER IT AND IT EVEN KEEPS THE RAIN OUT.
PLUS I CAN USE AS MUCH WATER AS I WANT IN THIS PARK AND IT'S FREE!
BUT IT'S DANGER-OUS!!
AND WHAT ABOUT BATHING AND FOOD?
BATHING? I HAVE A BATH-ROOM RIGHT THERE.
THERE'S A WALL, NOBODY CAN SEE.
AHHHH!
MIYAZAKI-SAN!
ガッし

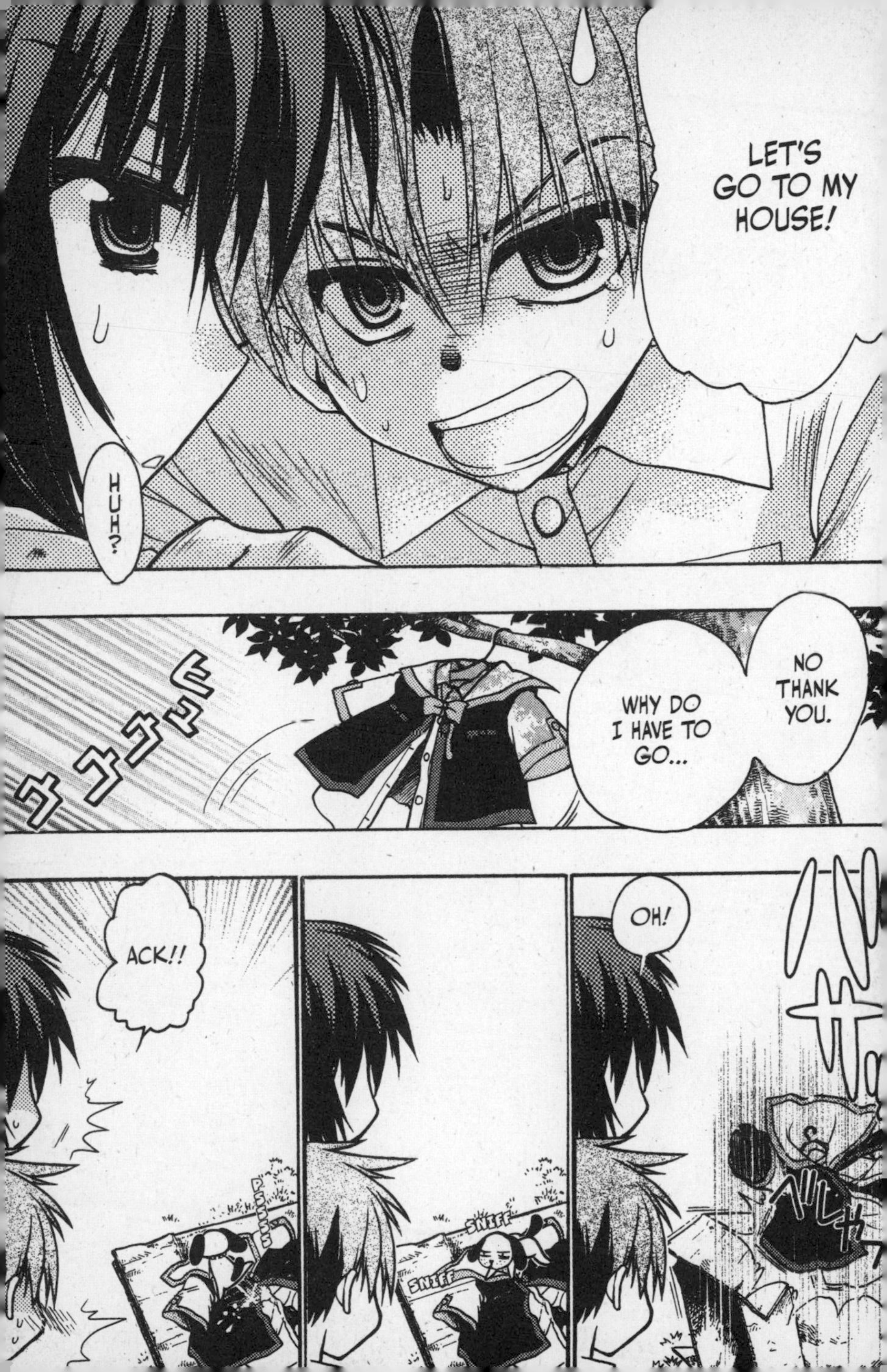
LET'S GO TO MY HOUSE!
HUH?
NO THANK YOU.
WHY DO I HAVE TO GO...
ヒュウウウ
OH!
SNIFF
SNIFF
ACK!!

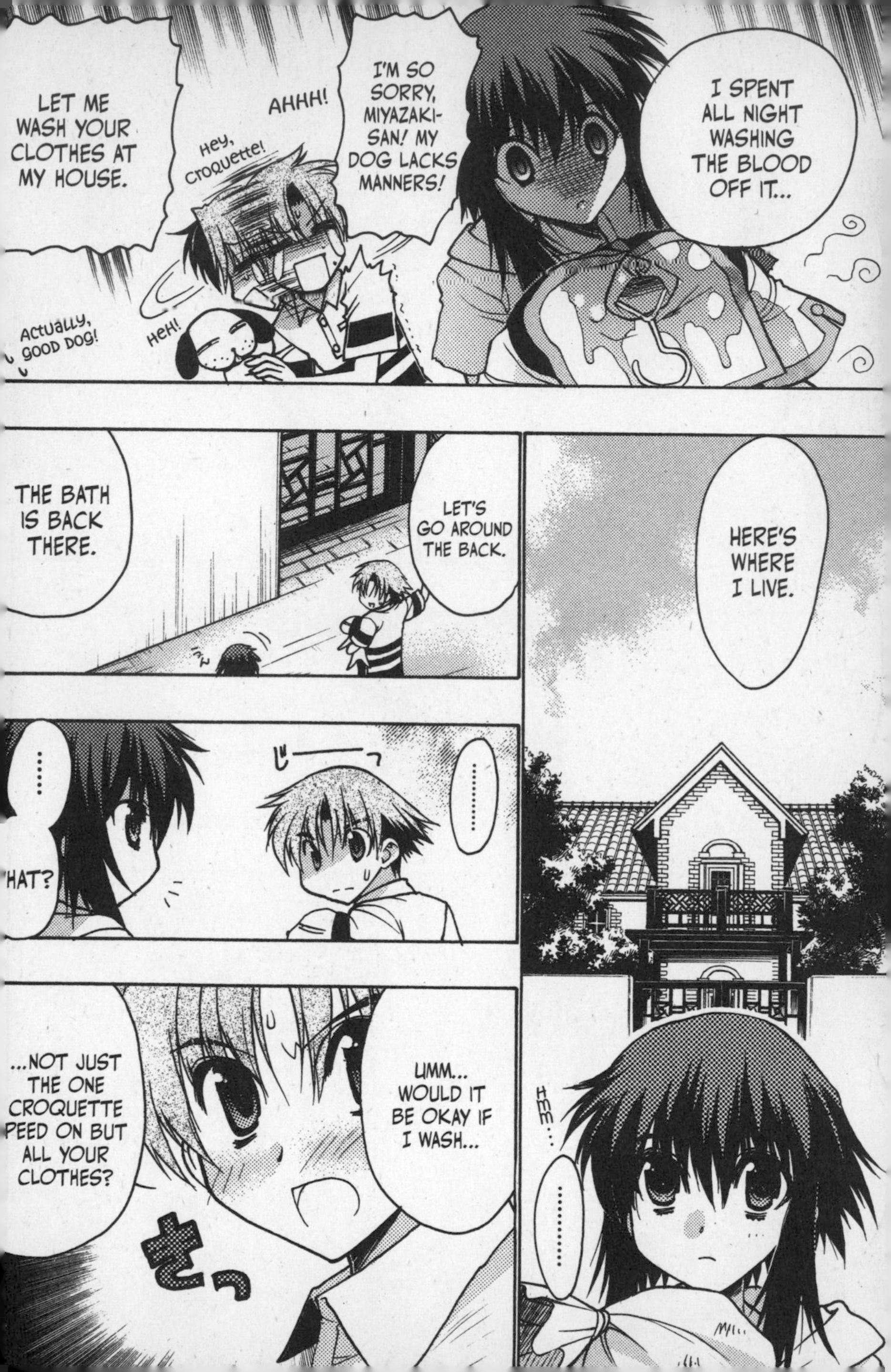
I SPENT ALL NIGHT WASHING THE BLOOD OFF IT...
I'M SO SORRY, MIYAZAKI-SAN! MY DOG LACKS MANNERS!
AHHH!
Hey, Croquette!
LET ME WASH YOUR CLOTHES AT MY HOUSE.
Heh!
Actually, good dog!
HERE'S WHERE I LIVE.
Hmm...
......
LET'S GO AROUND THE BACK.
THE BATH IS BACK THERE.
......
じーーっ
......
HAT?
UMM... WOULD IT BE OKAY IF I WASH...
...NOT JUST THE ONE CROQUETTE PEED ON BUT ALL YOUR CLOTHES?
さっ

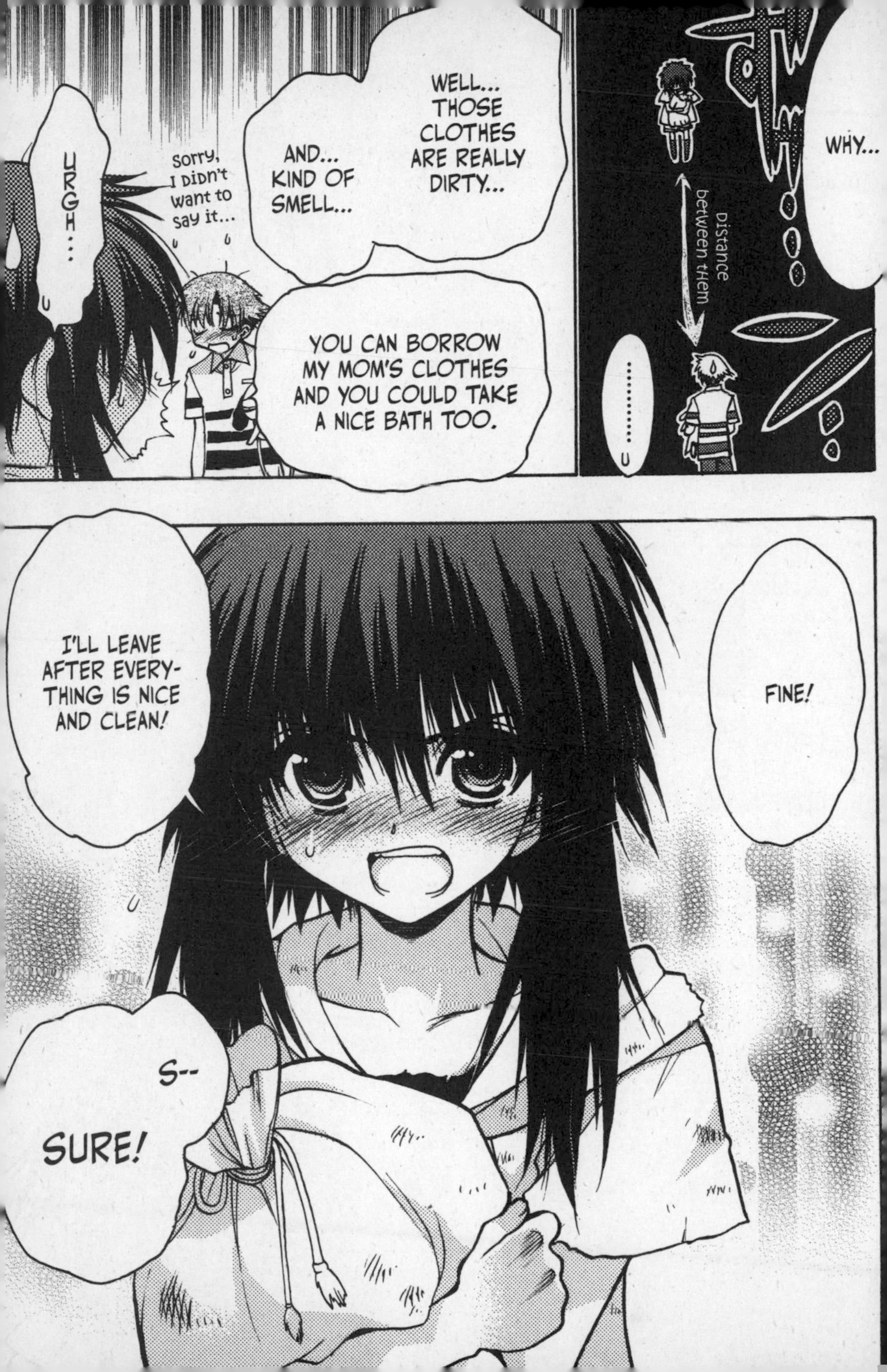
WHY...
Distance between them
......
WELL... THOSE CLOTHES ARE REALLY DIRTY...
AND... KIND OF SMELL...
Sorry, I didn't want to say it...
URGH...
YOU CAN BORROW MY MOM'S CLOTHES AND YOU COULD TAKE A NICE BATH TOO.
FINE!
I'LL LEAVE AFTER EVERY-THING IS NICE AND CLEAN!
S--
SURE!

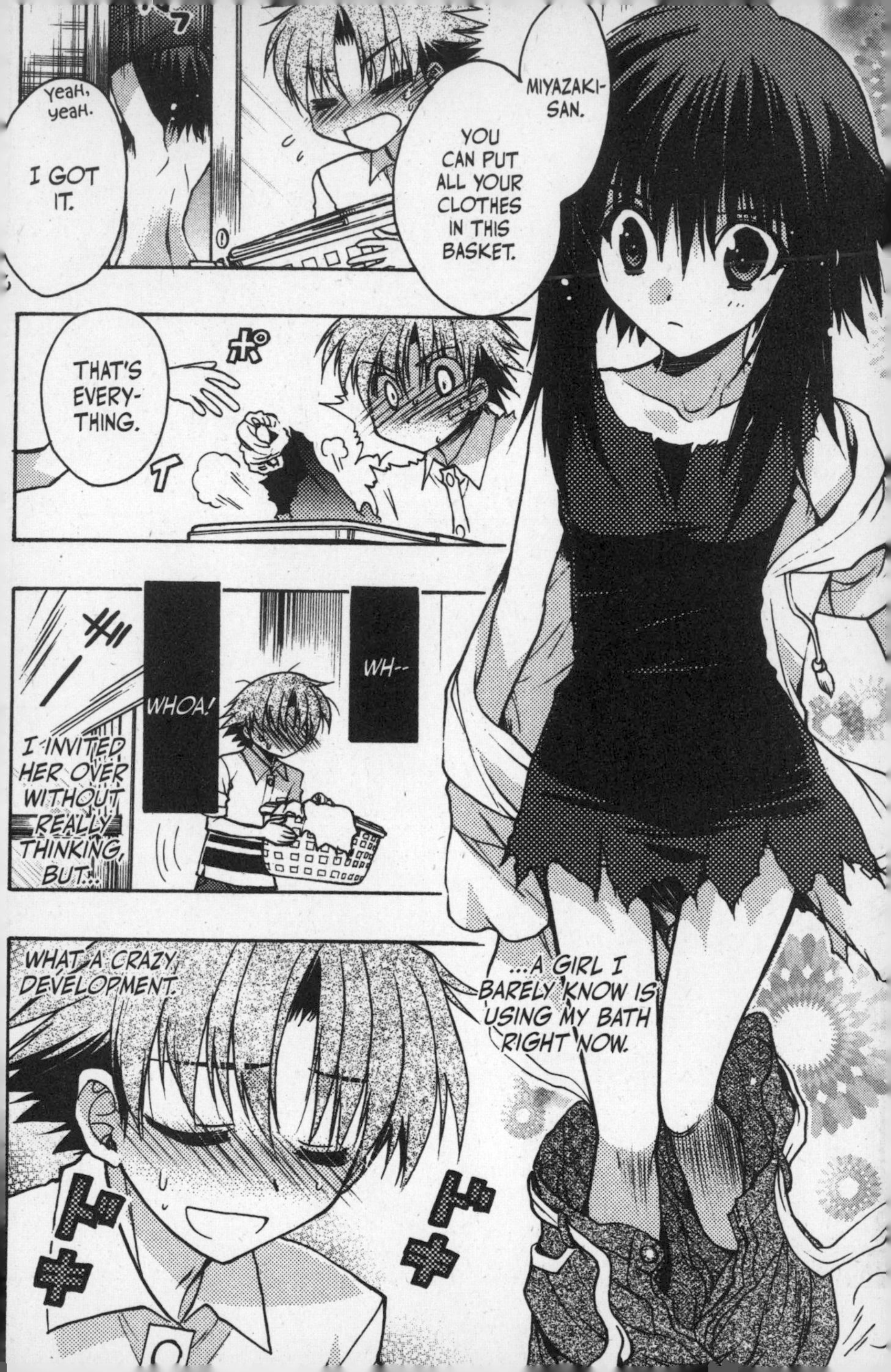
MIYAZAKI-SAN.
YOU CAN PUT ALL YOUR CLOTHES IN THIS BASKET.
Yeah, yeah.
I GOT IT.
THAT'S EVERYTHING.
WH--
WHOA!
I INVITED HER OVER WITHOUT REALLY THINKING, BUT...
...A GIRL I BARELY KNOW IS USING MY BATH RIGHT NOW.
WHAT A CRAZY DEVELOPMENT.

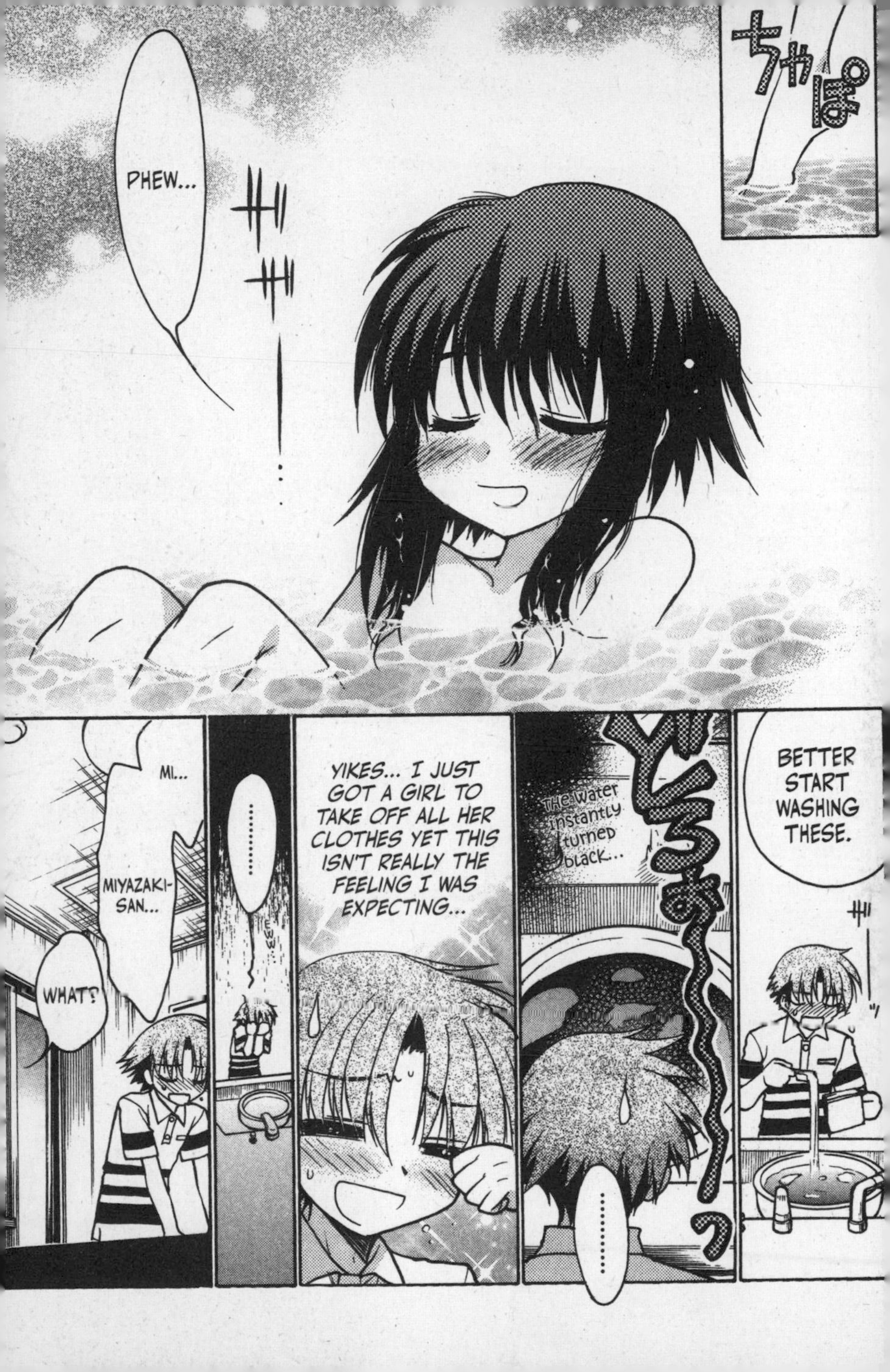
ちゃぽ
PHEW...
BETTER START WASHING THESE.
THE water instantly turned black...
......
YIKES... I JUST GOT A GIRL TO TAKE OFF ALL HER CLOTHES YET THIS ISN'T REALLY THE FEELING I WAS EXPECTING...
......
EWW
MI...
MIYAZAKI-SAN...
WHAT?

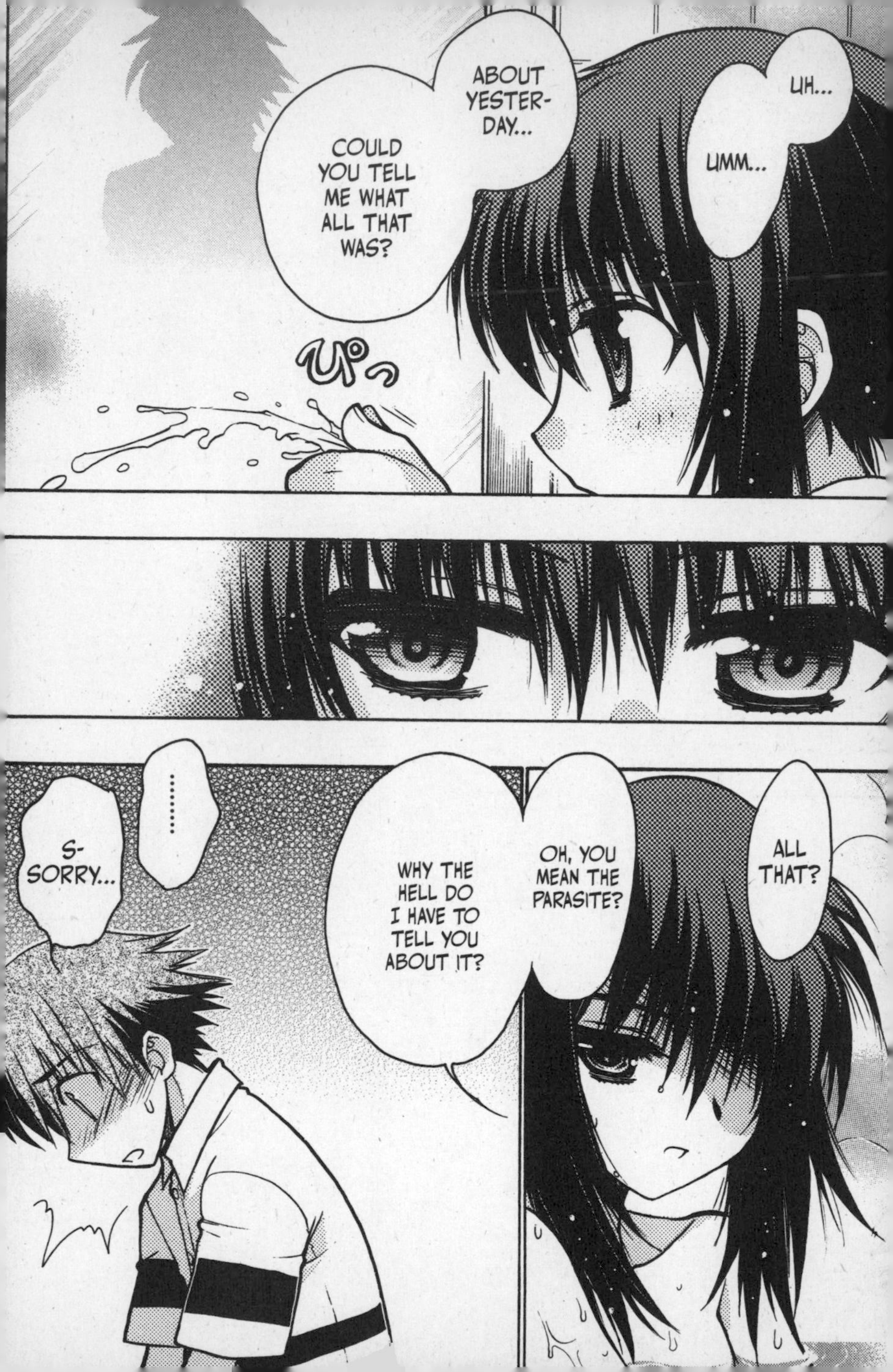
UH... UMM...
ABOUT YESTER-DAY... COULD YOU TELL ME WHAT ALL THAT WAS?
ぴっ
ALL THAT?
OH, YOU MEAN THE PARASITE? WHY THE HELL DO I HAVE TO TELL YOU ABOUT IT?
......
S-SORRY...

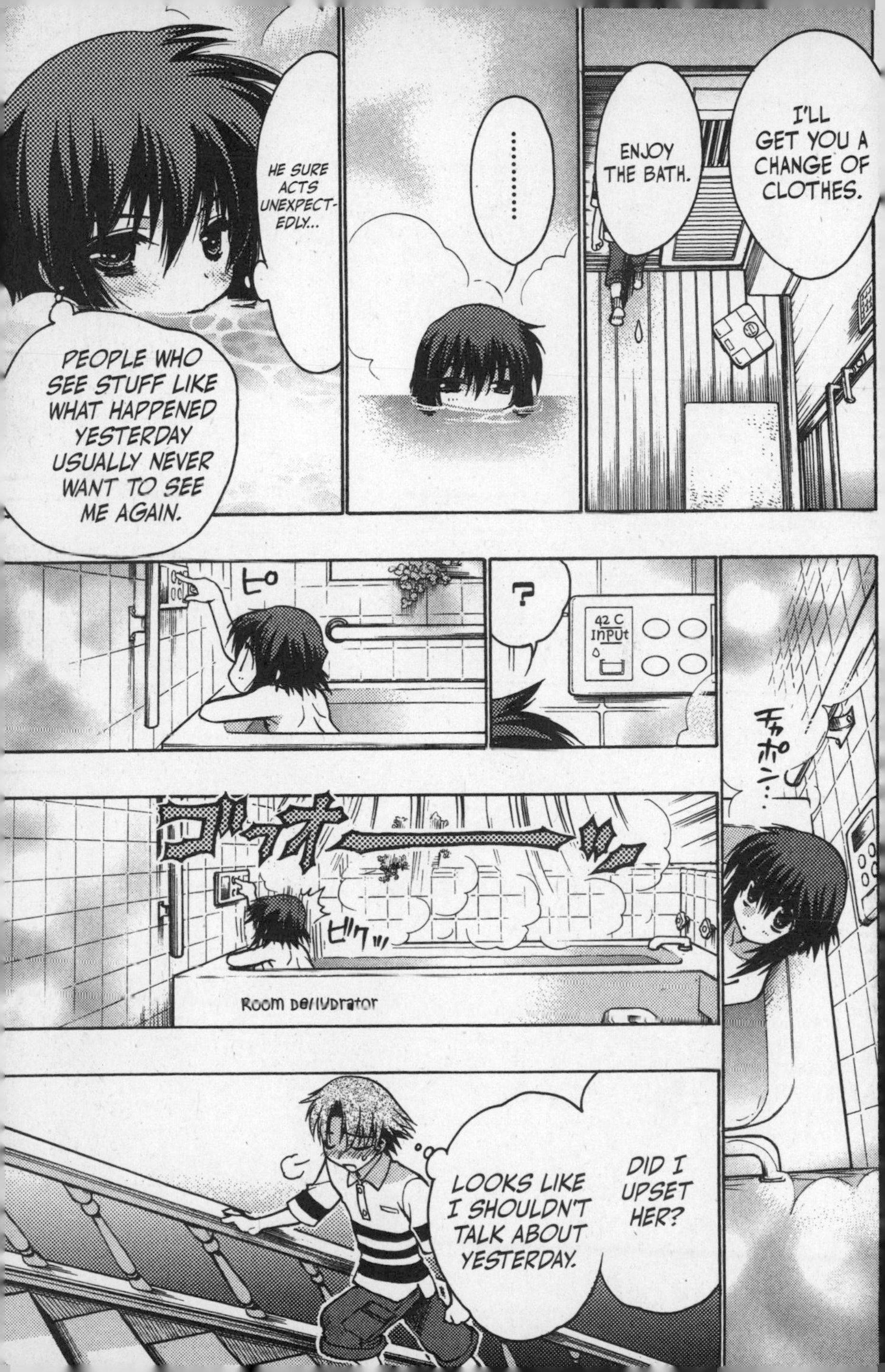
I'LL GET YOU A CHANGE OF CLOTHES.
ENJOY THE BATH.
......
HE SURE ACTS UNEXPECTEDLY...
PEOPLE WHO SEE STUFF LIKE WHAT HAPPENED YESTERDAY USUALLY NEVER WANT TO SEE ME AGAIN.
チャポン…
?
42 C
InPUt
ピ
ゴッオーーーッ
ビクッ
Room DeHydrator
DID I UPSET HER?
LOOKS LIKE I SHOULDN'T TALK ABOUT YESTERDAY.

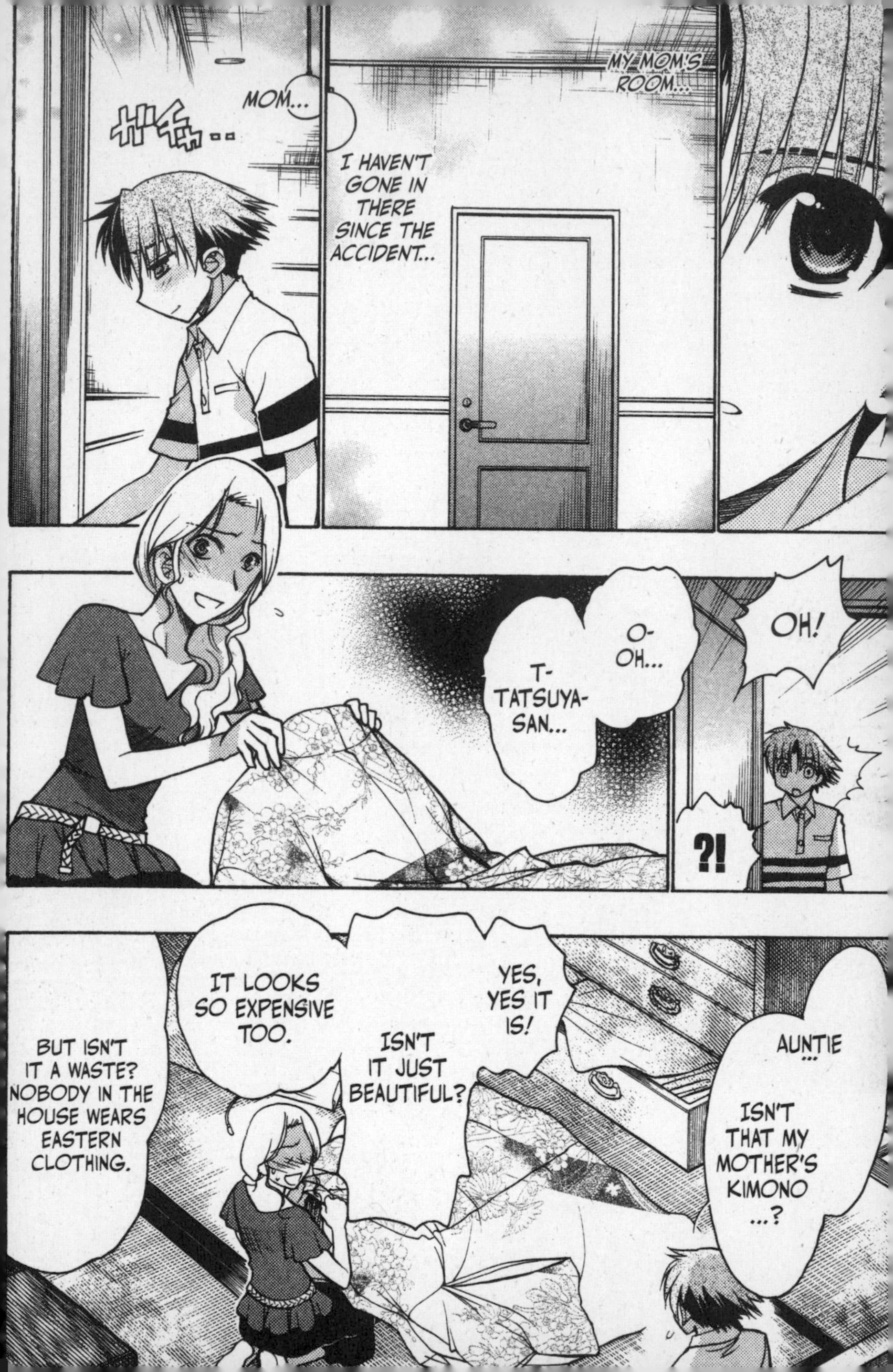
MY MOM'S ROOM...
I HAVEN'T GONE IN THERE SINCE THE ACCIDENT...
MOM...
OH!
?!
O-OH...
T-TATSUYA-SAN...
AUNTIE...
ISN'T THAT MY MOTHER'S KIMONO...?
YES, YES IT IS!
ISN'T IT JUST BEAUTIFUL?
IT LOOKS SO EXPENSIVE TOO.
BUT ISN'T IT A WASTE? NOBODY IN THE HOUSE WEARS EASTERN CLOTHING.

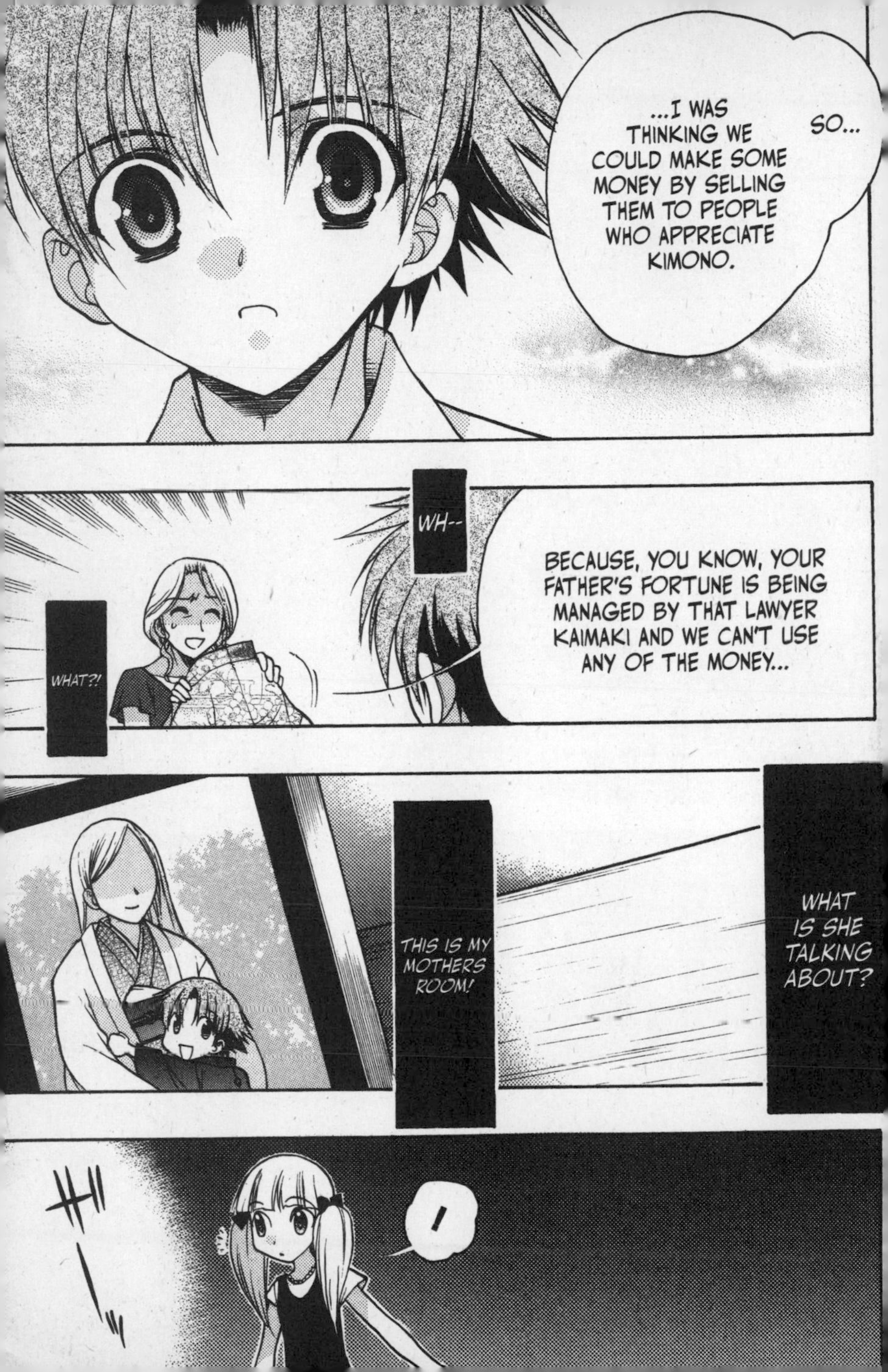
SO...
...I WAS THINKING WE COULD MAKE SOME MONEY BY SELLING THEM TO PEOPLE WHO APPRECIATE KIMONO.
BECAUSE, YOU KNOW, YOUR FATHER'S FORTUNE IS BEING MANAGED BY THAT LAWYER KAIMAKI AND WE CAN'T USE ANY OF THE MONEY...
WH--
WHAT?!
WHAT IS SHE TALKING ABOUT?
THIS IS MY MOTHERS ROOM!
!

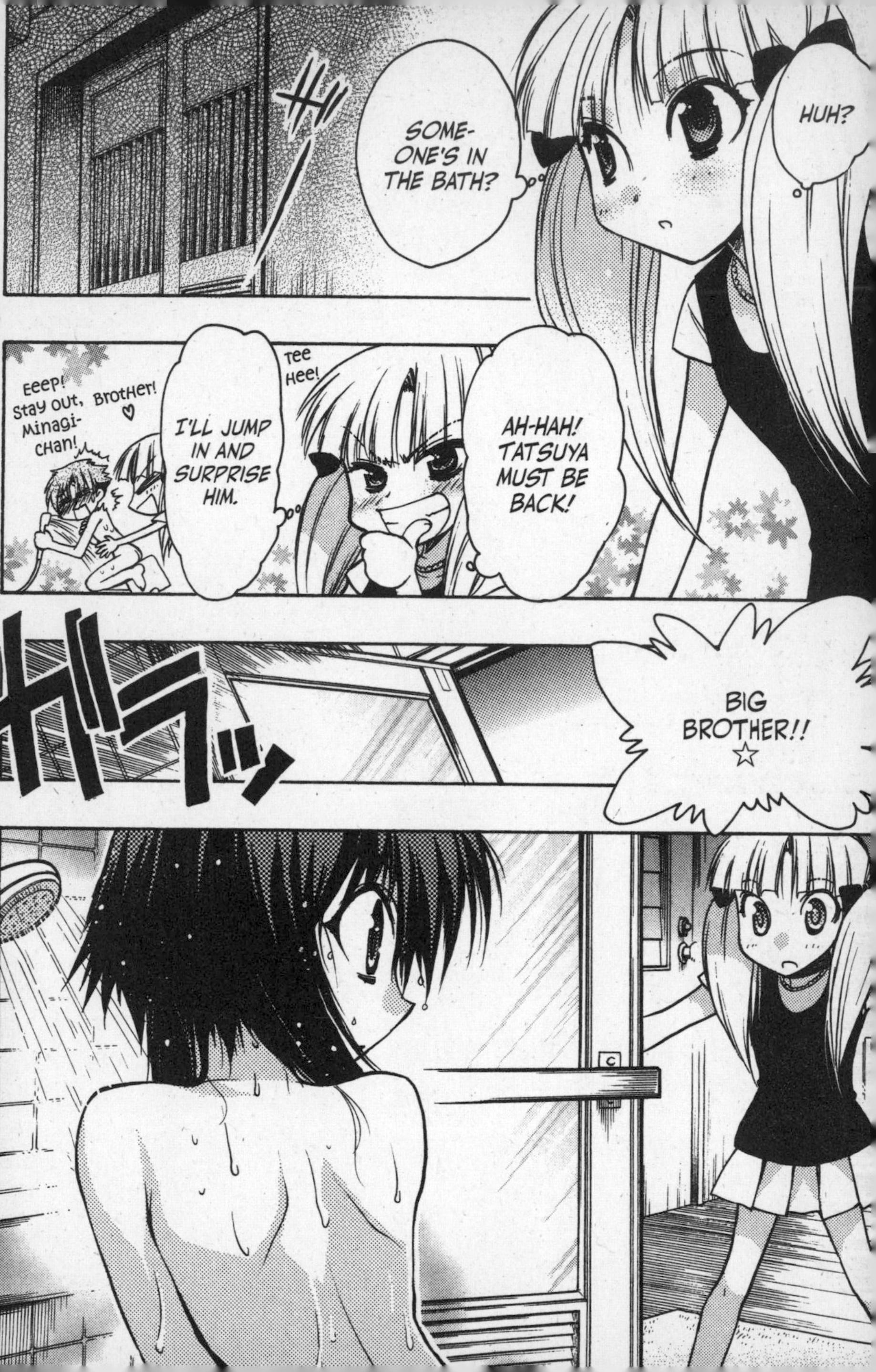
HUH?
SOME-ONE'S IN THE BATH?
AH-HAH! TATSUYA MUST BE BACK!
TEE HEE!
I'LL JUMP IN AND SURPRISE HIM.
Brother! ♥
Eeep! Stay out, Minagi-chan!
BIG BROTHER!! ☆
ガラッ

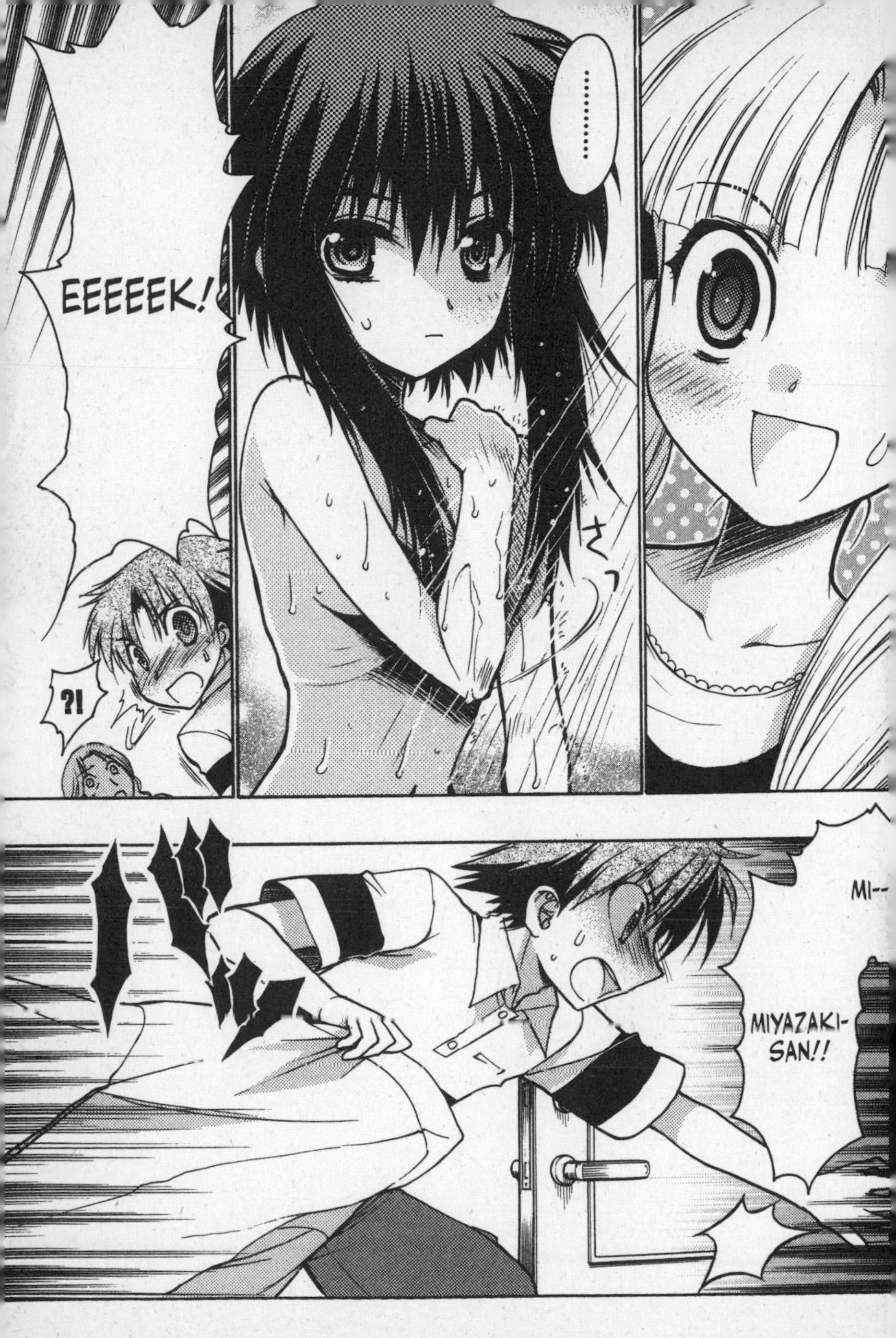
......
さっ
EEEEEK!
?!
MI--
MIYAZAKI-SAN!!

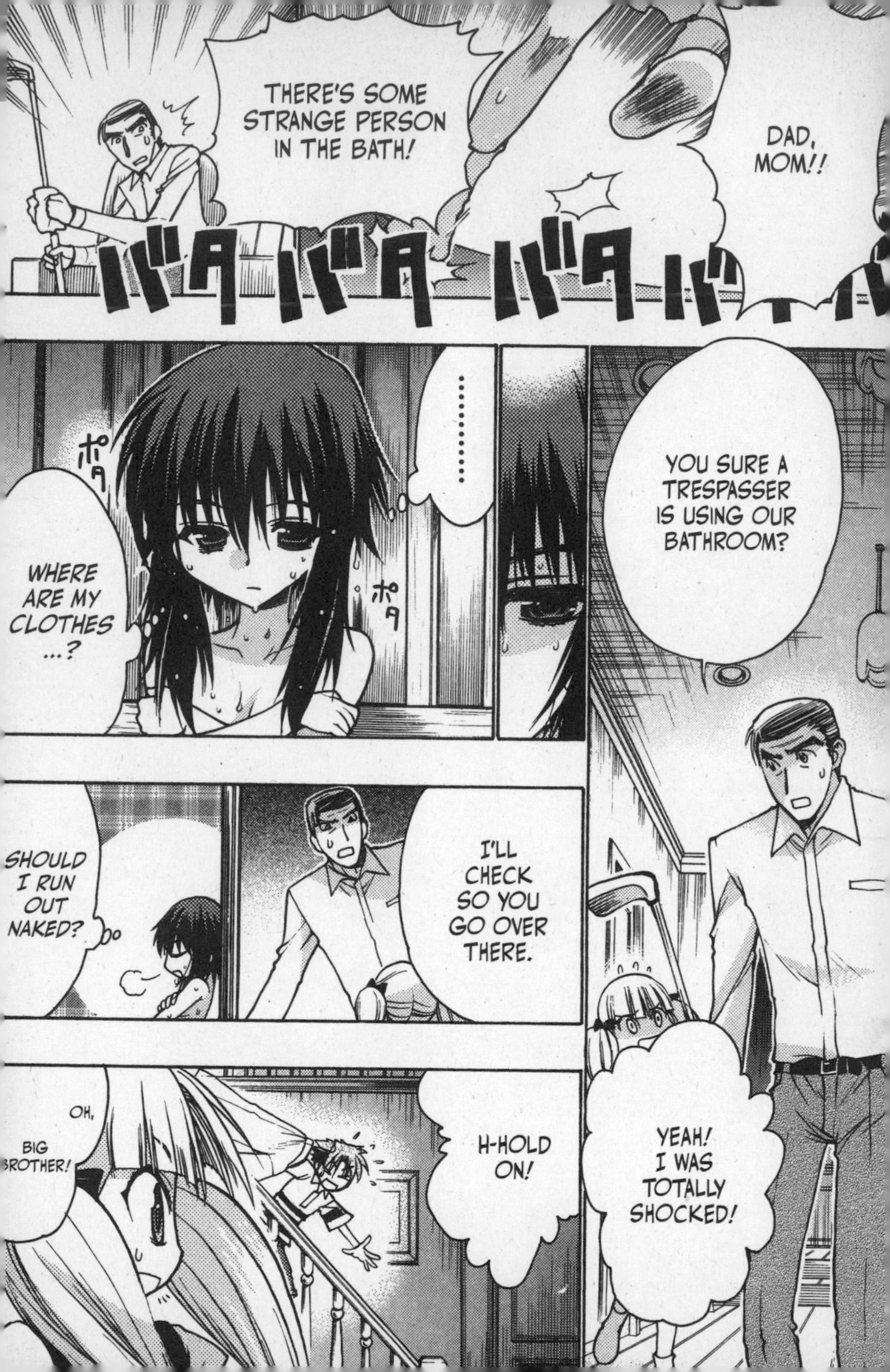
DAD, MOM!!
THERE'S SOME STRANGE PERSON IN THE BATH!
バタバタバタバ
YOU SURE A TRESPASSER IS USING OUR BATHROOM?
YEAH! I WAS TOTALLY SHOCKED!
......
ポタ
ポタ
WHERE ARE MY CLOTHES ...?
I'LL CHECK SO YOU GO OVER THERE.
SHOULD I RUN OUT NAKED?
H-HOLD ON!
OH, BIG BROTHER!

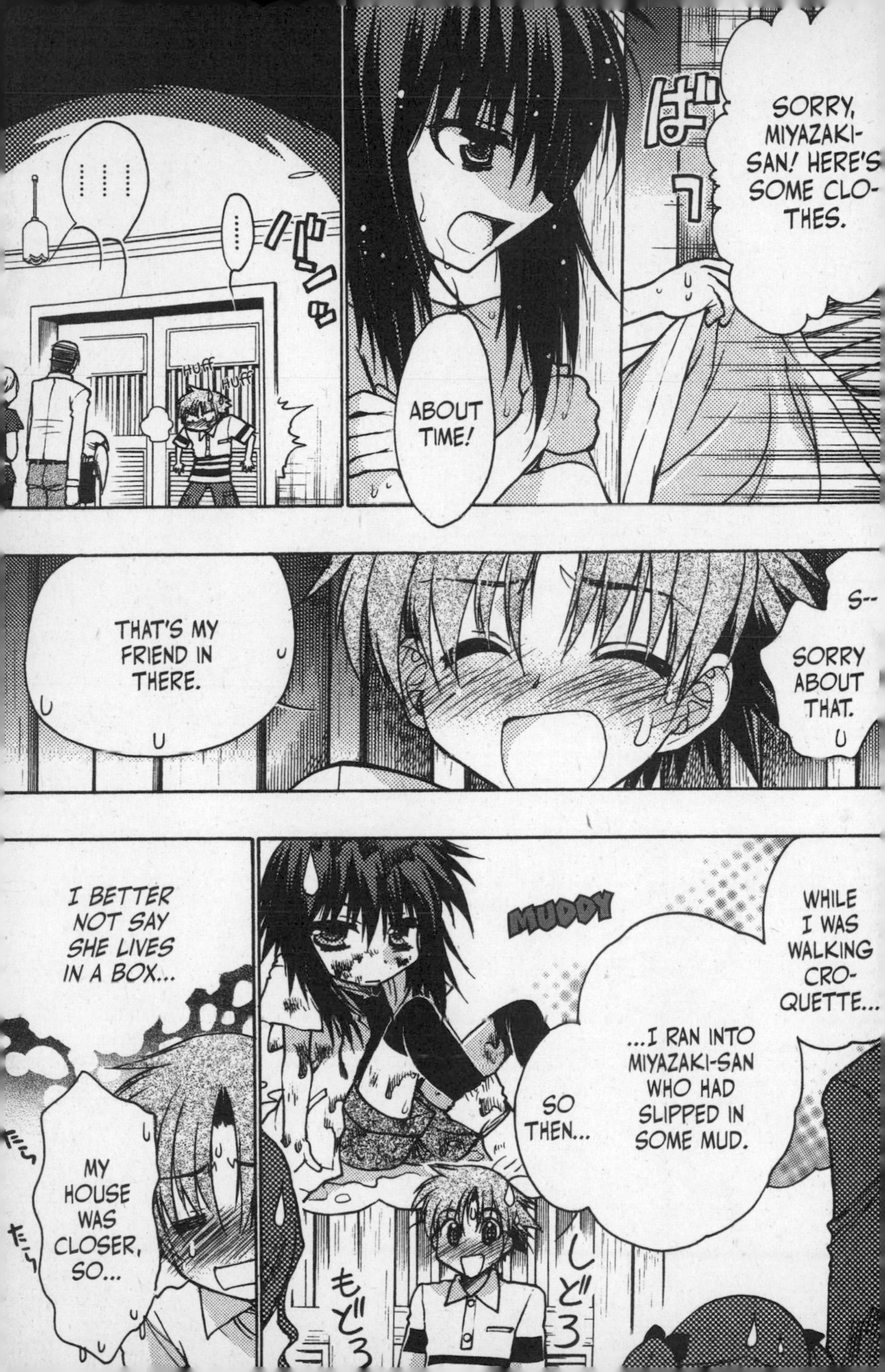

ばっ
SORRY, MIYAZAKI-SAN! HERE'S SOME CLO-THES.
ABOUT TIME!
......
...
HUFF HUFF
S-- SORRY ABOUT THAT.
THAT'S MY FRIEND IN THERE.
WHILE I WAS WALKING CRO-QUETTE...
...I RAN INTO MIYAZAKI-SAN WHO HAD SLIPPED IN SOME MUD.
SO THEN...
MUDDY
しどろ
もどろ
I BETTER NOT SAY SHE LIVES IN A BOX...
MY HOUSE WAS CLOSER, SO...

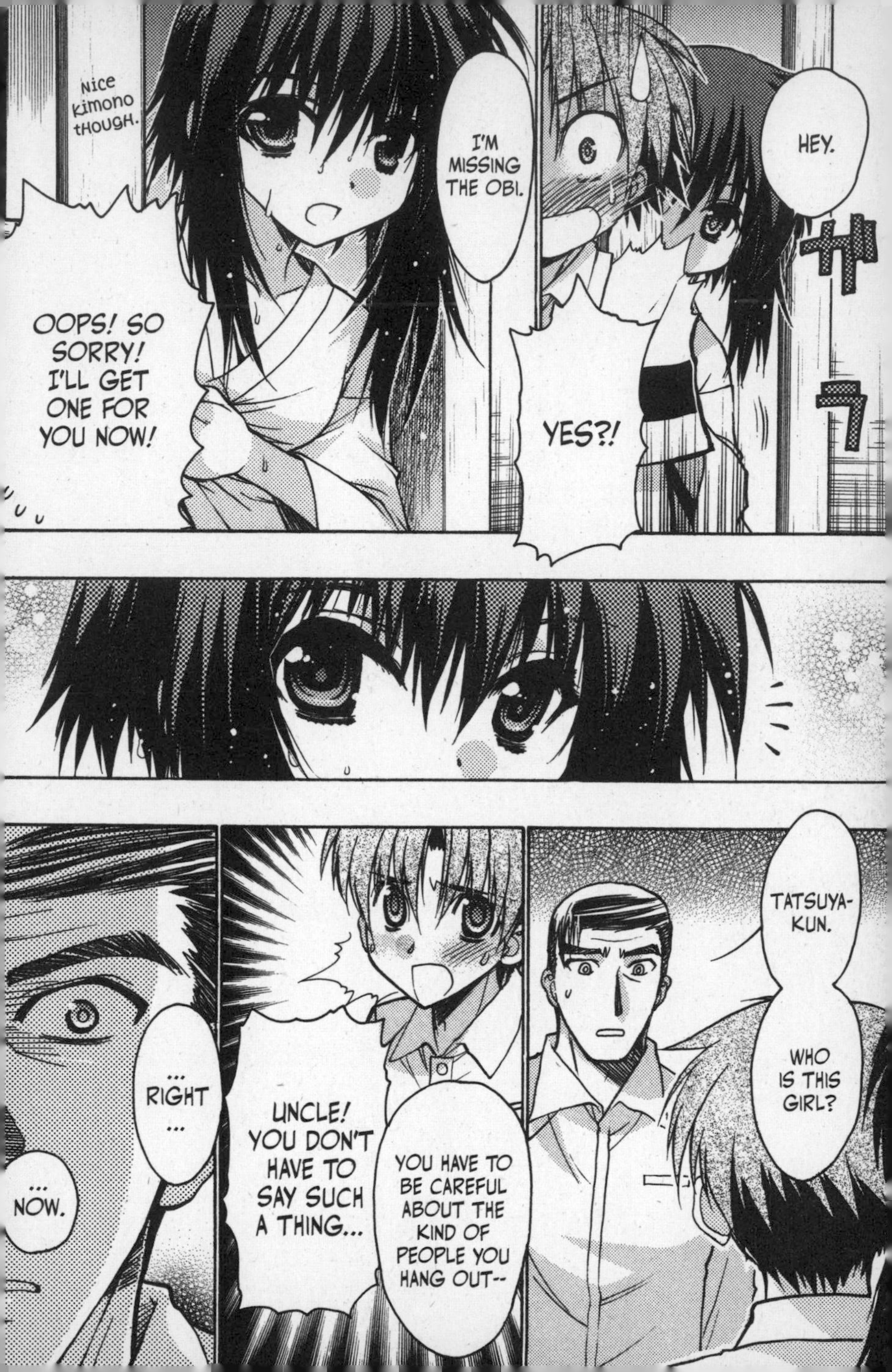
HEY.
YES?!
I'M MISSING THE OBI.
Nice kimono though.
OOPS! SO SORRY! I'LL GET ONE FOR YOU NOW!
TATSUYA-KUN.
WHO IS THIS GIRL?
YOU HAVE TO BE CAREFUL ABOUT THE KIND OF PEOPLE YOU HANG OUT--
UNCLE! YOU DON'T HAVE TO SAY SUCH A THING...
... RIGHT ...
... NOW.

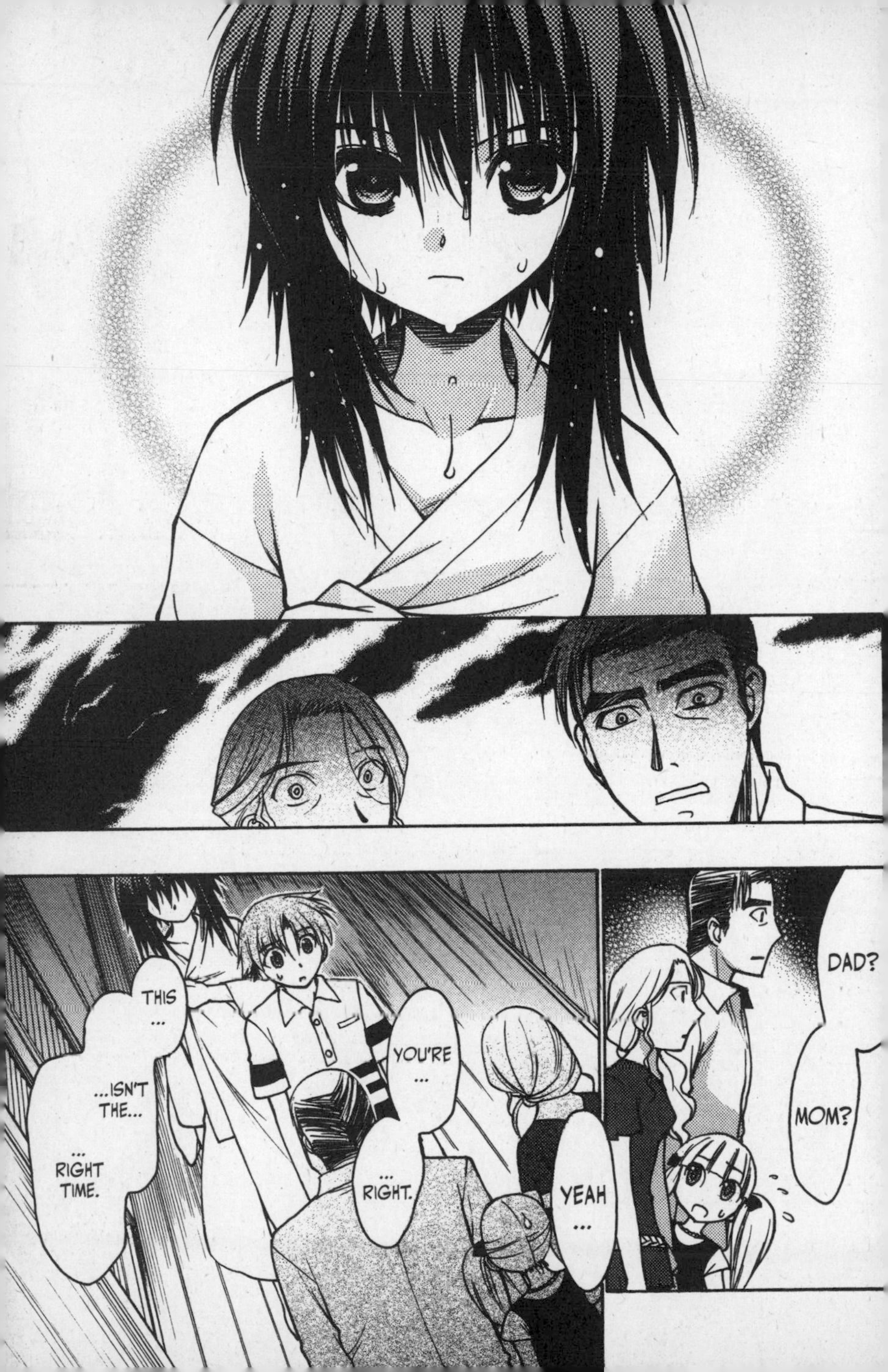
DAD?
MOM?
YEAH ...
YOU'RE ...
... RIGHT.
THIS ...
...ISN'T THE...
... RIGHT TIME.

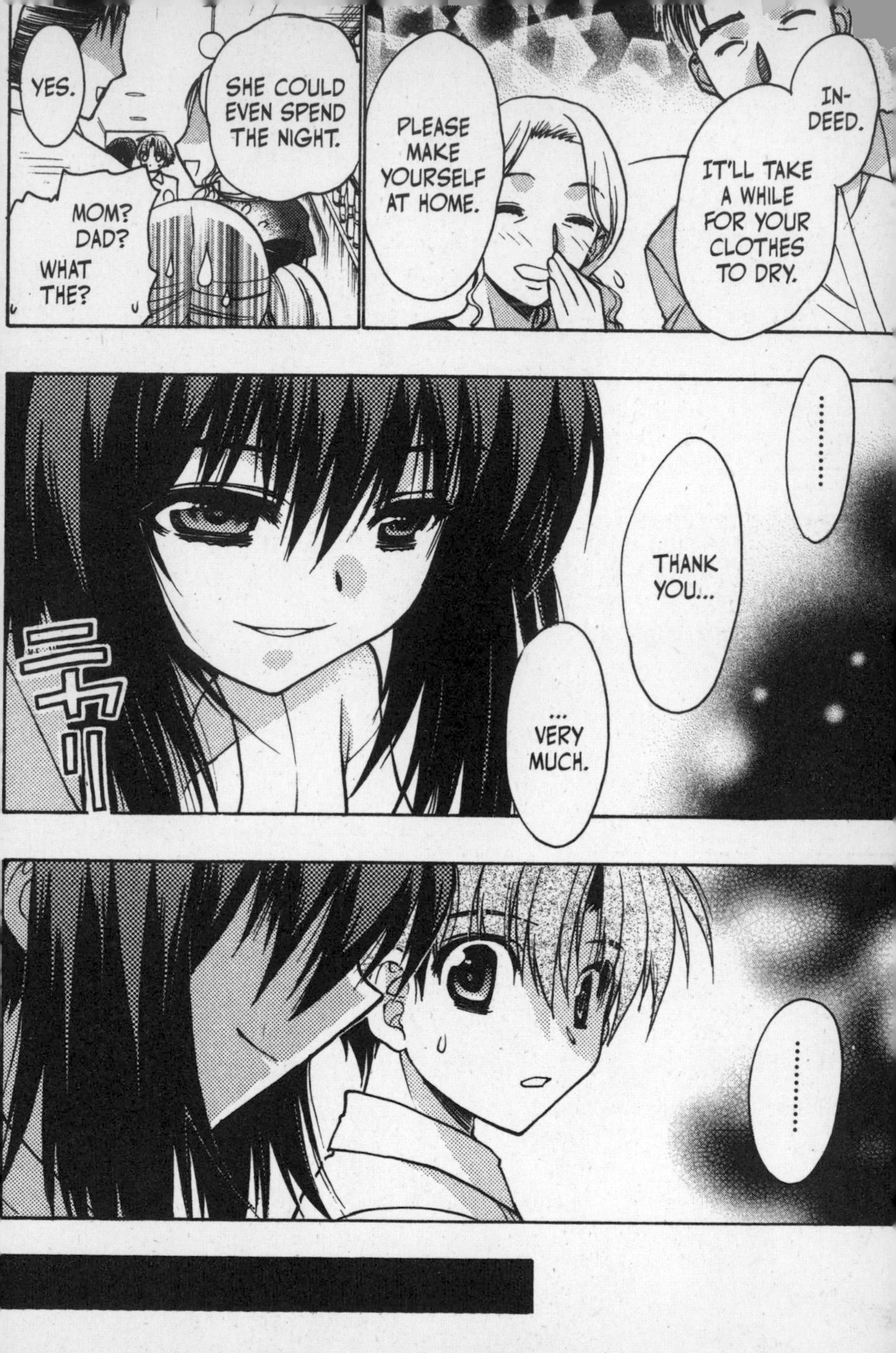
IN-DEED.
IT'LL TAKE A WHILE FOR YOUR CLOTHES TO DRY.
PLEASE MAKE YOURSELF AT HOME.
SHE COULD EVEN SPEND THE NIGHT.
YES.
MOM? DAD? WHAT THE?
......
THANK YOU...
... VERY MUCH.
ニヤリ
......

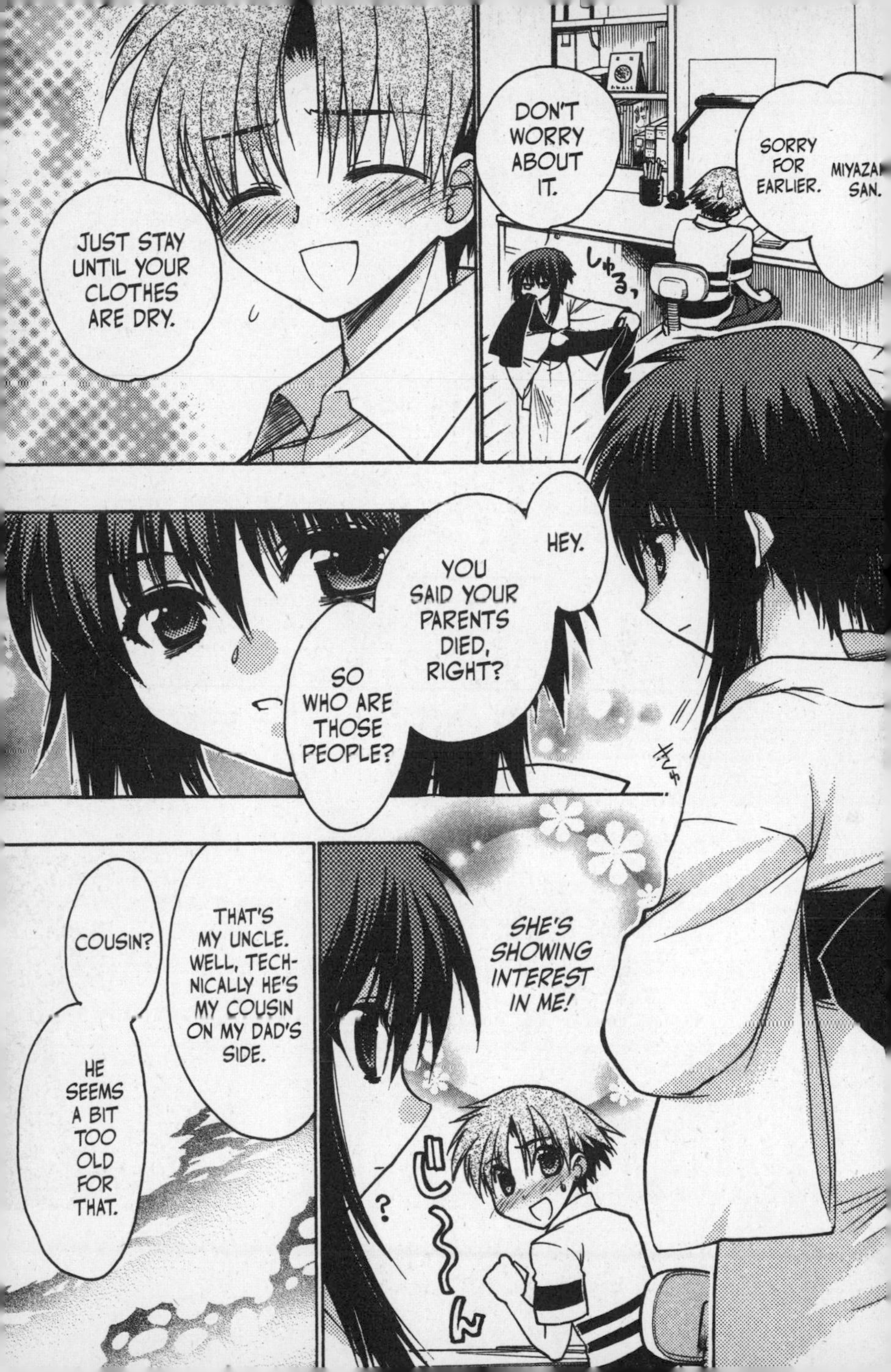
SORRY FOR EARLIER.
MIYAZA SAN.
DON'T WORRY ABOUT IT.
JUST STAY UNTIL YOUR CLOTHES ARE DRY.
HEY.
YOU SAID YOUR PARENTS DIED, RIGHT?
SO WHO ARE THOSE PEOPLE?
SHE'S SHOWING INTEREST IN ME!
THAT'S MY UNCLE. WELL, TECH-NICALLY HE'S MY COUSIN ON MY DAD'S SIDE.
COUSIN?
HE SEEMS A BIT TOO OLD FOR THAT.
?

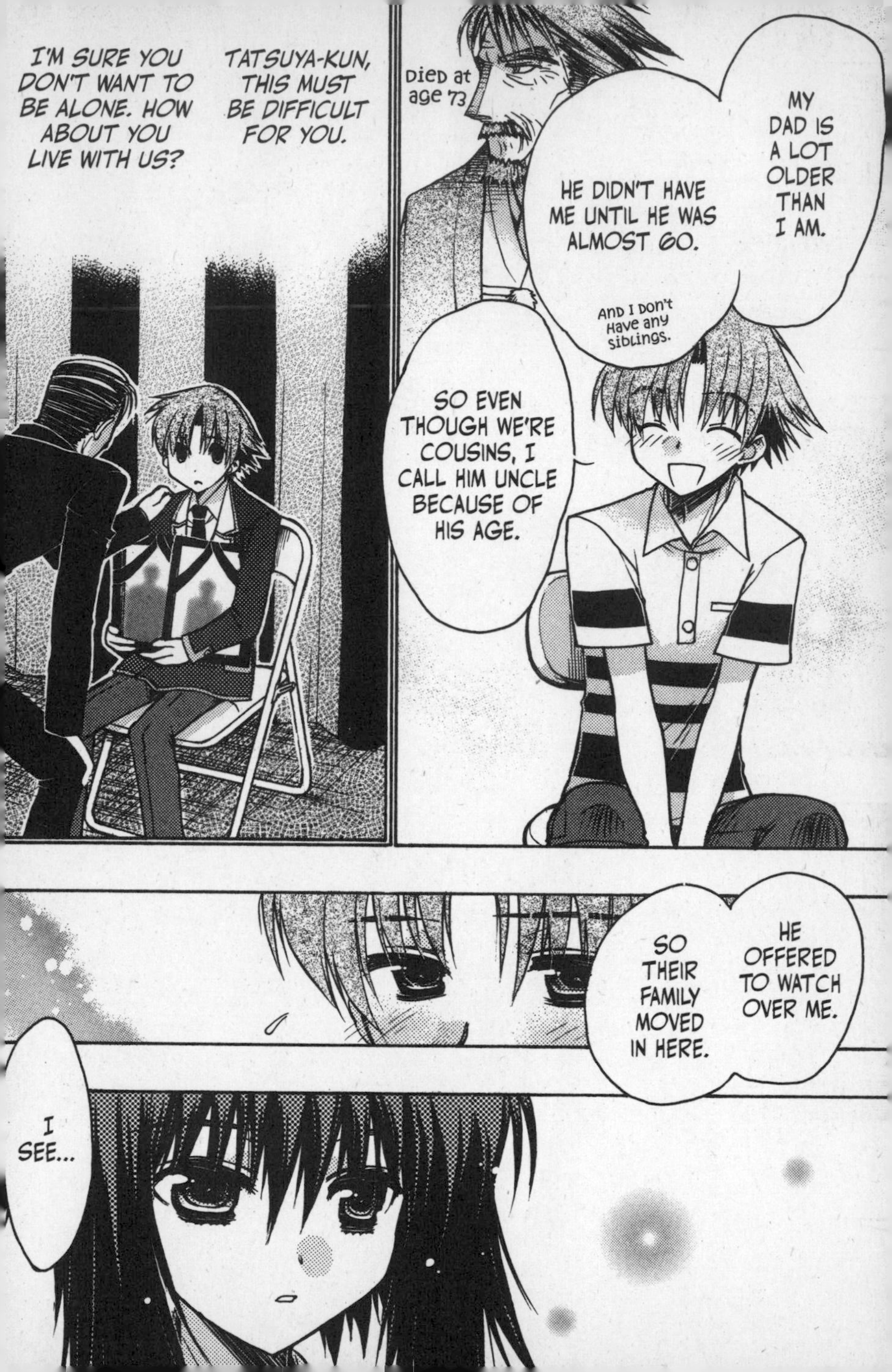
MY DAD IS A LOT OLDER THAN I AM.
HE DIDN'T HAVE ME UNTIL HE WAS ALMOST 60.
Died at age 73
And I don't have any siblings.
SO EVEN THOUGH WE'RE COUSINS, I CALL HIM UNCLE BECAUSE OF HIS AGE.
TATSUYA-KUN, THIS MUST BE DIFFICULT FOR YOU.
I'M SURE YOU DON'T WANT TO BE ALONE. HOW ABOUT YOU LIVE WITH US?
HE OFFERED TO WATCH OVER ME.
SO THEIR FAMILY MOVED IN HERE.
I SEE...

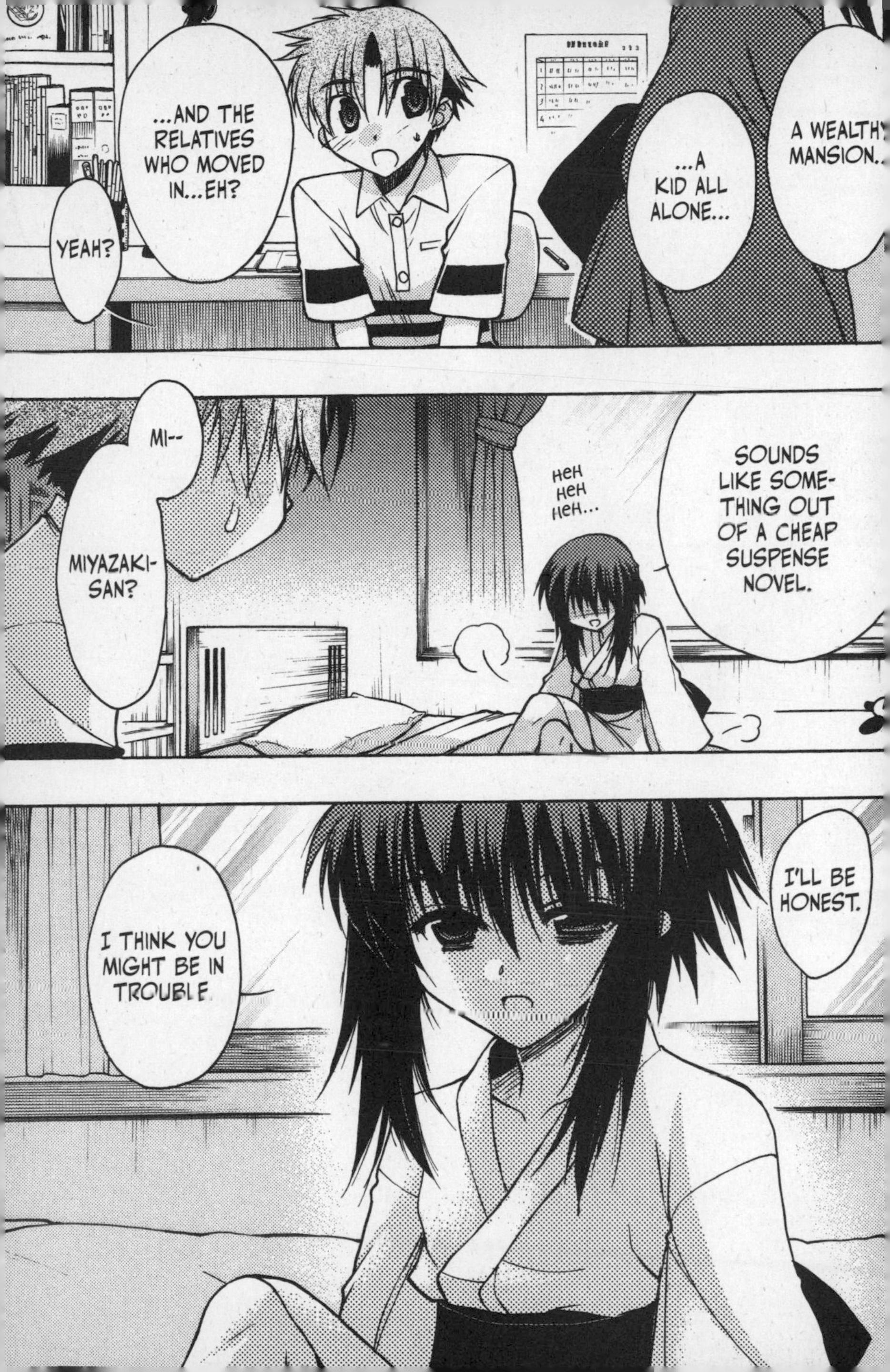
A WEALTHY MANSION..
...A KID ALL ALONE...
...AND THE RELATIVES WHO MOVED IN...EH?
YEAH?
SOUNDS LIKE SOME-THING OUT OF A CHEAP SUSPENSE NOVEL.
HEH HEH HEH...
MI--
MIYAZAKI-SAN?
I'LL BE HONEST.
I THINK YOU MIGHT BE IN TROUBLE.

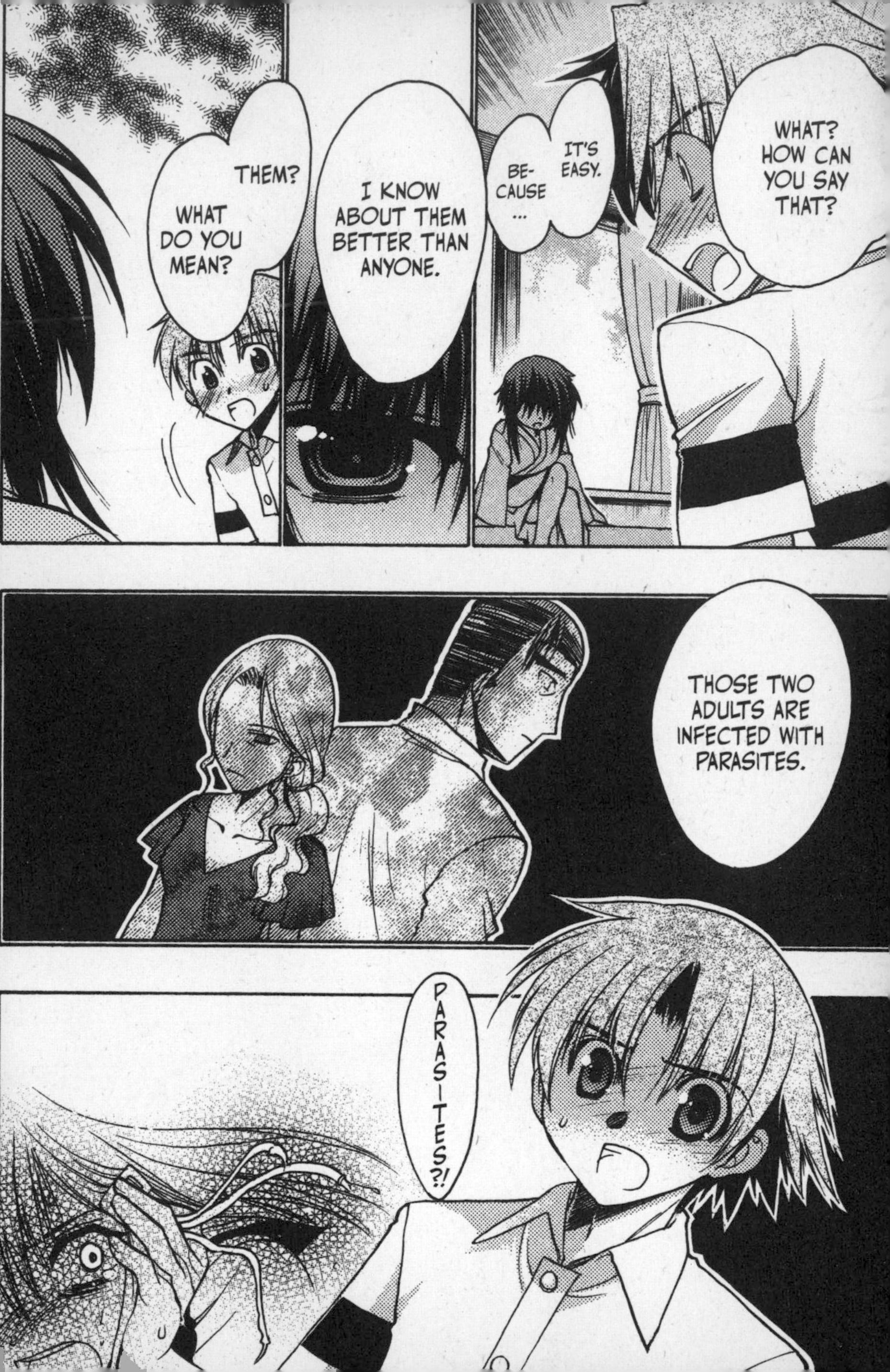
WHAT? HOW CAN YOU SAY THAT?
IT'S EASY.
BE-CAUSE ...
I KNOW ABOUT THEM BETTER THAN ANYONE.
THEM?
WHAT DO YOU MEAN?
THOSE TWO ADULTS ARE INFECTED WITH PARASITES.
PARASITES?!

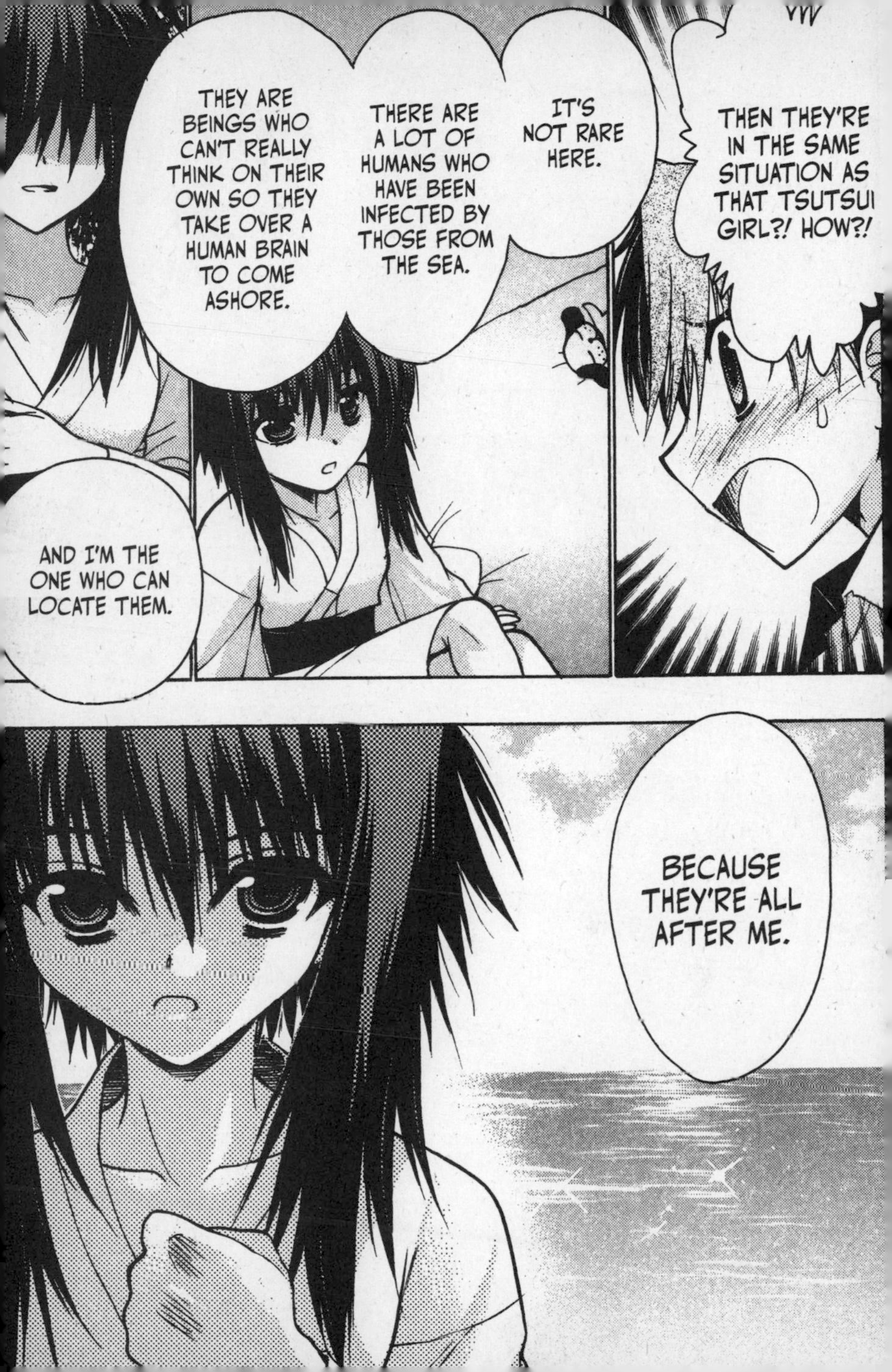
THEN THEY'RE IN THE SAME SITUATION AS THAT TSUTSUI GIRL?! HOW?!
IT'S NOT RARE HERE.
THERE ARE A LOT OF HUMANS WHO HAVE BEEN INFECTED BY THOSE FROM THE SEA.
THEY ARE BEINGS WHO CAN'T REALLY THINK ON THEIR OWN SO THEY TAKE OVER A HUMAN BRAIN TO COME ASHORE.
AND I'M THE ONE WHO CAN LOCATE THEM.
BECAUSE THEY'RE ALL AFTER ME.

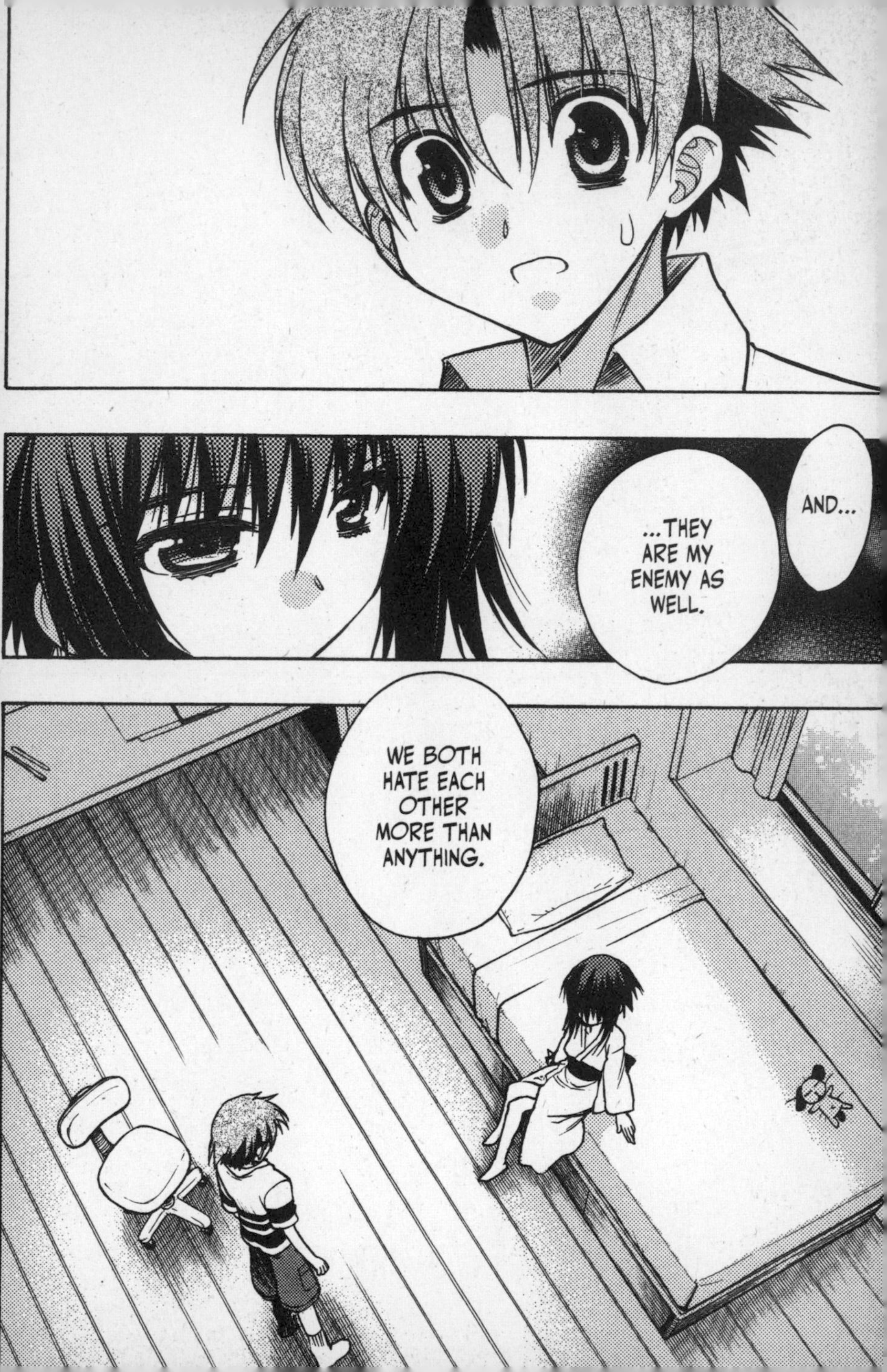
AND...
...THEY ARE MY ENEMY AS WELL.
WE BOTH HATE EACH OTHER MORE THAN ANYTHING.

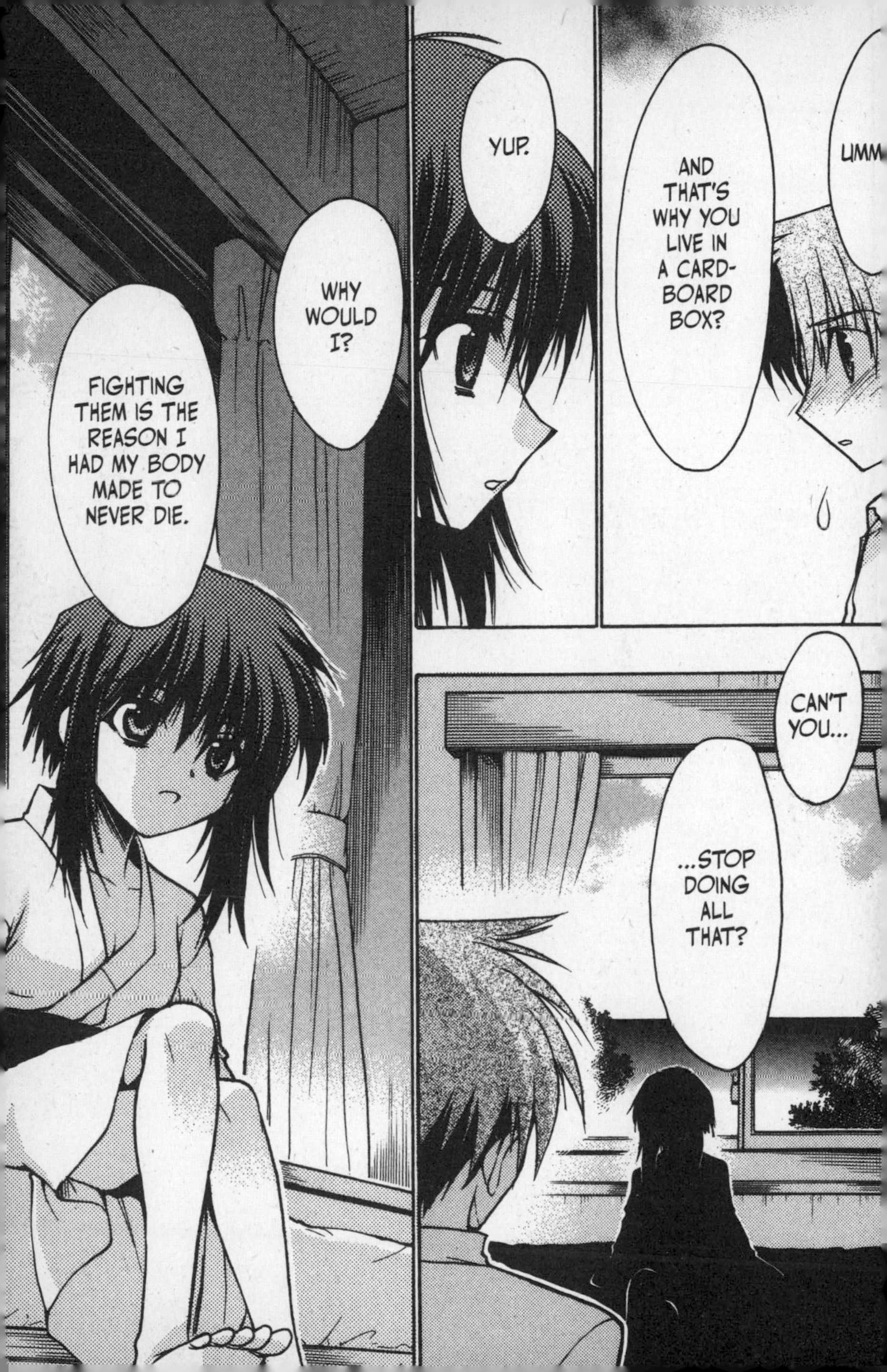
UMM
AND THAT'S WHY YOU LIVE IN A CARD-BOARD BOX?
YUP.
CAN'T YOU...
...STOP DOING ALL THAT?
WHY WOULD I?
FIGHTING THEM IS THE REASON I HAD MY BODY MADE TO NEVER DIE.

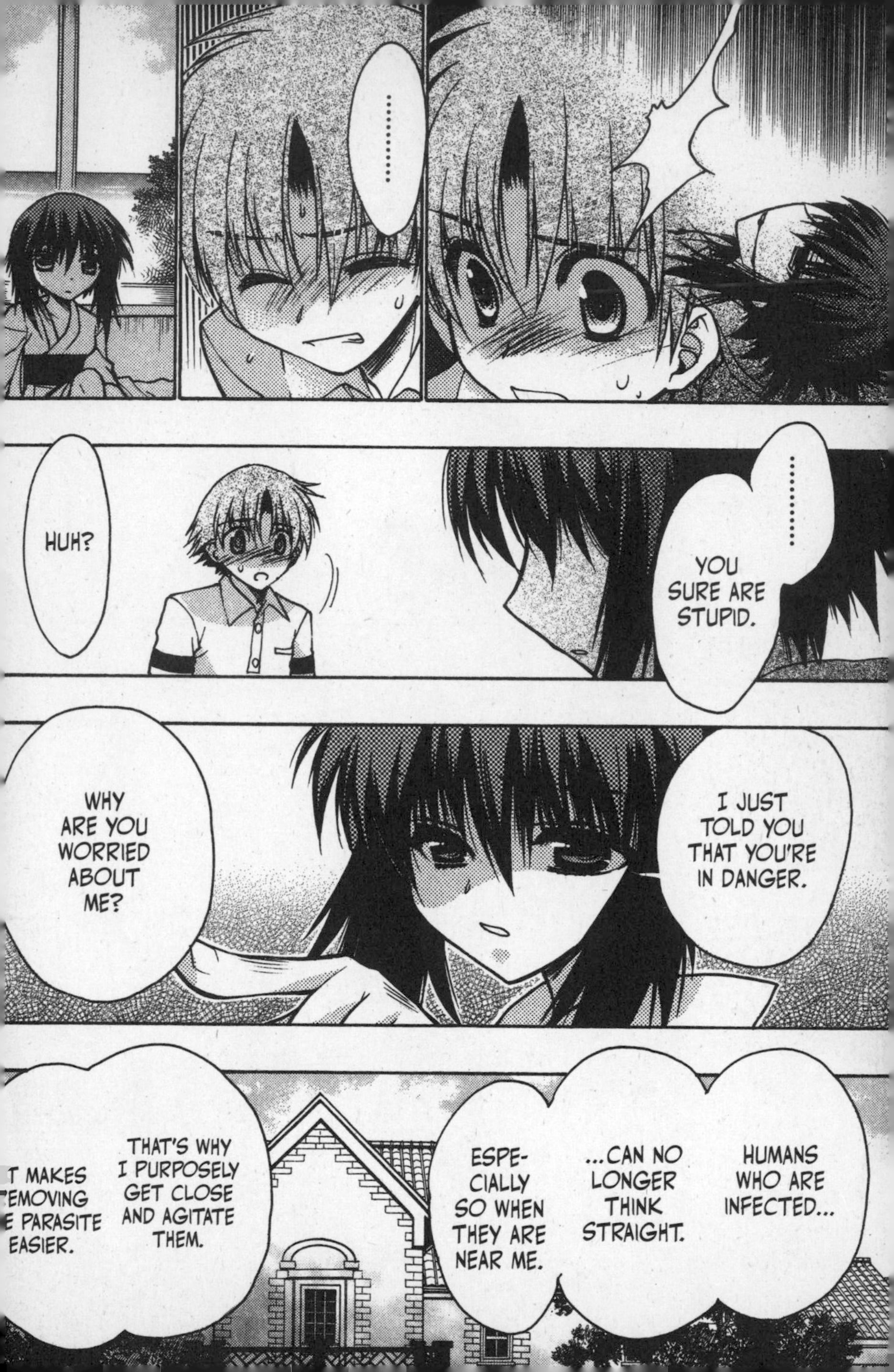
......
......
YOU SURE ARE STUPID.
HUH?
I JUST TOLD YOU THAT YOU'RE IN DANGER.
WHY ARE YOU WORRIED ABOUT ME?
HUMANS WHO ARE INFECTED...
...CAN NO LONGER THINK STRAIGHT.
ESPE-CIALLY SO WHEN THEY ARE NEAR ME.
THAT'S WHY I PURPOSELY GET CLOSE AND AGITATE THEM.
T MAKES EMOVING E PARASITE EASIER.

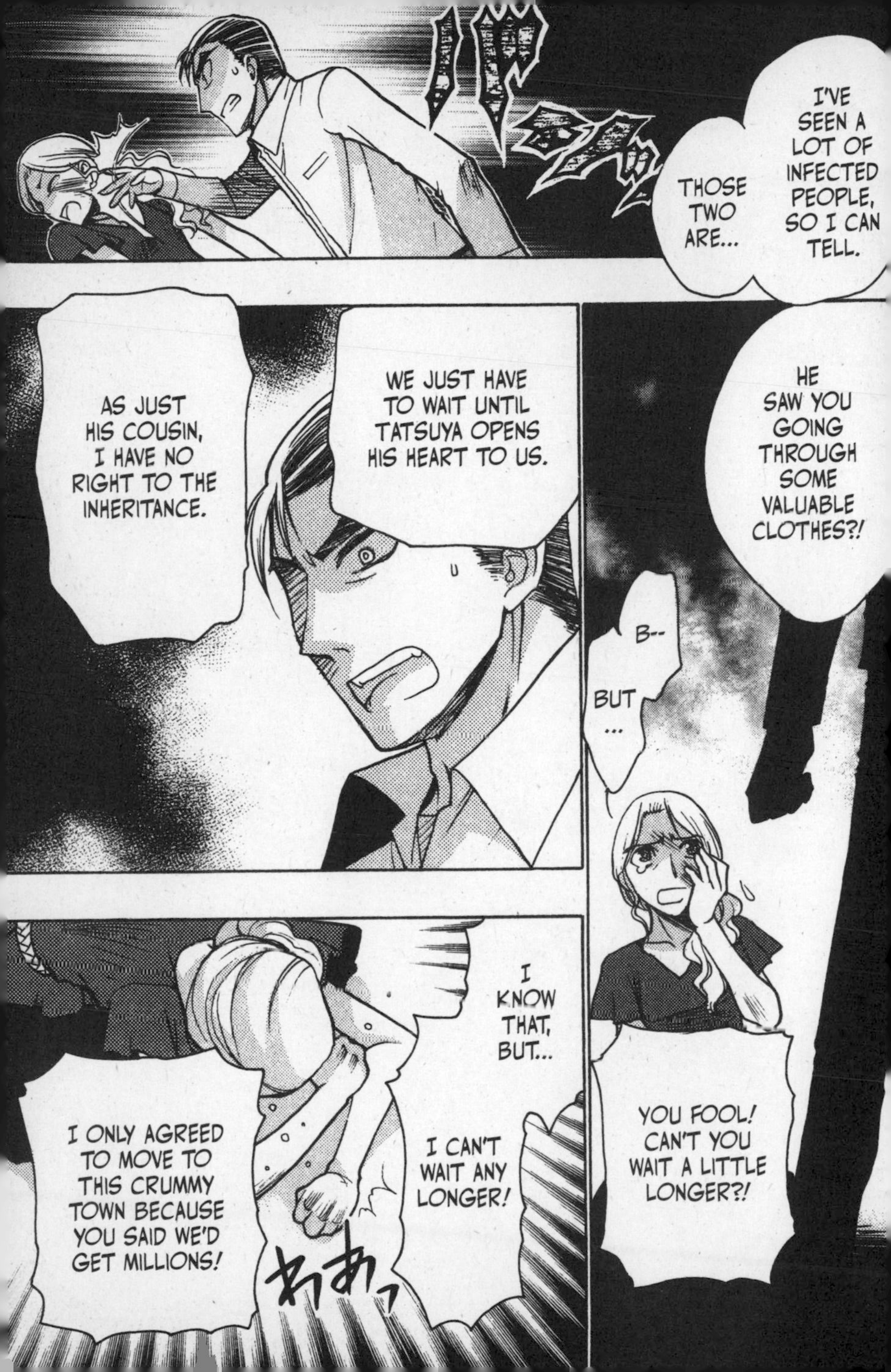
I'VE SEEN A LOT OF INFECTED PEOPLE, SO I CAN TELL.
THOSE TWO ARE...
HE SAW YOU GOING THROUGH SOME VALUABLE CLOTHES?!
B-- BUT ...
YOU FOOL! CAN'T YOU WAIT A LITTLE LONGER?!
WE JUST HAVE TO WAIT UNTIL TATSUYA OPENS HIS HEART TO US.
AS JUST HIS COUSIN, I HAVE NO RIGHT TO THE INHERITANCE.
I KNOW THAT, BUT...
I CAN'T WAIT ANY LONGER!
I ONLY AGREED TO MOVE TO THIS CRUMMY TOWN BECAUSE YOU SAID WE'D GET MILLIONS!
わあっ

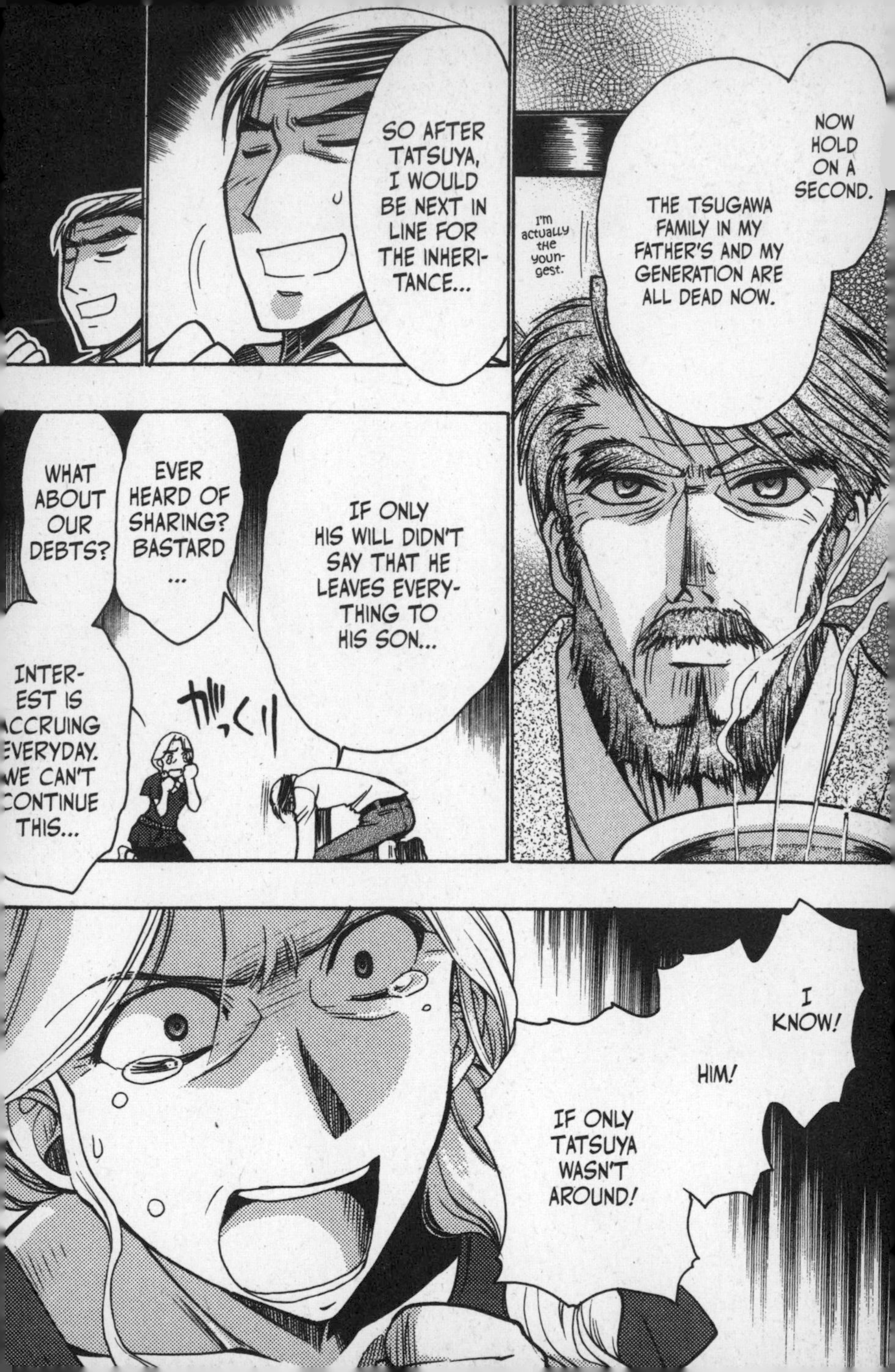
NOW HOLD ON A SECOND.
THE TSUGAWA FAMILY IN MY FATHER'S AND MY GENERATION ARE ALL DEAD NOW.
I'm actually the youngest.
SO AFTER TATSUYA, I WOULD BE NEXT IN LINE FOR THE INHERITANCE...
IF ONLY HIS WILL DIDN'T SAY THAT HE LEAVES EVERYTHING TO HIS SON...
EVER HEARD OF SHARING? BASTARD...
WHAT ABOUT OUR DEBTS?
INTEREST IS ACCRUING EVERYDAY. WE CAN'T CONTINUE THIS...
I KNOW!
HIM!
IF ONLY TATSUYA WASN'T AROUND!

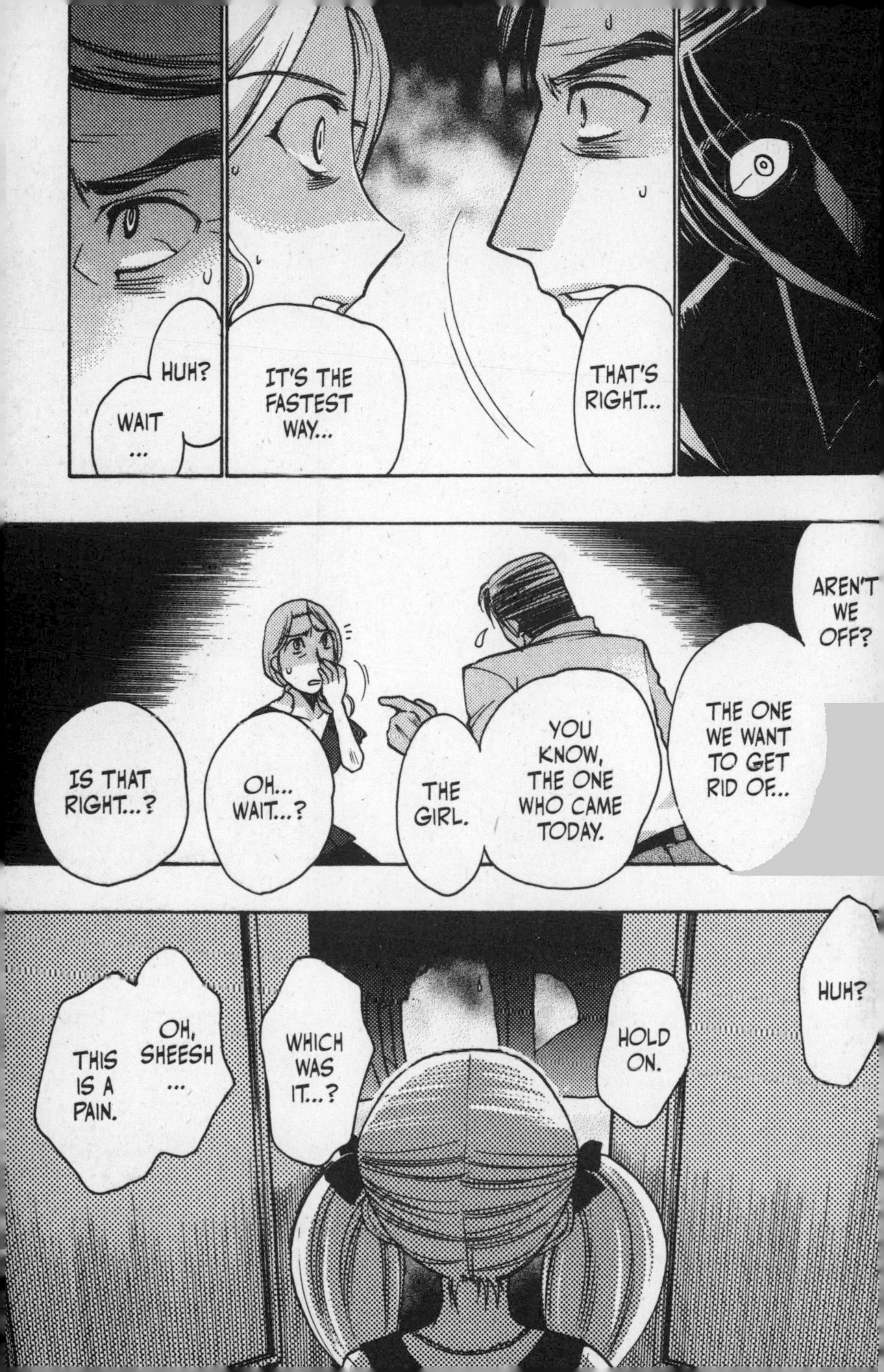
THAT'S RIGHT...
IT'S THE FASTEST WAY...
HUH?
WAIT ...
AREN'T WE OFF?
THE ONE WE WANT TO GET RID OF...
YOU KNOW, THE ONE WHO CAME TODAY.
THE GIRL.
OH... WAIT...?
IS THAT RIGHT...?
HUH?
HOLD ON.
WHICH WAS IT...?
OH, SHEESH ...
THIS IS A PAIN.

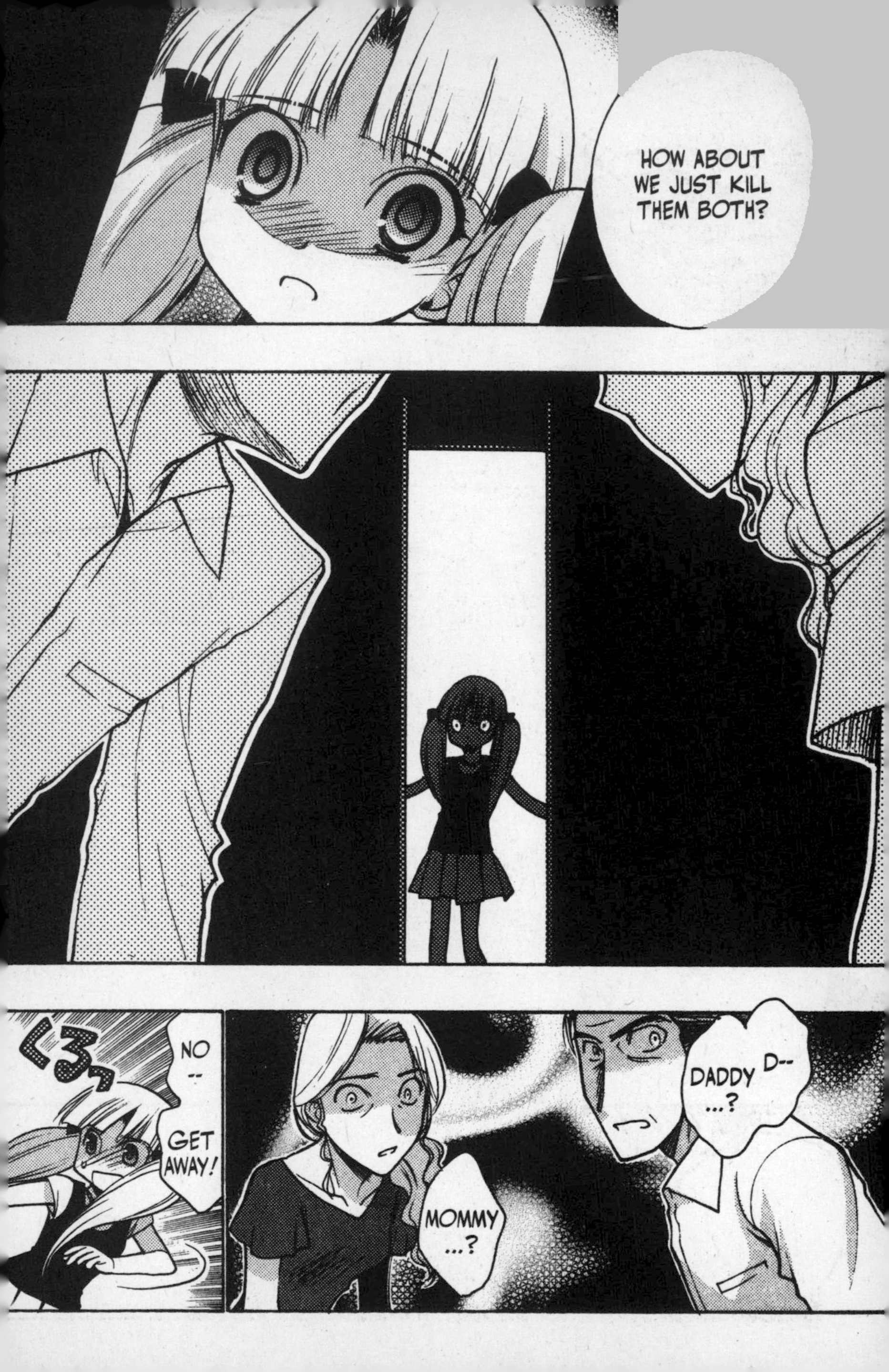
HOW ABOUT WE JUST KILL THEM BOTH?
D--
DADDY ...?
MOMMY ...?
NO --
GET AWAY!

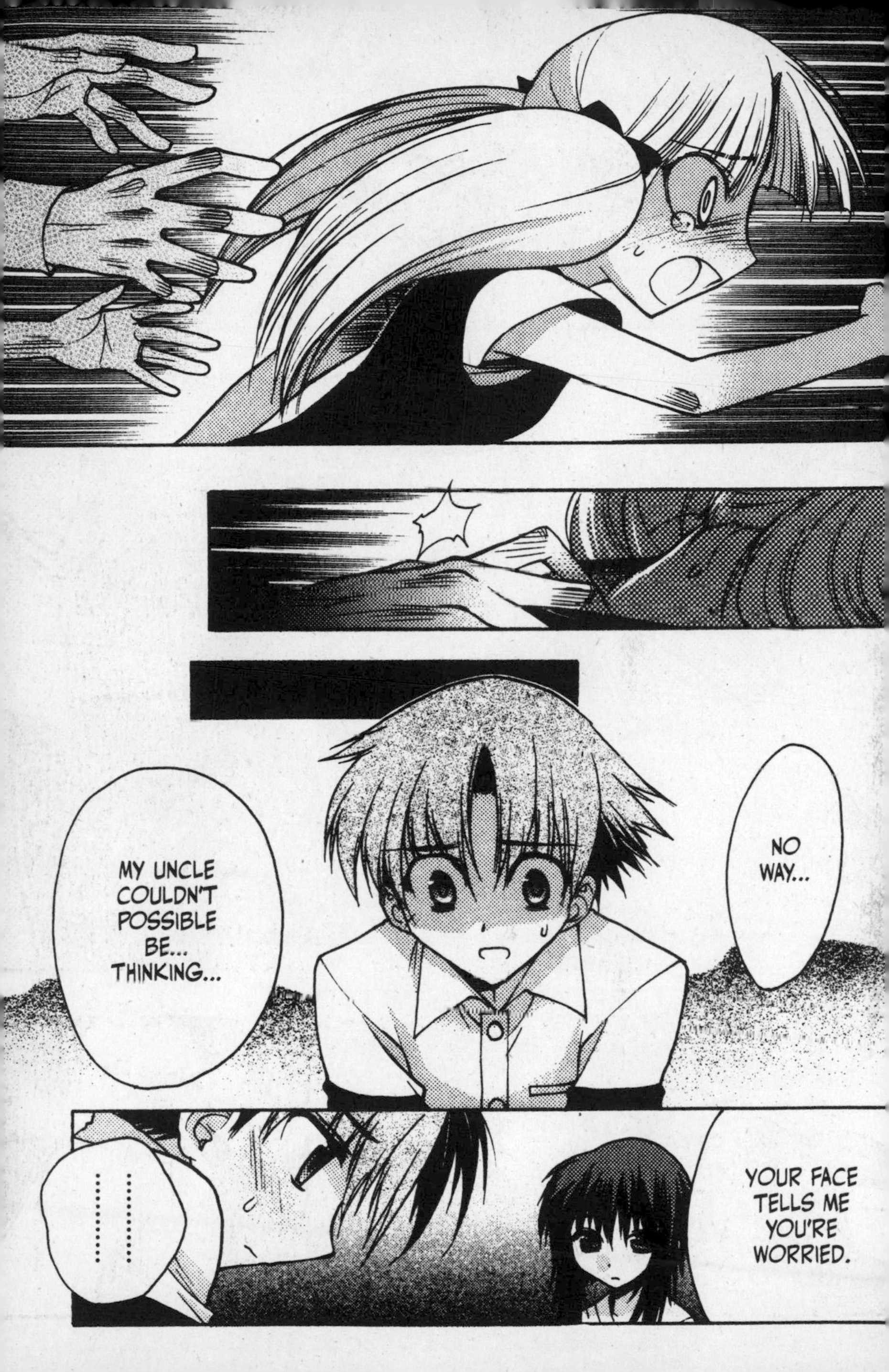
NO WAY...
MY UNCLE COULDN'T POSSIBLE BE... THINKING...
YOUR FACE TELLS ME YOU'RE WORRIED.
......

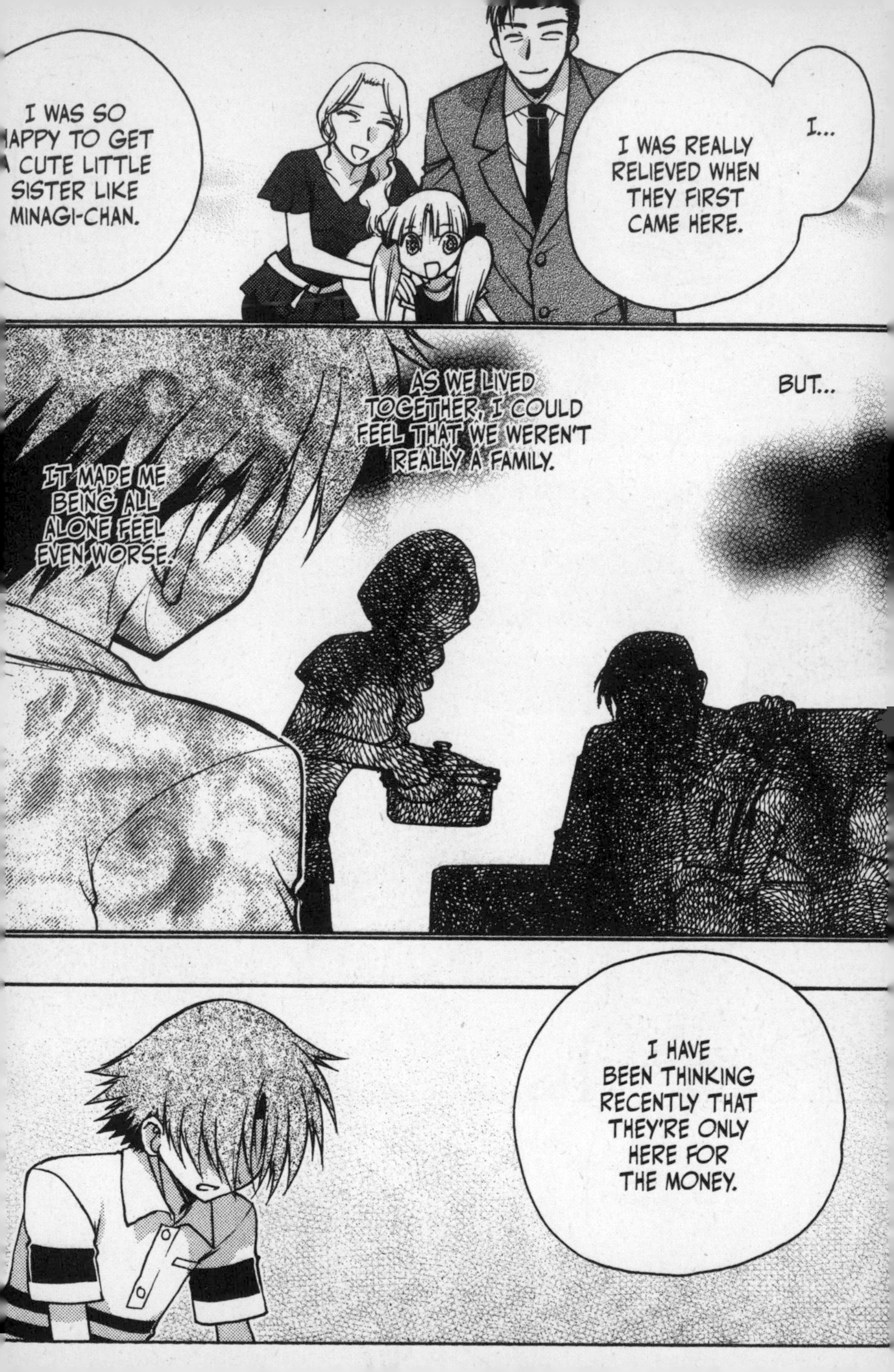
I...
I WAS REALLY RELIEVED WHEN THEY FIRST CAME HERE.
I WAS SO HAPPY TO GET A CUTE LITTLE SISTER LIKE MINAGI-CHAN.
BUT...
AS WE LIVED TOGETHER, I COULD FEEL THAT WE WEREN'T REALLY A FAMILY.
IT MADE ME BEING ALL ALONE FEEL EVEN WORSE.
I HAVE BEEN THINKING RECENTLY THAT THEY'RE ONLY HERE FOR THE MONEY.

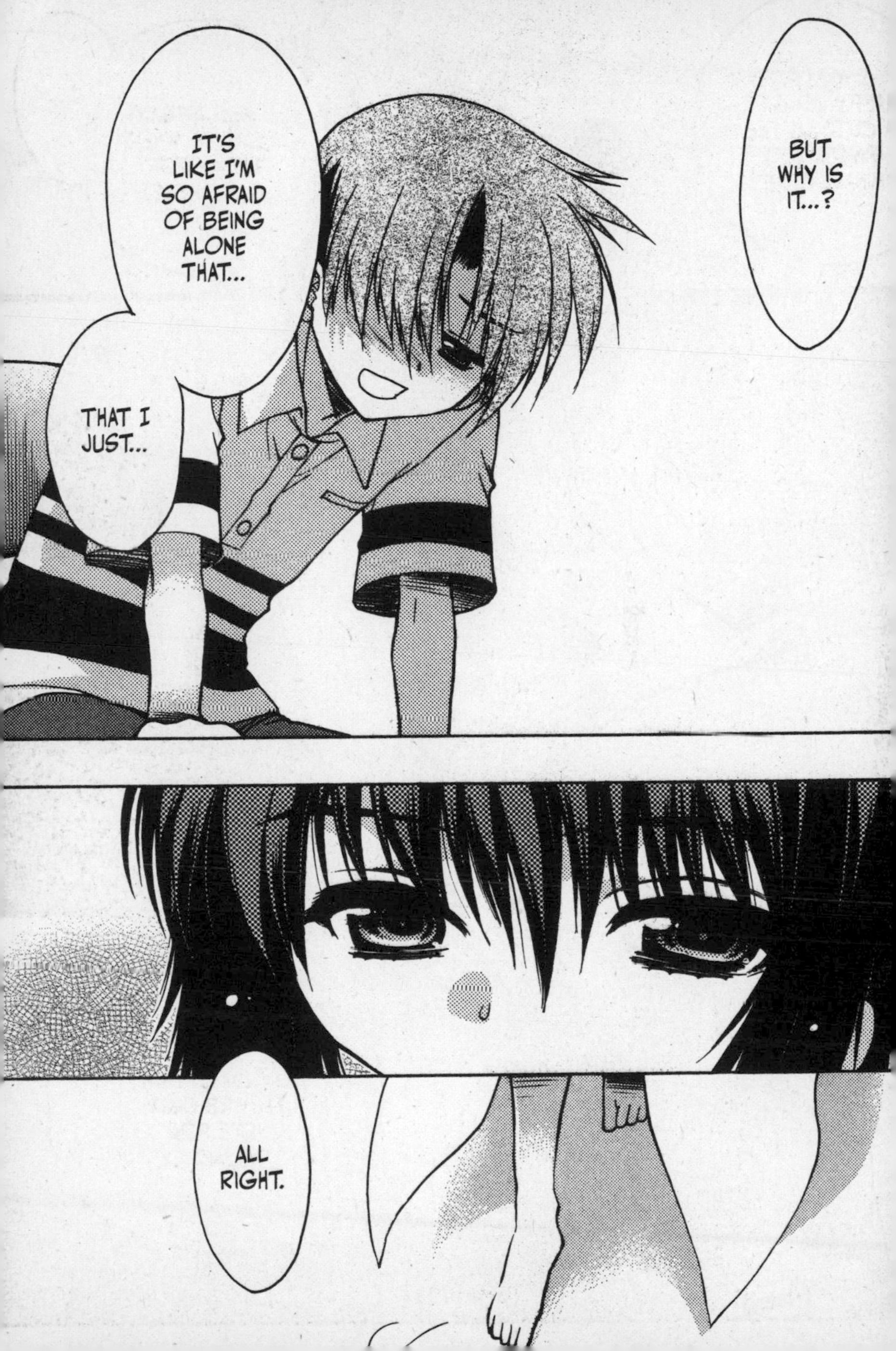
BUT WHY IS IT...?
IT'S LIKE I'M SO AFRAID OF BEING ALONE THAT...
THAT I JUST...
ALL RIGHT.

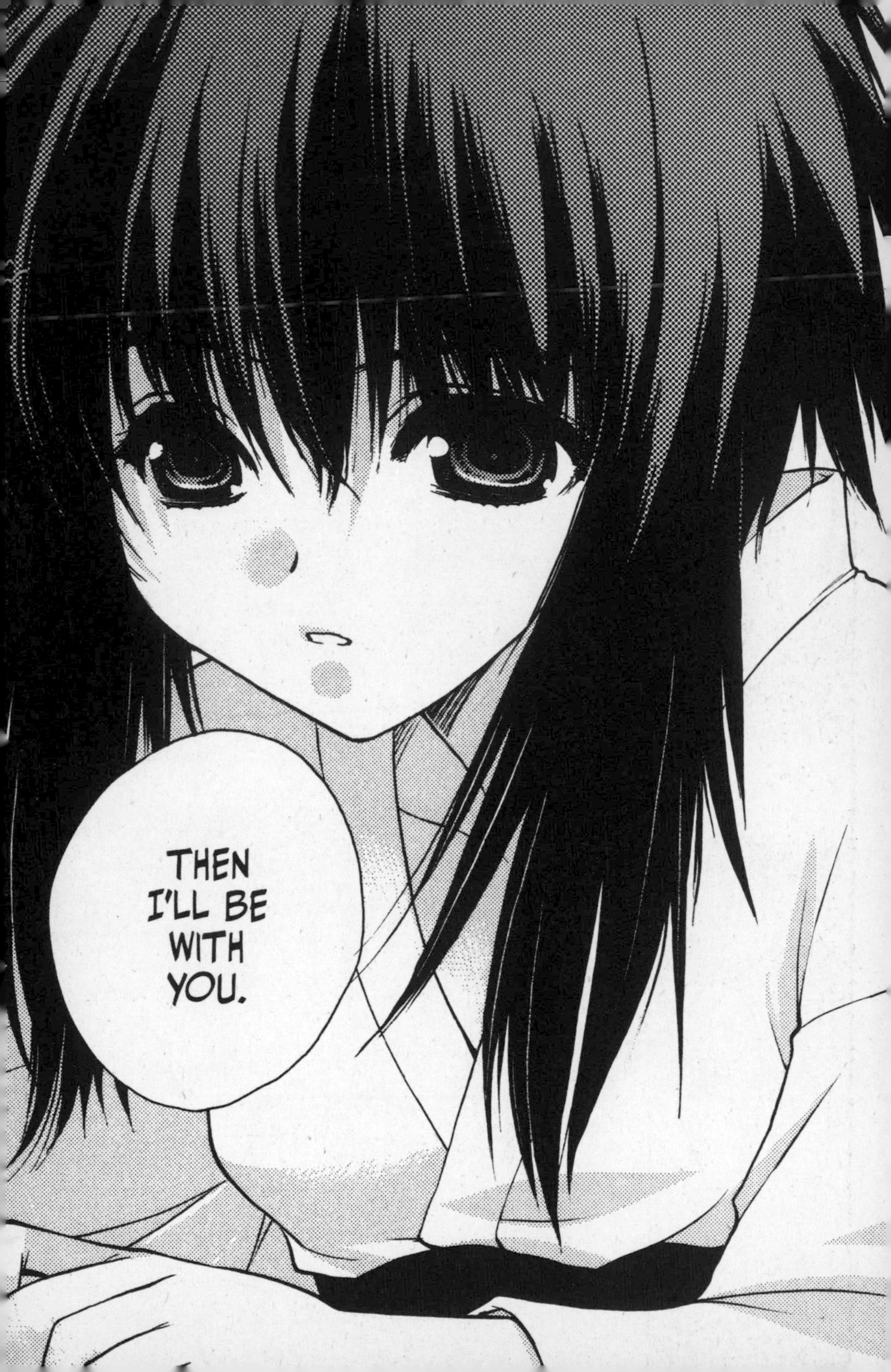
THEN I'LL BE WITH YOU.

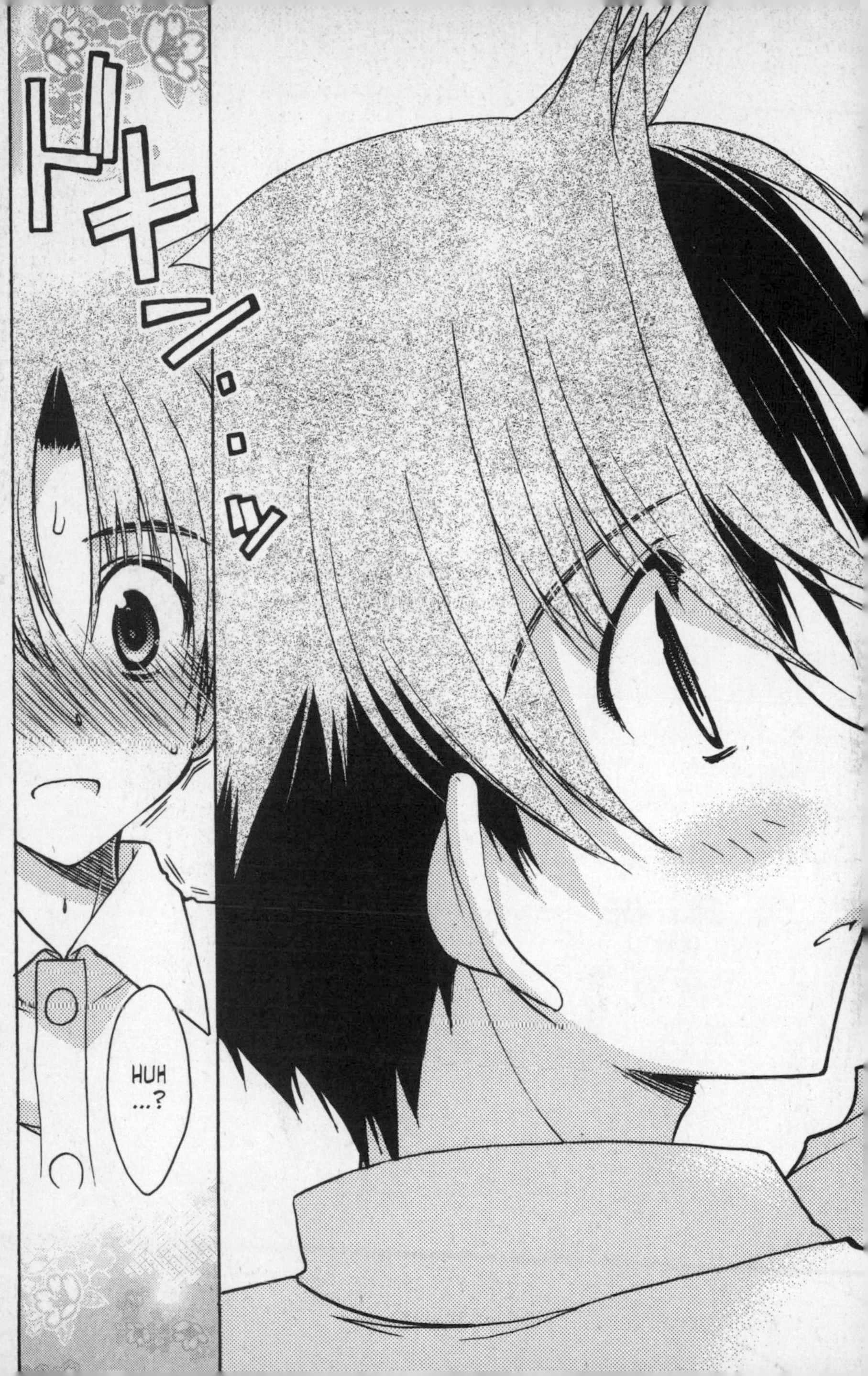
ドキーン・・ッ
HUH ...?

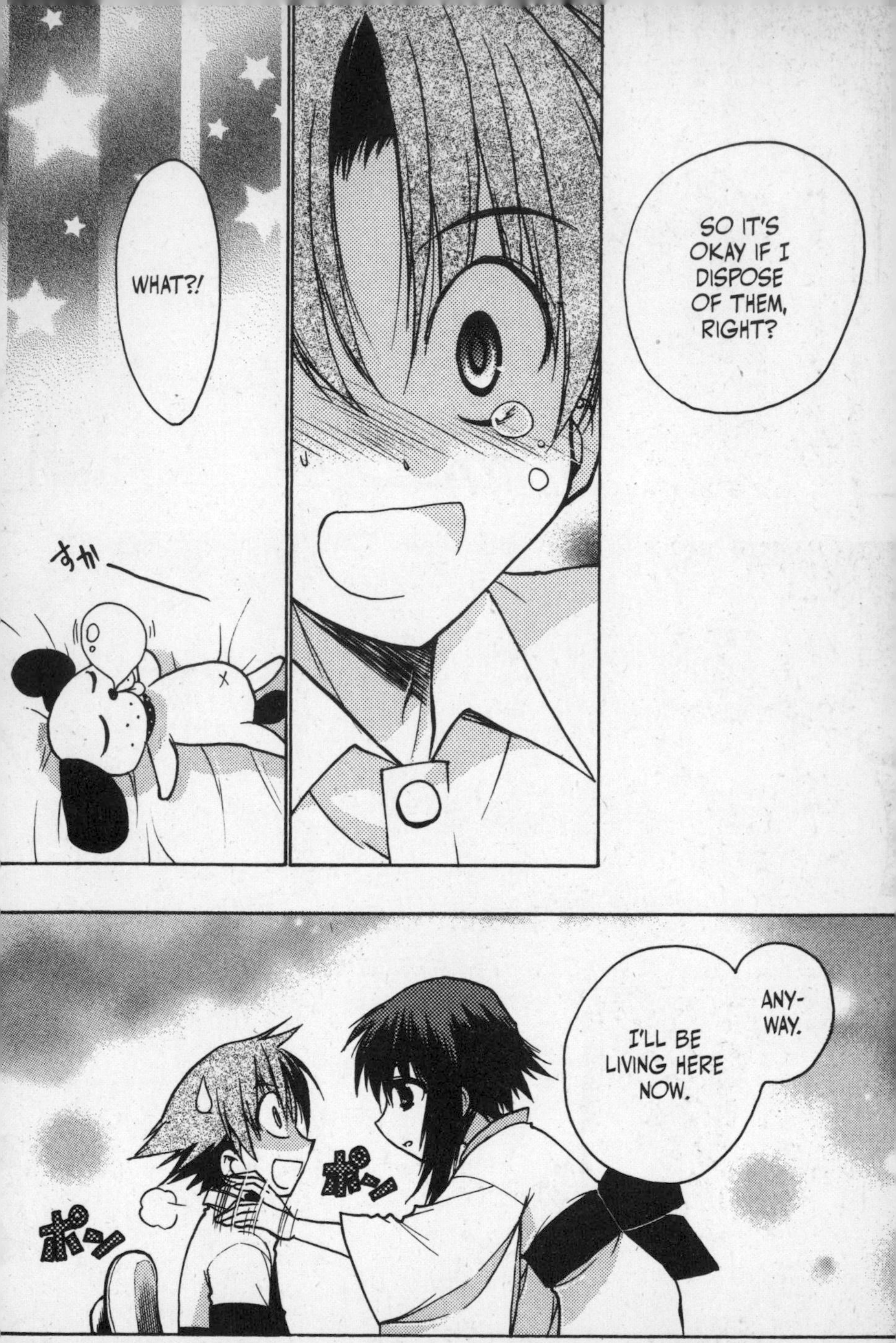
SO IT'S OKAY IF I DISPOSE OF THEM, RIGHT?
WHAT?!
すか
ANY-WAY.
I'LL BE LIVING HERE NOW.
ポッ
ポッ

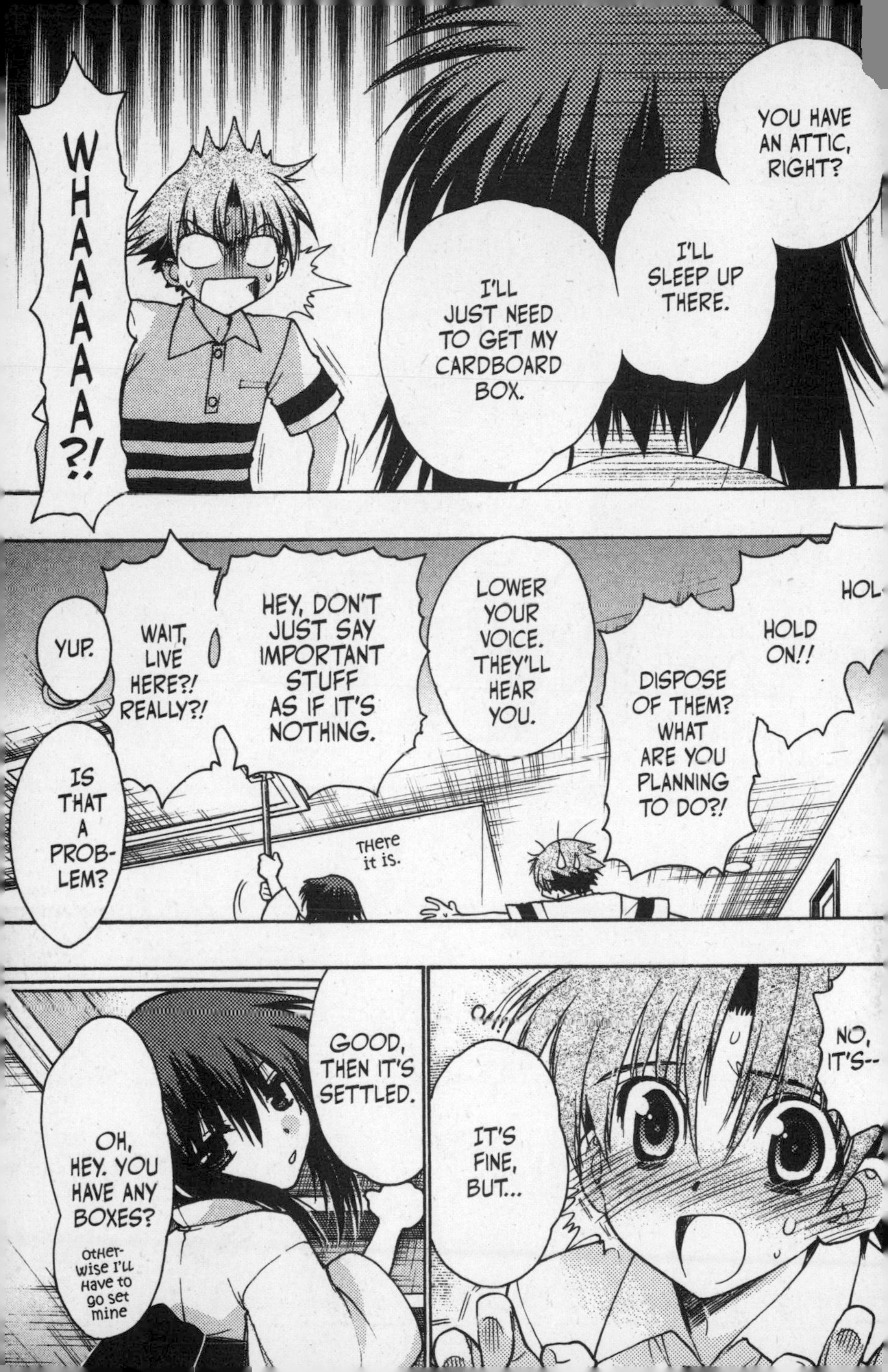
YOU HAVE AN ATTIC, RIGHT?
I'LL SLEEP UP THERE.
I'LL JUST NEED TO GET MY CARDBOARD BOX.
WHAAAAAA?!
HOL-
HOLD ON!!
DISPOSE OF THEM? WHAT ARE YOU PLANNING TO DO?!
LOWER YOUR VOICE. THEY'LL HEAR YOU.
HEY, DON'T JUST SAY IMPORTANT STUFF AS IF IT'S NOTHING.
There it is.
WAIT, LIVE HERE?! REALLY?!
YUP.
IS THAT A PROBLEM?
NO, IT'S--
IT'S FINE, BUT...
GOOD, THEN IT'S SETTLED.
OH, HEY. YOU HAVE ANY BOXES?
Otherwise I'll have to go set mine

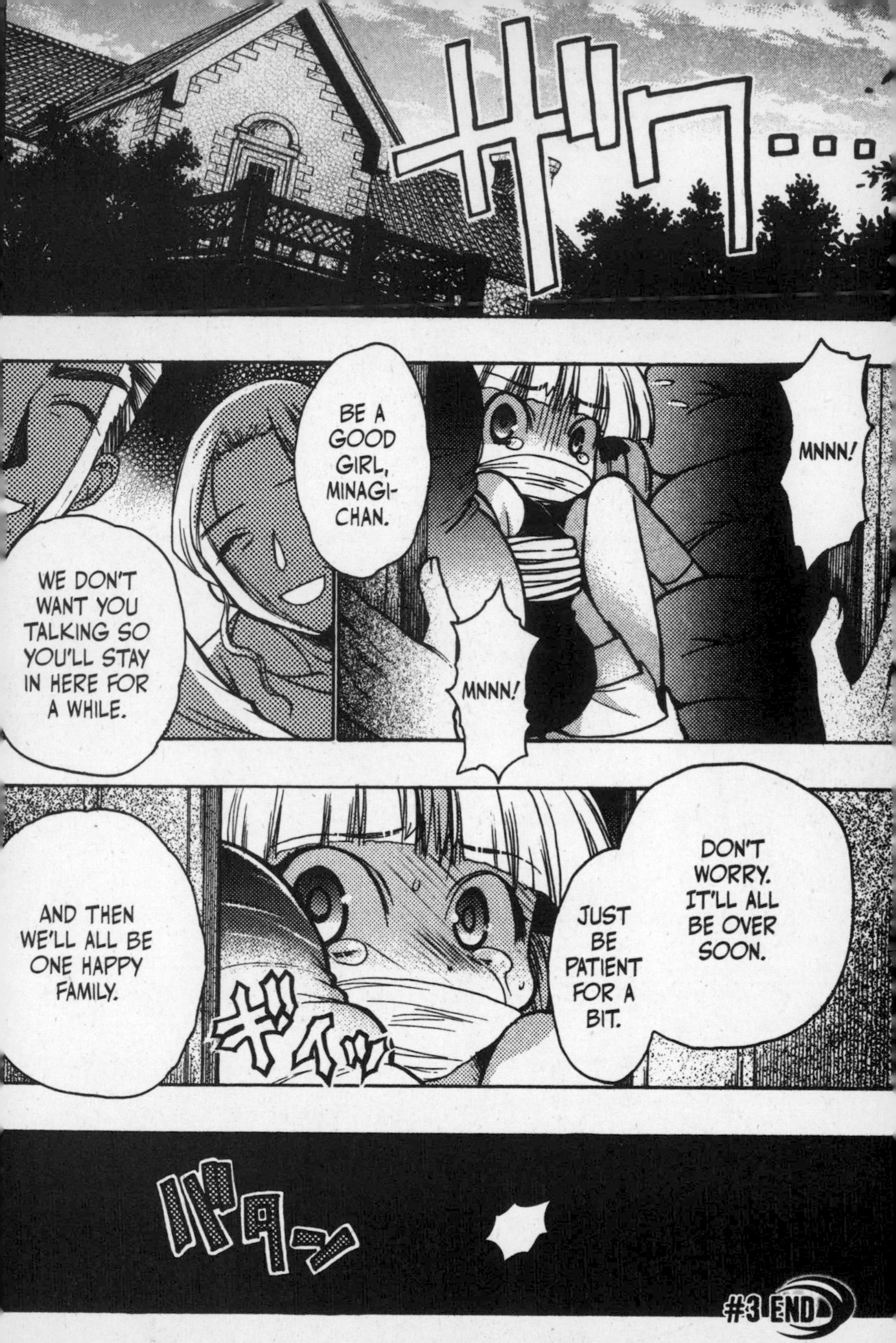
ザワ…
MNNN!
BE A GOOD GIRL, MINAGI-CHAN.
MNNN!
WE DON'T WANT YOU TALKING SO YOU'LL STAY IN HERE FOR A WHILE.
DON'T WORRY. IT'LL ALL BE OVER SOON.
JUST BE PATIENT FOR A BIT.
ギィッ
AND THEN WE'LL ALL BE ONE HAPPY FAMILY.
バタン
#3 END

#4Family Reversal

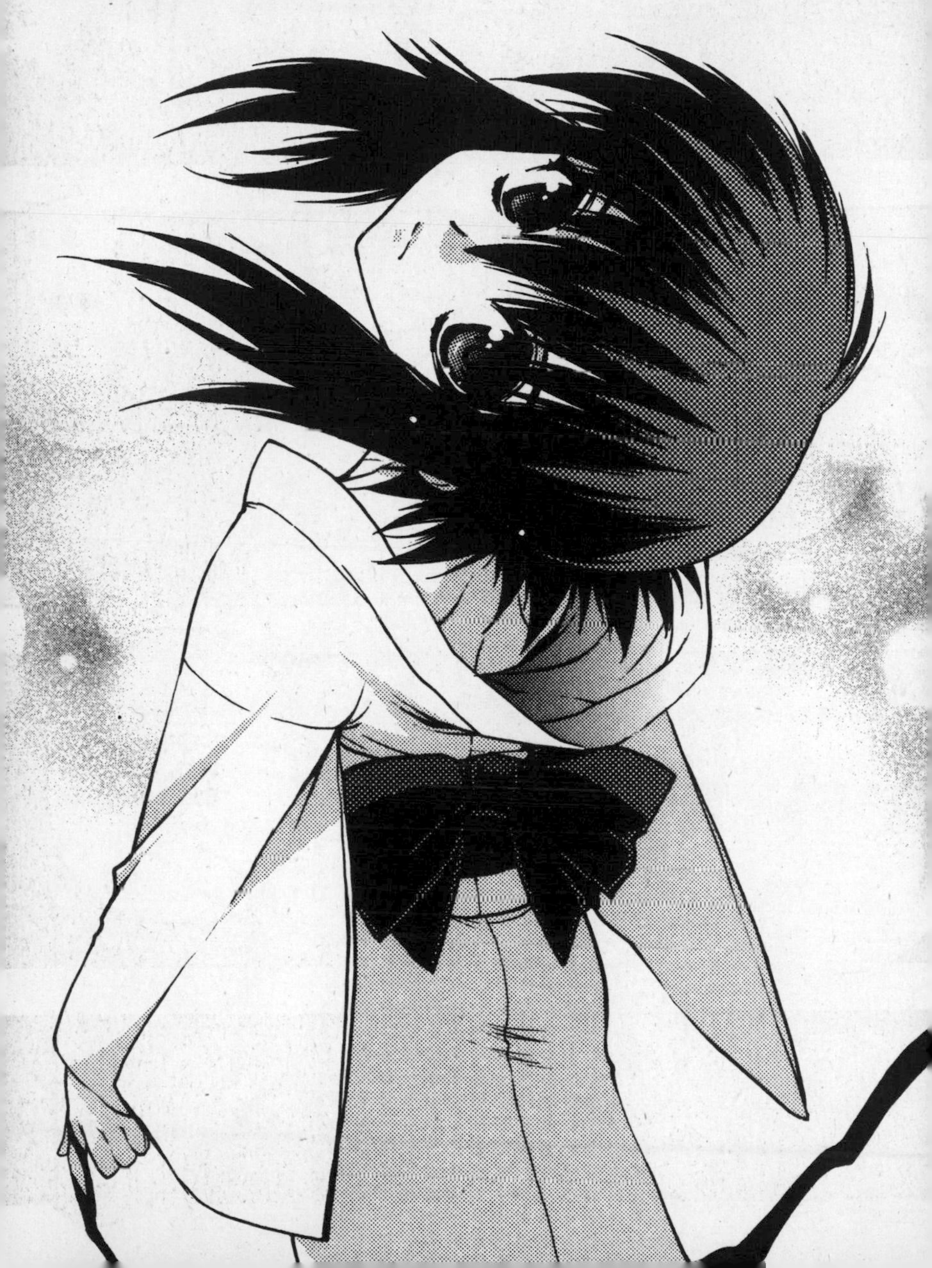

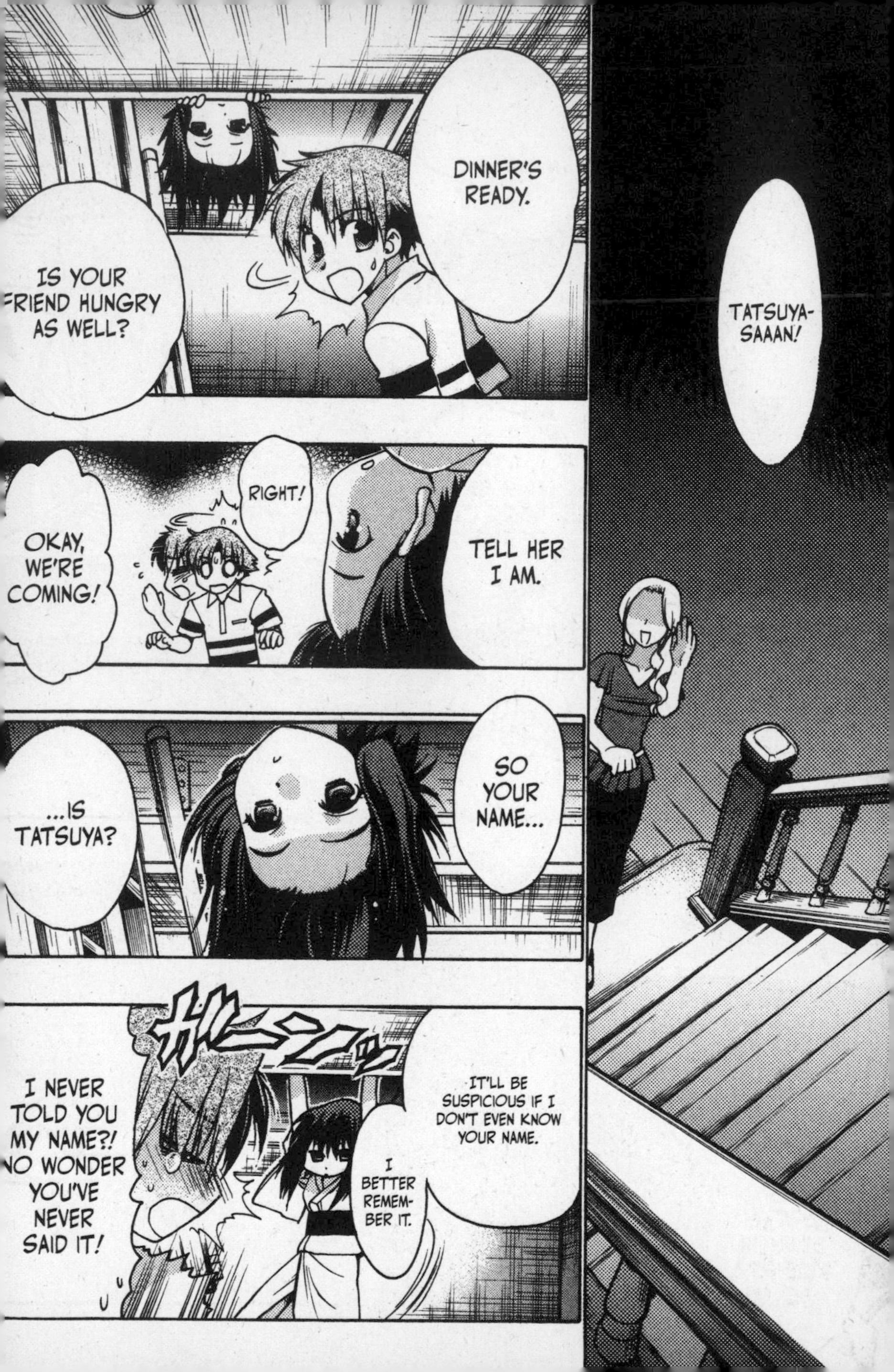
TATSUYA-SAAAN!
DINNER'S READY.
IS YOUR FRIEND HUNGRY AS WELL?
TELL HER I AM.
RIGHT!
OKAY, WE'RE COMING!
SO YOUR NAME...
...IS TATSUYA?
IT'LL BE SUSPICIOUS IF I DON'T EVEN KNOW YOUR NAME.
I BETTER REMEMBER IT.
I NEVER TOLD YOU MY NAME?! NO WONDER YOU'VE NEVER SAID IT!

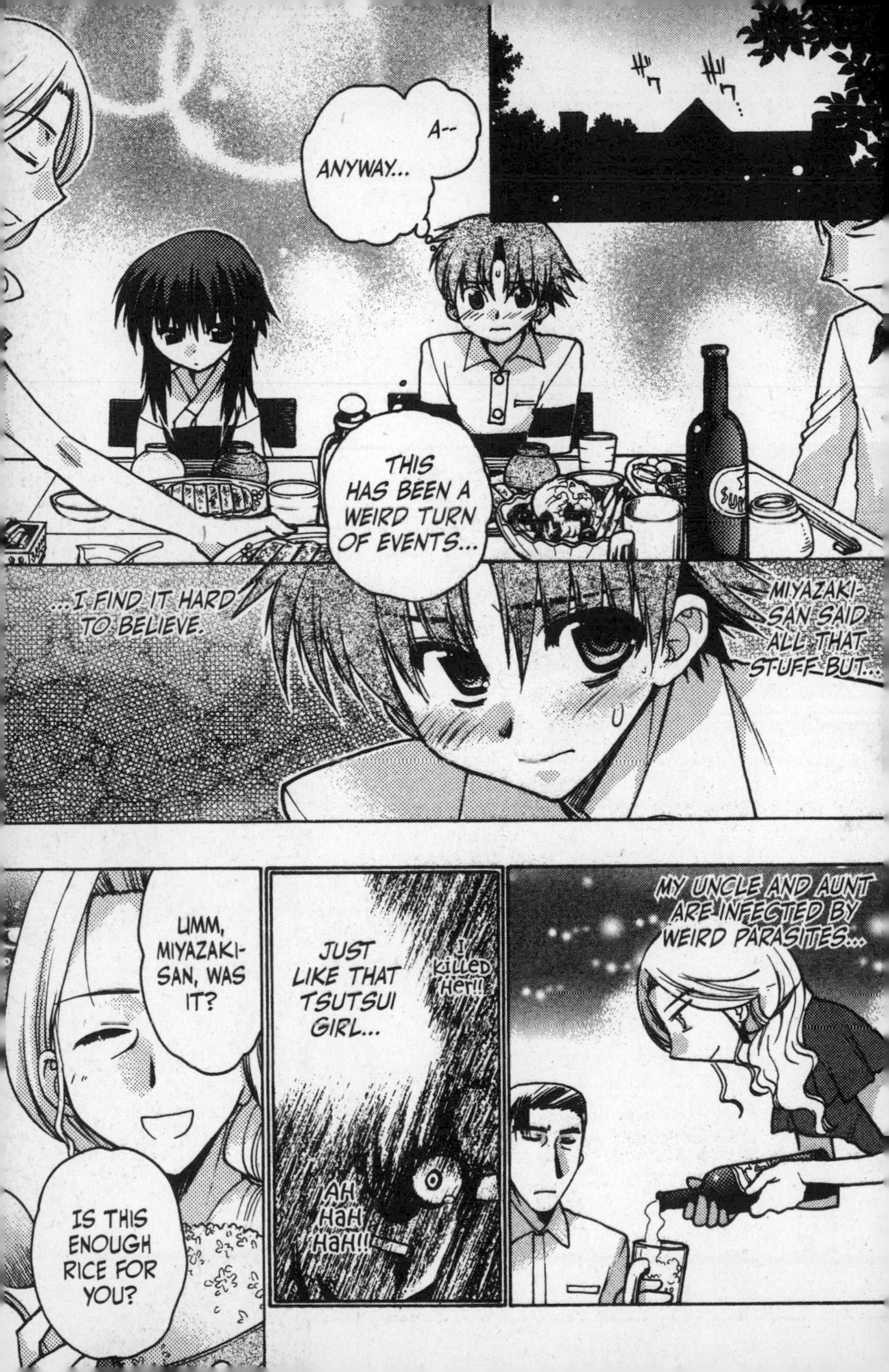
ギク
ギク...
A-- ANYWAY...
THIS HAS BEEN A WEIRD TURN OF EVENTS...
MIYAZAKI-SAN SAID ALL THAT STUFF BUT...
...I FIND IT HARD TO BELIEVE.
MY UNCLE AND AUNT ARE INFECTED BY WEIRD PARASITES...
JUST LIKE THAT TSUTSUI GIRL...
I killed her!!
AH HaH HaH!!
UMM, MIYAZAKI-SAN, WAS IT?
IS THIS ENOUGH RICE FOR YOU?

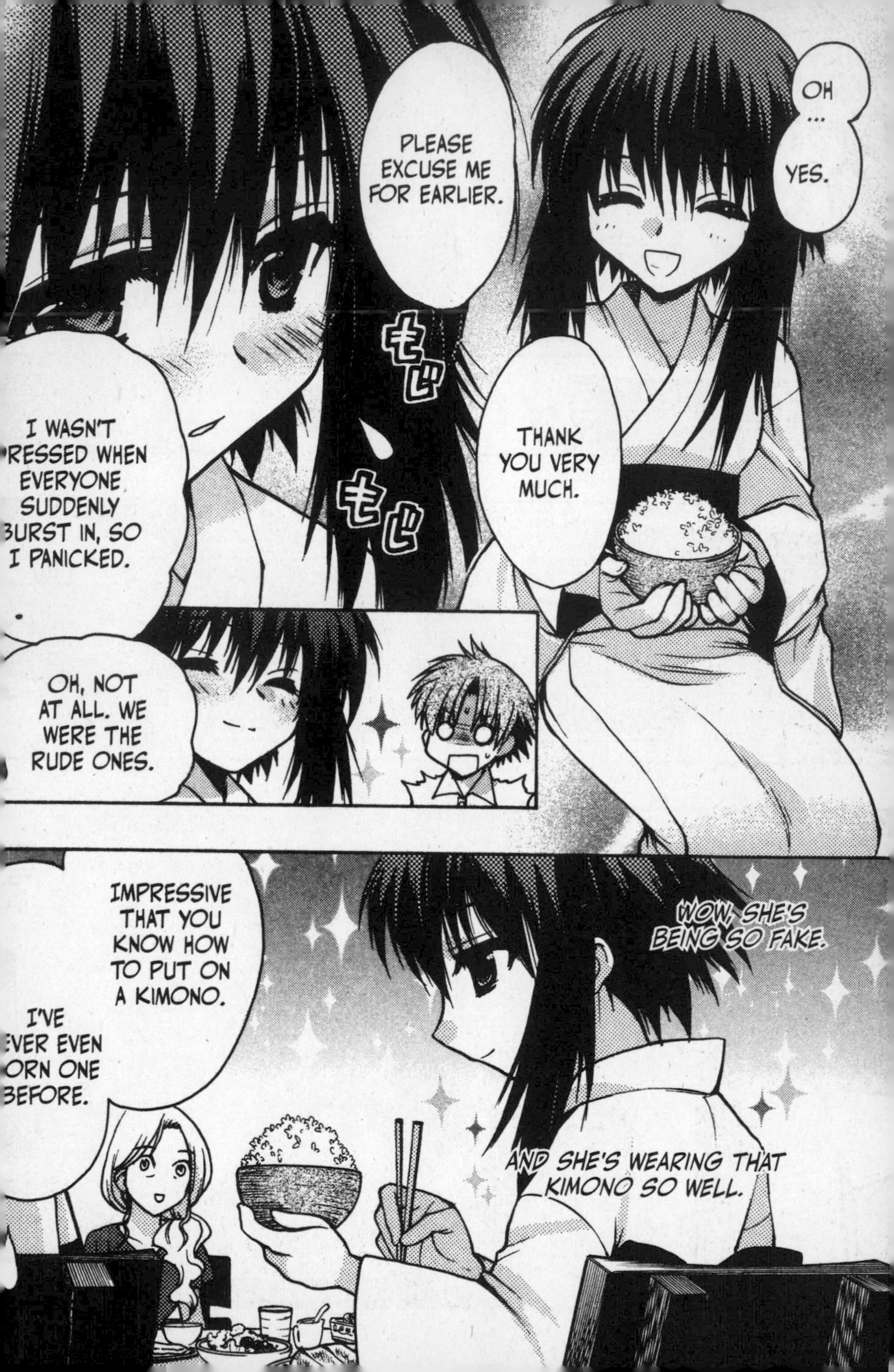
OH ... YES.
PLEASE EXCUSE ME FOR EARLIER.
もじ
もじ
THANK YOU VERY MUCH.
I WASN'T RESSED WHEN EVERYONE SUDDENLY URST IN, SO I PANICKED.
OH, NOT AT ALL. WE WERE THE RUDE ONES.
WOW, SHE'S BEING SO FAKE.
AND SHE'S WEARING THAT KIMONO SO WELL.
IMPRESSIVE THAT YOU KNOW HOW TO PUT ON A KIMONO.
I'VE VER EVEN ORN ONE BEFORE.

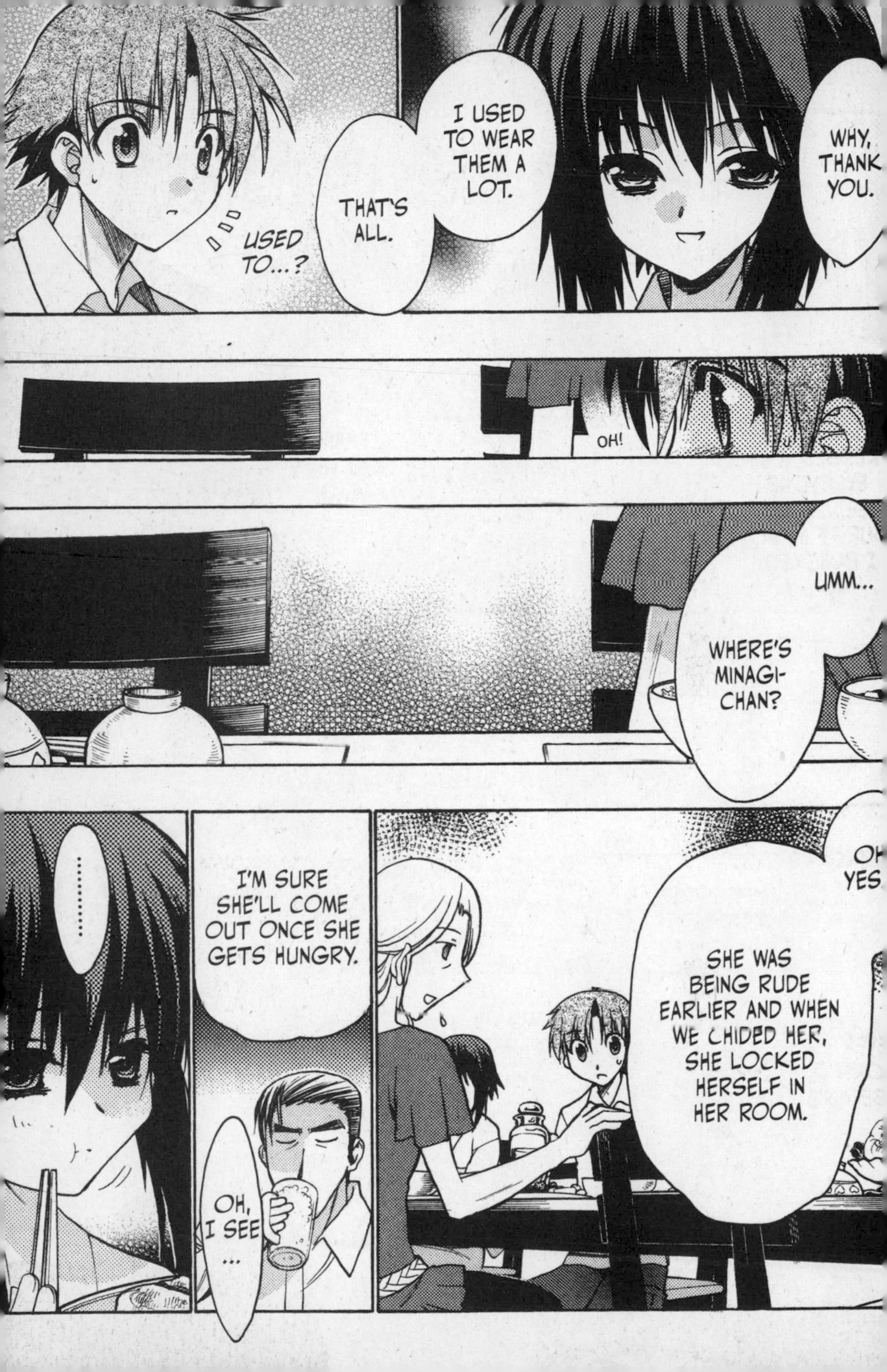
WHY, THANK YOU.
I USED TO WEAR THEM A LOT.
THAT'S ALL.
USED TO...?
OH!
UMM...
WHERE'S MINAGI-CHAN?
OH YES.
SHE WAS BEING RUDE EARLIER AND WHEN WE CHIDED HER, SHE LOCKED HERSELF IN HER ROOM.
I'M SURE SHE'LL COME OUT ONCE SHE GETS HUNGRY.
OH, I SEE ...
......

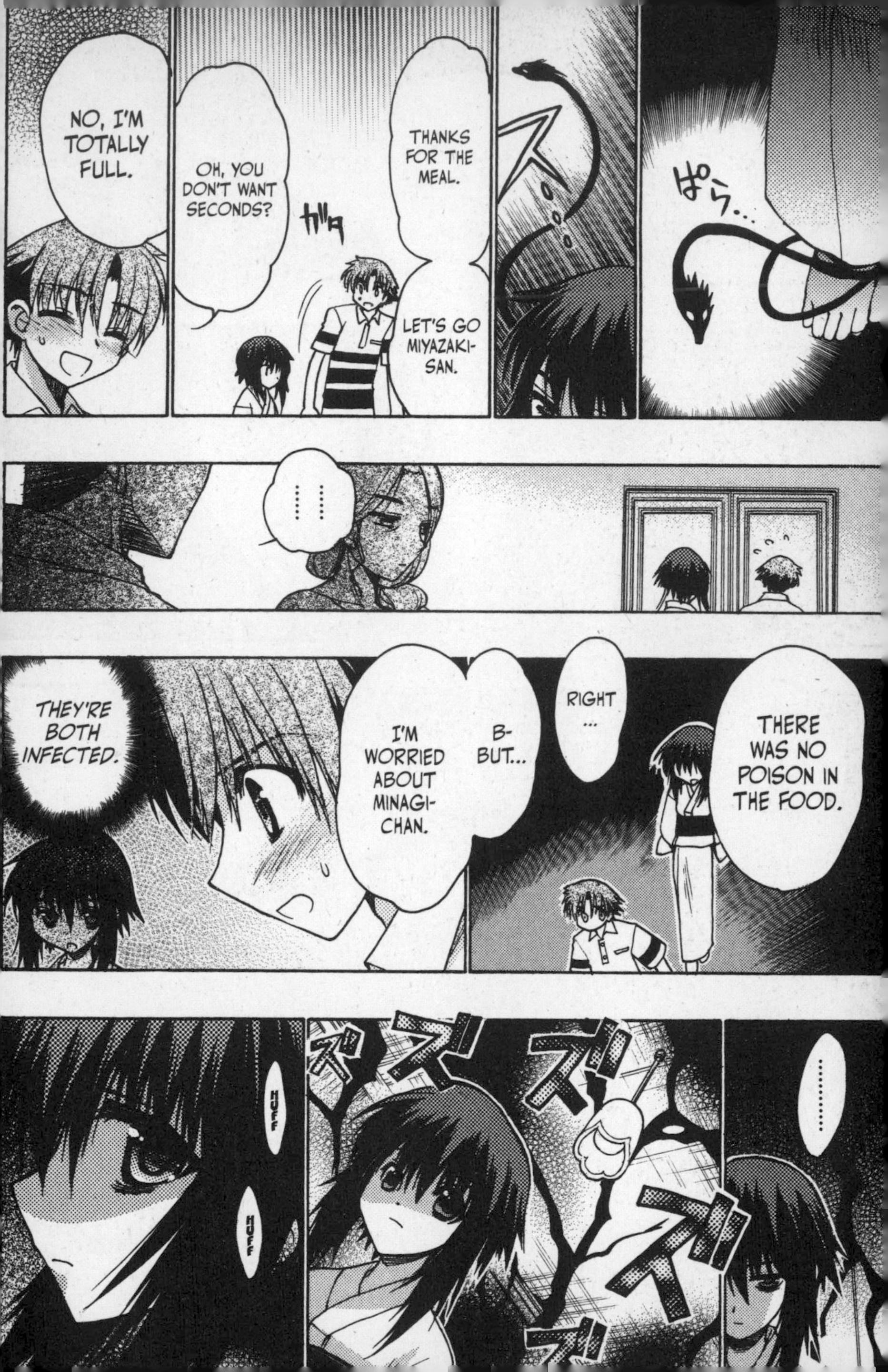
ぱら…
THANKS FOR THE MEAL.
ガタ
LET'S GO MIYAZAKI-SAN.
OH, YOU DON'T WANT SECONDS?
NO, I'M TOTALLY FULL.
……
THERE WAS NO POISON IN THE FOOD.
RIGHT ...
B- BUT...
I'M WORRIED ABOUT MINAGI-CHAN.
THEY'RE BOTH INFECTED.
....
HUFF
HUFF

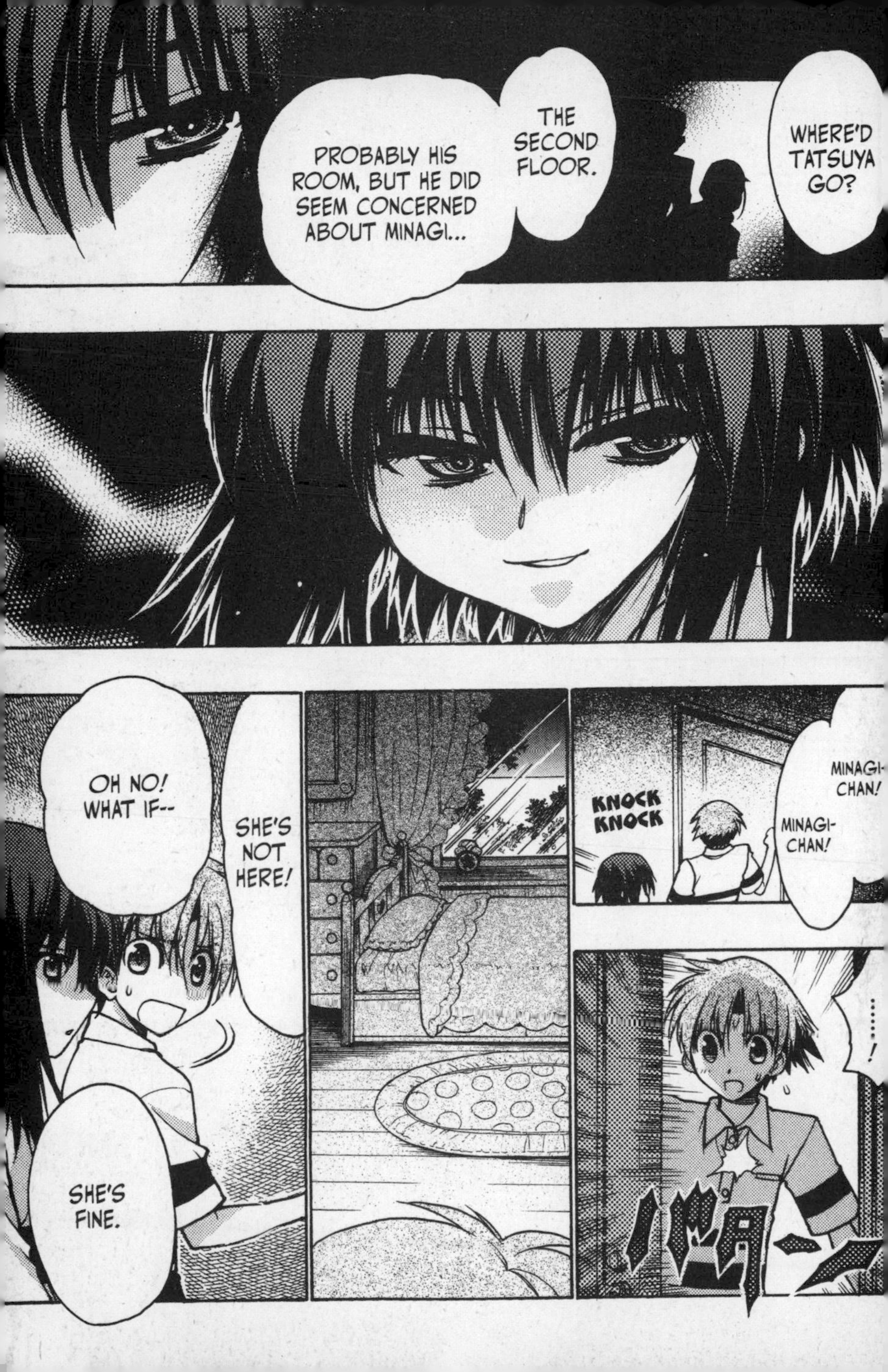
WHERE'D TATSUYA GO?
THE SECOND FLOOR.
PROBABLY HIS ROOM, BUT HE DID SEEM CONCERNED ABOUT MINAGI...
MINAGI-CHAN!
MINAGI-CHAN!
KNOCK KNOCK
......!
SHE'S NOT HERE!
OH NO! WHAT IF--
SHE'S FINE.

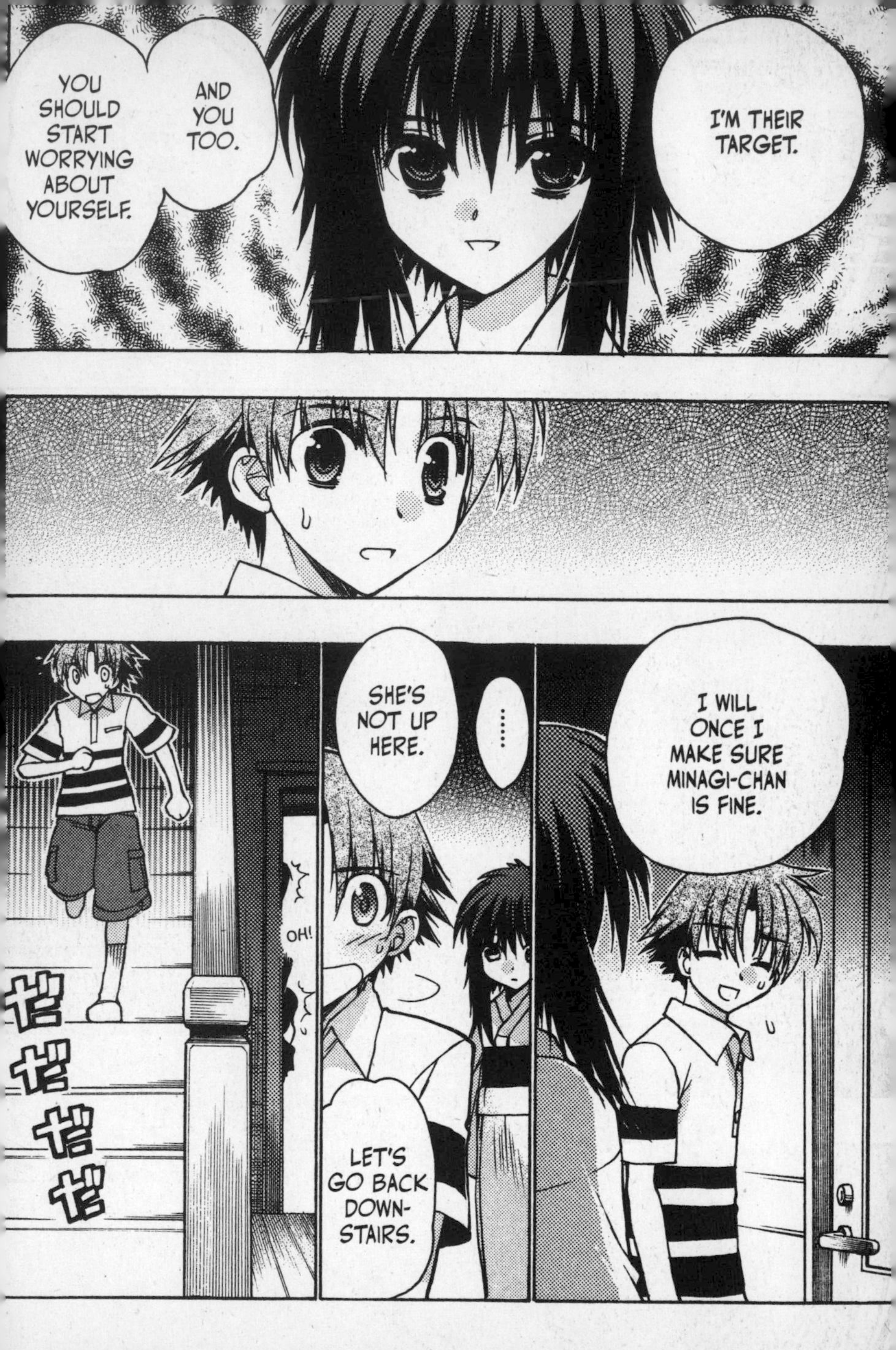
I'M THEIR TARGET.
AND YOU TOO.
YOU SHOULD START WORRYING ABOUT YOURSELF.
I WILL ONCE I MAKE SURE MINAGI-CHAN IS FINE.
......
SHE'S NOT UP HERE.
LET'S GO BACK DOWN-STAIRS.
OH!
だだだだ

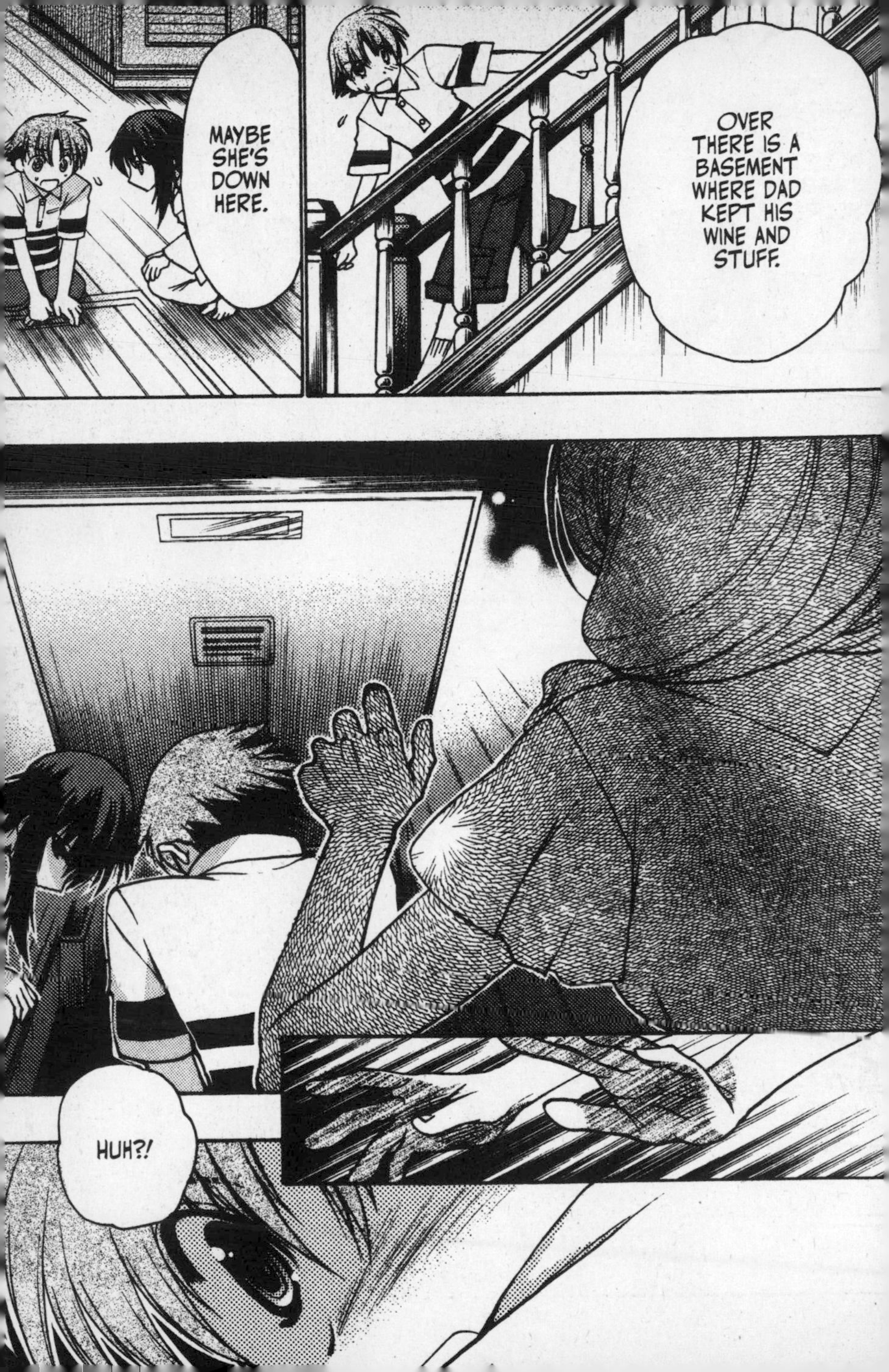
OVER THERE IS A BASEMENT WHERE DAD KEPT HIS WINE AND STUFF.
MAYBE SHE'S DOWN HERE.
HUH?!

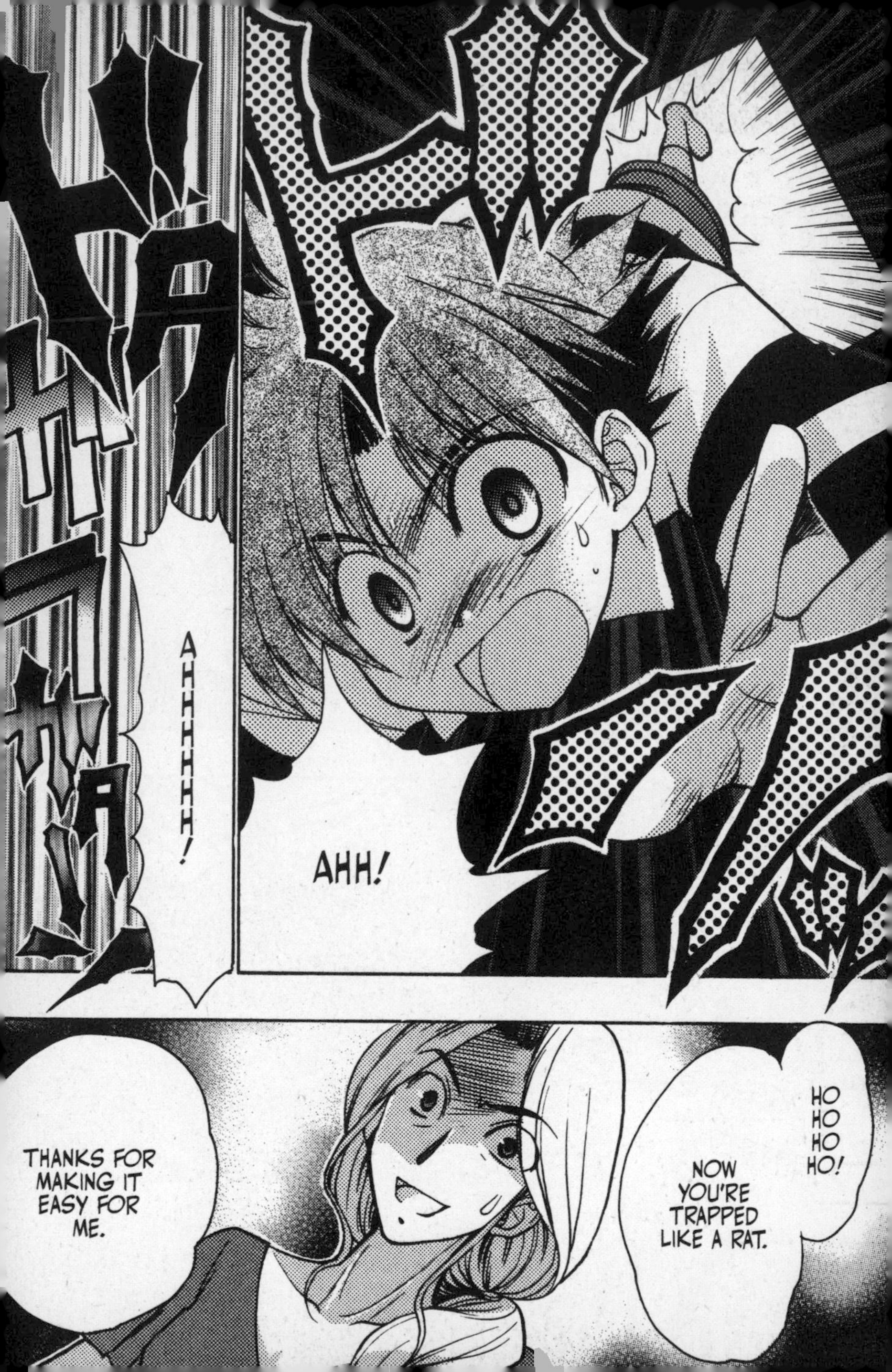
AHH!
AHHHHHHH!
HO HO HO HO!
NOW YOU'RE TRAPPED LIKE A RAT.
THANKS FOR MAKING IT EASY FOR ME.

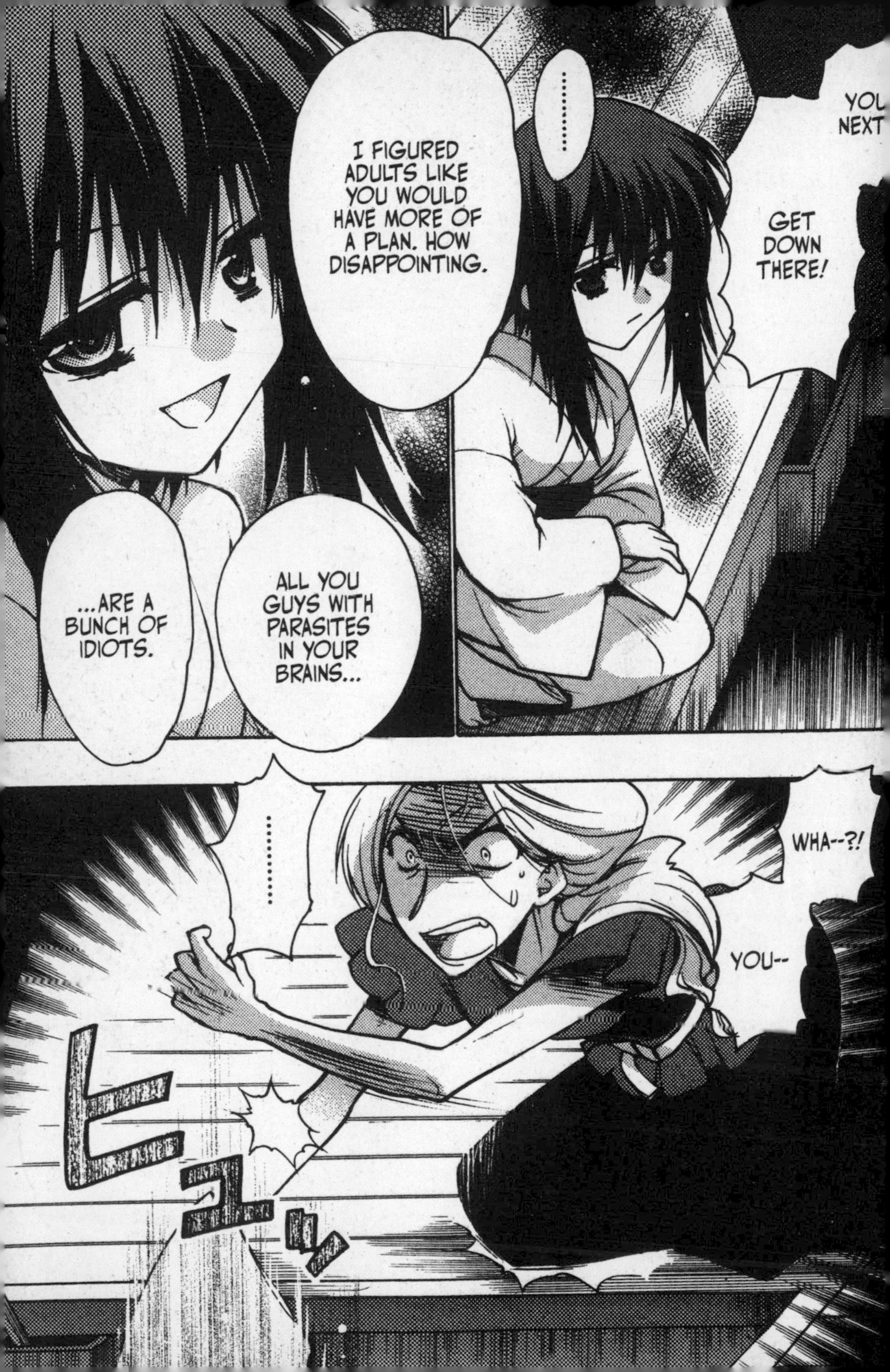

YOU NEXT
GET DOWN THERE!
......
I FIGURED ADULTS LIKE YOU WOULD HAVE MORE OF A PLAN. HOW DISAPPOINTING.
ALL YOU GUYS WITH PARASITES IN YOUR BRAINS...
...ARE A BUNCH OF IDIOTS.
WHA--?!
YOU--
......
ヒュッ

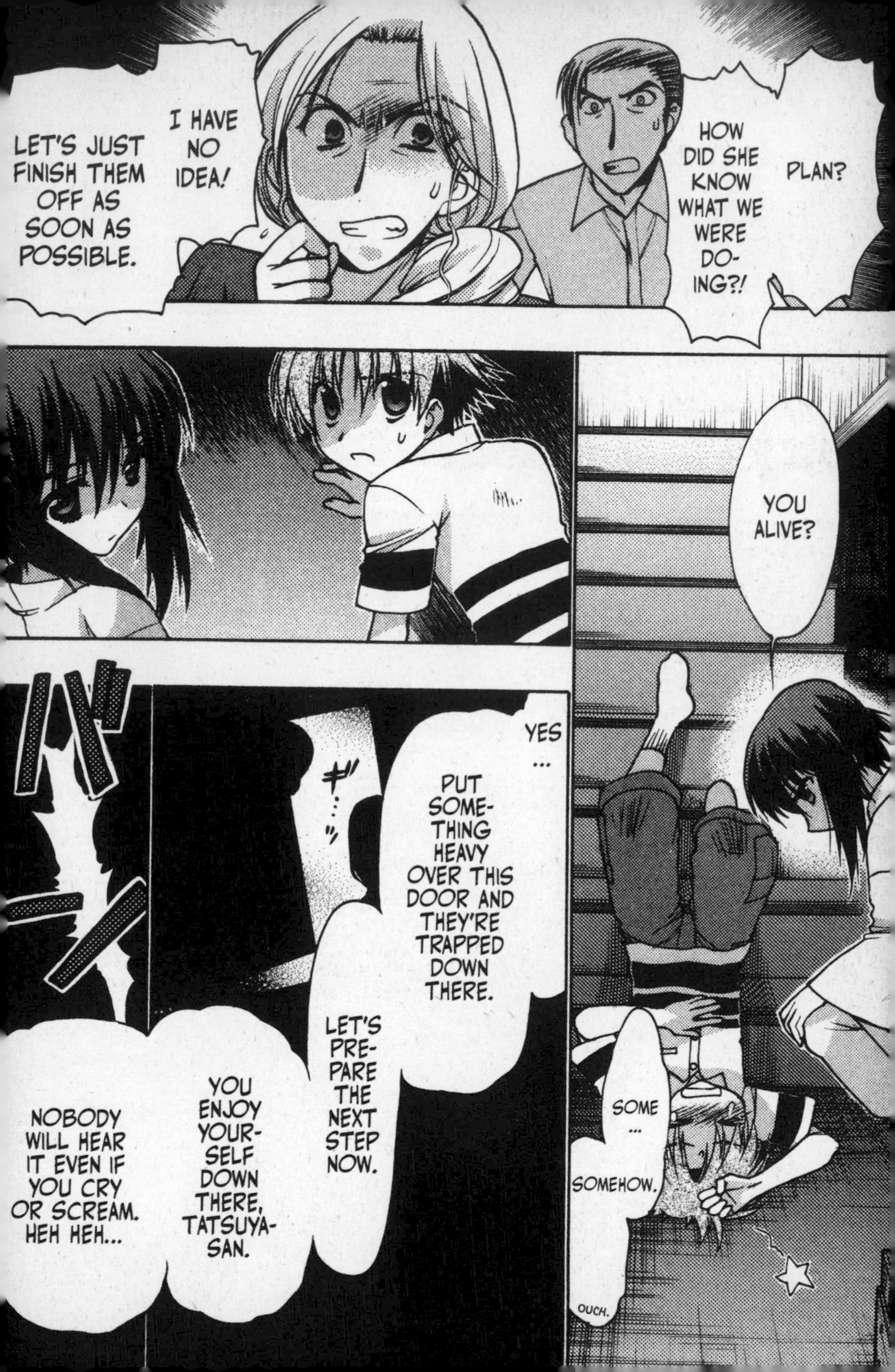
PLAN?
HOW DID SHE KNOW WHAT WE WERE DO-ING?!
I HAVE NO IDEA!
LET'S JUST FINISH THEM OFF AS SOON AS POSSIBLE.
YOU ALIVE?
SOME... SOMEHOW.
OUCH.
YES...
PUT SOME-THING HEAVY OVER THIS DOOR AND THEY'RE TRAPPED DOWN THERE.
LET'S PRE-PARE THE NEXT STEP NOW.
YOU ENJOY YOUR-SELF DOWN THERE, TATSUYA-SAN.
NOBODY WILL HEAR IT EVEN IF YOU CRY OR SCREAM. HEH HEH...

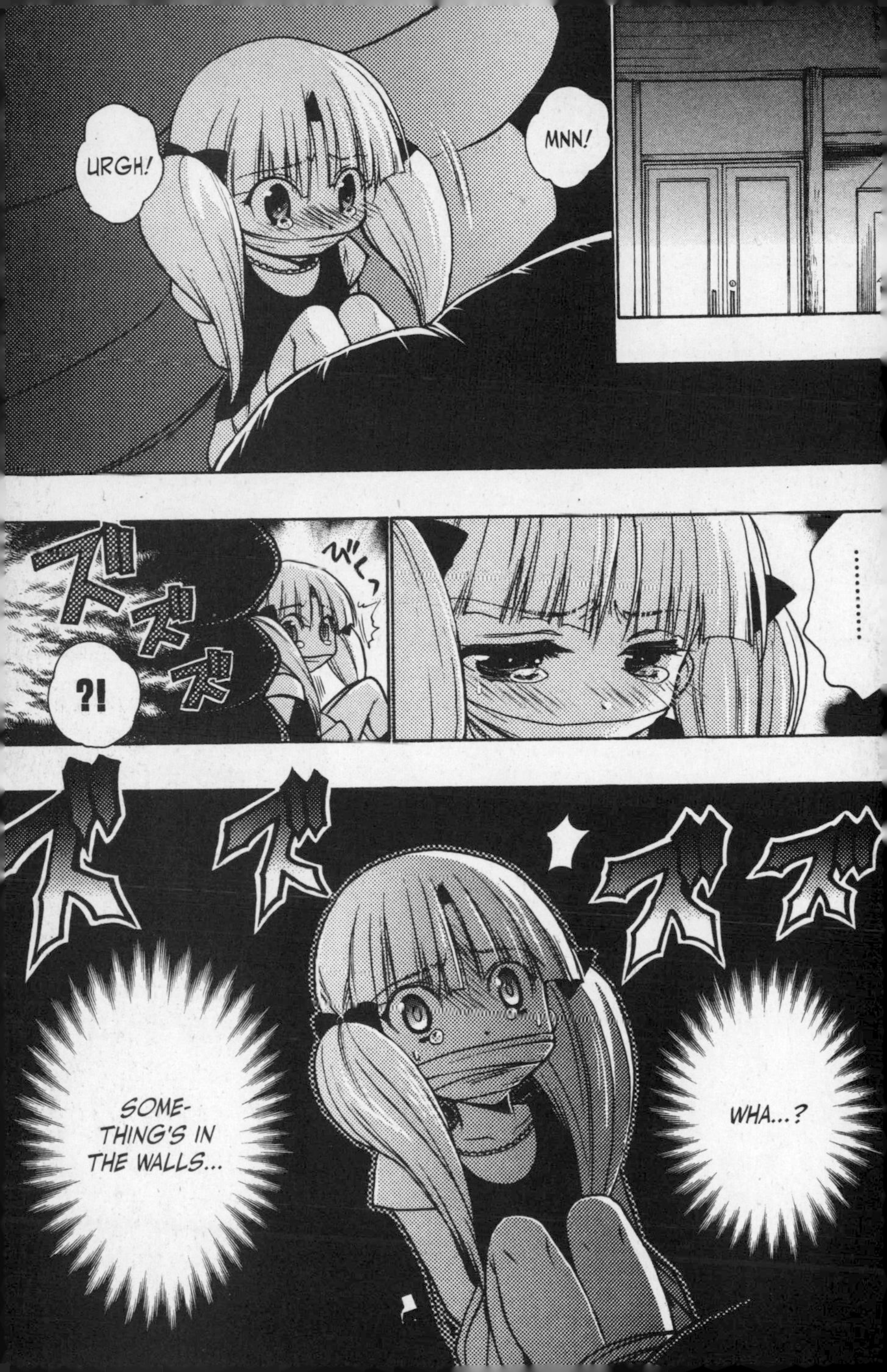
MNN!
URGH!
......
?!
WHA...?
SOME-THING'S IN THE WALLS...

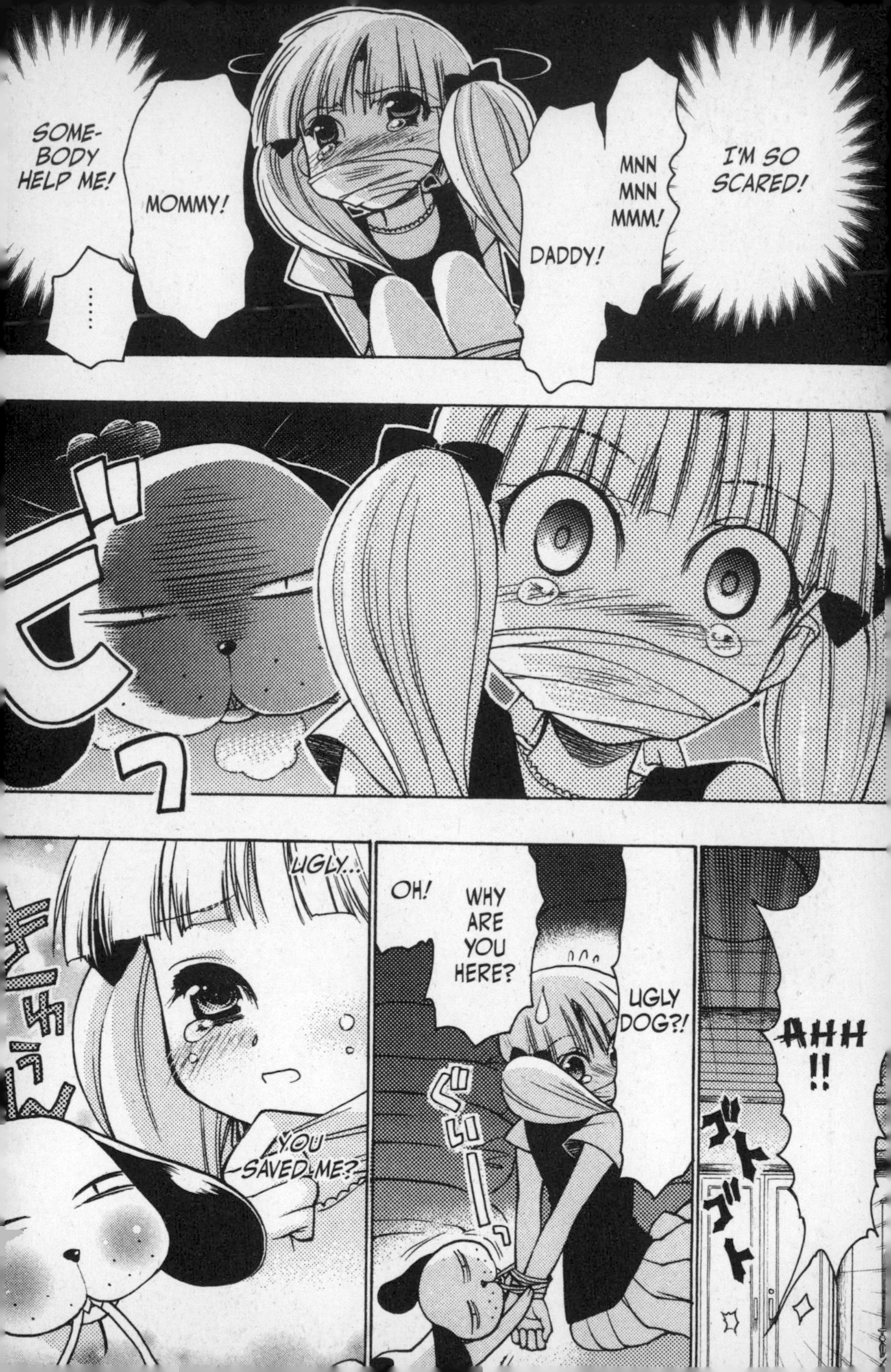
I'M SO SCARED!
MNN MNN MMM!
DADDY!
MOMMY!
SOME-BODY HELP ME!
......
AHH!!
OH!
WHY ARE YOU HERE?
UGLY DOG?!
UGLY...
YOU SAVED ME?

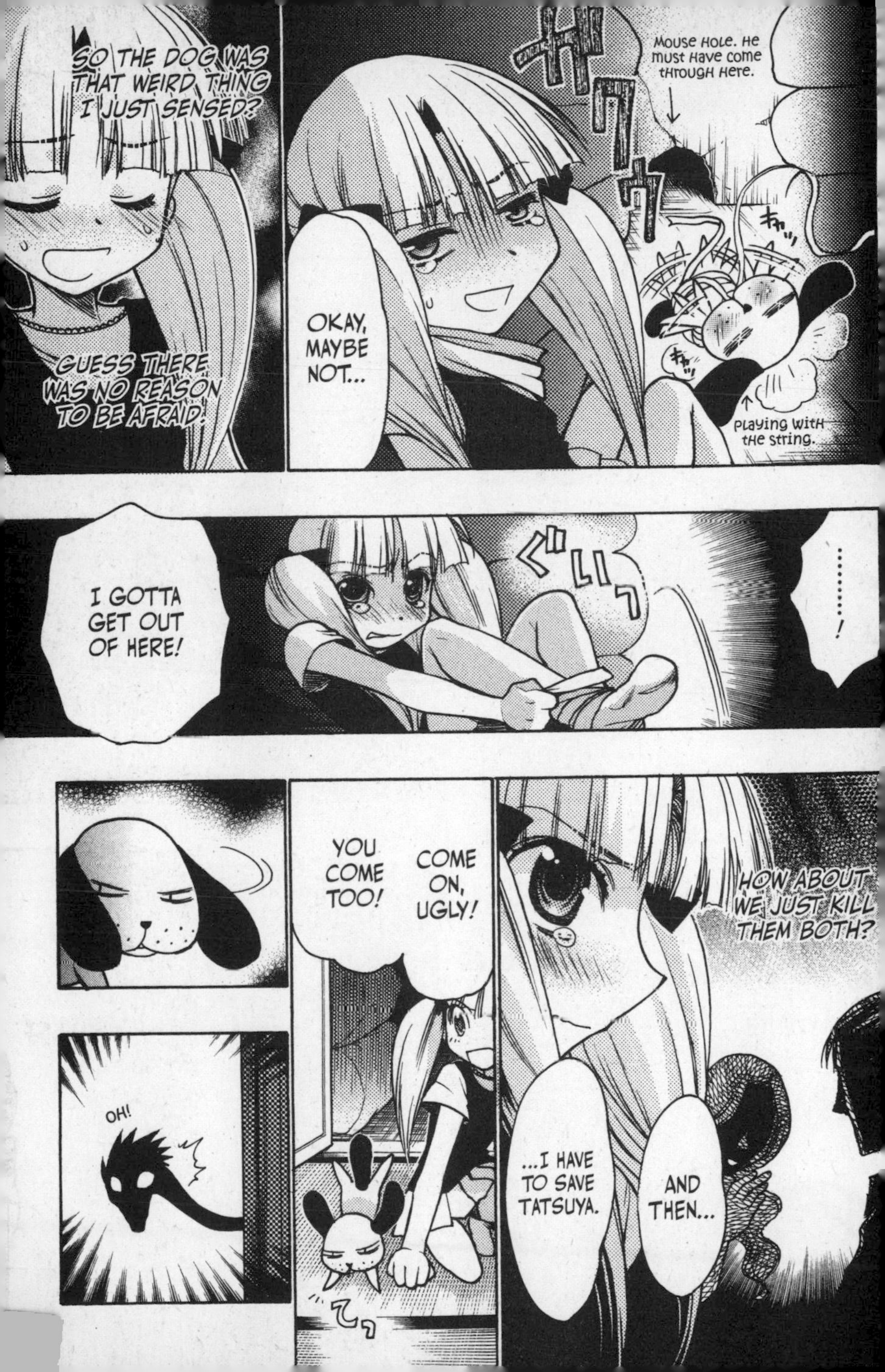
Mouse hole. He must have come through here.
Playing with the string.
OKAY, MAYBE NOT...
SO THE DOG WAS THAT WEIRD THING I JUST SENSED?
GUESS THERE WAS NO REASON TO BE AFRAID!
......!
I GOTTA GET OUT OF HERE!
HOW ABOUT WE JUST KILL THEM BOTH?
AND THEN...
...I HAVE TO SAVE TATSUYA.
COME ON, UGLY!
YOU COME TOO!
OH!

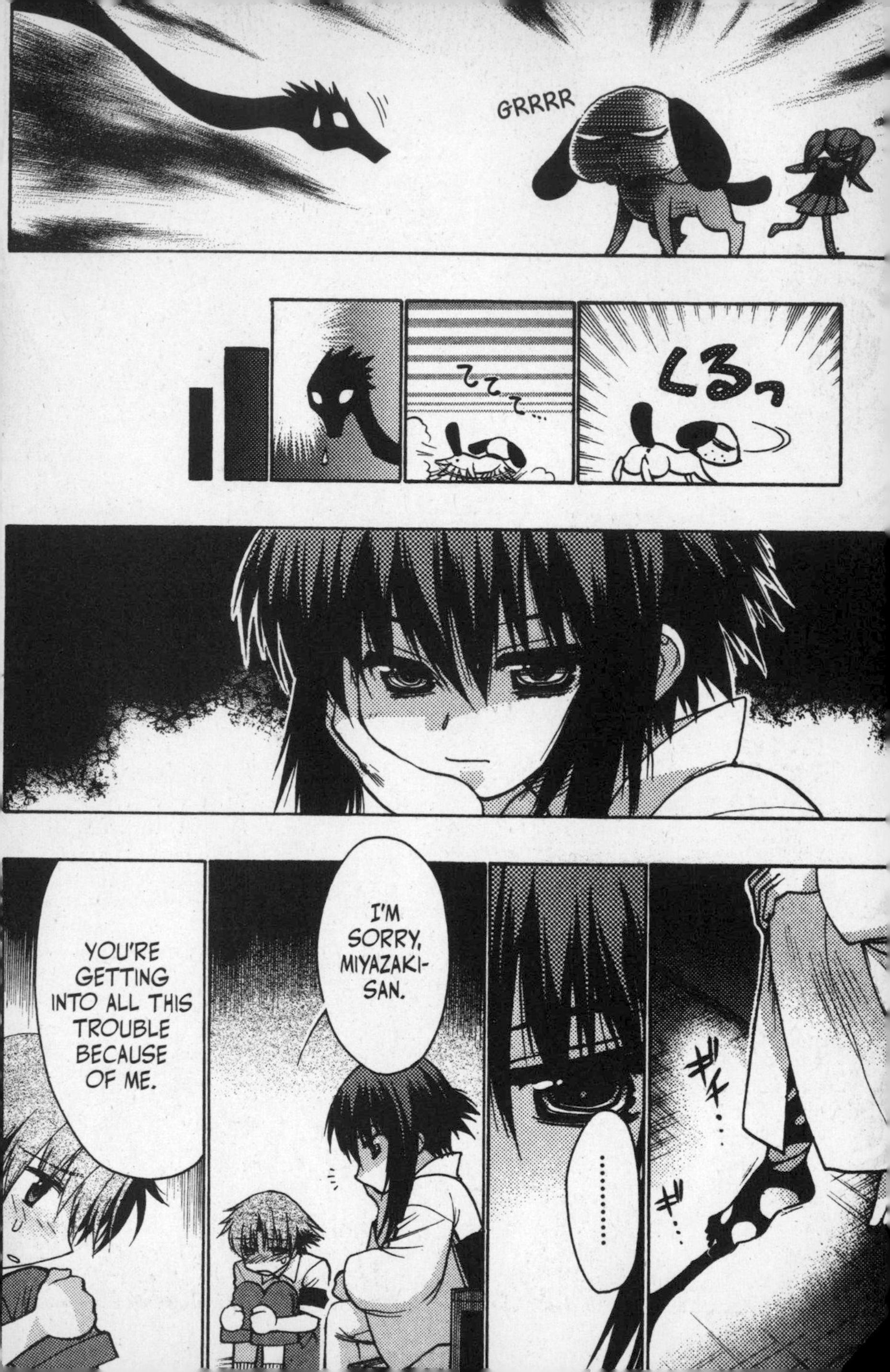
GRRRR
くるっ
ててて…
ギチ…
ギ…
……
I'M SORRY, MIYAZAKI-SAN.
YOU'RE GETTING INTO ALL THIS TROUBLE BECAUSE OF ME.

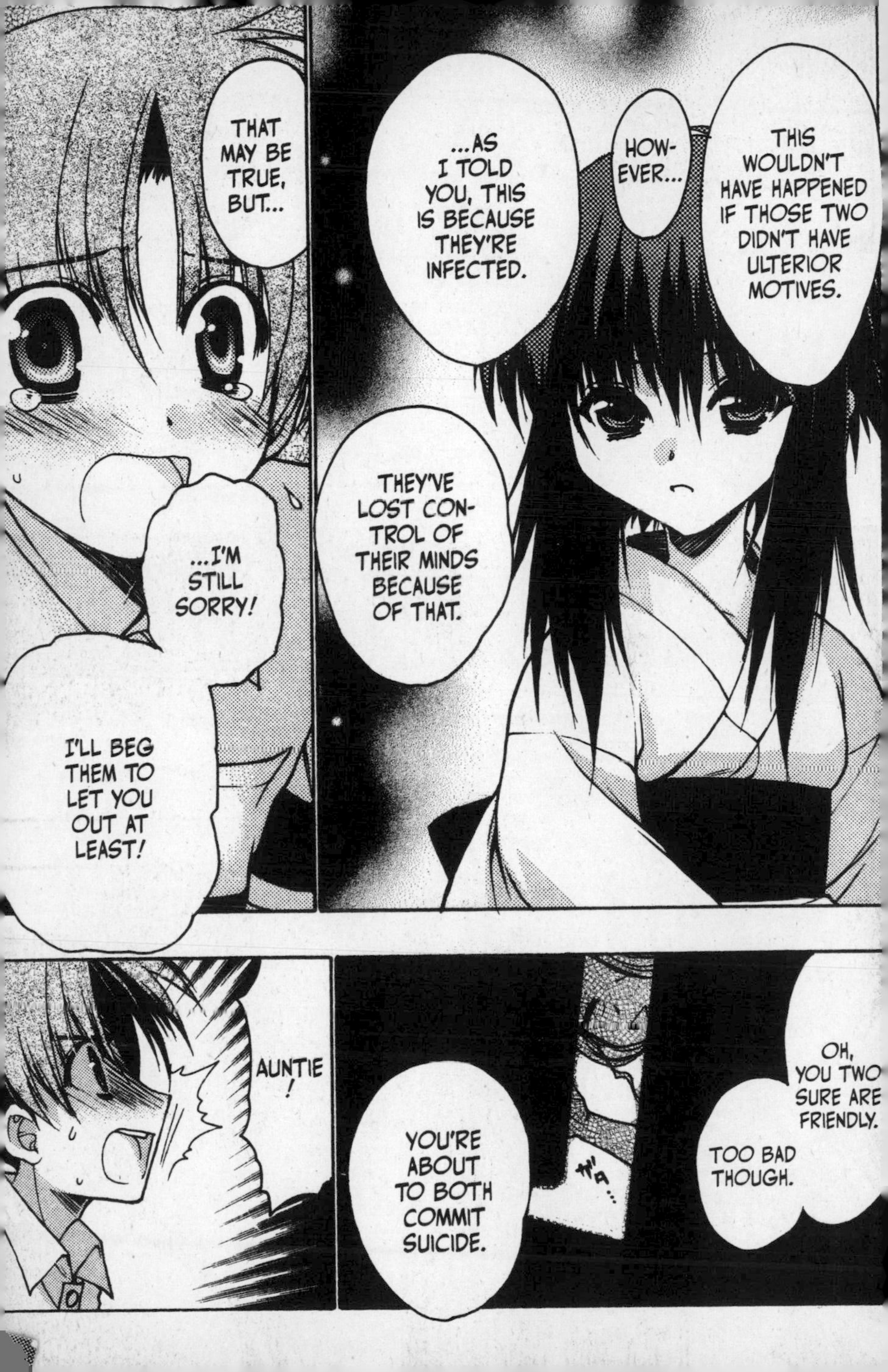

THIS WOULDN'T HAVE HAPPENED IF THOSE TWO DIDN'T HAVE ULTERIOR MOTIVES.
HOW-EVER...
...AS I TOLD YOU, THIS IS BECAUSE THEY'RE INFECTED.
THEY'VE LOST CON-TROL OF THEIR MINDS BECAUSE OF THAT.
THAT MAY BE TRUE, BUT...
...I'M STILL SORRY!
I'LL BEG THEM TO LET YOU OUT AT LEAST!
OH, YOU TWO SURE ARE FRIENDLY.
TOO BAD THOUGH.
YOU'RE ABOUT TO BOTH COMMIT SUICIDE.
AUNTIE!

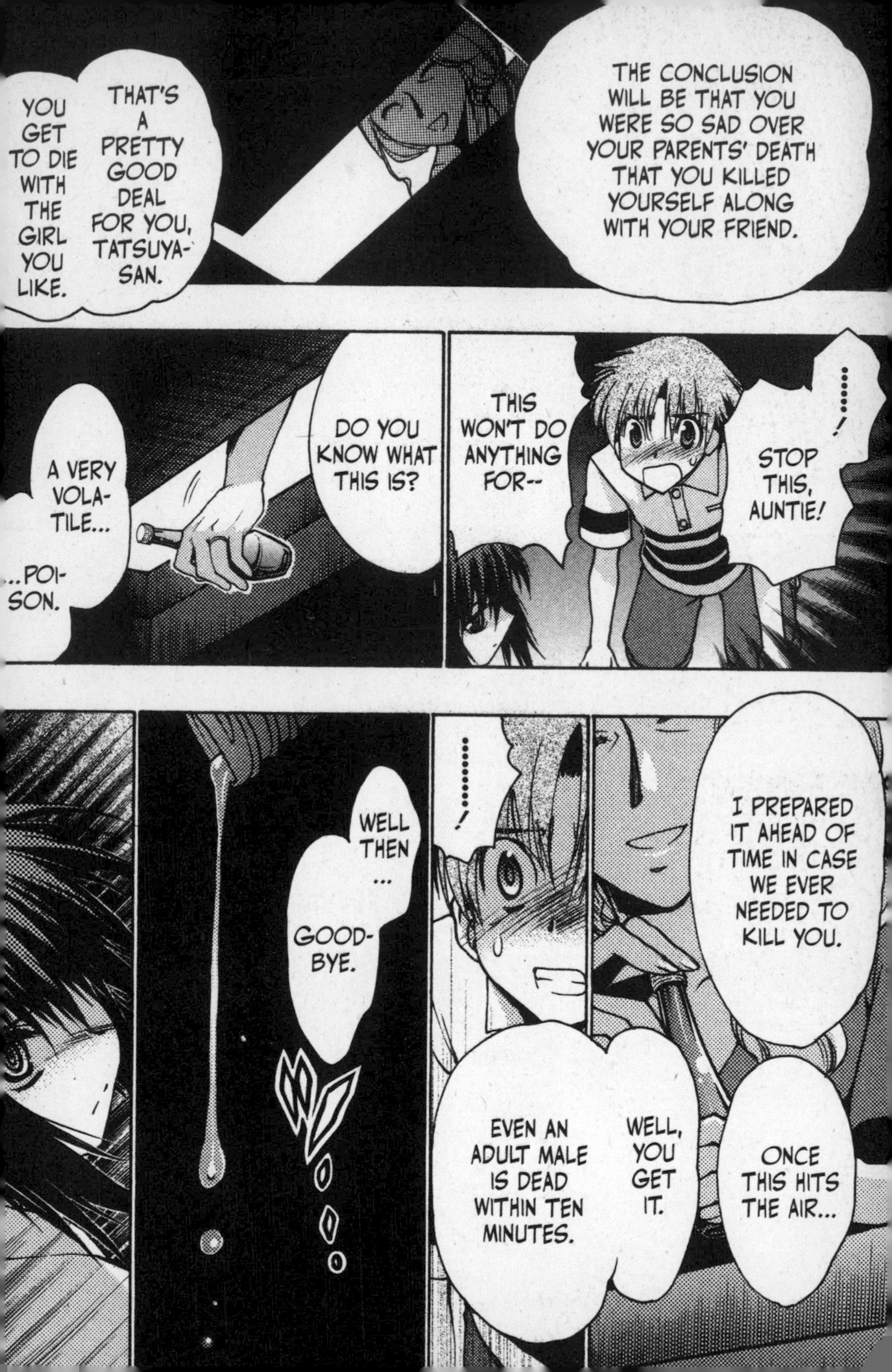
THE CONCLUSION WILL BE THAT YOU WERE SO SAD OVER YOUR PARENTS' DEATH THAT YOU KILLED YOURSELF ALONG WITH YOUR FRIEND.
THAT'S A PRETTY GOOD DEAL FOR YOU, TATSUYA-SAN.
YOU GET TO DIE WITH THE GIRL YOU LIKE.
......!
STOP THIS, AUNTIE!
THIS WON'T DO ANYTHING FOR--
DO YOU KNOW WHAT THIS IS?
A VERY VOLATILE...
...POISON.
I PREPARED IT AHEAD OF TIME IN CASE WE EVER NEEDED TO KILL YOU.
ONCE THIS HITS THE AIR...
WELL, YOU GET IT.
EVEN AN ADULT MALE IS DEAD WITHIN TEN MINUTES.
......!
WELL THEN ...
GOOD-BYE.

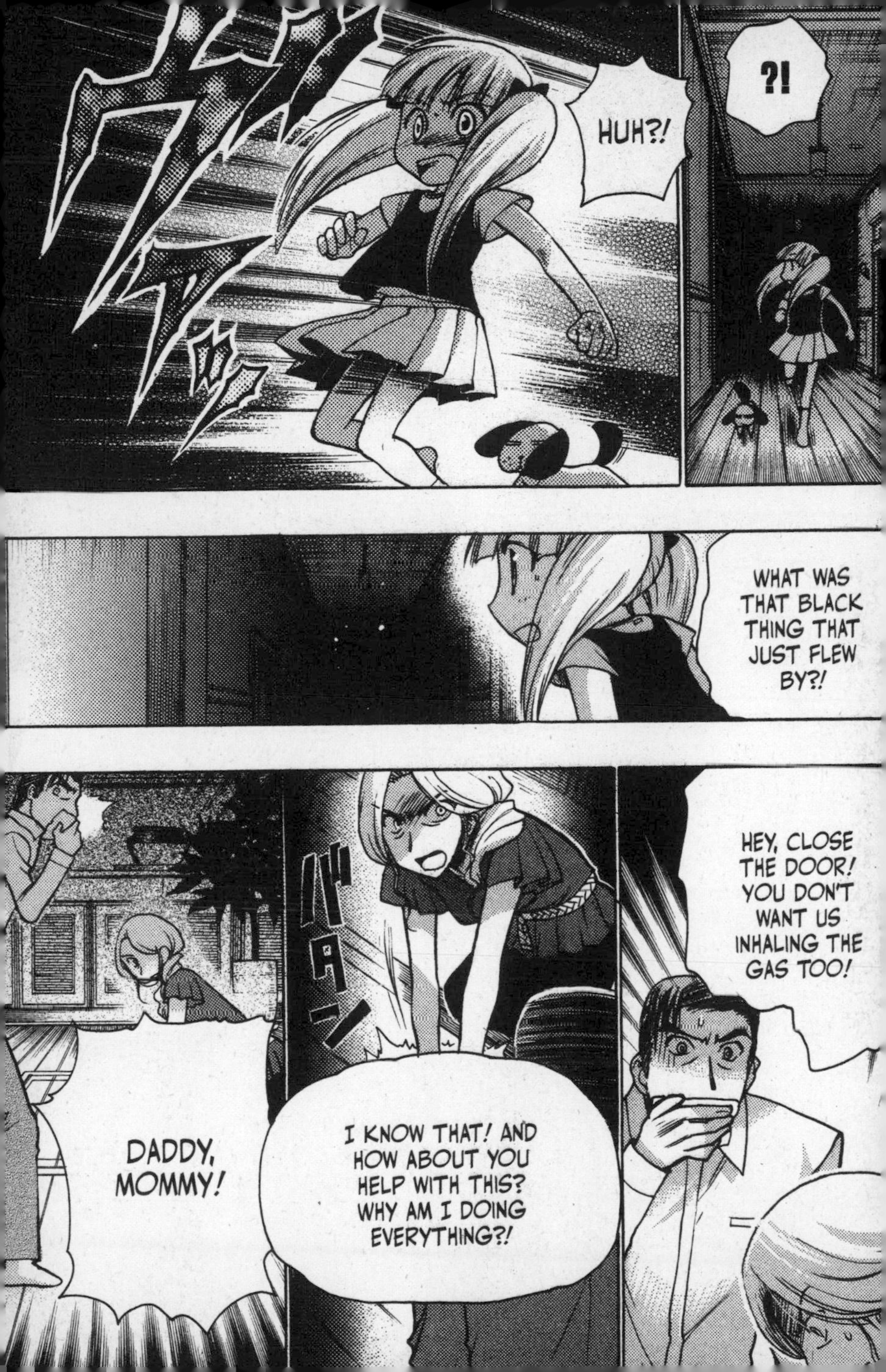
?!
HUH?!
WHAT WAS THAT BLACK THING THAT JUST FLEW BY?!
HEY, CLOSE THE DOOR! YOU DON'T WANT US INHALING THE GAS TOO!
I KNOW THAT! AND HOW ABOUT YOU HELP WITH THIS? WHY AM I DOING EVERYTHING?!
DADDY, MOMMY!

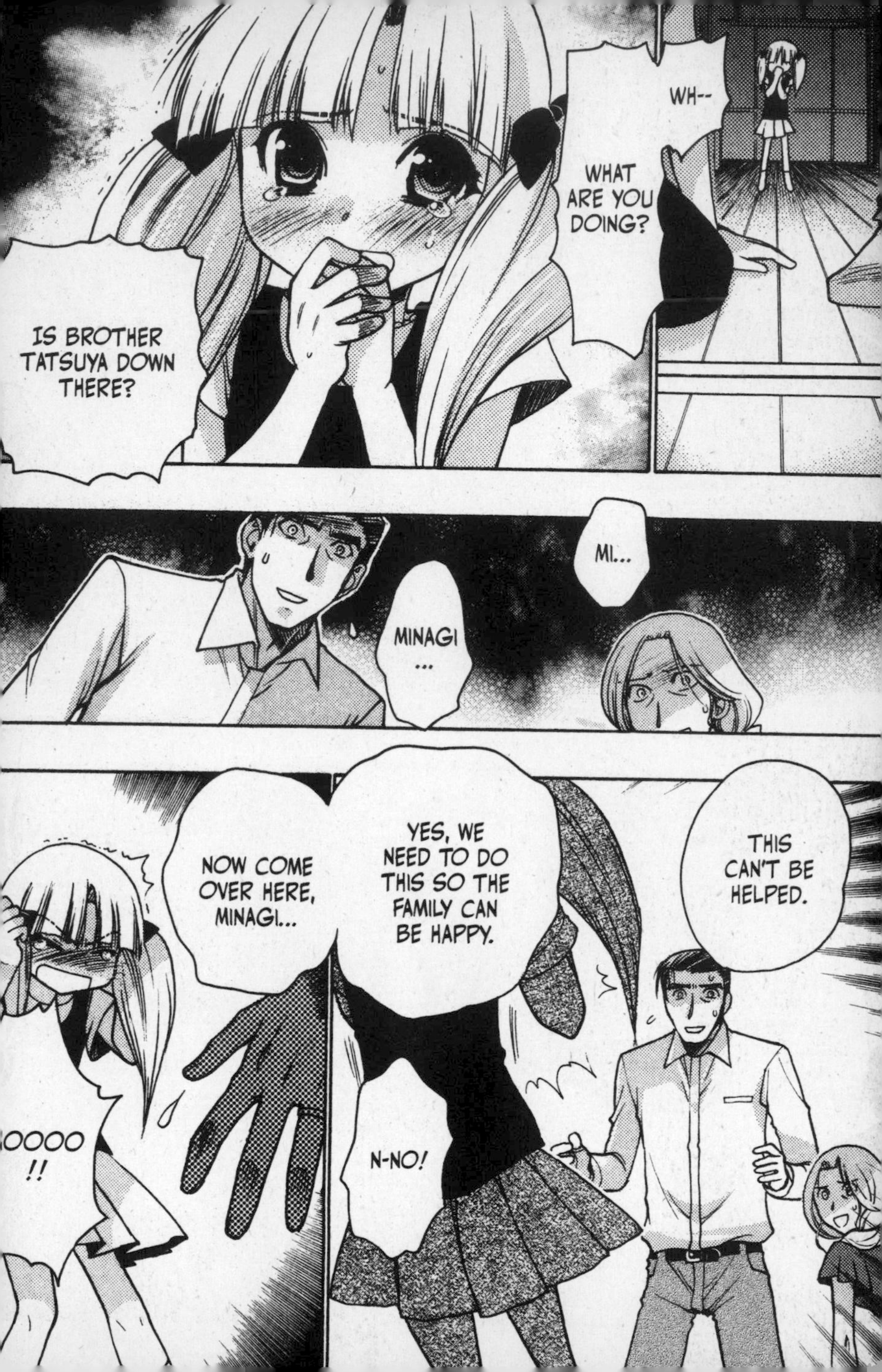
WH--
WHAT ARE YOU DOING?
IS BROTHER TATSUYA DOWN THERE?
MI...
MINAGI ...
THIS CAN'T BE HELPED.
YES, WE NEED TO DO THIS SO THE FAMILY CAN BE HAPPY.
NOW COME OVER HERE, MINAGI...
N-NO!
OOOO !!

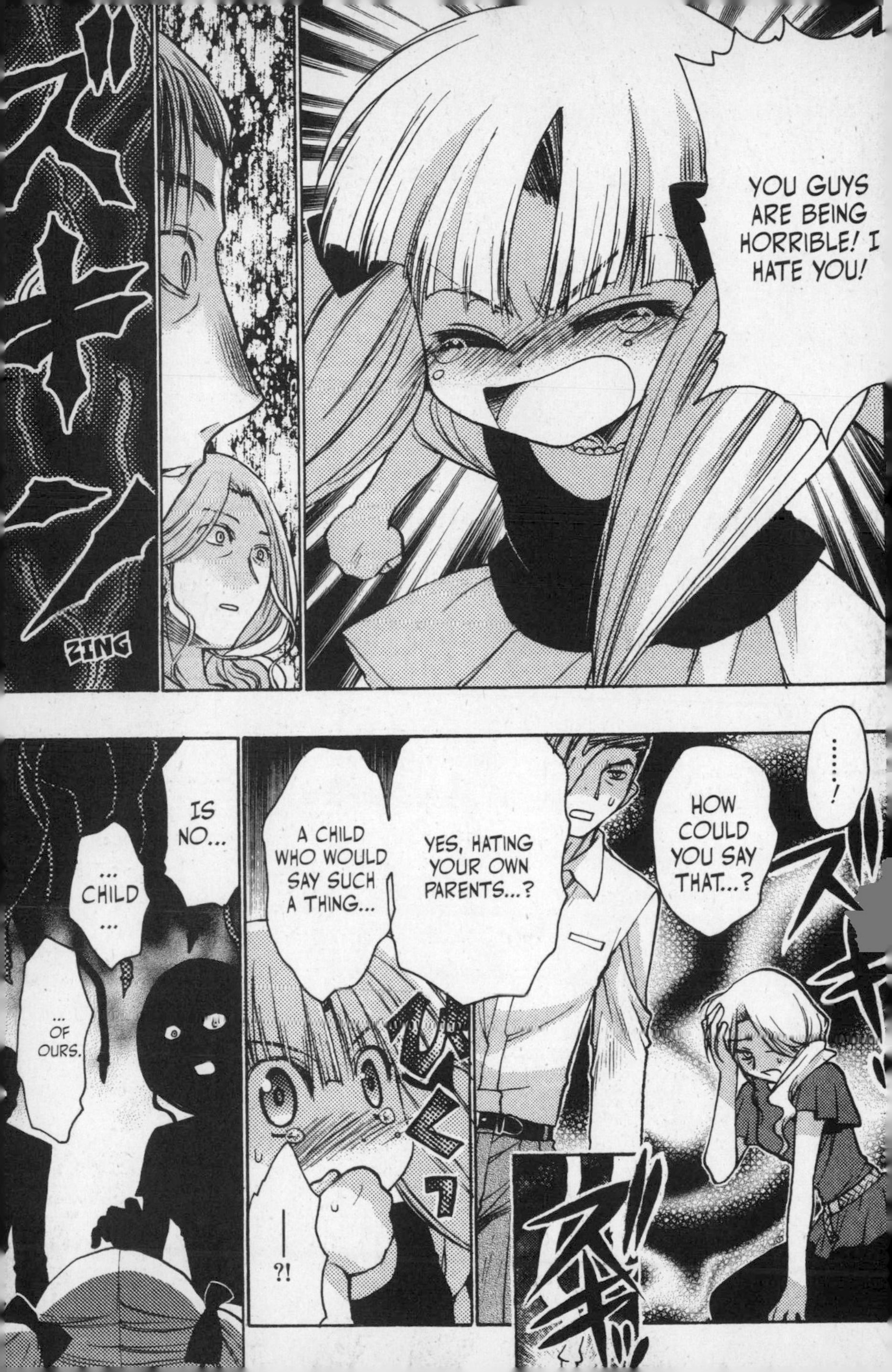
YOU GUYS ARE BEING HORRIBLE! I HATE YOU!
ZING
......!
HOW COULD YOU SAY THAT...?
YES, HATING YOUR OWN PARENTS...?
A CHILD WHO WOULD SAY SUCH A THING...
—?!
IS NO...
...CHILD...
...OF OURS.

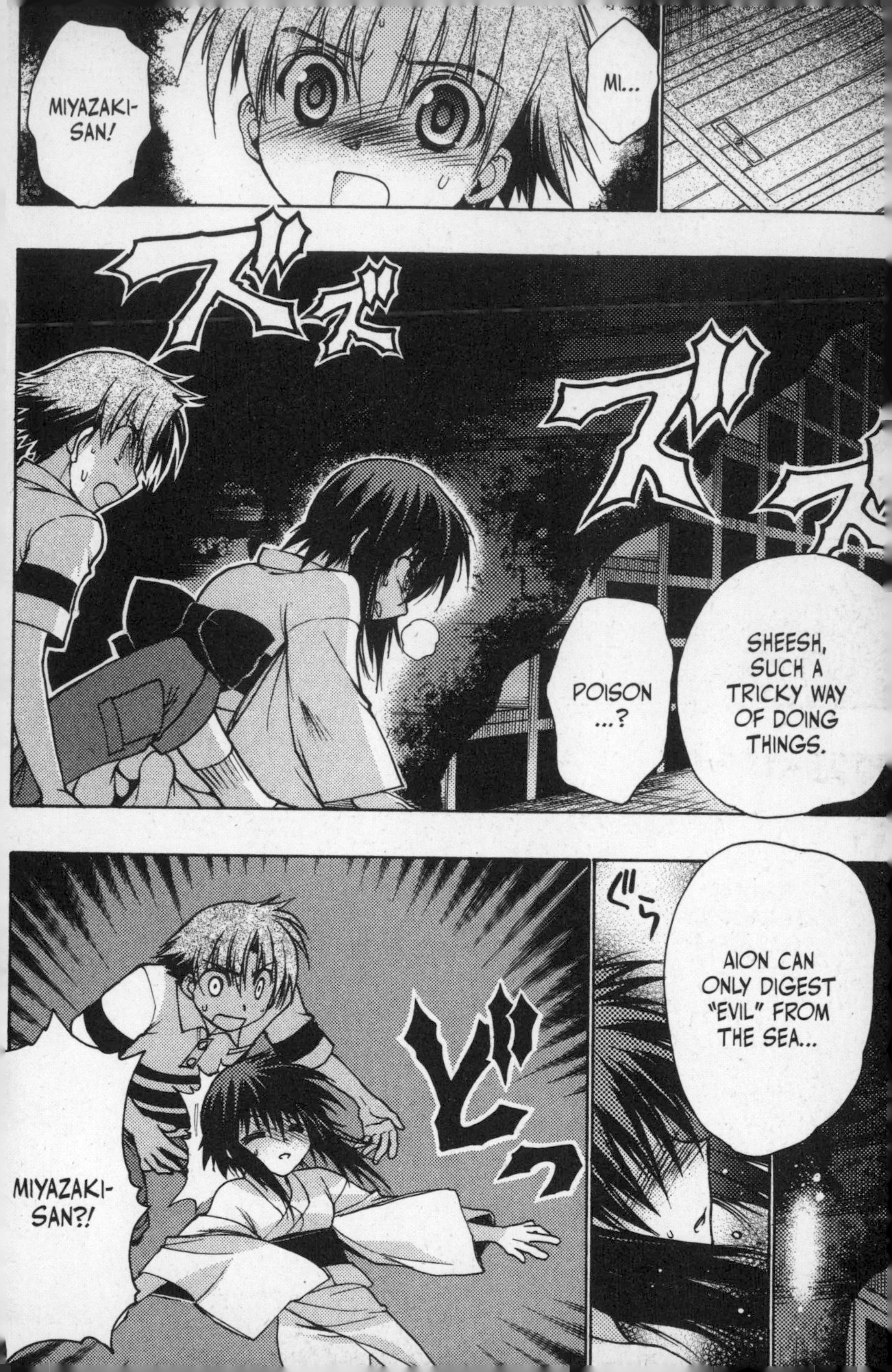
MI...
MIYAZAKI-SAN!
SHEESH, SUCH A TRICKY WAY OF DOING THINGS.
POISON ...?
AION CAN ONLY DIGEST "EVIL" FROM THE SEA...
MIYAZAKI-SAN?!

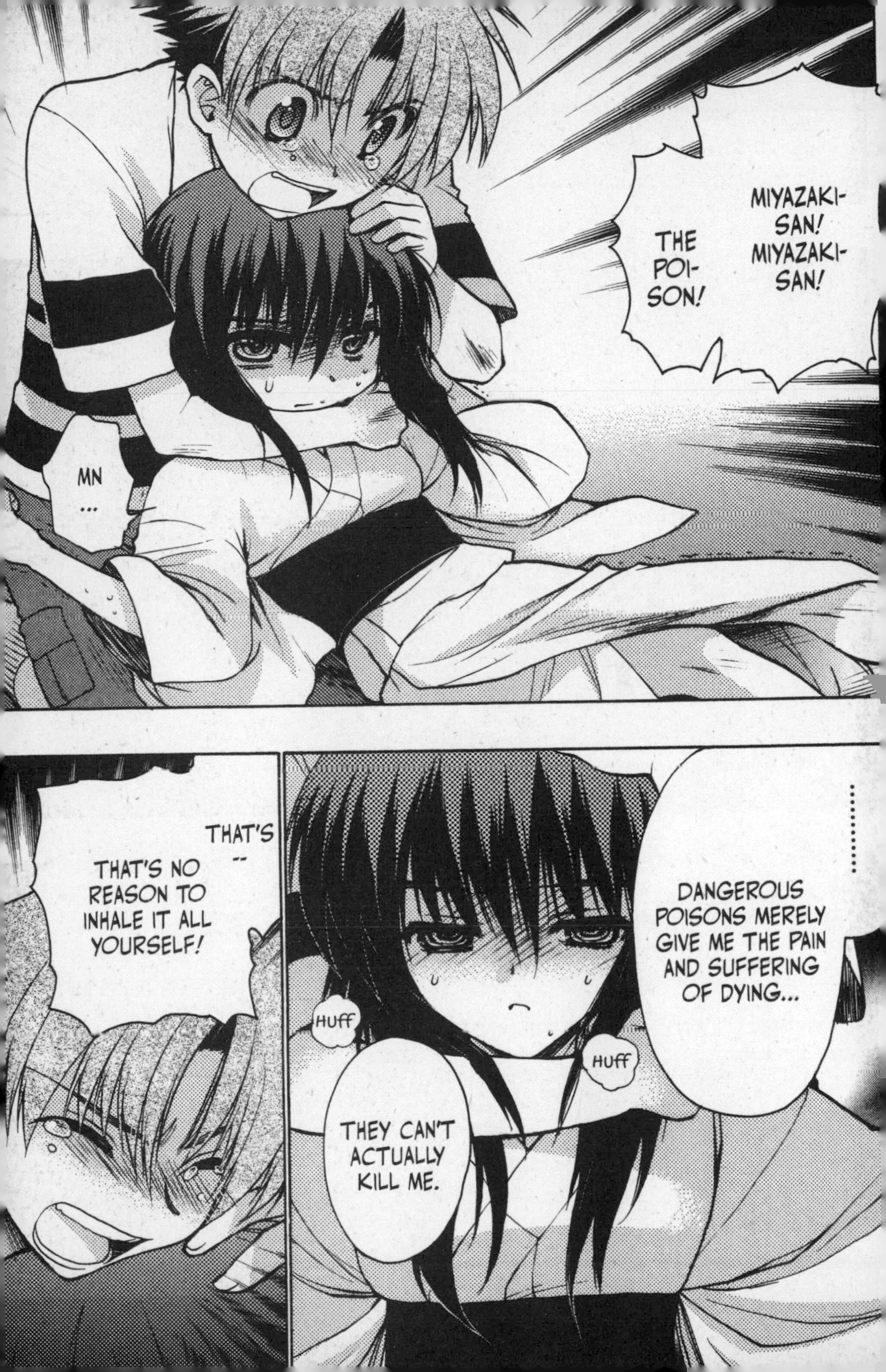
MIYAZAKI-SAN! MIYAZAKI-SAN!
THE POI-SON!
MN ...
DANGEROUS POISONS MERELY GIVE ME THE PAIN AND SUFFERING OF DYING...
HUFF
HUFF
THEY CAN'T ACTUALLY KILL ME.
THAT'S --
THAT'S NO REASON TO INHALE IT ALL YOURSELF!

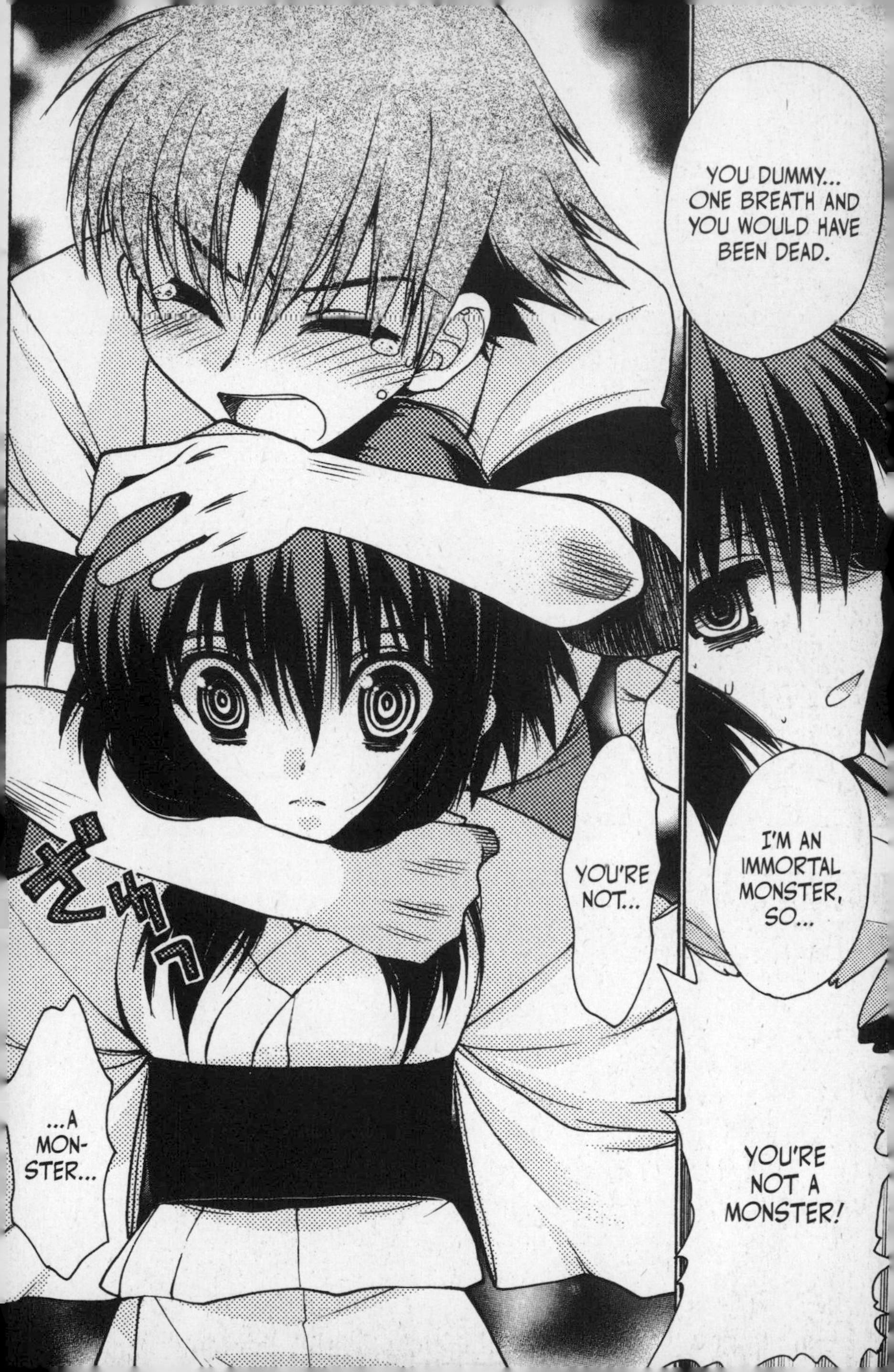
YOU DUMMY... ONE BREATH AND YOU WOULD HAVE BEEN DEAD.
I'M AN IMMORTAL MONSTER, SO...
YOU'RE NOT...
...A MON-STER...
YOU'RE NOT A MONSTER!

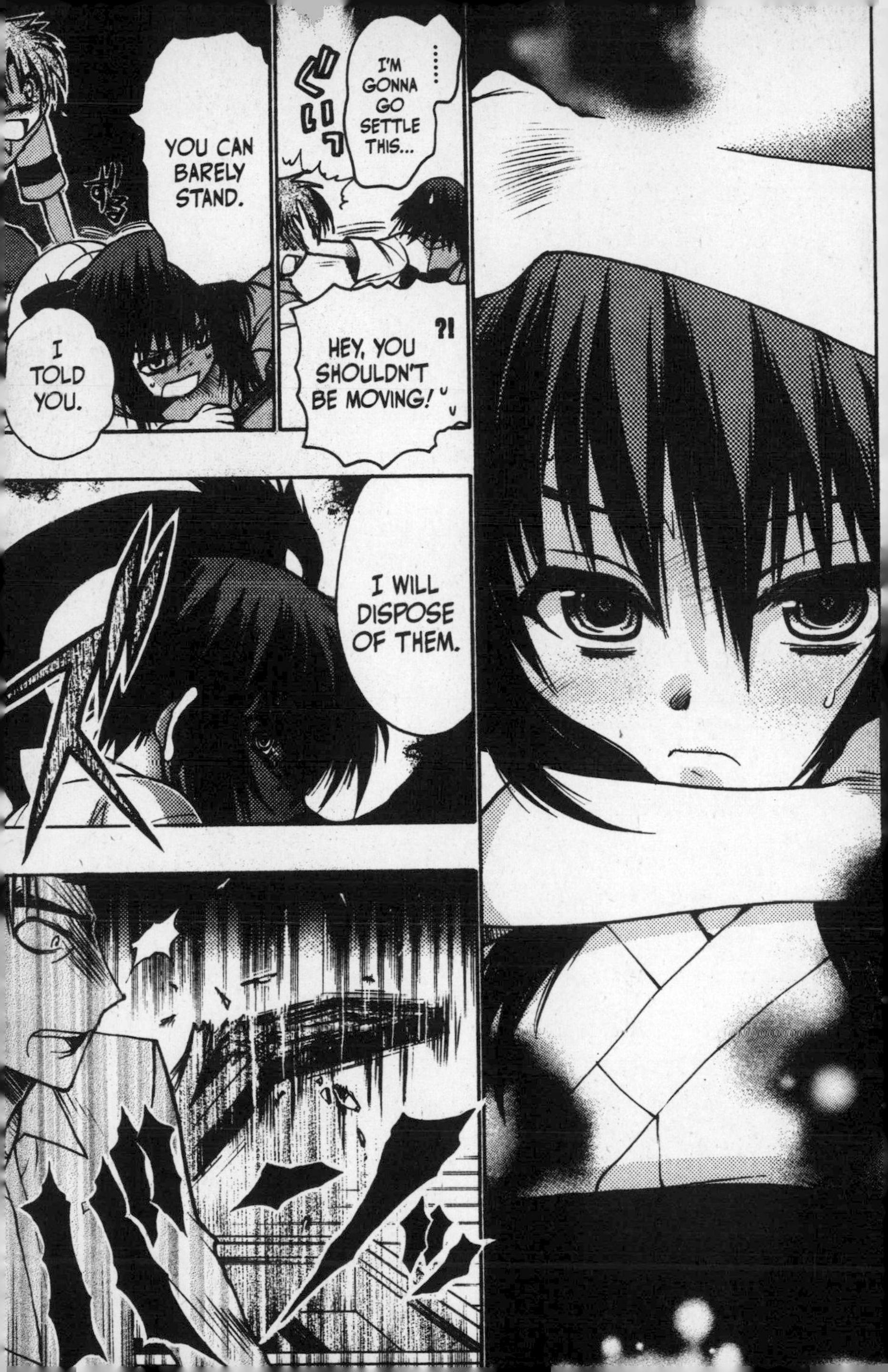
……
I'M GONNA GO SETTLE THIS...
?!
HEY, YOU SHOULDN'T BE MOVING!
YOU CAN BARELY STAND.
I TOLD YOU.
I WILL DISPOSE OF THEM.

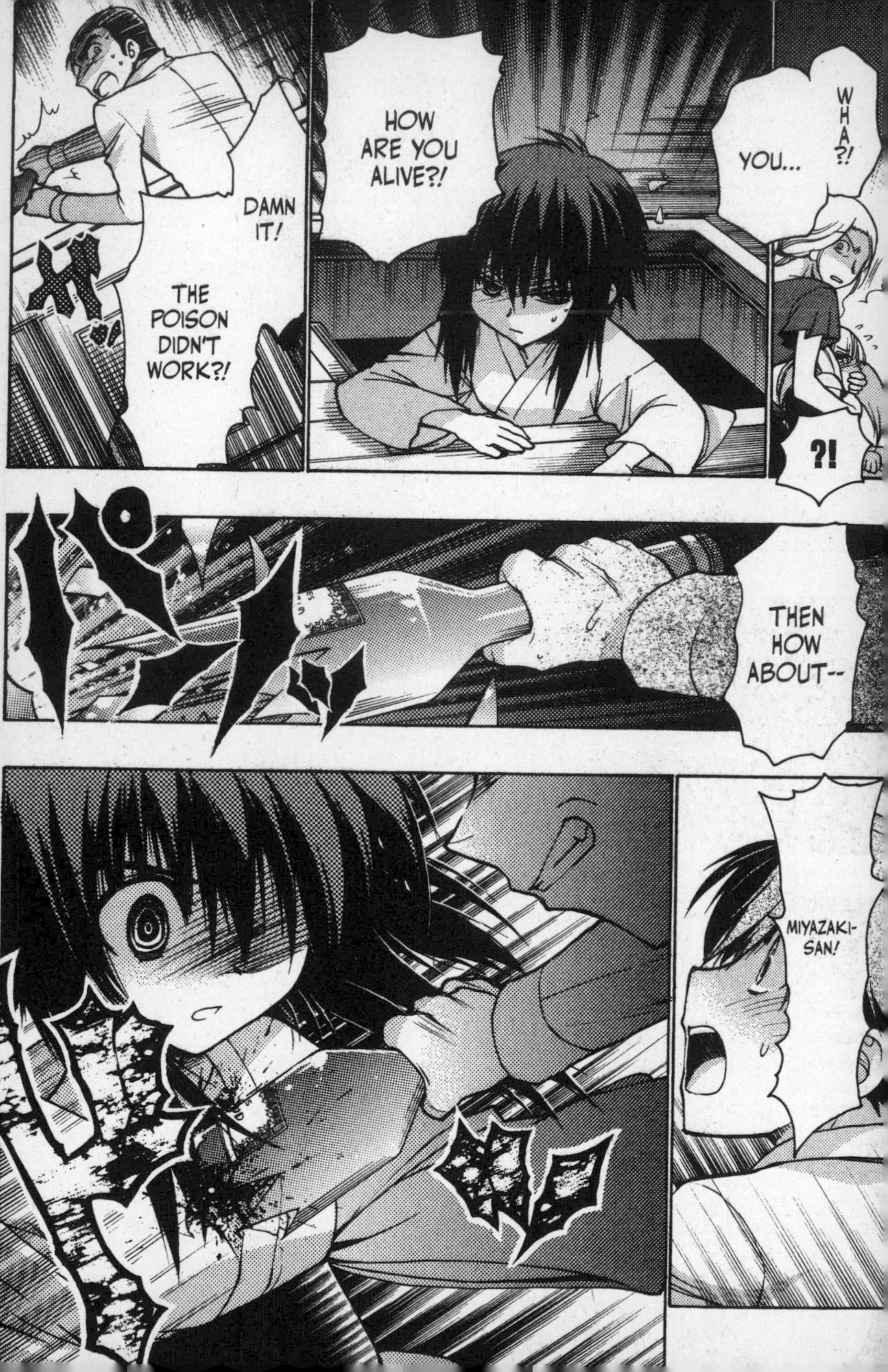
WHA?!
YOU...
?!
HOW ARE YOU ALIVE?!
DAMN IT!
THE POISON DIDN'T WORK?!
THEN HOW ABOUT--
MIYAZAKI-SAN!

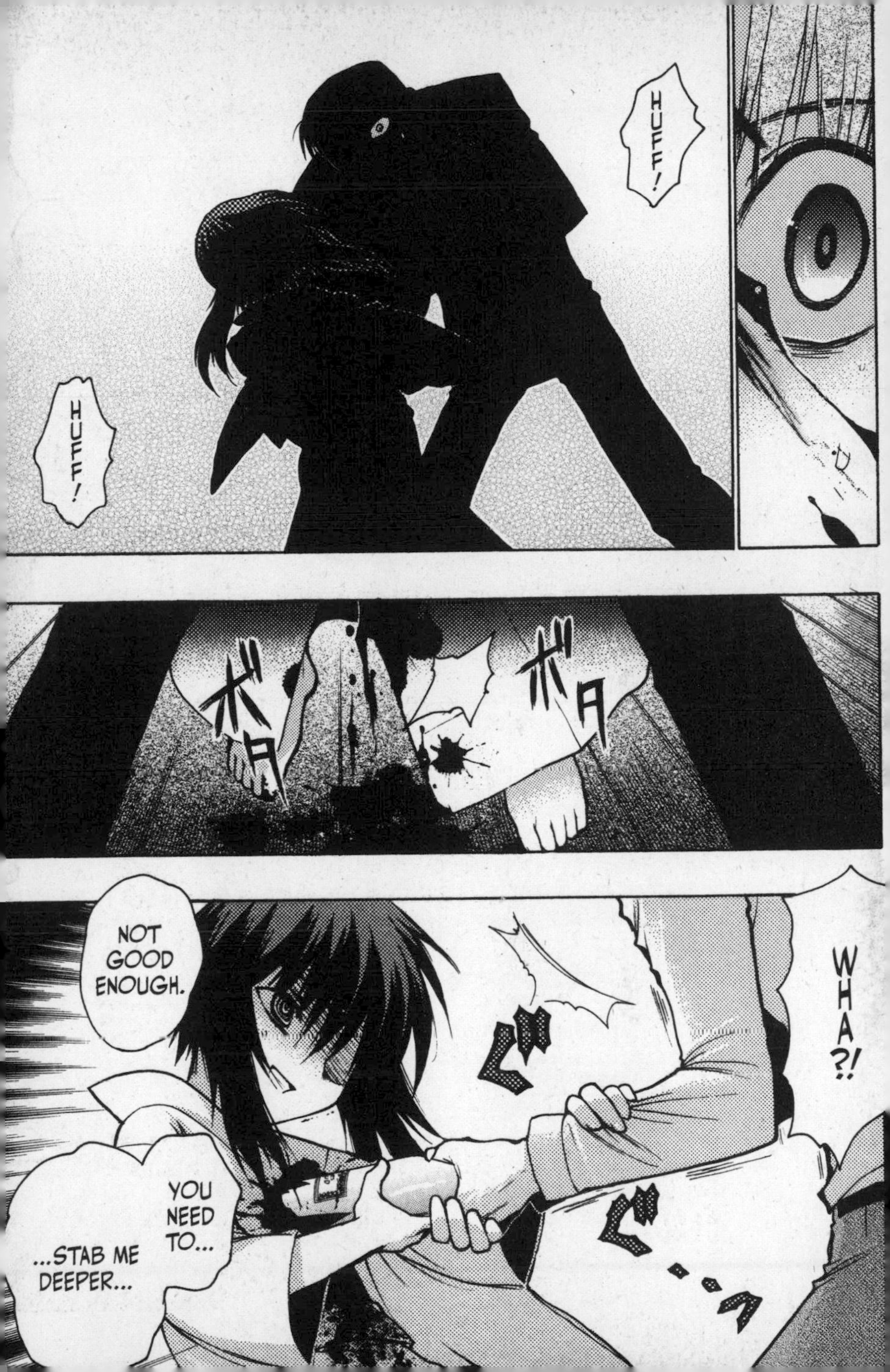
HUFF!
HUFF!
ボタ
ボタ
WHA?!
ぐ
NOT GOOD ENOUGH.
YOU NEED TO...
...STAB ME DEEPER...

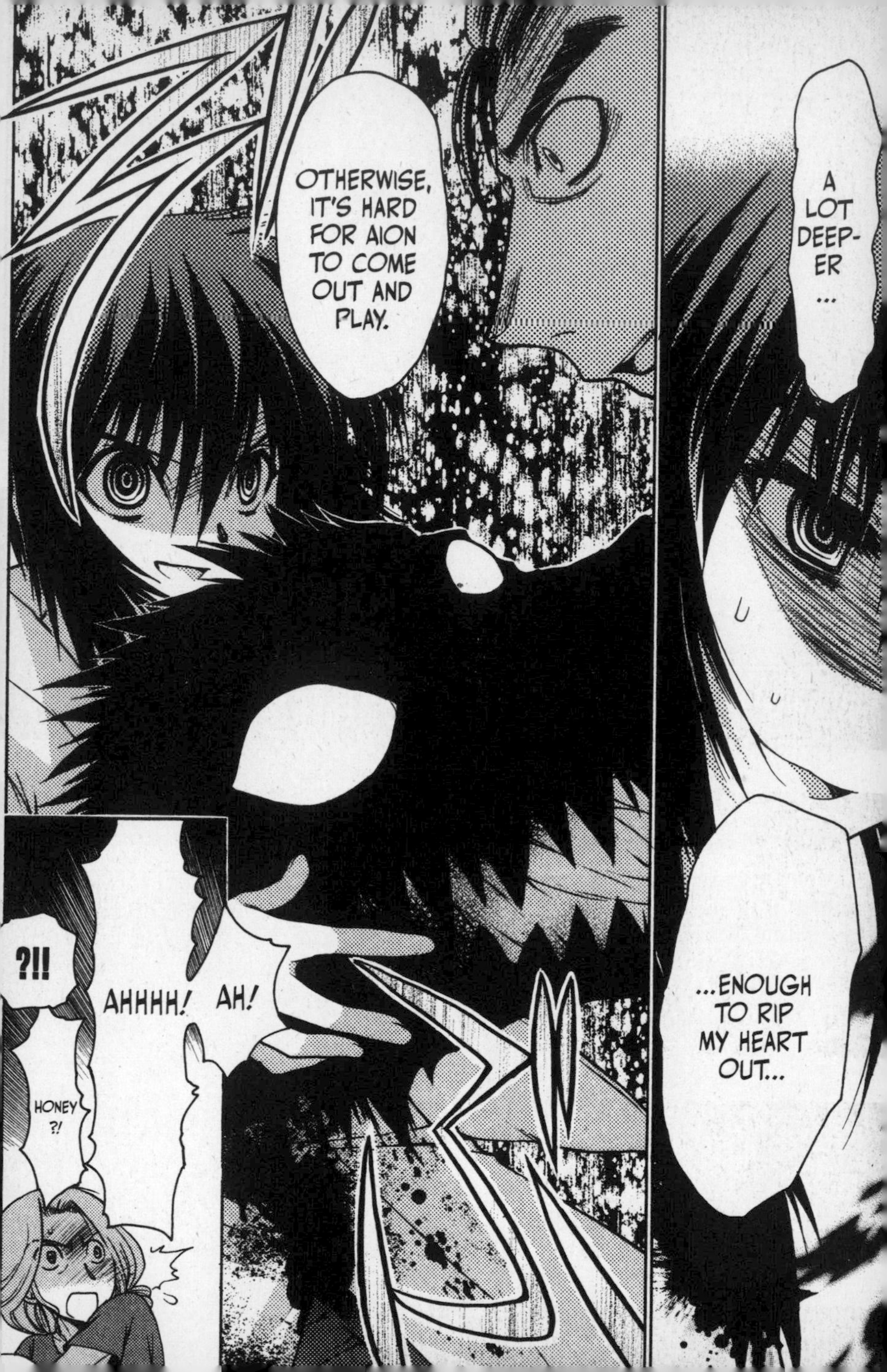

A LOT DEEPER-ER ...
...ENOUGH TO RIP MY HEART OUT...
OTHERWISE, IT'S HARD FOR AION TO COME OUT AND PLAY.
AH!
AHHHH!
?!!
HONEY ?!

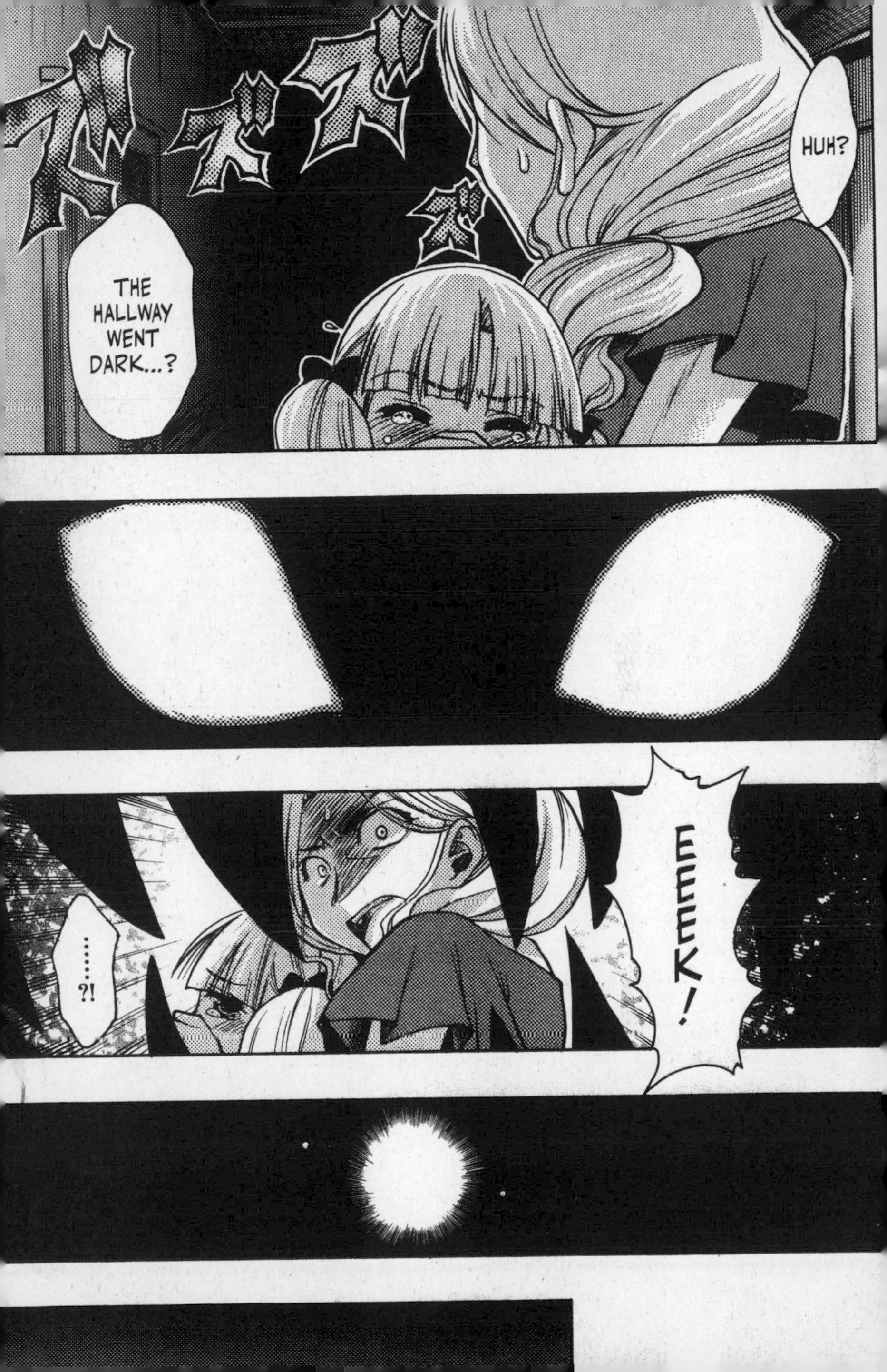
HUH?
THE HALLWAY WENT DARK...?
EEEK!
......?!

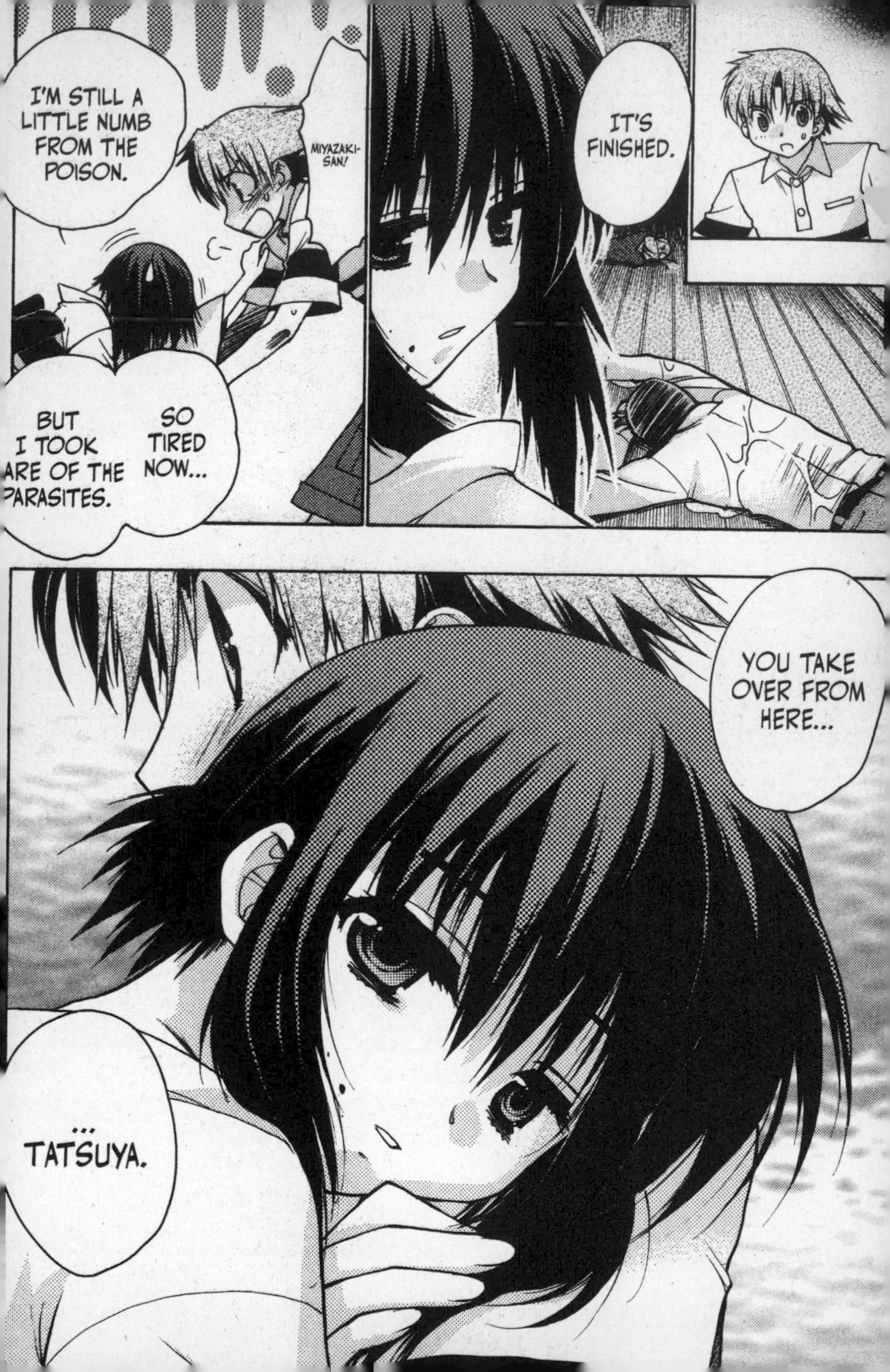
IT'S FINISHED.
MIYAZAKI-SAN!
I'M STILL A LITTLE NUMB FROM THE POISON.
SO TIRED NOW...
BUT I TOOK ARE OF THE PARASITES.
YOU TAKE OVER FROM HERE...
... TATSUYA.

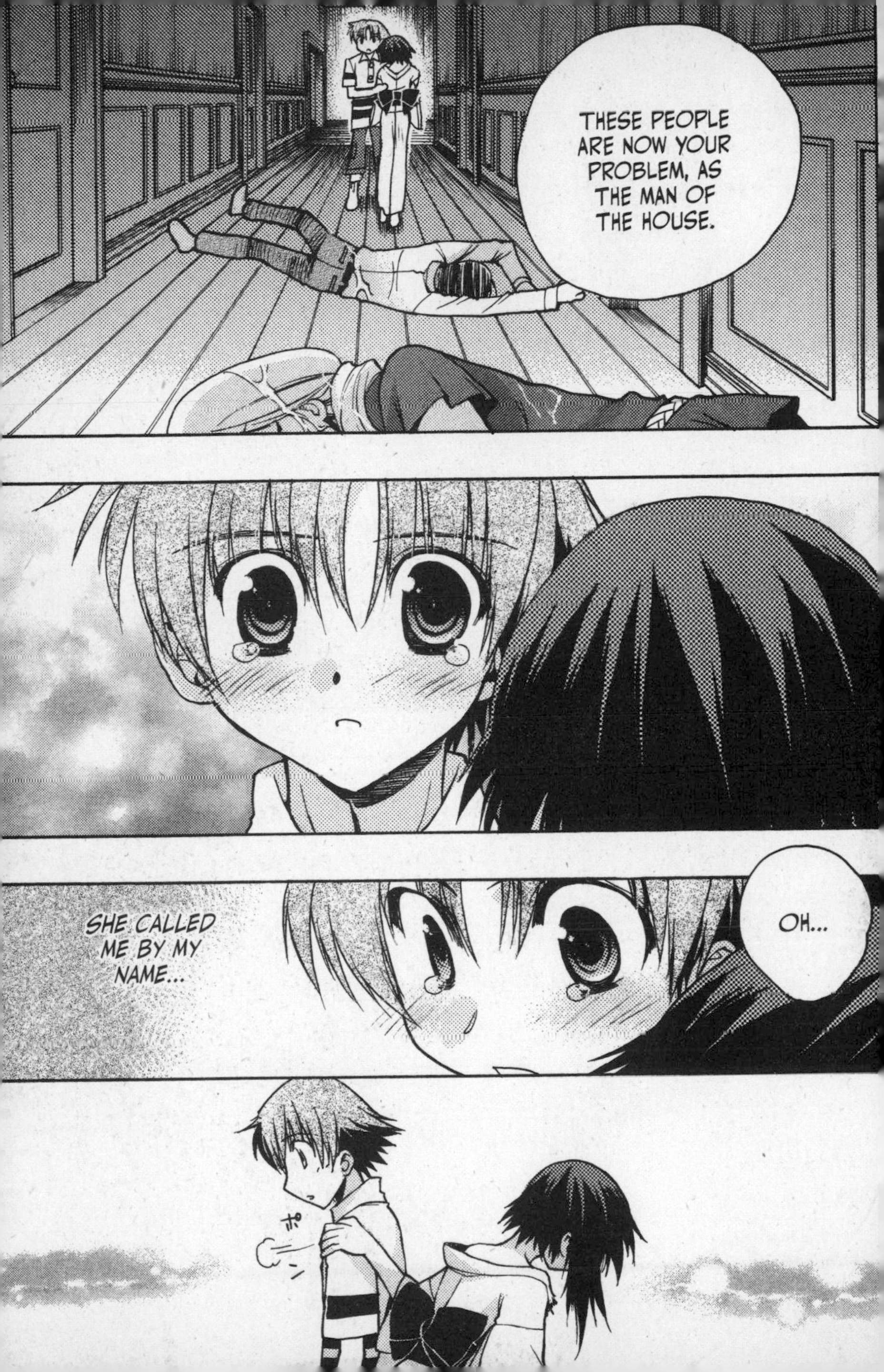
THESE PEOPLE ARE NOW YOUR PROBLEM, AS THE MAN OF THE HOUSE.
OH...
SHE CALLED ME BY MY NAME...
ポン

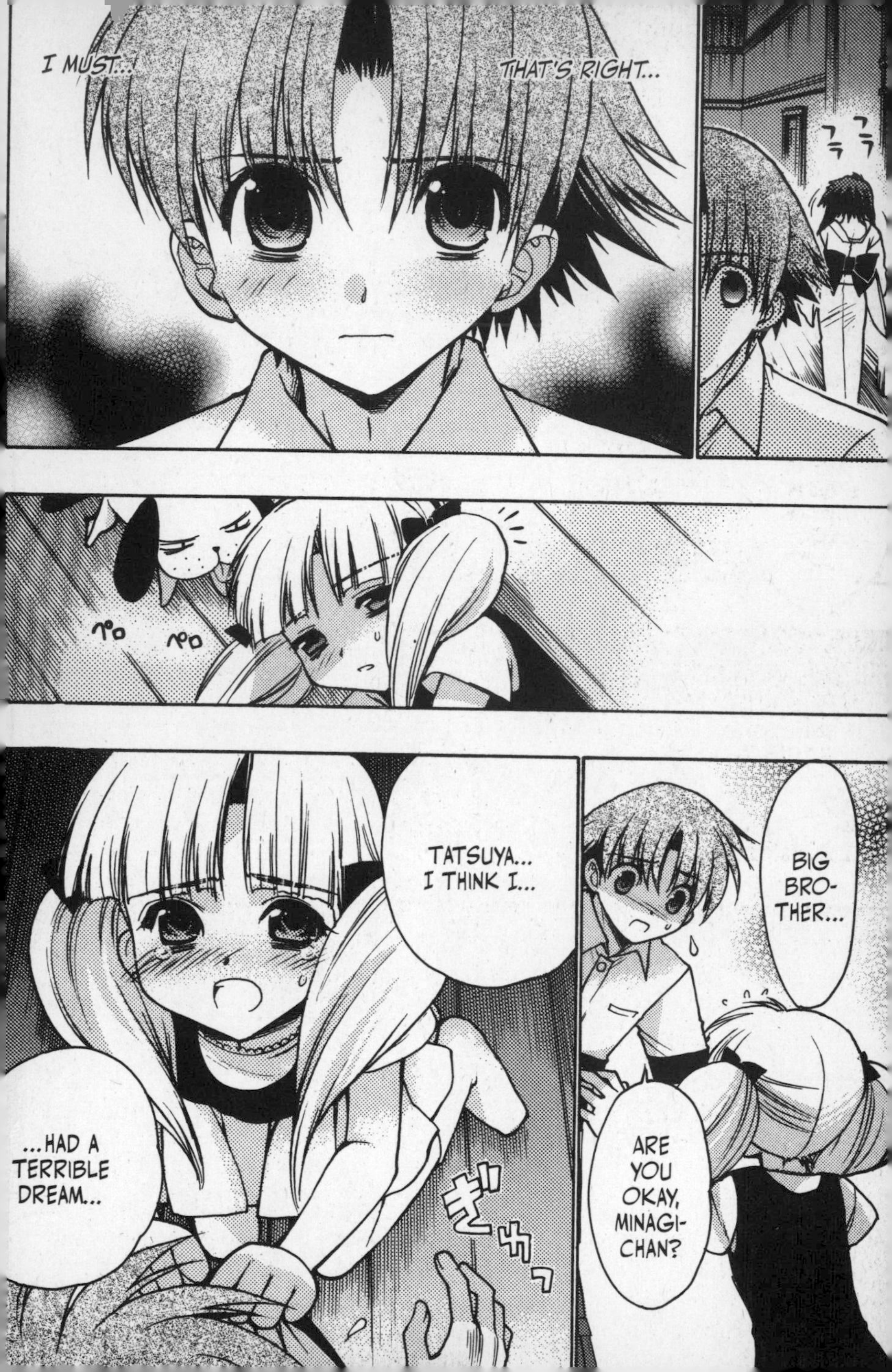

フラ フラ
THAT'S RIGHT...
I MUST...
ペロ ペロ
BIG BROTHER...
ARE YOU OKAY, MINAGI-CHAN?
TATSUYA... I THINK I...
...HAD A TERRIBLE DREAM...
ぎゅッ

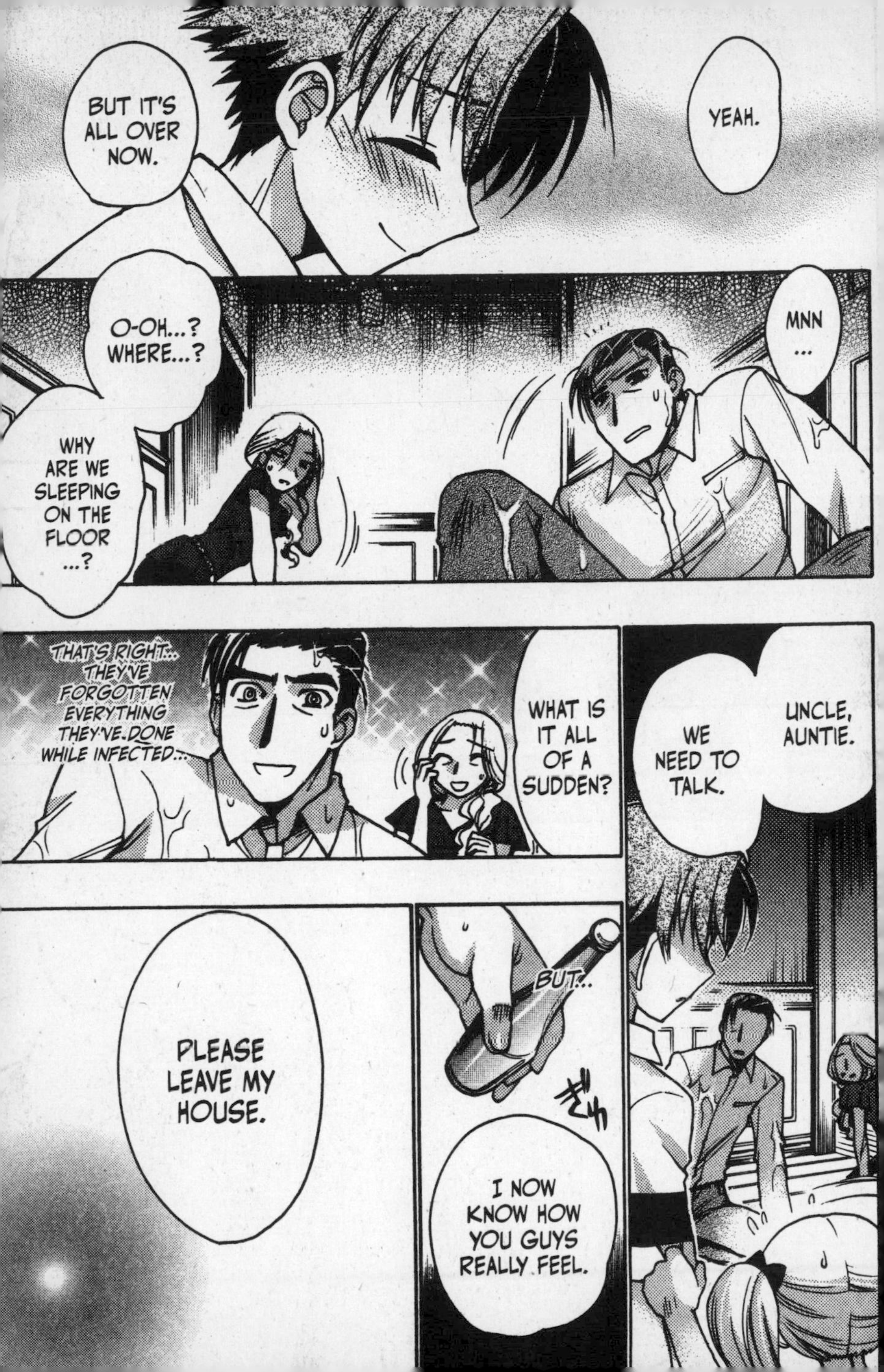
YEAH.
BUT IT'S ALL OVER NOW.
MNN...
O-OH...? WHERE...?
WHY ARE WE SLEEPING ON THE FLOOR...?
UNCLE, AUNTIE.
WE NEED TO TALK.
WHAT IS IT ALL OF A SUDDEN?
THAT'S RIGHT... THEY'VE FORGOTTEN EVERYTHING THEY'VE DONE WHILE INFECTED...
BUT...
ぎゅ
I NOW KNOW HOW YOU GUYS REALLY FEEL.
PLEASE LEAVE MY HOUSE.

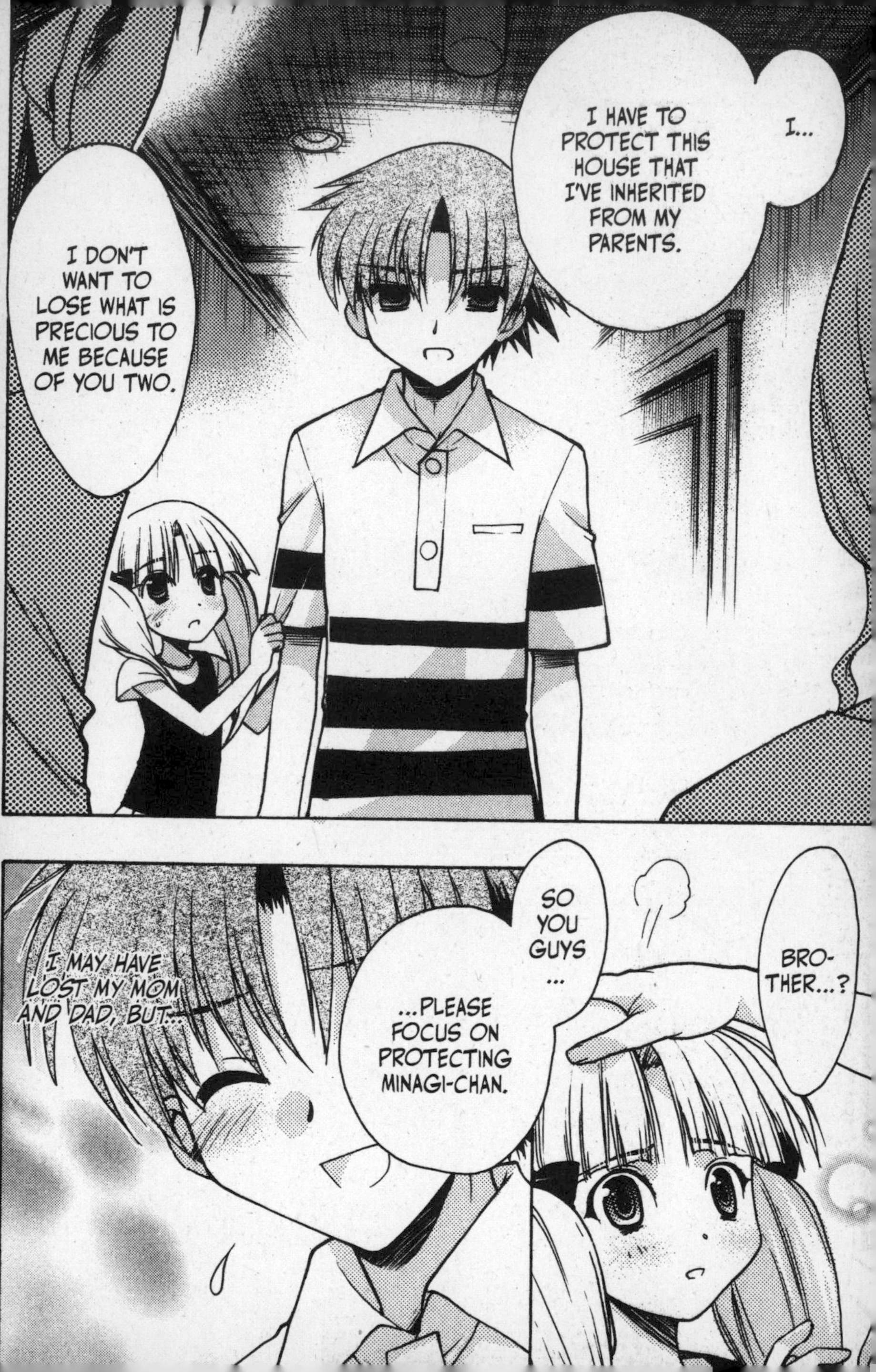
I...
I HAVE TO PROTECT THIS HOUSE THAT I'VE INHERITED FROM MY PARENTS.
I DON'T WANT TO LOSE WHAT IS PRECIOUS TO ME BECAUSE OF YOU TWO.
BRO-THER...?
I MAY HAVE LOST MY MOM AND DAD, BUT...
SO YOU GUYS ...
...PLEASE FOCUS ON PROTECTING MINAGI-CHAN.

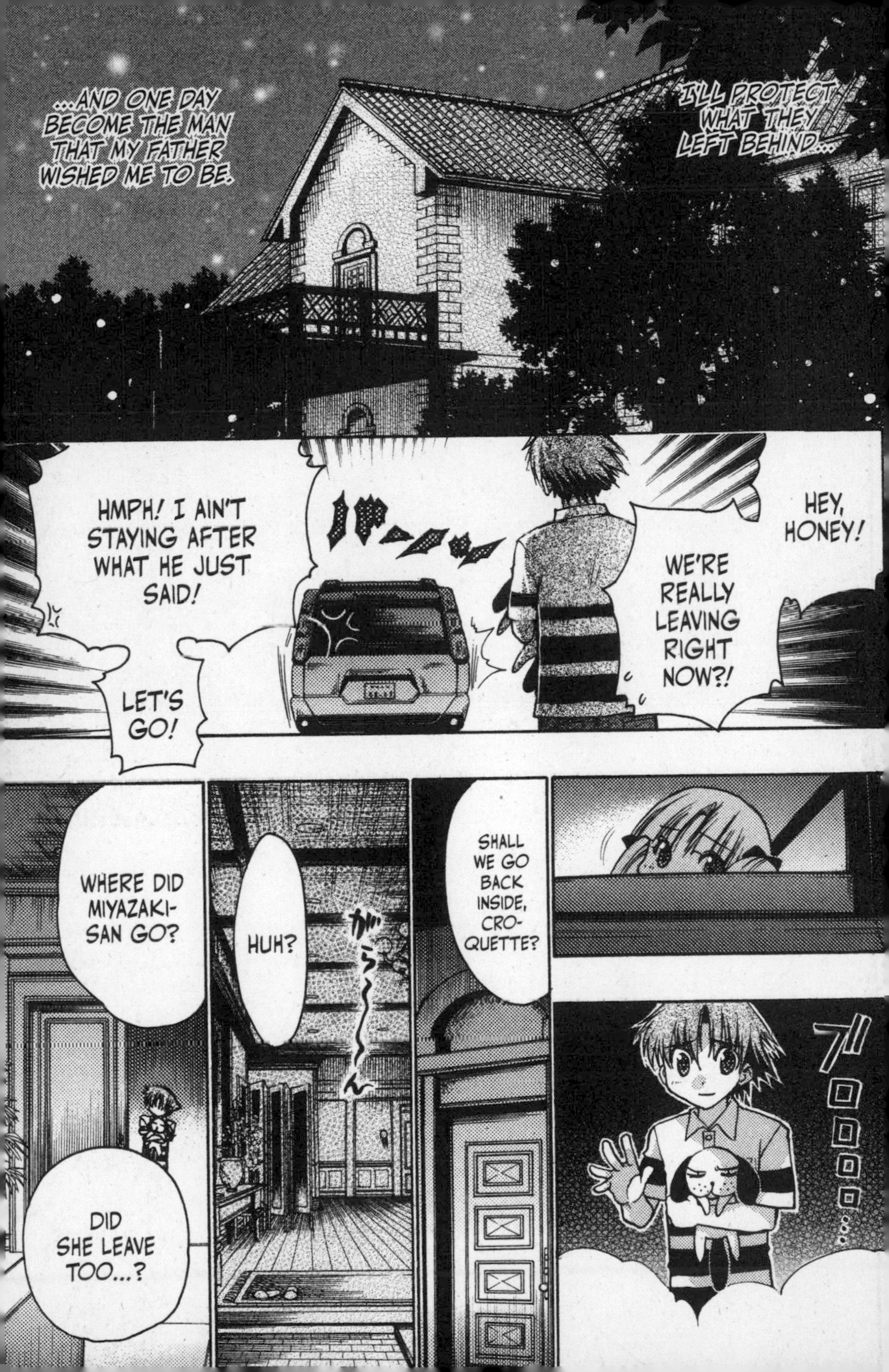
I'LL PROTECT WHAT THEY LEFT BEHIND...
...AND ONE DAY BECOME THE MAN THAT MY FATHER WISHED ME TO BE.
HEY, HONEY!
WE'RE REALLY LEAVING RIGHT NOW?!
HMPH! I AIN'T STAYING AFTER WHAT HE JUST SAID!
LET'S GO!
ブロロロ...
SHALL WE GO BACK INSIDE, CRO-QUETTE?
HUH?
がら〜ん
WHERE DID MIYAZAKI-SAN GO?
DID SHE LEAVE TOO...?

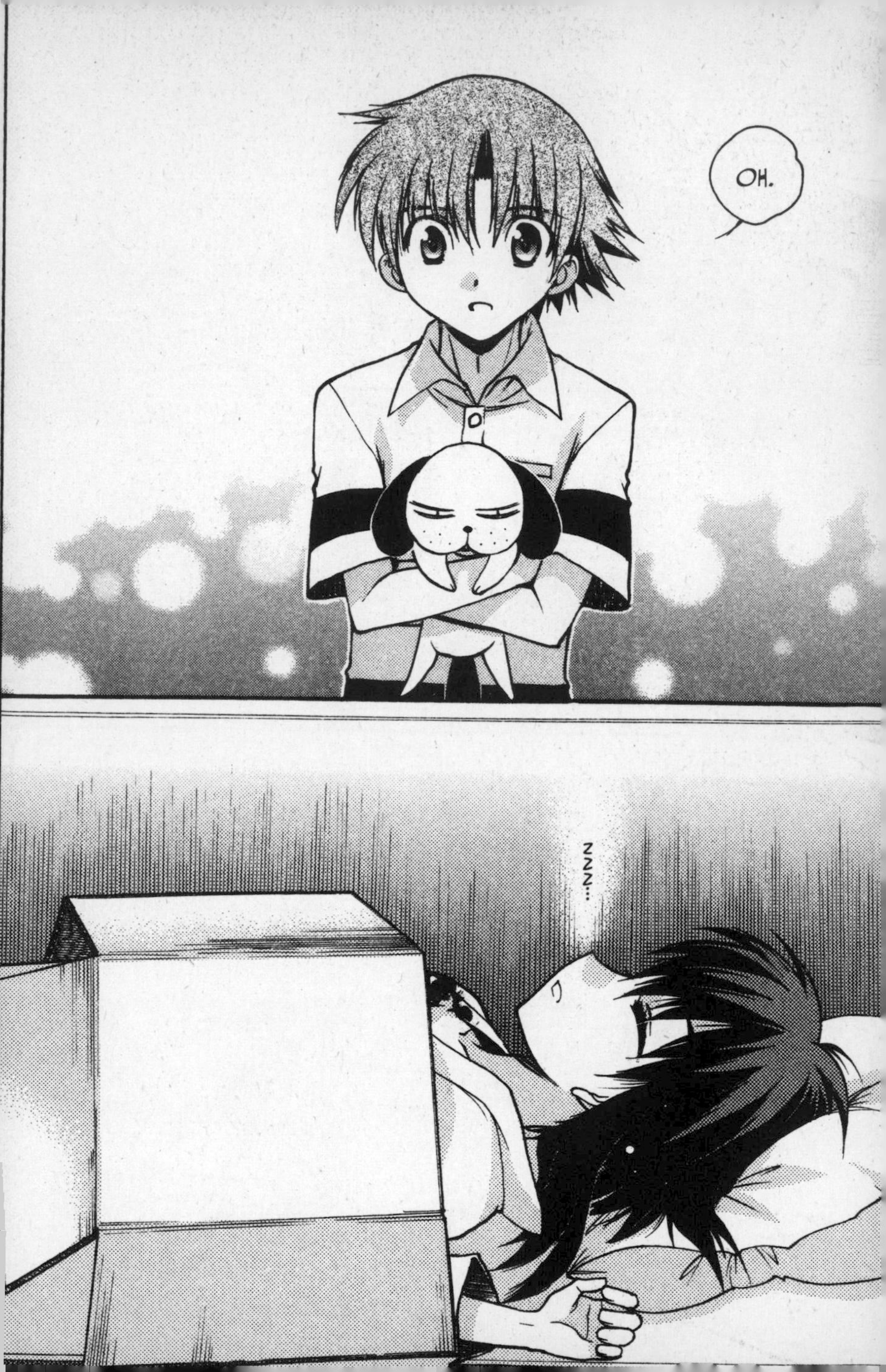
OH.
ZZZ...

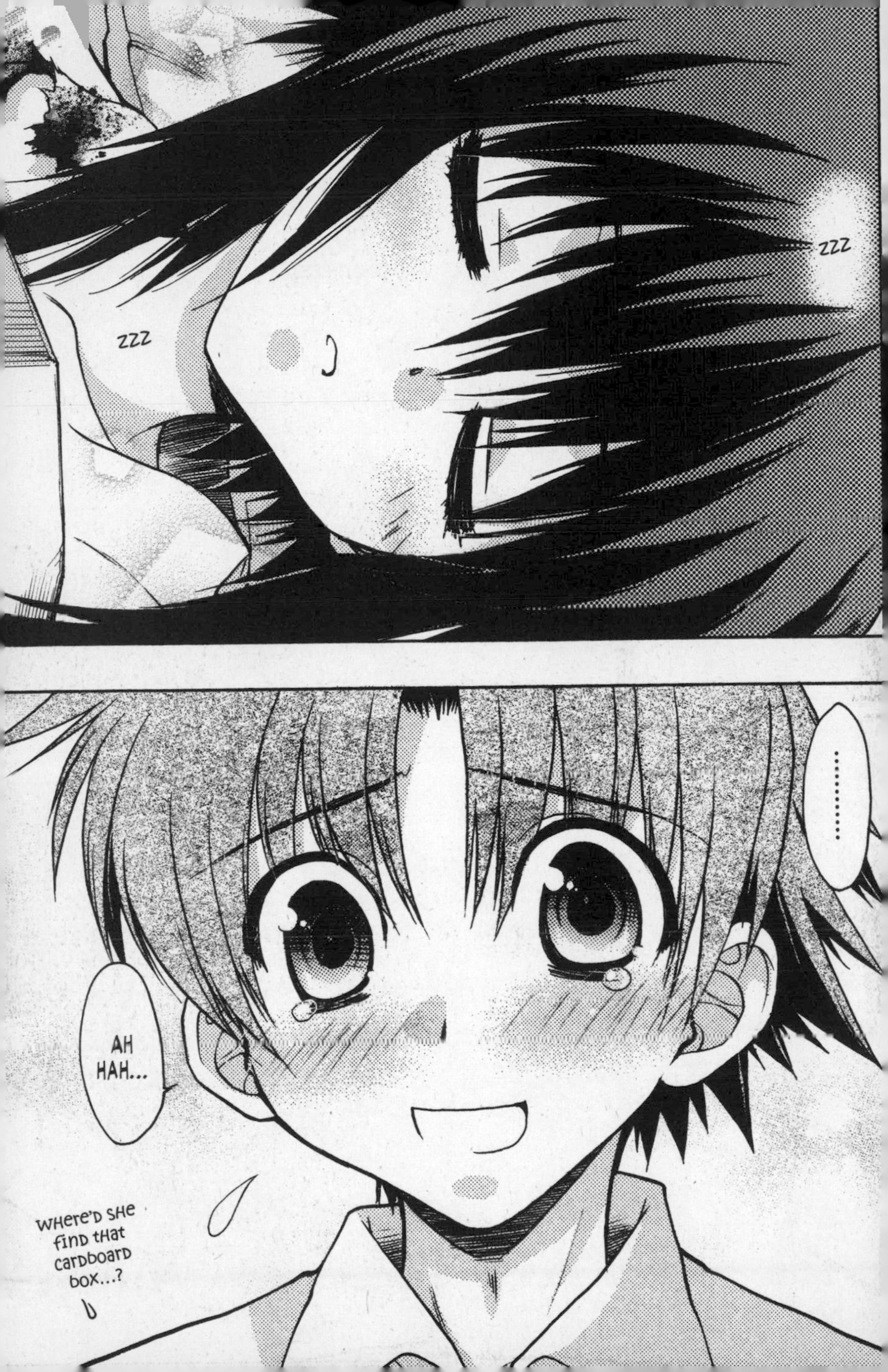
ZZZ
ZZZ
......
AH HAH...
WHERE'D SHE FIND THAT CARDBOARD BOX...?

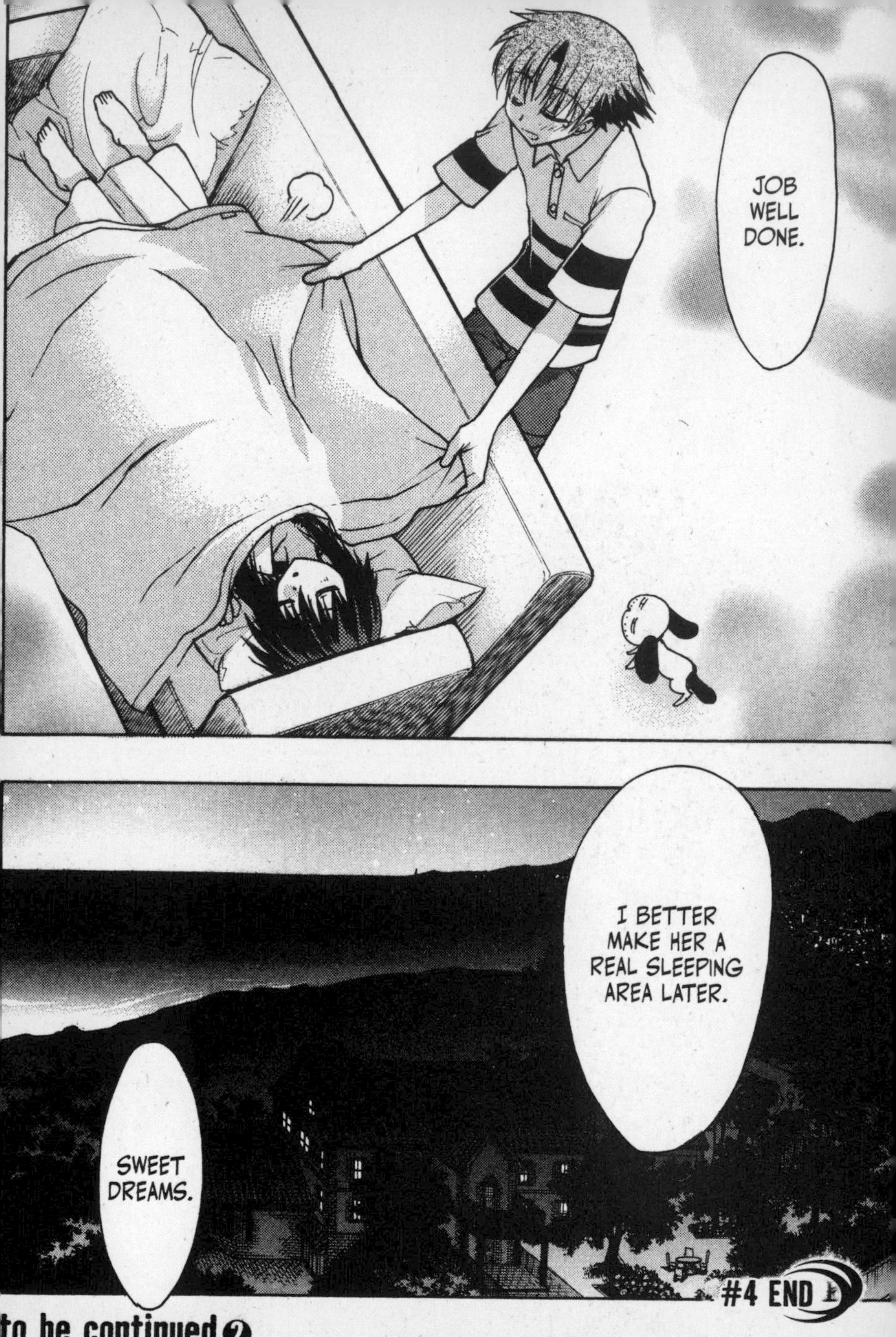
JOB WELL DONE.
I BETTER MAKE HER A REAL SLEEPING AREA LATER.
SWEET DREAMS.
#4 END

to be continued ②

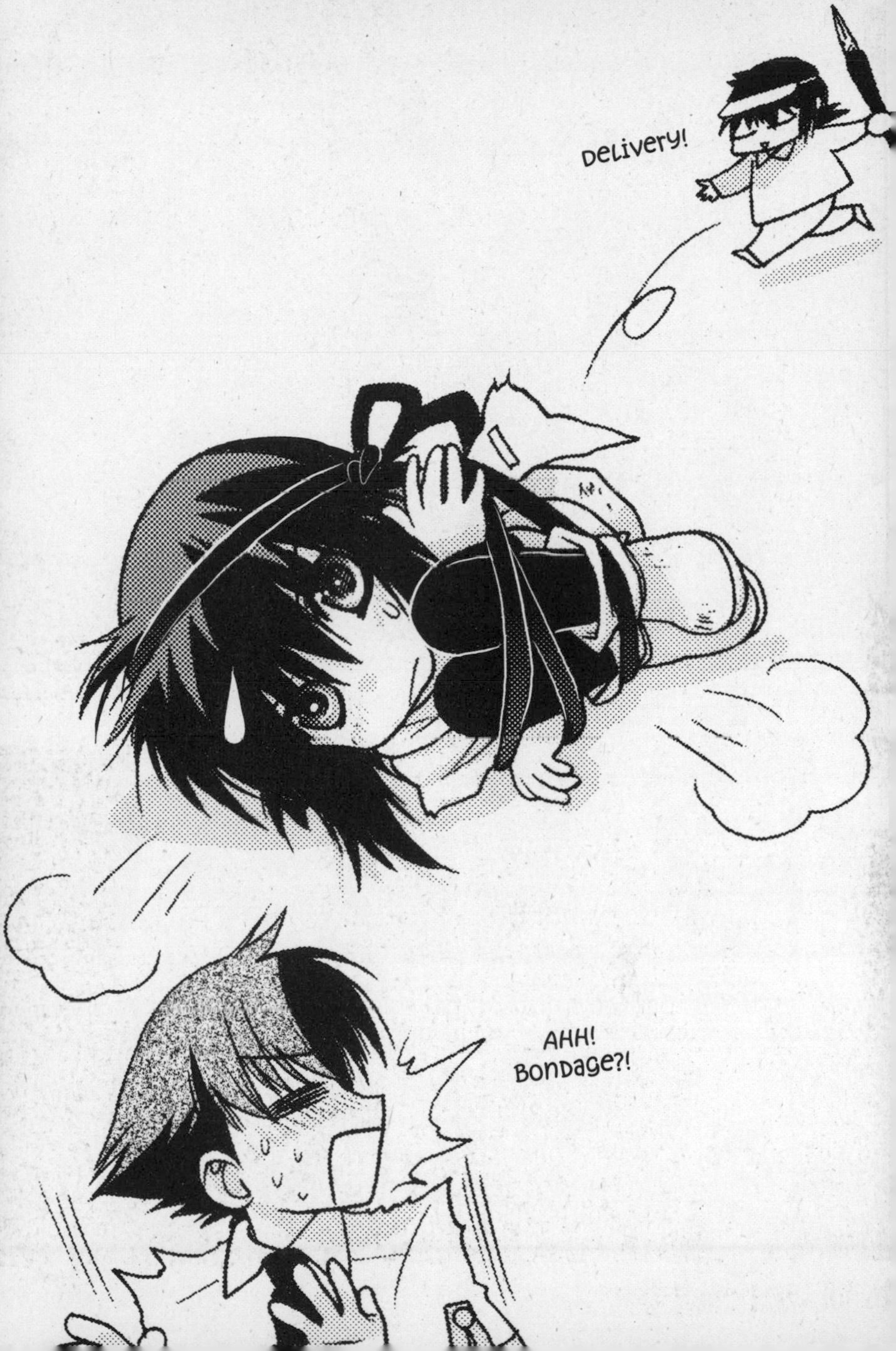
Delivery!
AHH! Bondage?!

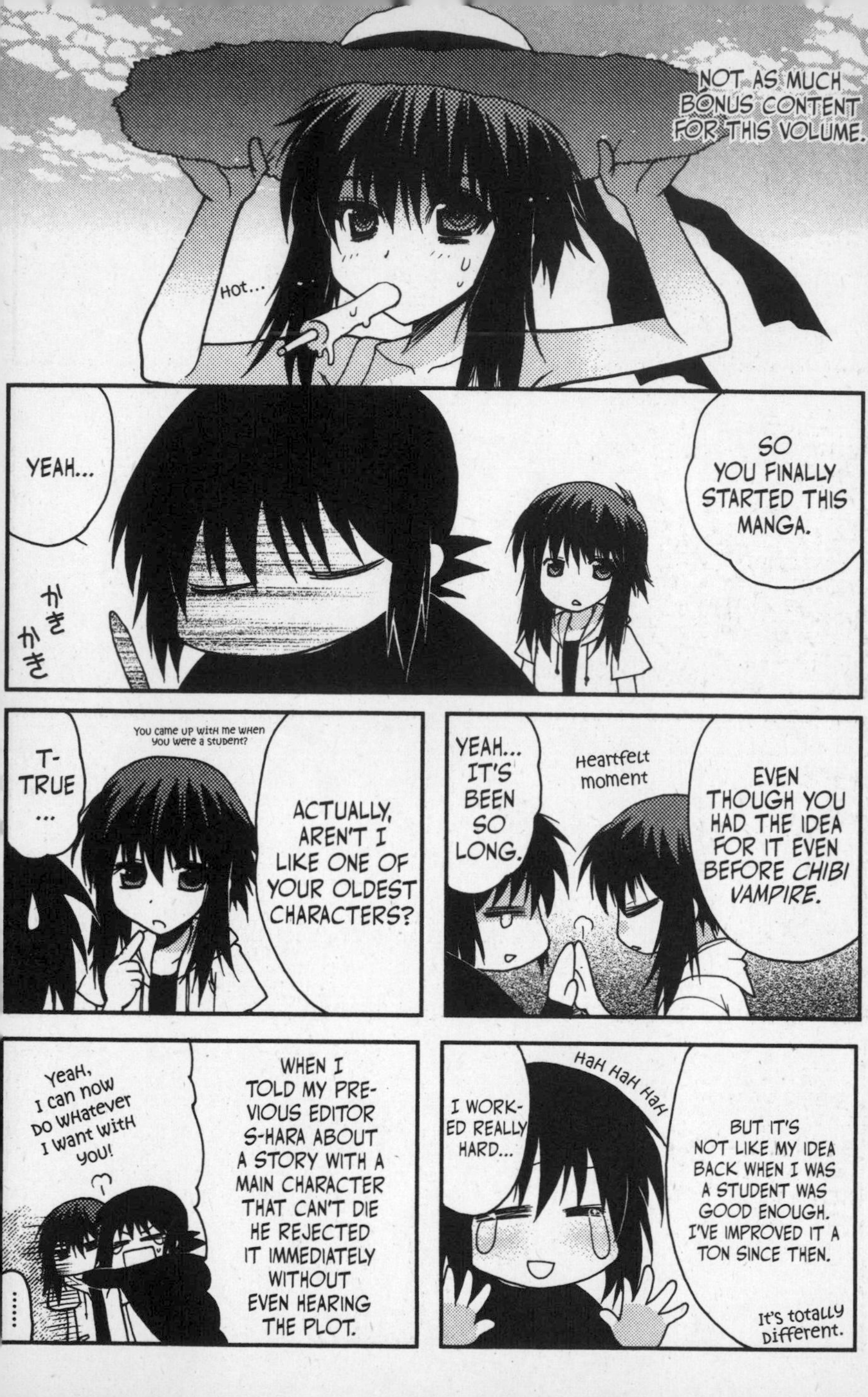
NOT AS MUCH BONUS CONTENT FOR THIS VOLUME.
Hot...
SO YOU FINALLY STARTED THIS MANGA.
YEAH...
かき かき
EVEN THOUGH YOU HAD THE IDEA FOR IT EVEN BEFORE CHIBI VAMPIRE.
Heartfelt moment
YEAH... IT'S BEEN SO LONG.
ACTUALLY, AREN'T I LIKE ONE OF YOUR OLDEST CHARACTERS?
You came up with me when you were a student?
T-TRUE...
BUT IT'S NOT LIKE MY IDEA BACK WHEN I WAS A STUDENT WAS GOOD ENOUGH. I'VE IMPROVED IT A TON SINCE THEN.
HaH HaH HaH
I WORKED REALLY HARD...
It's totally Different.
WHEN I TOLD MY PREVIOUS EDITOR S-HARA ABOUT A STORY WITH A MAIN CHARACTER THAT CAN'T DIE HE REJECTED IT IMMEDIATELY WITHOUT EVEN HEARING THE PLOT.
Yeah, I can now do whatever I want with you!
......

The Secret of Croquette's Birth

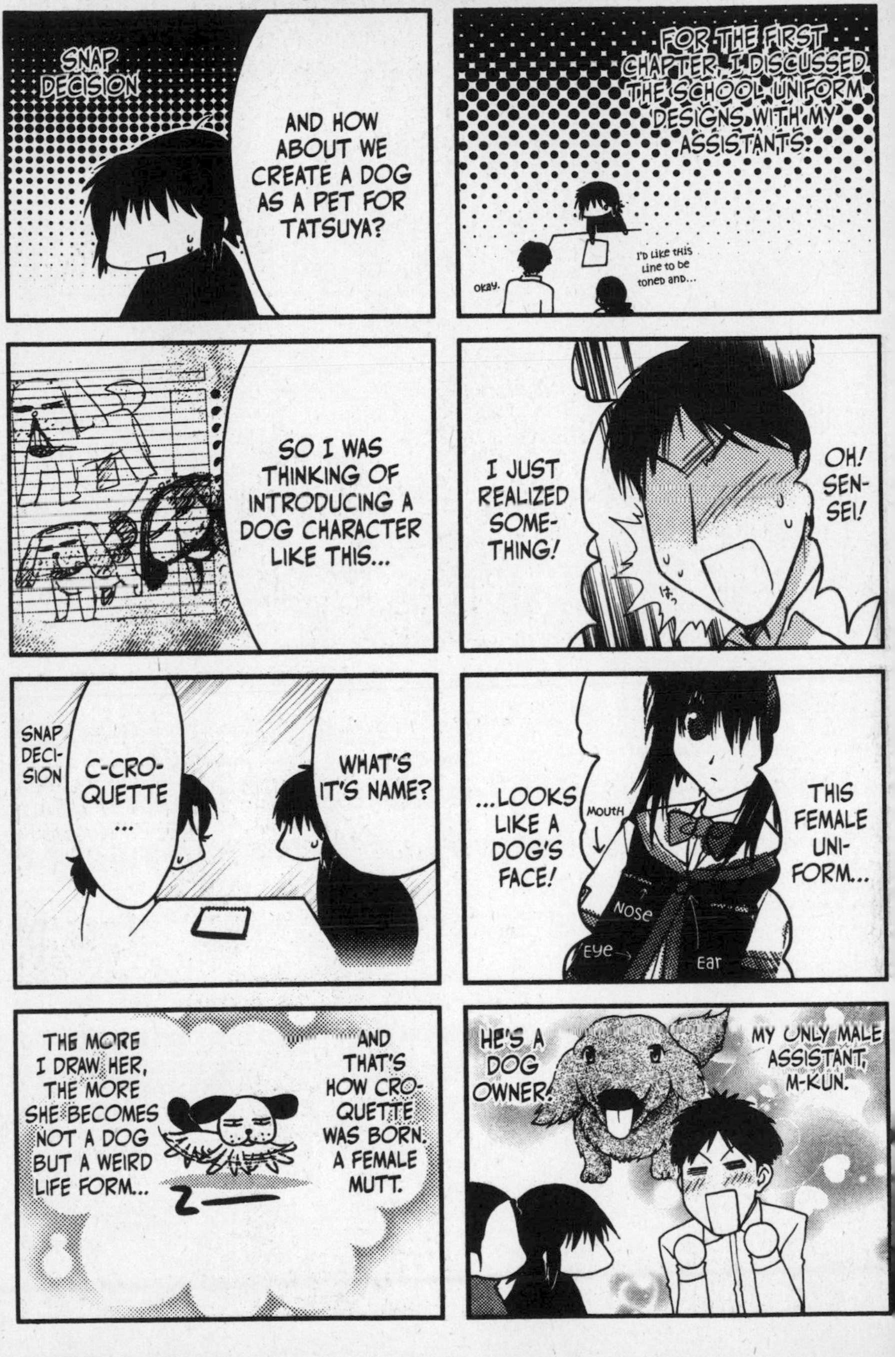
FOR THE FIRST CHAPTER, I DISCUSSED THE SCHOOL UNIFORM DESIGNS WITH MY ASSISTANTS.
I'D LIKE THIS LINE TO BE TONED AND...
OKAY.
OH! SEN-SEI!
I JUST REALIZED SOME-THING!
はっ
THIS FEMALE UNI-FORM...
...LOOKS LIKE A DOG'S FACE!
MOUTH
NOSE
EYE
EAR
MY ONLY MALE ASSISTANT, M-KUN.
HE'S A DOG OWNER.
AND HOW ABOUT WE CREATE A DOG AS A PET FOR TATSUYA?
SNAP DECISION
SO I WAS THINKING OF INTRODUCING A DOG CHARACTER LIKE THIS...
WHAT'S IT'S NAME?
C-CRO-QUETTE...
SNAP DECISION
AND THAT'S HOW CROQUETTE WAS BORN. A FEMALE MUTT.
THE MORE I DRAW HER, THE MORE SHE BECOMES NOT A DOG BUT A WEIRD LIFE FORM...
Z—

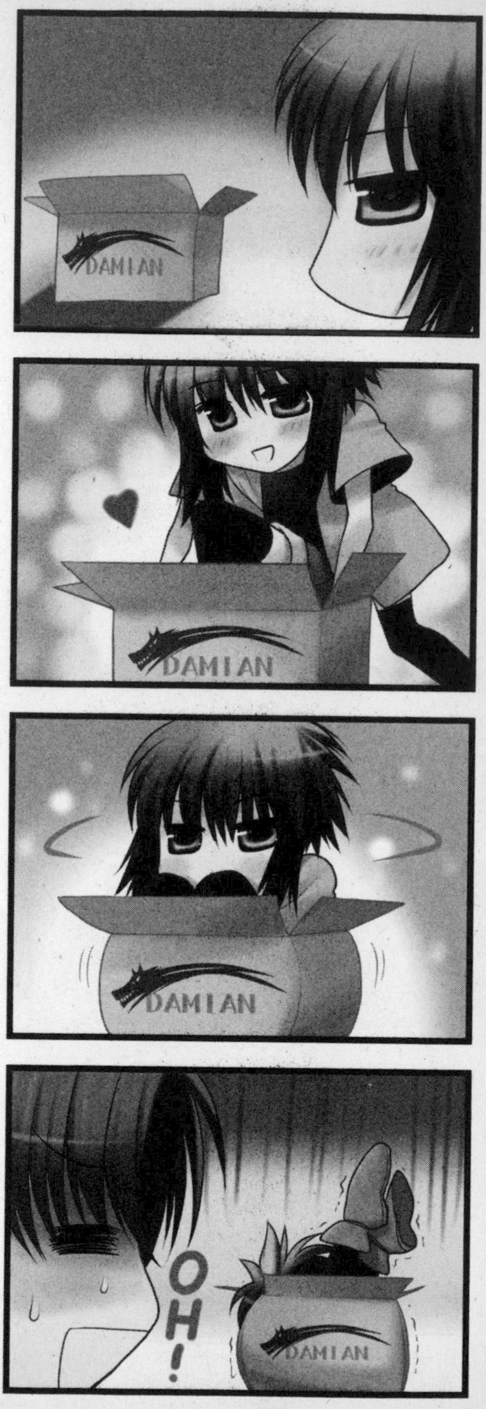
DAMIAN
DAMIAN
DAMIAN
DAMIAN
OH!

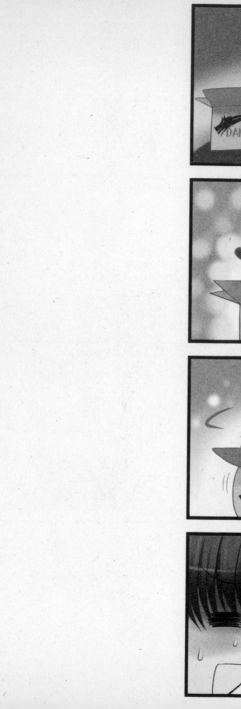

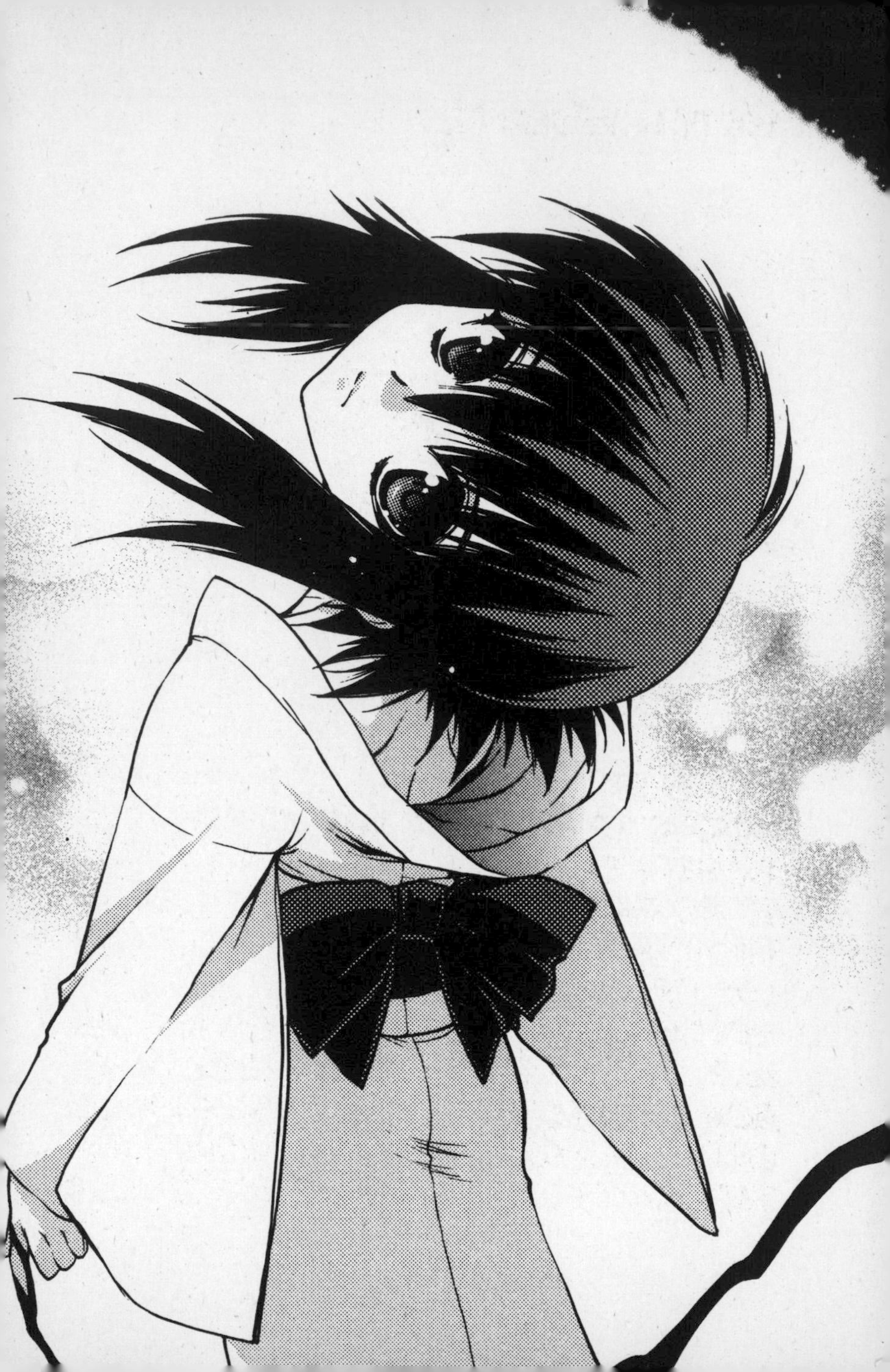

In the next volume of...

AiON

WITH MYSTERIOUS SCHOOLMATE SEINE NOW LIVING AT HIS HOUSE, TATSUYA'S LIFE IS ABOUT TO GET EVEN WEIRDER. SEINE IS ON A MISSION TO RID THE WORLD OF MALICIOUS MERMAIDS WHO CAN CONTROL HUMANS THROUGH THE USE OF PARASITES. ONLY SEINE SEEMS TO HAVE THE POWER TO DESTROY THEM WITH THE HELP OF HER SNAKE-LIKE CREATURE NAMED AiON. BUT WHEN SOME WEIRD TWINS SHOW UP CALLING THEMSELVES SEINE'S GUARDIANS, WILL TATSUYA LOSE HIS NEW FRIEND FOR GOOD?

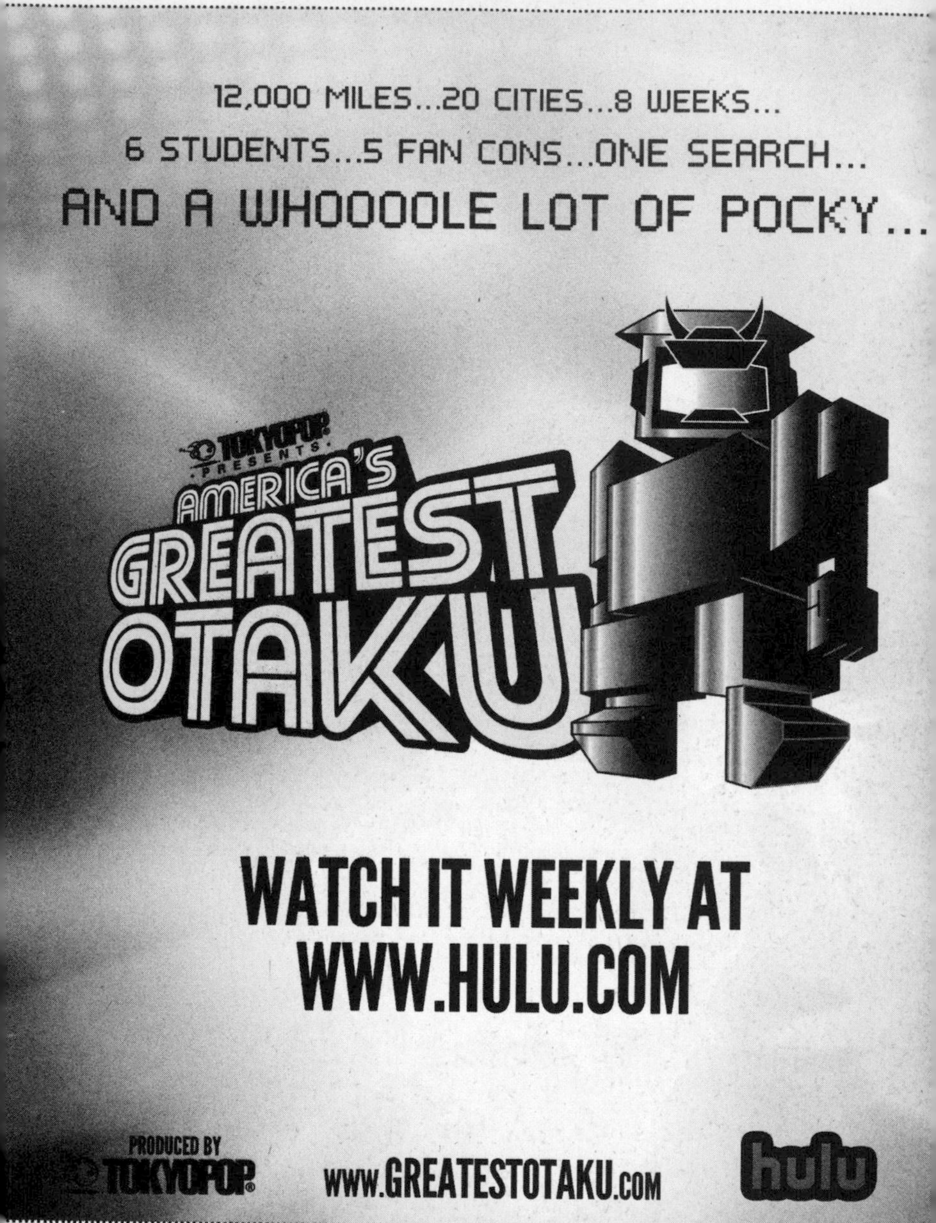
12,000 MILES...20 CITIES...8 WEEKS...
6 STUDENTS...5 FAN CONS...ONE SEARCH...
AND A WHOOOOLE LOT OF POCKY...
TOKYOPOP PRESENTS
AMERICA'S GREATEST OTAKU
WATCH IT WEEKLY AT WWW.HULU.COM
PRODUCED BY TOKYOPOP®
www.GREATESTOTAKU.com
hulu

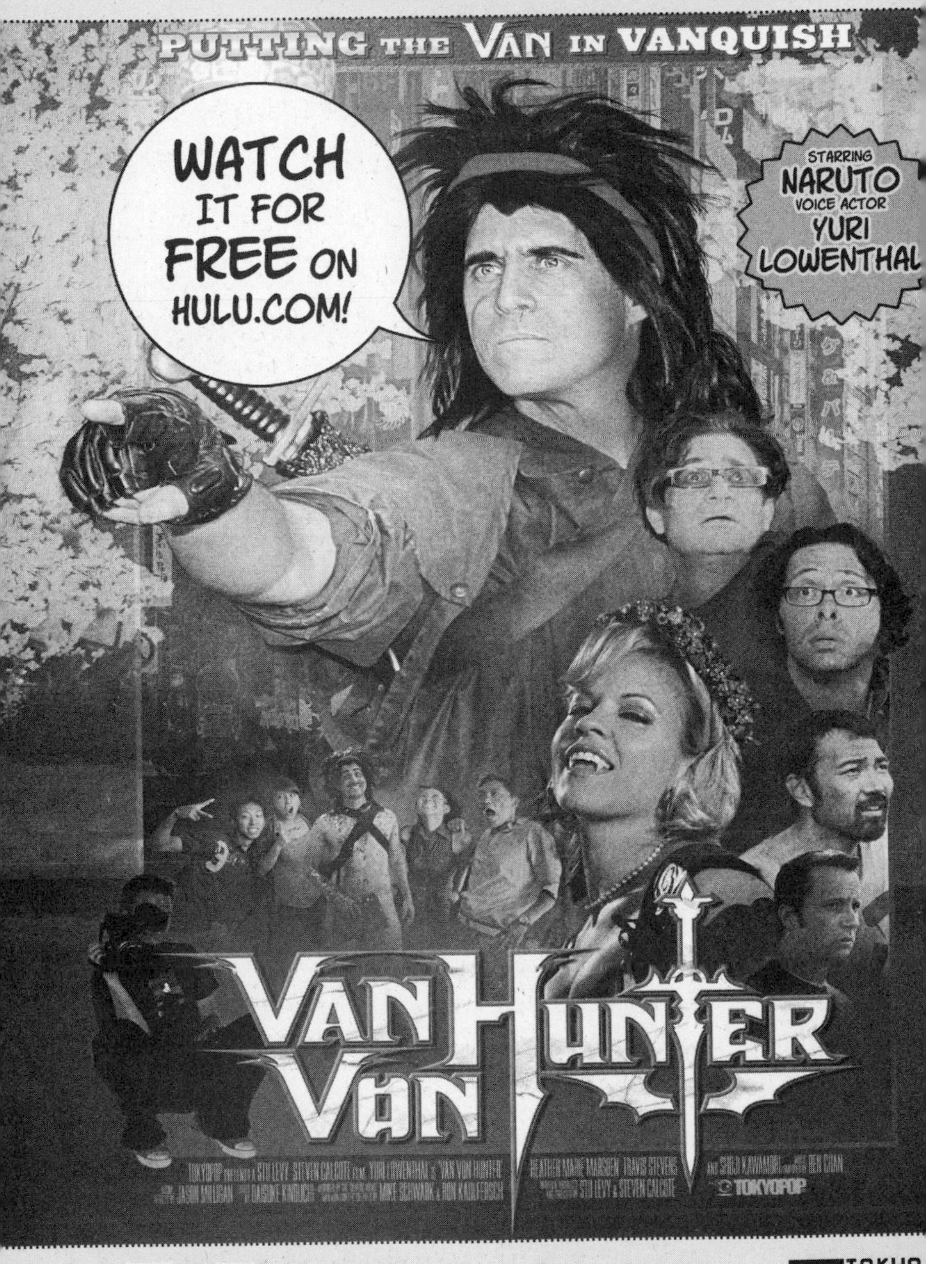
PUTTING THE VAN IN VANQUISH
WATCH IT FOR FREE ON HULU.COM!
STARRING NARUTO VOICE ACTOR YURI LOWENTHAL
VAN VON HUNTER
TOKYOPOP PRESENTS A STU LEVY STEVEN CALCOTE FILM YURI LOWENTHAL IS "VAN VON HUNTER"
HEATHER MARIE MARSDEN TRAVIS STEVENS
AND SHOJI KAWAMORI BEN CHAN
STU LEVY & STEVEN CALCOTE
TOKYOPOP

Hetalia goes Digital!
MOBILE
Hetalia on Comics by
COMIXOLOGY™
Search for "Hetalia" on iTunes!
First issue is FREE
DESKTOP
Hetalia on zinio™
For Mac and PC platforms
www.zinio.com/TOKYOPOP
HETALIA Axis Powers

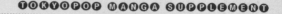

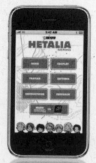

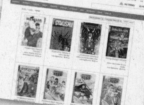

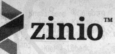

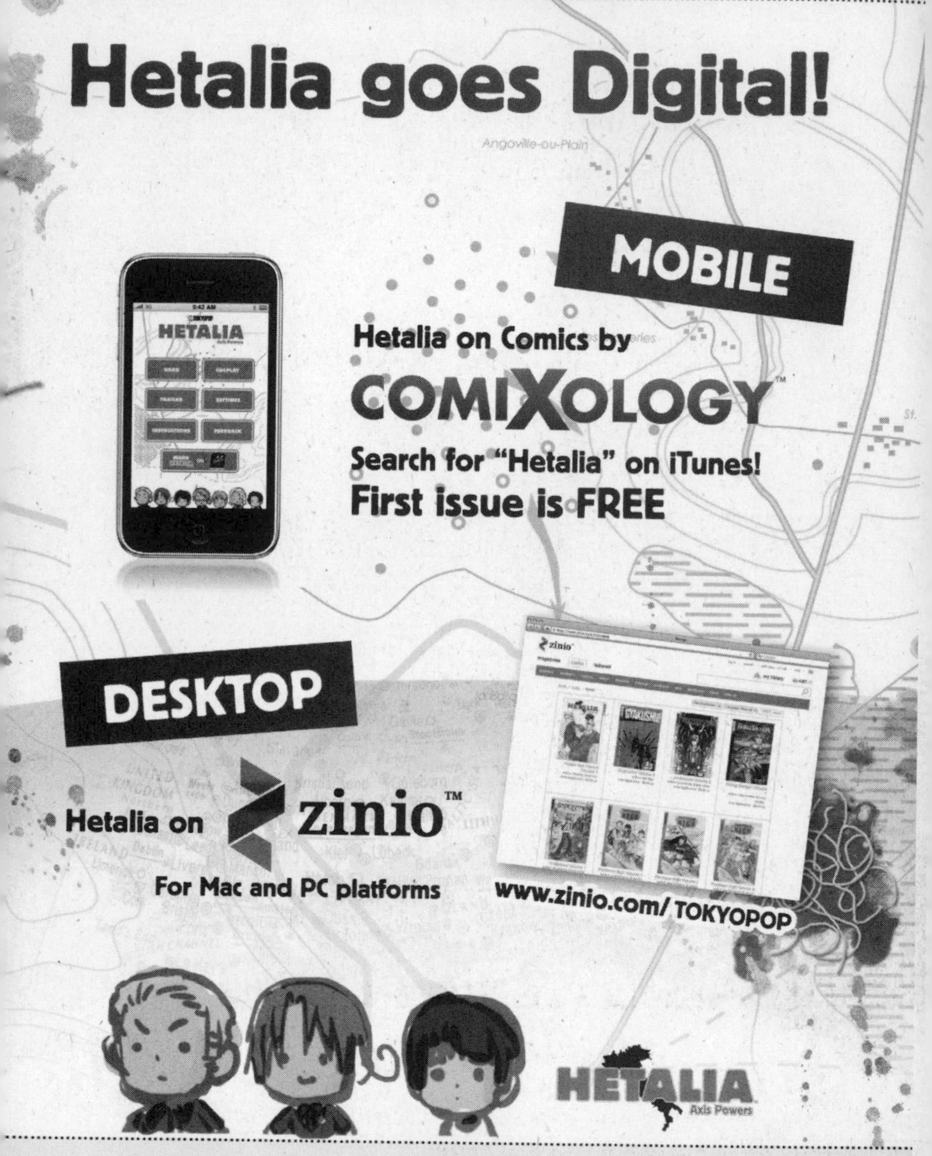

#1 on the New York Times Manga Bestseller List!
HETALIA
Axis Powers
TOKYOPOP
VOL. 2
Hidekaz Himaruya

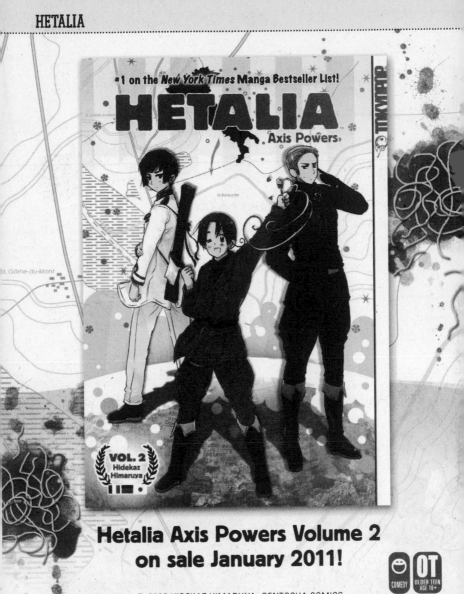

DISCOVER HOW IT ALL BEGAN

AN EVIL, ANCIENT AND HUNGRY, IS ROAMING THE
BADLANDS OF THE OLD WEST. IT SPARES NOT MAN,
WOMAN NOR CHILD, DEVOURING ALL THAT STAND
BEFORE IT. ONLY ONE MAN CAN STOP IT...A MYSTERIOUS
PRIEST WITH A CROSS CARVED INTO HIS HEAD. HIS NAME
IS IVAN ISAACS, AND HE WILL SMOTE ALL EVIL IN
A HAIL OF HOT LEAD. HALLELUJAH.

MIN-WOO HYUNG'S INTERNATIONAL MANWHA SENSATION RETURNS
WITH SPECIAL COLLECTOR'S EDITIONS FOR FANS OLD & NEW!

STOP!

This is the back of the book. You wouldn't want to spoil a great ending!

This book is printed "manga-style," in the authentic Japanese right-to-left format. Since none of the artwork has been flipped or altered, readers get to experience the story just as the creator intended. You've been asking for it, so TOKYOPOP® delivered: authentic, hot-off-the-press, and far more fun!

1
2
3
4
5
6
7
8
9
10

DIRECTIONS

If this is your first time reading manga-style, here's a quick guide to help you understand how it works.

It's easy... just start in the top right panel and follow the numbers. Have fun, and look for more 100% authentic manga from TOKYOPOP®!

THE MANGA REVOLUTION • LEADING • 漫画革命 • LEADING • THE MANGA REVOLUTION